Advance Praise

"I was impressed and delightfully surprised with *The Future of Branding*. It is a senior marketing executive's bible for rigorous thinking and analysis for growth and profitability. It provides a vital range of systematic frameworks and techniques for managing brands not covered in other books. Get it before your competition does!"
—**Tan Suee Chieh**, Group Chief Executive, NTUC Enterprise Cooperative Limited, Singapore

"The book is a very useful tool for managers and practitioners involved in all aspects of branding. A lot of how to's and discussions of strategies from leading thinkers in the field of branding mean that this book can be used as a ready reference. Speaking as someone whose business is centered on building a brand, I'd make it available throughout my organization."
—**Richard Eu**, CEO, Eu Yan Sang International Ltd, Singapore

"*The Future of Branding* is already here and it is proving to be challenging, as markets are being transformed with digital technologies and advantages are increasingly transient. This book is a valuable guide to this demanding new reality for all brands. Srivastava and Thomas have assembled some of the best minds and their latest thinking on how to build, protect, and leverage brands to capture new opportunities and fully realize a brand's economic potential."
—**George S. Day**, Geoffrey T. Boisi Professor of Marketing, Co-Director of the Mack Institute for Innovation Management, Wharton School of the University of Pennsylvania

"The role of brands is changing rapidly and dramatically with the rise of digital marketing and addressability, the growing power of emerging markets, and the key role of value chains in providing ecosystems of products and services. A changing role does not mean a decreasing role, but it does provide an urgent call for creative adaptation. This book brings together some of the best minds in marketing to understand the issues involved in this turbulent environment and provide ideas as to how they might be addressed. As such, I consider it to be essential reading for both academics and managers."

—**John Roberts**, Professor of Marketing, Joint appointment at London Business School and Australian National University

"A nice, tight compilation of guru-inspired commentaries covering many of the foundations, facets, and fallacies of branding in a hyperconnected digital world. [This book] provides a multi-disciplinary view of how to build brand value using customer-centric, gratification strategies. Drawing on expert insight, [it] provides a banquet of views with a more palatable and enjoyable content snacking experience. Finally, we have a marketing treatise that makes brand strategy more meaningful and an essential part of business performance, innovation, and customer affinity building."

—**Donovan Neale-May**, Executive Director, Chief Marketing Officer (CMO) Council

"Today's consumers are confounded by an endless stream of product information in our always-connected, global economy resulting in choice fatigue and purchase indecision. [This book] is *the* definitive roadmap for the students and managers of enduring brands who are attempting to navigate this competitive landscape and consumer reality. It provides turn by turn guidance to help develop strategy, measure branding effectiveness, narrow focus on profitable customers, and assess the true value of a successful brand. Don't attempt to drive your brand without it."

—**Jim Anhut**, SVP Design, InterContinental Hotels Group and Serial Hospitality Brand Builder

"This book comes at a time when brand owners are being challenged by technologies that are changing consumer behaviors and new business models that are disrupting traditional markets. One thing remains the same, consumers still need products to buy and ideas to buy into, but how we build branded relationships with consumers has changed forever. This book is an essential guide for marketers today.

Brand marketing is changing and Lluis Martinez-Ribes' chapter gets straight to the point. Retailers are no longer destinations that sell branded products, they are brands in their own right. That requires new thinking and new approaches, this book signposts the way."

—**Simon Hathaway**, Global Chief Retail Officer, Cheil Worldwide Inc.

THE FUTURE OF BRANDING

THE
FUTURE
OF
RELIGION

THE FUTURE OF BRANDING

Edited by
RAJENDRA K. SRIVASTAVA
GREGORY METZ THOMAS

www.sagepublications.com
Los Angeles • London • New Delhi • Singapore • Washington DC

Copyright © Rajendra K. Srivastava and Gregory Metz Thomas, 2016

All rights reserved. No part of this book may be reproduced or utilized in any form or by any means, electronic or mechanical, including photocopying, recording, or by any information storage or retrieval system, without permission in writing from the publisher.

First published in 2016 by

SAGE Publications India Pvt Ltd
B1/I-1 Mohan Cooperative Industrial Area
Mathura Road, New Delhi 110 044, India
www.sagepub.in

SAGE Publications Inc
2455 Teller Road
Thousand Oaks, California 91320, USA

SAGE Publications Ltd
1 Oliver's Yard, 55 City Road
London EC1Y 1SP, United Kingdom

SAGE Publications Asia-Pacific Pte Ltd
3 Church Street
#10-04 Samsung Hub
Singapore 049483

Published by Vivek Mehra for SAGE Publications India Pvt Ltd, typeset in 11/13 pt Baskerville by RECTO Graphics, Delhi, and printed at Chaman Enterprises, New Delhi.

Library of Congress Cataloging-in-Publication Data

The future of branding/edited by Rajendra K. Srivastava and Gregory Metz Thomas.
   pages cm
   Includes bibliographical references and index.
  1. Branding (Marketing) 2. Strategic planning. I. Srivastava, Rajendra K., editor. II. Thomas, Gregory Metz, editor.
   HF5415.1255.F88   658.8'27—dc23   2016   2015033678

ISBN: 978-93-515-0316-3 (HB)

The SAGE Team: Sachin Sharma, Sandhya Gola, Nand Kumar Jha, and Rajinder Kaur

We dedicate this book to Tricia and Kiki for their support, encouragement, and affection.

Thank you for choosing a SAGE product!
If you have any comment, observation or feedback,
I would like to personally hear from you.
Please write to me at **contactceo@sagepub.in**

Vivek Mehra, Managing Director and CEO, SAGE India.

Bulk Sales

SAGE India offers special discounts
for purchase of books in bulk.
We also make available special imprints
and excerpts from our books on demand.

For orders and enquiries, write to us at

Marketing Department
SAGE Publications India Pvt Ltd
B1/I-1, Mohan Cooperative Industrial Area
Mathura Road, Post Bag 7
New Delhi 110044, India

E-mail us at **marketing@sagepub.in**

Get to know more about SAGE
Be invited to SAGE events, get on our mailing list.
Write today to **marketing@sagepub.in**

This book is also available as an e-book.

Contents

List of Tables	ix
List of Figures	xi
List of Abbreviations	xv
Preface	xvii
Acknowledgments	xix

Section I: Brand Strategy

1. Selecting the Brand Architecture to Match Your Strategy   3
   Jean-Noël Kapferer

2. A Strategic Approach to Grow Profits: Defining, Measuring, and Maximizing Customer Value   34
   V. Kumar and Bharath Rajan

3. Branding in Retail   68
   Lluis Martinez-Ribes

Section II: Brand Building

4. Brand Identity: Brand Naming Process and Brand Linguistics in the International Context   99
   Bernd Schmitt and Shi Zhang

5. The Six-station Model of Corporate Identity: Developing and Assessing the Model   119
   Jean Yannis Suvatjis and Leslie de Chernatony

6. Brand Development Processes and Planning   149
   Kevin Lane Keller

7. Managing the Brand Experience   177
   Bernd Schmitt

8. Rethinking Brand Development in an
   Interactive Marketplace 199
   Don E. Schultz

9. Luxury Brands 217
   Vanessa M. Patrick and Henrik Hagtvedt

10. The Dynamics of Brand Trust 237
    Gregory Metz Thomas

Section III: Leveraging Brands

11. Branding and Emerging Markets 271
    Martin Roll

12. Opportunities and Risks in Co-branding and Licensing 300
    Jeffrey Parkhurst

13. Brand Revitalization 314
    Kevin Lane Keller

14. Brand Identity Strategy for Mergers and Acquisitions 335
    Srinivas Reddy and Anupam Jaju

Section IV: Brand Performance Management

15. The Great Debate: Managing Brands versus
    Managing Customers 377
    Werner Reinartz

16. Brand Imperative: Protecting Your Most Valuable Assets 392
    Jeffery Andrien, Paul Benoit, and Philip C. Zerrillo

17. Hidden Value of Brands: Brands in Mergers and
    Acquisitions 420
    S. Cem Bahadir

18. Role of Brands in Managing Innovations 430
    Rajendra K. Srivastava

About the Editors and Contributors 447

Index 458

List of Tables

1.1	"House of Brands" versus "Branded House" in Perspective	17
2.1	Tom's Referral Behavior in a Financial Services Company (Semi-annual Data)	58
2.2	Customer Deciles of CLV and CRV for a Telecommunications Company	60
2.3	Campaign for "Misers," "Advocates," and "Affluents" for a Telecommunications Company	65
2.4	Campaign Results for "Misers," "Advocates," and "Affluents"	66
4.1	Stimuli Brand Names for Study 1	110
5A.1	Rotated Factor Matrix: Sorted Form of Variables Loadings	142
5A.2	Total Variance Explained	144
5A.3	Confirmatory Factor Analysis	145
6.1	Summary of Qualitative Techniques	152
6.2	Example of Brand Association Ratings in Terms of Strength, Favorability, and Uniqueness	154
6.3	Brand Element Choice Criteria	164
6.4	Sample Customer-performance Scorecard Measures	171
8.1	Market Performance of Stores and Products	201
8.2	Top Leading Brand Categories Characteristics	202

10.1	Sources of Risk	244
10.2	Examples of Advertising Lines Relating to "Trust"	250
10.3	Trust-building Programs	259
14.1	Descriptive Results: Categorical Measures (Market Relatedness, Ownership Status, and Diversification)	356
14.2	Descriptive Results: Continuous Variables (Relative Standing and Relatedness)	357
14.3	Descriptive Results: Categorical Measures (Control Variables)	358
14.4	Multinomial Logistic Model Results: Parameter Estimates—Acquirer-dominated versus Target-dominated	360
14.5	Multinomial Logistic Model Results: Parameter Estimates—Concatenated Synergistic versus Non-synergistic	361
15.1	Go-to-market Strategies	379
16.1	Brand Risks	402
16.2	Brand Valuation Methodologies	404
17.1	Illustrative Transactions and Brand Portfolio Value	421

List of Figures

1.1	Integrative Role of Brands	9
1.2	The Six Typical Brand Architectures	13
1.3	Positioning the Six Typical Brand Architectures	16
1.4	How to Brand Innovations	28
1.5	Progressive Integration of Innovations	29
2.1	Inter-linkages between CLV, CBV, and CRV	39
2.2	The Wheel of Fortune	46
2.3	Components of CBV	50
2.4	Sample Output of Customer A's Observed Brand Value	51
2.5	Optimized Brand Value of Customer	54
2.6	Sample Referral Program from AT&T	61
2.7	Sample Referral Program from DIRECTV	62
2.8	CLV–CRV Matrix of a Telecommunications Company	63
4.1	Brand Name Evaluation as a Function of Name Emphasis, Sound, and Meaning in Study 1	112
5.1	The Six-station Corporate Identity Model	125
6.1	Accenture's Competitive Positioning Map	158
6.2	Accenture Straddle Positioning	159
6.3	Brand Positioning Worksheet	161
6.4.	Hypothetical Starbucks Positioning Worksheet	162
8.1	Positioning Map for Cereal Brands Using BAV Measures of Brand Stature and Brand Strength	204

8.2	Positioning Map for Cosmetics Brands Using BAV Measures of Brand Stature and Brand Strength	205
8.3	Positioning Map for OTC Allergy Brands Using BAV Measures of Brand Stature and Brand Strength	206
10.1	The Personalization–Privacy Tradeoff	246
10.2	Four Types of Mass Customization	247
10.3	Law and the Court of Public Opinion	251
10.4	Brand Trust: The Conceptual Model	251
10.5	Corruption Perceptions Index 2014	253
10.6	Brand Trust Reputation Building	255
10.7	Trust by Industry	257
10.8	Levels of Trust in Ads for the Given Products	258
10.9	Brand Trust Breach Event and Impact	262
12.1	Value of Duration with Brand	304
12.2	Drivers of Future Growth: Brand Value, Opportunity Space, and Resilience	307
12.3	Creating Future Options	312
13.1	Brand Revitalization Strategies	333
14.1	Framework of Brand Redeployment Strategy	345
14.2	Antecedents of Brand Redeployment Strategy	351
14.3	Post-merger Brand Equity: Comparison across Redeployment Strategies	366
15.1	Distribution of Customers' Contribution	385
15.2	Distribution of Individual Customer's Contribution (in $) across Customer Base (Stylized Illustration)	386
15.3	Link between Brand Management and Customer Management	389
16.1	Brand Value as a Percent of Market Capitalization	395
16.2	Trademark Protection under the Law	412

17.1	Diversity in Acquirer's Brand Portfolio—Brand Value Relationship: Impact of Redundancy	426
17.2	Target Marketing Capability: Brand Value Relationship—Impact of Redundancy	427
18.1	Impact of Brands and Marketing on Financial Performance	435
18.2	Role of Brands at Different Stages of the Product Life Cycle (Contingent Strategies and Relevant Metrics)	437
18.3	Strategies, Relevant Metrics Depend on Stage of Product Life Cycle and Competition	439
18.4	Brand Platforms as Strategic Growth Options	441

List of Abbreviations

AGR	average growth rate
AIT	average inter-purchase time
AMA	American Medical Association
B2B	business-to-business
B2C	business-to-customer
CBV	customer brand value
CE	customer equity
CLV	customer lifetime value
CPG	consumer package goods
CRM	customer relationship management
CRV	customer referral value
CV	customer value
CVM	customer value management
FIR	Firms-In-Retailing
FMCG	fast moving consumer goods
GC	average gross contribution margin
IOC	International Olympic Committee
NBP	No Brand Preference
OEM	original equipment manufacturer
PCV	past customer value
RFM	recency-frequency-monetary
ROI	return on investment
SOW	share of wallet
SUR	seemingly unrelated regression
WASS	weighted average cost of capital
WOM	word of mouth

Preface

THE GENESIS

The objective of developing this book was to bring to light the latest thinking on brand management with chapters contributed by many of the most accomplished and well-known thought leaders in the marketing discipline. After what seems like a long journey, our goal is finally realized due to the excellent collaborative spirit of the authors.

New ideas change the world. From social movements to scientific discovery, the power of an idea can reshape the world, who we are, and how we live. The aim of this book is to provide an outlet for cogent ideas that may not be easily conveyed within the bounds of other formats (academic journals or in shorter formats in business periodicals).

As language developed, it was found that humans needed a way to capture ideas more permanently, and thereby, writing came into being aeons ago. Today, there are several well-regarded journals in every discipline that lead to advancement in management and do a fine job of enabling peer-reviewed articles to be published. Books, when written by a single author, can provide an outlet for a subject to be treated robustly and in depth. What this book does is that it provides an outlet for ideas in each chapter and does not require a full-length book to express itself. This format provides more freedom for expression than is typically found in journals.

We view marketing and branding not merely as a department, but as a managerial practice that pervades business. Consequently, our target audience includes executives, managers, and prospective managers in organizations.

The managerial implications of this book have cross-industry application in management as well as across market sectors of both business-to-business (B2B) and business-to-consumer (B2C).

Those who will find this book of interest include board of directors, chairmen, CEOs, CFOs, CMOs, COOs, general managers, presidents, senior vice presidents, vice presidents, directors, consultants, product development managers, marketing managers, marketing analysts, channel managers, product marketing managers, solutions managers, brand managers, financial managers, operations managers, and others in companies. The book was developed to serve the general business as well as the academic market. It can also be used as a textbook in business schools at the undergraduate and graduate levels.

HIGHLIGHTS OF THE BOOK

This book aims to become a classic in marketing literature. It presents the latest thinking on key concepts in brand management, including brand performance management, brand strategy, brand-building, revitalization of brands, valuation of brands, analysis of brands, protection of brands, and brand experience. This book is an authoritative anthology with relevant input from leading experts in the field. The information in it will provide managers with the knowledge they need to build and maintain brands with a linkage to superior business performance.

SUMMARY

This book is the source for engaging the perspectives of leading minds on branding. It is the essential roadmap to the future of brand and customer management.

Acknowledgments

We wish to recognize and appreciate the expertise, commitment, and collaborative spirit of the authors who have made this book possible by generously devoting their time to write the chapters. We are proud to be associated with the world's leading thought leaders and management scientists who address challenges faced in management of brands. The collective effort of this distinguished group has resulted in a book with great depth and perspective, which goes far beyond what a single author could produce.

We would like to thank the companies that collaborated to develop brand insights over the years. These include Kimberly Clark, DuPont, Milliken & Co., Marriott, Leading Hotels of the World, Banyan Tree Hotels, Avaya, Lucent Technologies, the InterContinental Hotel Group, Palladium, Sprint, Home Depot, ING, UPS, Electronic Arts, Coca-Cola, the CMO Council, and Equifax. Conversations and projects with managers at these companies helped us develop a more comprehensive view of marketing challenges facing senior management.

A special "thank you" to Professor Jagdish Sheth, whose advice was of prime importance for the book!

We would like to thank Sachin Sharma, Chandra Sekhar, and the team at SAGE for their active support in publishing this book.

We dedicate this book to Roberto C. Goizueta, whose support of management education provided a platform for the initiation of this book.

Section I
Brand Strategy

Chapter 1
Selecting the Brand Architecture to Match Your Strategy

Jean-Noël Kapferer

To grow, companies need to expand their number of products and create new brands to address a particular market. As soon as a company decides to launch a second product line, brand architecture issues arise. Should the second product have a name or just a designator? Is it a brand? Should its identity be related to the first product line? How should this be done? In the same way, as soon as a company acquires another organization, the question of renaming the acquired unit arises—should it keep its name, immediately adopt the name of the acquiring company or choose a middle ground by being endorsed by the former?

Brand architecture decisions relate to identification of products within a range in order to maximize their value and brand equity. This is the way a company structures and presents:

- Products/Services within their brands
- Brands within the company

Brand architecture is the visible identity that specifies the degree of relation between all the parts together. In business-to-business (B2B), it is the identity system that relates (or not) the constituents of the company (branches, activities, poles and subsidiaries) to the corporate brand. In brief, brand architecture is the parental system a company or group chooses to maximize the flows of the image and trust between its different parts. It is not a mirror of its financial or legal structure or of its organization: it aims at building reputation in an efficient manner.

Today, brand architecture issues have become more complex because companies and brands have diversified their activities. However, there are principles that need to be adopted to solve these issues as rationally as possible.

It is the purpose of this chapter to present working models and criteria relating to brand architecture. We will keep a balance between business-to-customer (B2C) and B2B examples. This is no more a solely marketing issue or a communication one. It has implications on the governance of companies as well (Rao et al., 2004; Balmer, 2011; Fetscherin and Usunier, 2012).

A STRATEGIC DECISION, YET TOO UNDERRATED

Brand architecture issues are largely ignored in companies and they do not attract much of academic research. Yet they have a long-lasting effect on the reputation of a brand or company as well as on its financial returns (Morgan and Rego, 2009; Chang and Park, 2013). Philips is a typical example. In 2004, T. Kleisterlee, the CEO of this consumer electronics company, decided to incorporate a new branding policy in it. This was summarized by his slogan "one brand." It was evident that the stock market was strongly undervaluing Philips compared to its world competitors from Asia. Most of the innovations the company brought to the market were attributed to Sony or Samsung by consumers. As a result, Philips was made to look like a market follower, a regional player and not the pioneer and leader it actually was.

How could such a situation have developed? Philips' brand architecture decisions were largely at fault. For years, the company had grown worldwide by its acquisition of local brands and companies, all of which were market leaders in their home countries, as this was the best way to enter a country and its distribution networks. That is why Philips bought Norelco, the No.1 razor brand in the USA, or Walitta the No.1 white goods brand in Brazil. Unfortunately, instead of immediately planning and putting in place a phased brand substitution plan from the local name of the acquired company to its new global name or at least some kind of endorsement or co-branding between Norelco and Philips or Walitta and Philips, the latter's local marketing teams were strong advocates of a no-change policy in keeping with the local name of the acquired company. Worse, since Philips was not known to local consumers, and consequently, brought no added value to them, the management of the acquired company refused to include Philips' name (even subtly) on its products and their packaging. And like a self-fulfilling prophecy, Philips retained its image of a regional European player, whereas its operations were truly global. However, its brand was not global. These brands included Sony and well-known global companies and brands including Samsung, LG, and Haier.

Another historical brand architecture decision that was questioned by the CEO of Philips was that of naming the company's razors "Philishave." While Braun simply calls its razors "Braun razors," Philips had, a long time ago, decided on Philishave. A sub-brand such as Philishave may retain the positive brand image traits without passing them on to the "mother brand" (Sullivan, 1990; Erdem and Sun, 2002).

EVERY TYPE OF ORGANIZATION FACING BRAND ARCHITECTURE ISSUES

Brand architecture issues are not limited to industrial groups, conglomerates, and big companies. These are also faced by small companies. The only difference is that they become quite complex in large groups, especially if enterprises are diversified and different sets of rules may have to be used from one branch to another (Balmer, 2011). Brand architecture decisions arise as soon as one creates a start-up company. For instance, Bookeen, a young start-up company in the booming digital or electronic book market, invented a brilliant product called Cybook and markets a range of such merchandize including Cybook Opus. This engineer-led company had already created a somewhat inefficient brand architecture. It was vital for it to concentrate its resources on building a single brand name to quickly enhance awareness of its brand—the first requisite step in brand building. However, in this case, one wonders what the brand actually is. Is it Cybook or Bookeen? Bookeen's managers should have benchmarked a former famous start-up of the Silicon Valley called Apple. What did Steve Jobs and Steve Wozniak, Apple's founders, call their first products? Apple. They came out with Apple II and Apple III, and only much later (more than eight years) did they change this policy with the launch of a real disruption in the market called "MacIntosh."

Brand architecture decisions need to be made, even in organizations that refuse to use the word "brand" for cultural reasons or even in their marketing. Although mainly known because of its world-entertaining event, the Olympic Games, the Olympic movement is in fact developing high ideals and goals to foster peace through sport. The International Olympic Committee operates through a world network of partners, organizations, stakeholders and sponsors who act at the local level to implement actions, for example, the National Olympic Committees in each country, the Games Organizing Committee in each town selected to run the next Olympic Games, official sponsors such as Coca Cola or Samsung, and official technical partners such as Atos. Decisions regularly need to be made as to the signature that should be used and the occasions on which the partners have the right to use the Olympic Rings. When can a partner use the word "Olympic" (which belongs exclusively to IOC [International Olympic Committee])? Other questions are still more specific. Since the Olympic rings have five colors to symbolize the five continents, when can there be exceptions and the use of a single color?

One cannot answer on a case-by-case ad hoc basis. The IOC needs a framework with guiding principles to be shared within the organization and outside vis-à-vis all third parties and stakeholders.

BUILDING BLOCKS OF BRAND ARCHITECTURE

To start working successfully and collaboratively on brand architecture, one needs to acquire a common understanding with the help of a glossary on the subject. Words are related to very precise notions and acts. Because authors on brands tend to introduce their own terminology, some confusion exists in this domain (Aaker and Joachimsthaler, 2000a; Douglas et al., 2001; Rajagopal and Sanchez, 2004; Strebinger, 2004). Therefore, it is necessary to clarify the terminology once and for all. This is the goal of this section.

What is a brand? It is a name with power, the power to influence behavior. The source of this power is the fame attached to a name, making it the perceived champion of either a product class or of a set of values. Brand identifiers go beyond the name. They encompass a logotype—how a brand is written and designed. The cursive letters used in the brand Coca Cola or the bold capital letters in IBM are examples of famous logotypes. A brand can benefit from a symbol. For example, Generali, the insurance brand and company, is symbolized by a Venetian Lion, and Royal Dutch Shell, the petroleum company commonly known at Shell, by its red and yellow seashell.

We use the word "brand image" to refer to what a brand evokes now in people's minds, as measured through opinion surveys or qualitative interviews. This is just a description of the current mindset of consumers and what people think about a brand or company. Brand decisions are aimed at achieving competitiveness in the future; they aim to build a strong perception of its uniqueness and relevance. Therefore, the word "corporate brand" does not refer to the present image of a company, but to what it wants to stand for in the future. There may be a gap between the two, and its marketing communication needs to reduce this gap.

Business growth is obtained by launching new products to match new needs and attract new clients. This leads to the issue of organizing a new range (with old and new products) to make it clearer to consumers or buyers, prescribers, engineering departments in B2B markets (Muylle et al., 2012). We will use the word "mother brand," which is similar to a family surname name in its social reputation, to refer to the integrating role a brand fulfils. Brands are here to not only differentiate themselves versus their competition, but also to integrate their products under their umbrella, as parent brands. Nivea has named all the products in its wide range as Nivea Cream, Nivea Shampoo, Nivea Deodorant, and so on. This structure means that they have been "approved" by Nivea and that each product contains adequate *"Niveaness"* to warrant its being called Nivea.

Brand architecture issues focus on "what do you write after the brand." Samsung has named its digital high-end products (smartphone, pads and watches) "Galaxy" all over the world. The company did not feel obligated to launch a sub-brand, although its managers are often tempted to do this when a new product is to be launched. However, managers should resist over-indulging in naming their innovations. There is nothing more value-destroying than giving a new product a special distinctive name if one can instead use its generic name. This is one of the trickiest decisions a company has to take, for example, should 3M have called Post'it simply "Scotch Notes"? Creating a new brand name can have strategic implications. To build awareness of its brand, a company has to divert million dollars from nurturing its existing "masterbrands," which need to be permanently reinforced through innovation.

The word "masterbrand" has emerged from the fact that today, companies want to capitalize on a few names, which cover a large number of products and services within their umbrellas, instead of multiplying brands, each one with a limited scope. These masterbrands tend to generate over a billion dollars in revenue and are global (managed worldwide as one organization versus multinational (or multiregional), which implies a different approach on a national basis).

To summarize, a clear picture emerges from this discussion in that the global range of any company should be organized under masterbrands acting as an integrating force to cover and tie together a range of either products or "sub brands." All these masterbrands should be themselves either nested below the corporate brand or managed independently as brands, which implies that the corporation is a financially driven holding company and does not wish to stand out by advertising its name on its products or on those of its acquired companies. A masterbrand exerts its integrating effect, as shown in the pyramidal model (Figure 1.1).

Organizational Structure Is Not to Be Confused

In B2B and in corporate branding in general, much confusion arises from the fact that at the board of directors' level, the dominant vision is legal, financial or organizational, but not symbolic. Brand

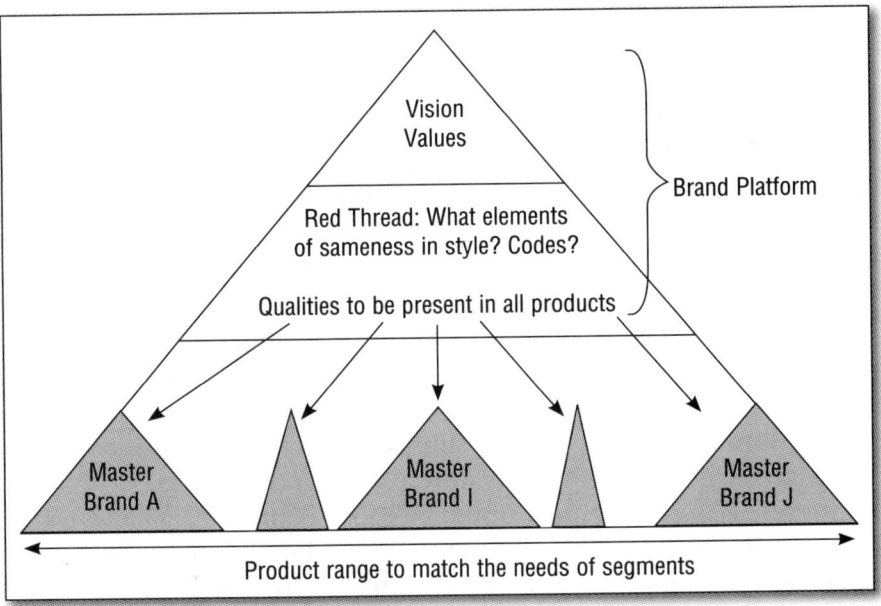

Figure 1.1 Integrative Role of Brands

architecture decisions are those that relate to communication of relationships between the parts and the whole. How can these be managed to maximize their share value? For a lawyer, these words (parts and whole) evoke the notion of groups, subsidiaries, sub-subsidiaries or holdings. From the perspective of organizational behavior or administration, these words evoke the notion of groups, branches, divisions, business units, poles, companies, departments or activities.

That is why much pedagogy is needed when introducing brand architecture to groups and companies. One should not confuse the branding system with organizational or legal structures. How often have we seen the word "group" in a corporate brand name? Outside its walls, who cares about how an organization is structured internally? No brand should ever include the word "group." Poles, divisions, branches or activities are organizational decisions that are generally not long-lasting. CEOs need to change organization of their companies and or the way they are strategically segmented. That is why it is dangerous to believe that organizational constituents are brands. They are the active arms of companies. Consequently, it is not because each subsidiary has a legal name that this name is a brand. Its legal name may be used to sign a contract, but it is not necessarily a brand. For example, Zodiac Aircraft Systems may be the name of a company, but the overarching brand is Zodiac Aerospace. Taking Vishnu, the Indian Hindu deity as a metaphor, all these company names are its arms, but there is only one God.

In another example, one of the largest groups selling environmental services in the world is Veolia Environment. Aiming at mayors in major cities, this private operator delivers what is known as "public utilities." It has three main activities, each with its own "masterbrand"—Veolia Water, Veolia Waste, and Veolia Transport. One of the many activities within its transportation unit is cargo-based, and is carried out by subsidiaries in European countries (Veolia Cargo Deutschland Gmbh. and Veolia Cargo UK, Ltd). However, it has only one brand, Veolia Transport. Veolia Cargo is not a brand, but the legal name of local companies. This holds true for a company called Veolia Water Solutions Inc., which has subsidiaries around the world to provide drinkable water in major cities. Here again, the company name is not the brand. The brand is Veolia Water. This should be very clear on its business cards, since the brand should stand alone at the top, followed by the managers' name and function, and then by the name of the specific local company of which they are an acting member.

The implications of taking a brand as a highly symbolic sign are simple. Brand architectures do not describe legal linkages or proximities in terms of subsidiaries, only proximity to the intended meaning of the brand.

Six Types of Brand Architecture

All groups or companies need to answer the following four questions to maximize their creation of value and share valuation:

1. What is the role of the corporate brand? Should it stay hidden, explicitly endorse or be the commercial name of some specific activity in the company's portfolio? For instance, the German pharmaceutical company Bayer, known for its famous medical blockbusters, signs its generics division

directly as it is called: Bayer Classics. Bayer is the group name, but is also used as commercial name for some of the company's divisions. This also holds true for Danone, which is both the name of the group (with other brands such as Evian Water) and the commercial brand of the company's dairies.

2. Does the company want to support a single reputation or a plural set of reputations? Should it follow a "branded house" structure, also referred to as a "one brand" policy, or conquer markets by using a "house of brands" structure through a portfolio of well-targeted and leading brands. IBM has a "one brand" policy called "branded house." It competes through a single corporate masterbrand with the company acting as a single entity in promoting its uniqueness and relevance to lead in markets. Examples of companies following a "branded house" policy include Virgin, EasyJet, GE, Samsung, Sony, Intel, and Nokia. Many others use segmented and independent masterbrands because they operate in distinct markets, each to meet a specific set of clients' needs. Typical examples of such companies include Procter and Gamble with its famous portfolio of unrelated masterbrands (Ariel, Tide, Pampers, Oil of Olay, Head and Shoulders, Always, Gillette, Braun, Tampax, etc.), GM with its many automobile masterbrands, and L'Oréal with its brand portfolio (Lancôme, L'Oréal, Garnier, Kiehl's, BodyShop, and Maybelline). That is why this second structure is called the "house of brands," since the company houses a set of brands within its enterprise.

3. What are the explicit links that should be established between the corporate brand and masterbrands? One very explicit link needs to be put in place when a corporation decides to take the name of its flagship product to clarify what it stands for. Coca-Cola Corporation is named after the world's No.1 soft drink brand, but also owns other major masterbrands such as Fanta, Minute Maid, Dasani Water, the Burn energy drink, and Innocent Smoothies. Nestlé Corporation has chosen the name of its historical founding line Nestlé Baby Food (the nest symbol for its logo), but

the firm also markets other masterbrands such as Nescafé, Nespresso, Buitoni, Friskies, San Pellegrino, Acqua Panna Waters, nuts, and KitKat. A company such as LVMH, the world's No.1 luxury group, is never visible in the operations of its 60 brands (Louis Vuitton, Givenchy, Tag Heuer, Fendi and Bulgar, to name a few), so as to not destroy their mystique.

4. What is the link that should be established between masterbrands and their products or services? Should some of these products be held as sub-brands or as variants of the masterbrand, and consequently, by called by their generic names? In the smartphone business, Galaxy is a sub-brand of Samsung, but iPhone is a variant of the Apple brand.

Decisions about sub-branding are made after examining the role each product or service should play in the construction of a masterbrand. Is it a variant of the latter? Is it the prototype or best exemplar of the masterbrand or a transformation? A variant means that all the product's differentiating qualities are the same as those promised by the masterbrand. The prototype is the icon of the masterbrand. A transformation means that some of the masterbrand's values are not present as differentiators of a particular product, and the product has differentiating attributes of its own. Only a transformation should normally have the right to become a sub-brand. For instance, Venus is a sub-brand of the masculine Gillette brand.

Questions 1–3 relate to corporate decisions and question 4 to marketing ones. These questions lead not to an infinite number of brand architectures, but to a finite number of these. In practice, we find six types, which designate how sublevels are explicitly related to hierarchial levels (products to brands, activities to corporate, etc.) (see Figure 1.2):

The selection of a brand architecture is not a formal exercise, nor is it something that is driven by mathematical modeling. In real life, brand architecture expresses a company's strategy. For instance, recent research recommends the "one brand only" policy (with the corporate masterbrand as the only brand) because this is the most correlated to Tobin's Q criterion, the ratio between a company's market value and its book value (Rao et al., 2004; Rubera and Drodge, 2013). This criterion measures what can be called "the

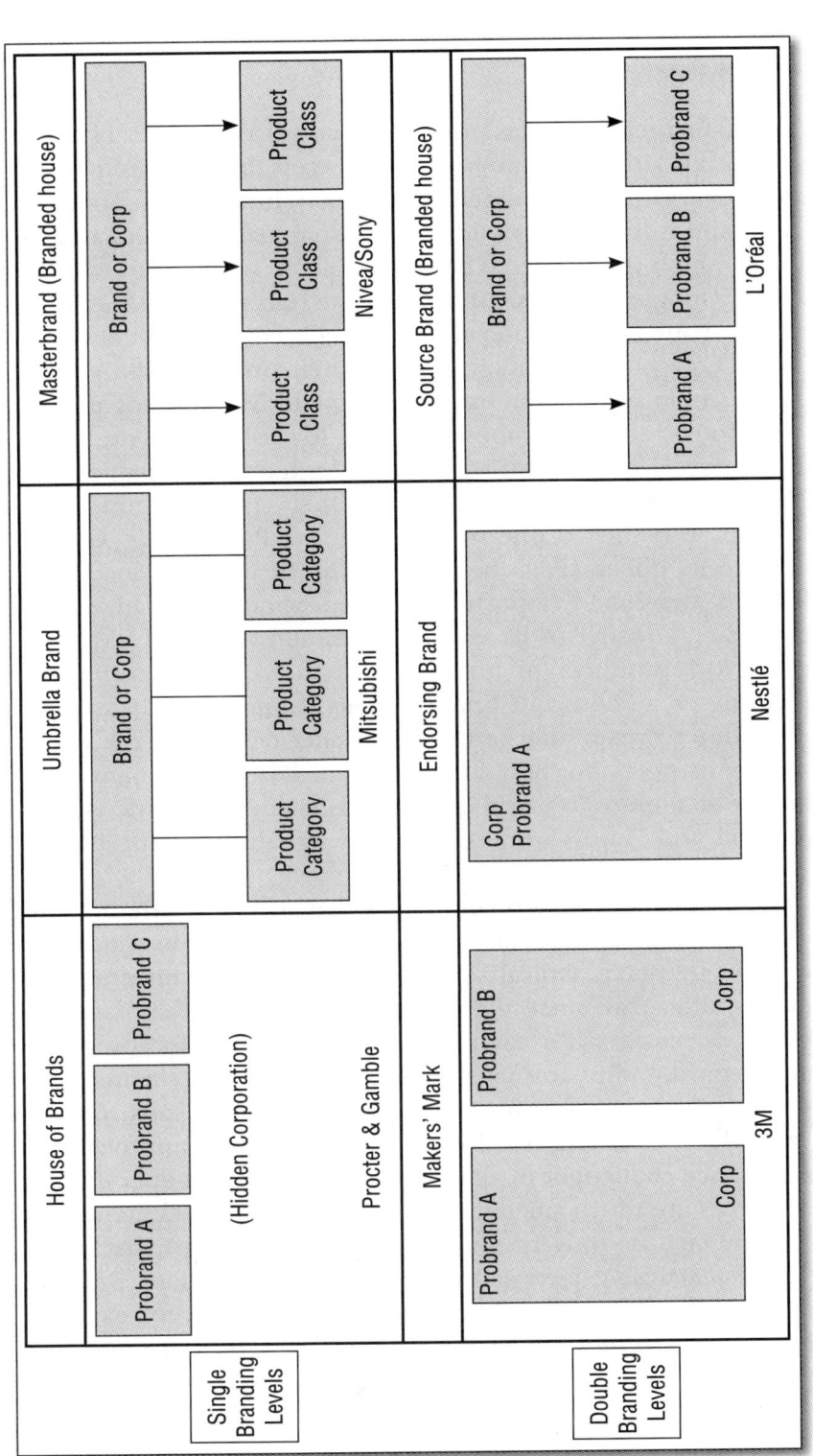

Figure 1.2 The Six Typical Brand Architectures

dream of financial markets" (Kapferer and Tabatoni, 2011). The danger of this kind of research is that it forgets that establishment of brand architecture is a competitive decision, linked to a company's strategy, and is highly dependent on its financial capacities and the sector in which it operates. The results of the research fit with the profile of Google and those of many of the stars of NASDAQ. When they were young, these internet or biotech companies needed to follow a "One brand" strategy, with all their products and services under a single brand, for example, Google Maps, Google View, Google Books, etc. The same holds true for IBM. Its "One brand" policy is typical of those of service and high-tech companies such as Nokia and Samsung, which change their entire product lines every year. But should one immediately ask Procter and Gamble to change its policy (P&G being a "house of brands" since 1890, which has developed a portfolio of independent world masterbrands, each a leader in its segment)? Should one ask LVMH, the world's No.1 producer of luxury products, to do the same, and stop acting as a "house of brands"? This would immediately ruin the consumer dream attached to the cachet of each of the luxury brands in its portfolio. Should the hidden Diageo company move out of the shadow of its world-class brands (such as Johnnie Walker, J&B, Ketel One, and Ciroc) and put its signature on the bottles? Of course not.

In the same sector, two companies may follow different routes just because they do not have the same resources. The Coca-Cola Company adopts a typical "house of brands" architecture. Its resources allow this, since the company can sustain the marketing investments required for each of its masterbrands. Moreover, consumers typically want to buy the "prototype" of the segment, the best exemplar being *Coke* for Cola, *Fanta* for orange soda, *Innocent* for smoothies, etc). Virgin follows a "branded house" approach and acts as a price challenger in all the markets in which it operates, but its resources are much smaller than those of the brands mentioned earlier. In fact, its only resource is its brand (Virgin), backed by the media-catalyzing personality of its founder, Richard Branson. That is why Virgin names all its products generically, for example, Virgin Cola, Virgin Orange, Virgin Vodka, Virgin Airways, and Virgin Stores.

Which Brand Architecture for Which Situation

A detailed analysis of the pros and cons of each of these six brand architectures has been exposed elsewhere (Kapferer, 2012). In this article, we focus on the criteria or situations that should orient a company toward one or the other of these brand architectures. Academic literature generally identifies only three of these: umbrella branding (with branded houses acting as umbrella brands), endorsing brand (dual branding), and hidden corporate (also called "house of brands"). But in practice, business executives are not satisfied with only these three types and want to add another type of architecture to the three mentioned above: the "source brand." This has been overlooked in branding literature or confused with the "endorsement brand." However, the difference is significant.

- In an "endorsement brand" architecture, the hero is the product, and the company is just endorsing it as a trust mark, which is a certification of quality. Graphically, the masterbrand logo or the corporate logo stands below in the media used (be it packaging, advertising, etc), and quite far from the product logo if any.
- In a "source brand" architecture, the brand projects its family's benefits and values onto the whole range, be they tangible or intangible. Therefore, it should never sign below its products as a endorsing brand does. For instance, L'Oreal Paris is a source brand and its name stands above the name Elseve (name of its haircare line). Lego is also the source brand (for example, Lego Scala, Lego Duplo, Lego Chima, Lego Friends, Lego Hero Factory).

An endorsement is not a binary variable, but it includes nuances of endorsement. Most authors do not make the distinction between the "makers' mark" architecture (a certificate of its authentic origin) and the "endorsing architecture" (a certificate of trust and satisfaction guarantee). Similarly, "umbrella branding" needs to be separated into two nuances, depending on the way a corporation is managed:

1. Some companies are fully decentralized and give significant freedom to their branches. This is typical of the Korean company Chaebols. Samsung cars are promoting a different image from Samsung consumer products, driven by 3D TVs and mobile smartphones. Each branch of the company is run in silo, independent of the other branches.
2. Some other companies communicate with slogans about what their umbrella brands want to portray across their divisions and product lines. As a result, they enforce strict alignment policies across all their activities, products, and ranges. A typical case is that of the Korean company LG, which has decided to give a common and very precise meaning, both tangible and intangible, to its umbrella brand name (LG = Life is Good).

The following mapping (Figure 1.3) compares the six brand architectures on their completeness. More in-depth analyses can be found elsewhere (Kapferer, 2012). Two dimensions structure these architectures. In fact, it all depends on whether companies use their

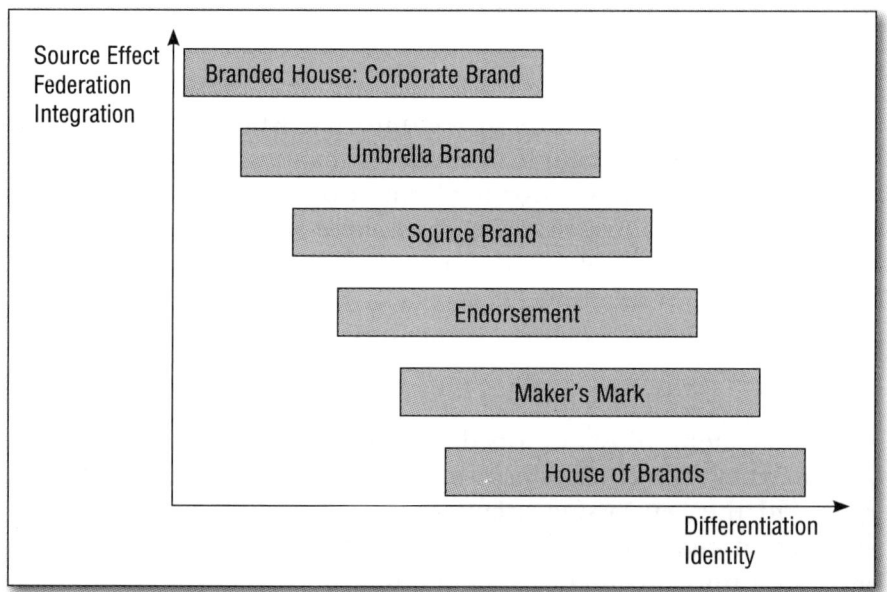

Figure 1.3 Positioning the Six Typical Brand Architectures

strength as their main driver of choice or if they rely more on their customers' identity.

1. When trust is of paramount importance, a corporation should adopt a "one brand" policy. That is why AXA (the world's No.1 insurance brand) immediately drops the names of local No.1 insurance and asset management companies it acquires to expand its operations geographically. Its management wants to make AXA the world's most trusted insurance company.
2. In the soft drink industry, pleasure comes first (thirst second). It is driven by product brands that encompass both taste-related promises and a high brand personality profile (Azoulay et al., 2005). That is why the corporation is either hidden or at best acts as a discreet maker's mark on the labels of its brands.

How do all these six architectures relate to the basic dichotomy, that of a house of brands vs branded house? See Table 1.1.

As we can see, "house of brands" does not solely relate to a hidden corporate brand and fully independent ones. It also applies to two other strategies. One can even say that in a very decentralized company, where silos are in place, and no transverse brand management exists, the same brand image is not built in all its divisions, despite their acting formally under a single umbrella name. It looks like a "branded house," but it is, in fact, managed like a "house of brands." This is the case with Asian brands. Does Samsung Fashion promote the same values as Samsung Cars or Samsung Phones? No.

Table 1.1 "House of Brands" versus "Branded House" in Perspective

House of Brands	Branded House
Endorsing brand	Source brand
Makers mark	Umbrella brand
Independent brands	Corporate masterbrand

Tying Brand Architecture to Company's Business Model

Establishment of a brand architecture is a strategic decision. It is decided over many years and has an immediate cost, which includes alignment of all the parts of the company worldwide to match the selected brand architecture. Which is then the best branding strategy? Procter & Gamble are firm supporters of the "house of brands" (many separate product brands, while the corporation remains hidden). The L'Oréal Group prefers a concentrated number of world masterbrands, which regroup all the brands, sub-brands, and products of the group, one of these masterbrands being L'Oreal Paris. The other brands include Maybelline, The BodyShop, Lancôme, Garnier and Kiehl's. Who is right? Both.

Each brand strategy has its own advantages and disadvantages. This has been described elsewhere (Kapferer, 2012). However, a simple list of the pros and cons does not provide a robust decision process to a company in a given market. The choice of a brand architecture is not an informal exercise, but a reflection of the corporate strategy selected by a company in a specific context. We will now analyze the parameters one should take into account when selecting a branding strategy.

The first and foremost parameter is corporate strategy, of which branding strategy is a visible symbol. In 2000, the CEO of the L'Oréal Group, Lindsay Owen Jones, said "only global." He meant that there should soon remain only global brands at the L'Oréal Group, with the understanding that broad brands are stronger (Meyvis and Janizewski, 2004). There would be local products such as whiteners in Asia, but most of the innovation should, from then on, be justified by their global scope and business plan. As to their remaining regional brands, they would have also to be nested in one of the supra brands. L'Oréal enacted its "only global" motto by deciding to concentrate its portfolio around 15 global masterbrands, each encompassing a very wide range of products.

In 2003, Schneider Electric's new CEO redefined the company's strategic positioning against those of GE, ABB and Siemens. Compared with these electrical giants, Schneider Electric was not a small general electrical company, but liked to see itself as a "multi-specialist" one. As a result of its "multi-specialist" positioning, these specialties had to be carried by its specialist masterbrands

Telemecanique and Merlin-Gerin, which were endorsed by the corporate brand. However, in 2012, Schneider Electric decided to move to a "one brand" architecture. The reason was that its corporate strategy had changed again. Electrical companies were now selling energy efficiency. The results were more important than the parts needed to achieve this. This ended the life of former world specialist masterbrands. There was only one now: Schneider Electric.

Group SEB, the world leader in small household appliances, decided to compete with four world brands—Moulinex, Tefal, Krups and Rowenta. SEB as a corporate name would remain hidden, only known in the trade and by financiers. It decided not to follow the same one-brand policy as Philips. Thus, the second parameter to take into account is the business model. In this respect, it is interesting to compare companies within the same sector, since their brand architectures are often a reflection of their business models, the driving force of their competitive edge and their profitability.

Brand Architecture and Corporate Culture

Culture is another key parameter for a company's choice of brand architecture. The United States have developed the culture of the "product brand"—a brand that sells a single product. Ivory, the founding brand of Procter & Gamble, is and continues to remain a soap brand. Pampers sells only diapers, Tide Detergent, and so on. This is possible in a wide domestic market for fast moving consumer goods (Saunders, 1994, 1999, 2007). In contrast, this explains why Europe and Japan have been the main advocates of the umbrella-brand policy with an extended multi-product range under each brand.

How do you grow a brand in a small country without extending it? You cannot. You launch it internationally or adopt a brand extension strategy, or both. Nivea and Nestlé are just two of many European examples. In Japan, apart from the size of its domestic market, the reputation of a company is also a major concern—an inheritance from Confucianism. The more products a company produces and the more sectors it services, the greater its reputation. It would simply not occur to the director of a Japanese company to not use the corporate name to promote all kinds of extensions. Yamaha is a typical example of this. It started as a company selling musical instruments (classical pianos and guitars), then it extended its product range to HiFi equipment and finally to recreation equipment and small motorbikes for the US market. No American management team would ever do this for cultural reasons only (Dacin and Smith, 1994; Van Osselaer and Alba, 2003; Völckner and Sattler, 2006). However, thinking global, its "One brand" policy proved helped Yamaha build its reputation worldwide.

Another parameter is the pace of innovation in the category. How do you develop product brands or sub-brands in a sector that renews its offer twice a year? You cannot. In this instance, a single-brand policy covering the entire range is preferable, as in the case of Nokia, Sony-Ericsson, and even Whirlpool and GE. Samsung is an exception because it wanted to put Galaxy in completion to i-Phone. The company's image did not have much in-depth content in the West at that time, which Galaxy now has.

Another key parameter is the type of added-value lever on which a product is based. This point is illustrated in Figure 1.3 and gives the relative positioning of the six different brand architectures. When the added value in a particular market is linked to reassurance, reputation and scale, a "branded house" single-brand umbrella strategy is recommended. (In the world of industry, this is often the corporate brand.) Another possibility is the "source-branding" strategy with two levels of branding—the architecture adopted by brands such as Garnier or L'Oréal Paris. However, the more segmented the market, with top-quality, highly personalized products, the more one needs to favor either a "house of brands" approach (like the Coca Cola Company's portfolio) or an "endorsing brand" architecture.

Finally, brand identity itself has to play a role. It is a cornerstone concept in brand management and was introduced through the *brand identity prism* in Europe (Kapferer, 1990) at a time when textbooks on brand equity never used the term even once (Aaker,1990) or used it in the manner design agencies speak about the word (which invokes the visual dress of the brand) (Olins, 1989). It appeared only lately in the US literature (Aaker and Joachimsthaler, 2000b; Aaker, 2004). Identity reminds us that brands have more than an image; they have an inner self, an inner truth, and a DNA.

They are not just a number of mental associations in consumers' memories, as developed by the cognitive approach to brand equity (Keller, 2012).

At Clarins, a skincare company, there are no single products as a rule. The company's 70 products are all grouped into lines. Why? Because of the brand's identity. Since its creation, Clarins' self-concept has been that of it being a Beauty Institute. This concept implies the use of a set of products belonging to the same line, just as in a prescription made by a specialist who has taken the time to listen to you. At Clarins, names constitute two or three words, for example, "Multi-Repair Restructuring Lotion." Clarins' brand identity is simple—not overpromising claims about its products. The company's brand architecture follows from this identity.

WHY CORPORATIONS WANT TO BE MORE VISIBLE TODAY

Today, corporations have a strong desire to be visible on their products. Gone is the time when they preferred to remain hidden or just be shadow endorsers. For example, pharmaceutical laboratories now regard themselves as brands in their own right and take great care to ensure that their laboratories' names are visible on the packaging of their medicines. They even want to directly sign some of their activities and branches. Bayer Classics, the name of the company's Generic Division, is an example of this. The back of all Nestlé products bears the company's corporate brand and its customer service phone number. It is the same in the case of Danone, which has taken great care to create a specific logo to differentiate its corporate brand from its commercial brand, which it uses for its dairies and waters.

This is part of a fundamental trend. Today big, as in large organizations, means an obligation to be responsible and act responsibly. This creates a public demand for transparency. A company presents itself as the ultimate endorsement and no longer hides itself behind its masterbrands. This also has the effect of increasing its visibility, and consequently, its attractiveness to students, executives and the employment market in general.

In Asia, one can read in big letters for a few seconds the signatures of Procter & Gamble and Unilever brands at the end of television commercials. This is not the case in the United States or in Europe, although—influenced by its Asian experience—Unilever is looking at increasing its visibility to boost its corporate brand profile in these regions. However, these two companies do not have a good reputation in Asia, and they are seeking to rectify this. Procter & Gamble needs to be known as a reputed company if it wants to hire the best students or managers in Japan, China or Korea.

Once a company is listed on a Stock Exchange, it must try to influence its share price beyond the financial results published on a regular basis. Market evaluations are influenced by its name and reputation. Therefore, anything that makes investors happy adds to its goodwill.

That is why companies change their names and adopt those of their flagship brands. For example, the company formerly known as BSN changed its name to Danone (after nearly choosing Evian, the other world brand in its portfolio). The Volkswagen Group and the L'Oréal Group have both taken their names from their flagship brands. Mars, on the other hand, changed its name and became known as Masterfoods in the manner of other companies called Bestfoods or General Foods. What are the reasons for these two diametrically opposite attitudes?

Apparently, it was difficult to sell brands of pet food such as Pedigree and Whiskas under the Mars corporate or group name, particularly since Mars conjures up the image of a legendary chocolate bar, which has growth limits in an extremely segmented market. There is also the risk of a negative halo effect on financial evaluations.

LVMH, the initials of Louis Vuitton and Moët Hennessy, uses both strategies. On the one hand, industry and financial experts are familiar with the acronym, which stands for three internationally renowned luxury brands. On the other, by retaining this acronym, the group demonstrates its intention of being discreet and placing the emphasis at the masterbrand level rather than the corporate one, thereby letting each brand develop its own charisma.

However, the demand for enhanced corporate visibility creates tensions between marketers and CEOs. At 3M, local marketers outside the USA have always been unwilling to put the marque 3M name on its products. Their argument is that consumers do not care about 3M, which is unknown and irrelevant to them. But they miss out on an important point—3M needs to build its own equity. If it does not, it may become the most innovative but unknown company in the world and have its share undervalued. Brand architectures therefore need to find a balance between all their stakeholders' viewpoints.

RATIONALIZING THE BRAND PORTFOLIO

Strategic questions generally arise after a phase of external growth when leading brands or companies have been bought for their market share, strong image and customer loyalty. After years of such growth, a look at their portfolios frequently reveals a mess that has been created by gross inefficiency. It is therefore clear that the portfolios of brands—global, regional and local—need to be rationalized. This can be done in three ways:

1. This can be achieved in a radical way by immediately shifting to a one-brand policy, which will entail moving all individual brands to this single brand over a short period of time.
2. A company can adopt the policy of co-branding (for example, Gemey-Maybelline or Philips-Whirlpool) to increase the local awareness of its global brand by attaching this to its local star.
3. It can organize its portfolio under a small number of masterbrands, each addressing an activity or segment. In this case, a second question arises. Should the former individual brands be retained as sub-brands or become variants of their new masterbrands? At Nestlé, all acquisitions must be nested in one of the group's strategic masterbrands. However, this generally results in their losing their status of being individual brands by becoming variants of the masterbrands.

To illustrate these strategies, let us analyze some significant cases. Philips still grows by external acquisitions. It has bought a Japanese leader in ultrasonic toothbrushes called Sonicare.

Now it is following a "one brand" policy, which means that in the mid-term, consumers and prescribers will talk about the "Philips ultra sonic toothbrush" and not "Sonicare" or "Sonicare by Philips," even if the latter may be used for a while during the re-branding transition phase.

Veolia is a spin-off of a conglomerate called Vivendi, which had two major branches—multimedia (known as Vivendi-Universal), and construction and public utilities concessions. Because its name could not legitimately endorse this second branch, the company developed it across the world by implementing a policy of individual brands that were positioned around a specific activity. For example, Connex was the brand for public transportation, Onyx for waste management, and Degremont for building industrial water filtering and treatment facilities. Once the tie-up with Vivendi was dropped, it became clear to the new spin-off company Veolia Environment that its main task was to build the brand equity of the new corporate brand as soon as possible. That is why all the former company's "activity masterbrands" were dropped in 2008.

The Nestlé Group portfolio is structured by nesting all its products into a limited number of masterbrands. However under each masterbrand, an open question remains—how to treat each individual product? Is it a variant of the masterbrand (needing no name, for example, "rice and milk chocolate bars" or "nuts and milk chocolate bars") or is it a transformation of the masterbrand and acts as a sub-brand (and therefore needs a name, for example, "Crunch" or "Nuts"). This entails balancing two considerations:

- A corporate one: how to build an attractive company profile and boost the company's financial market valuation
- A market-driven one: Nestlé sells commodities, so how can it make these not look like commodities, especially at the front of private labels? Carrefour and Tesco also sell rice and milk chocolate bars. Is the Nestlé brand strong enough to create a difference? Is it not better to build a "Crunch" brand equity, making it the reference product in its product class (rice chocolate bars and tablets), and thereby less prone to imitation and more desirable because of its pull-power among its youngest consumers who act as influencers? Moreover,

sometimes an innovation creates a market disruption and establishes a new segment. It is important to foresee potential competition with "me-too products" soon to be launched, and to weaken their standing in advance. However, to do so one needs to become the star in a new segment, its prototypical brand. That is why it is necessary to create a name that will marginalize all incoming copiers because they cannot use the name that in fact defines the segment. Sony did this 20 years ago with its "Walkman" and Apple with its "iPhone." To compete in the low CO_2 car market, Toyota has unfortunately chosen a generic word "Hybrid," which it cannot own.

HOW TO BRAND INNOVATIONS

The examples given above introduce a broad and sensitive issue. How should new products be named? Should they get names of their own? Let us now turn to a practical flowchart to aid new products-naming decisions. In B2B, these also apply to any company or brand acquired for its know-how, channel penetration or equity.

The intention of a decision flow chart is to have a clear vision of the masterbrand (referred to here as Brand A) and what it wants to achieve. If it is a corporate brand, what does it want to stand for? Acquisitions and new product opportunities should be evaluated vis-à-vis the corporate goal—the future image of the brand and its desired identity in the long run.

To change an image, a company needs new products or services, which will soon become the "prototypes" (best exemplars) of its new image. Audi moved from an entry price car brand to a super premium one by following a one-brand policy and investing in aggressive communication on and promotion of innovations that pulled its brand image upwards consistently over 25 years with aluminium engines (for example, Audi Quattro) and by following stringent designing norms. That is why companies buy new products and make acquisitions, not only for business reasons, but to turn around their image to revitalize their masterbrands.

Looking at the top of the decision flowchart, two filtering questions come to mind. Does the innovation or acquisition match the desired future identity of the masterbrand, and how large should its sales volume be?

If the first answer is "no," the project should be dropped. If it is "yes," a practical question arises. How far is this acquisition or innovation from the current image of the masterbrand? Clients are not aware of the company's plan to upgrade its image, trade up its brand or make it move like IBM from a product brand to a B2B service one. They base their choice on the company's current image. Three instances are generally encountered:

1. If the innovation falls within the present zone of legitimacy of the brand, its latitude of acceptance—a result of its perceived expertise and brand personality (Azoulay et al., 2005)—the brand should adopt a generic name. There should be no sub-brand or specific buffer-name. If there is already one, it should be removed and a simple product name adopted. Now all generic names need not to be bland. It is important that people realize what the company is trying to communicate. (Such names as Live Box and PlayStation are remarkable cases.) The brand architecture to be adopted should be the typical "umbrella architecture."
2. Looking at the bottom left part of the decision flowchart, what happens if the planned acquisition is remote from the current image of the masterbrand? In this case, one needs a sub-brand, at least for a while. Let us remember that a sub-brand is also a brand. Why is it called a sub-brand? Because its goal is to drive the image of the masterbrand, just as a maverick son or daughter makes a family's name image evolve. But to call this innovation by the masterbrand's name would kill its chances of commercial success and prevent it from playing its image repositioning role. For example, perhaps the most macho brand on earth is Gillette. In its commercials, women are depicted as adoring their demi-gods, their men. Today, there is a huge untapped market for hair removal products for women. If Gillette had launched "Gillette for women" (a typical illustration of umbrella branding with a single brand followed only by a product description) it would have failed.

How many women want to be identified as being masculine or having a severe hair problem? That is why the company launched "Venus by Gillette" with a large Venus identifier at the top of the product and a small Gillette endorsing name at the bottom.

What about the future? It is well known that because of changes in social trends within developed societies, the Gillette brand will need to evolve toward a less caricature-type style vision of man and woman relationships. However, its current image is far from meeting this need today. That is why the brand architecture, featuring at the far left bottom as shown in Figure 1.4, is being followed by the company. For Gillette to evolve its image, its architecture will need to move gradually through time (as depicted in the flow chart) from left to right.

3. The same flow chart can be applied to naming of brand extensions. A brand has a single main goal—to grow consistent profitably. It frequently capitalizes on the success of its founding product or service by implementing successive brand extensions and launching new products and services beyond its core business (Zook, 2004). This may deepen its relationship with its existing customers, or enable it to enter new customer segments or develop new distribution channels. These extensions may be narrow to begin with, for example, substitutes or complementary products, or broader in scope like its entering new product categories, for example, when the designer Armani also became a hotel brand.

When this extension occurs, strategic questions arise about the architecture to be adopted. The answers will have a considerable effect on value creation and construction of brand capital. This is not a problem of aesthetics, but of efficiency. Taking Tropicana as an example, it decided to enter the soup market, not of course with any soup, but gazpacho, a typical Spanish tomato soup, which is served chilled. For this purpose, it bought a company called Alvalle (No.1 in Spain) and launched its product in all supermarkets in Europe, with a big "Alvalle" at the top of the pack and a very small "Tropicana" just below as the maker's mark. This was followed by a big "Gazpacho" and "No.1 in Spain" credential support.

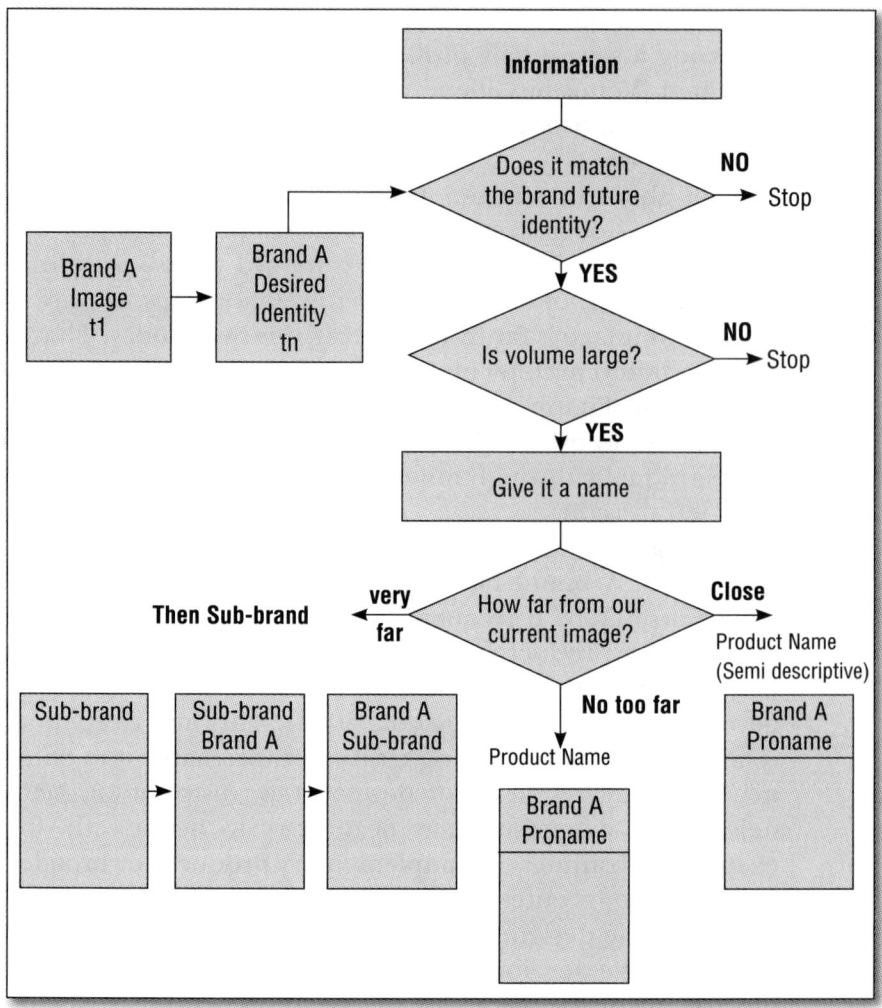

Figure 1.4 How to Brand Innovations

STEPWISE INTEGRATION OF DISRUPTIVE INNOVATIONS

Brand expansion is achieved by acquisition of companies or products, which would not be spontaneously expected from a brand due to the need for a dimension of surprise and disruption. At first the "product-fit" or "concept-fit" between both will seem shallow. As times goes on, however, the main brand will slowly see its own

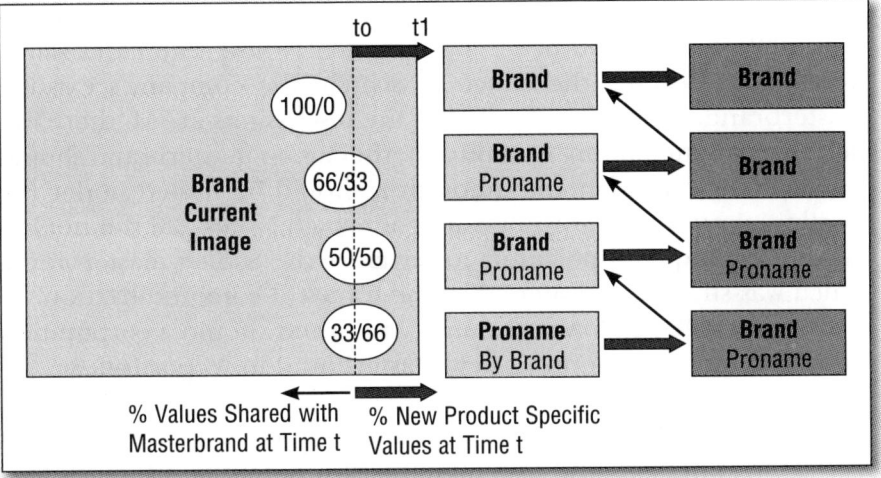

Figure 1.5 Progressive Integration of Innovations

image change. The gap between the innovation and the extension, once remote from the core, will gradually narrow. By checking the progression of its image, the masterbrand will be able to undertake the integration of the extension in its global image, as shown in Figure 1.5. It should be read bottom up. At the bottom is a situation where innovation shares little with the current values of the masterbrand. As a result, the innovation name ("proname") is used as a standalone name with the remote endorsement of the masterbrand. With time, however, the innovation and the masterbrand will share more values through transference of mental association. This will be the time to inverse the order, putting proname below, and still later, printing it in much smaller characters, to end up with a single "brand" (+ a generic wording for the innovation).

WHEN SHOULD COMPANIES CREATE NEW BRANDS

Innovation is the oxygen of brands. Innovation should first and foremost nurture existing masterbrands to increase their lifespan. However, there are situations where innovation should become a brand itself, a new masterbrand. Let us look at a well-known case.

Why then did 3M give a specific name to its breakthrough innovation "Post'it" instead of calling it Scotch Notes? The latter name would have boosted the image of Scotch, the company's existing masterbrand. In fact, till the end of the discussions at 3M, there was hesitance about naming it, about whether a new masterbrand should be created or whether the innovation should be nested under the existing masterbrand. By not calling it Scotch Notes, 3M did not leverage this unique opportunity to revitalize the Scotch masterbrand, which was strongly threatened by the forces of commoditization.

What was 3M follow reasoning? And when should a corporation be bold enough to launch a new masterbrand in its portfolio?

1. A new masterbrand is needed when it creates a new segment with high-growth and high- margin potential, which cannot be captured through an existing masterbrand at the same price. Post'it revealed B2B's information of the market. To look at it from an engineer's standpoint that Post'it should be a part of Scotch, since it is gummed at the back just as Scotch does, would miss the point. Brands are promises and also conjure up images for their clients. Scotch is a pupils' brand; Post 'it a business information device.
2. A masterbrand is needed when me-too products (imitations) are expected to come into the market sooner or later, despite the originals being protected by patents. To make it difficult for copiers to enter the market, a masterbrand needs to become the prototype in it. In cognitive psychology, a prototype is the best exemplar of a concept in its class. By naming an innovation with a new brand name, a company makes the whole product class proprietary and makes it difficult for the sales force of its possible competitors, with their employers asking questions such "What is your own Post'it?"
3. A masterbrand is needed when there are adequate financial resources to build the brand equity of a new brand. If this is not so, the idea needs to be put under the cover and budget of an existing masterbrand. That is why Bic named its innovative disposable razor "Bic." Although this innovation created a new market that Gillette had not identified, Bic did not look for another name despite the recommendations of consultants who said that a ball pen and a razor could

not have the same brand name. But one should recall that in the USA, the total turnover of Bic's disposable razors is relatively small, not higher than Gillette's total advertising budget in the country. As the CEO of Bic, Mr Bich, said, "We had better put all our money in building the most advanced and automated factory in the USA to create a competitive cost advantage, rather than exhaust ourselves in building another brand name worldwide. By doing so, Bic is no longer a product brand but becomes a life- style brand representing the easy and cool life."

4. In the service business, the main problem is in making intangibles tangible (Lei et al., 2004; Devlin and McKechnie, 2008). To do this, it is important to create names that serve as umbrella for a large array of services. For instance, EDF, the French national electricity supplier, launched "Bleu Ciel" (literally Blue Sky) as a major masterbrand to act as an umbrella for all its services that aimed to help households and small businesses save energy and adopt low CO_2 behaviors. This masterbrand has been endorsed by EDF, but is able to talk in a different tone of voice from this monopolistic company, and has brought its target audience closer to it. In addition, the brand Bleu Ciel is licensed to operators that actually sell the devices (solar roofs and windmills).

CONCLUSION: KEY TAKEAWAYS

This chapter aims to promote a more strategic vision of brand architecture-related decisions. Too often, a design agency is hired to make proposals on brand identity and elaborate graphic scenarios. But brand architecture needs to be first audited on business grounds. Does this help the business? Does it reinforce a company's competitiveness? In fact, this is not a design-related issue, but a strategic one. How many brands does a company want to develop including its corporate one? How should these be communicated for enhanced efficiency? In this chapter, we have delved into criteria, parameters and market situations that lead a company to choose a specific architecture instead of another.

REFERENCES

Aaker, D. A. (1990), *Brand Equity*. New York: Free Press.
——— (2004), *Brand Portfolio Strategy*. New York: The Free Press.
Aaker, D. A. and E. Joachimsthaler (2000a), *Brand Leadership*, Free Press, New York.
——— (2000b), "The Brand Relationship Spectrum: The Key to the Brand Architecture Challenge," *California Management Review*, 42(4), 8–23.
Azoulay, A. and J.-N. Kapferer (2003), "Do Brand Personality Scales Measure Brand Personality?" *Journal of Brand Management*, November, 11(2), 143–155.
Balmer, J. M. T. (2011), "Corporate Marketing Myopia and the Inexorable Rise of a Corporate Marketing Logic," *European Journal of Marketing*, 45(9/10), 1329–1352.
Chang, D. R. and S.-B. Park (2013), "The Effects of Brand Strategy and Technological Uncertainty on Pioneering Advantage in the Multigenerational Product Market," *Journal of Product Innovation Management*, 30(1), 82–95.
Dacin, P. A. and D. C. Smith (1994), "The Effect of Brand Portfolio Characteristics on Consumer Evaluations of Brand Extensions," *Journal of Marketing Research*, 31(2), 229–242.
Devlin, J. F. and S. McKechnie (2008), "Consumer Perceptions of Brand Architecture in Financial services," *European Journal of Marketing*, 42(5/6), 654–666.
Douglas, S. P., C. S. Craig, and Nijssen, E. J. (2001), "Integrating Branding Strategy Across Markets: Building International Brand Architecture," *Journal of International Marketing*, 9(2), 97–114.
Erdem, T. and B. Sun (2002), "An Empirical Investigation of the Spillover Effects of Advertising and Sales Promotions in Umbrella Branding," *Journal of Marketing Research*, 39(4), 408–420.
Fetscherin, M. and J.-C. Usunier (2012), "Corporate Branding: An Interdisciplinary Literature Review," *European Journal of Marketing*, 46(5), 733–753.
Kapferer, J.-N. (1990), *Les Marques, Capital de l'Entreprise*. Paris: Eyrolles.
——— (2012), *The New Strategic Brand Management: Advanced Insights and Strategic Thinking*. London: Kogan Page.
Kapferer, J.-N. and O. Tabatoni (2011), "Is Luxury a Financial Dream?" *Journal of Strategic Management Education*, 7(4), 1–16. Senate Hall Academic Publishing.
Keller, K. L. (2012), *Strategic Brand Management*. Upper Saddle River, NJ: Pearson/Prentice-Hall.
Laforet, S. and J. Saunders (1994), "Managing Brand Portfolios: How the Leaders Do It," *Journal of Advertising Research*, 34(5), 64–76.
——— (1999), "Managing Brand Portfolios: Why Leaders Do What They Do," *Journal of Advertising Research*, 39(1), 51–66.
——— (2007), "How Brand Portfolios Have Changed: A Study of Grocery Suppliers Brands from 1994 to 2004," *Journal of Marketing Management*, 23(1/2), 39–58.
Lei, J., R. Pruppers, H. Ouwersloot, and J. Lemmink (2004), "Service Intensiveness and Brand Extension Evaluations," *Journal of Service Research*, 6(3), 243–255.
Meyvis, T. and C. Janiszewski (2004), "When are Broader Brands Stronger Brands? An Accessibility Perspective on the Success of Brand Extensions," *Journal of Consumer Research*, 31(2), 346–357.

Morgan, N. A. and L. L. Rego (2009), "Brand Portfolio Strategy and Firm Performance," *Journal of Marketing*, 73(1), 59–74.

Muylle, S., N. Dawar, and D. Rangarajan (2012), "B2B Brand Architecture," *California Management Review*, 54(2), 58–71.

Olins, W. (1989), *Corporate Identity: Making Business Strategy Visible Through Design*, Boston: Harvard Business School Press.

Rajagopal and R. Sanchez (2004), "Conceptual Analysis of Brand Architecture and Relationships within Product Categories," *Journal of Brand Management*, 11(3), 233–247.

Rao, V. R., M. K. Agarwal, and D. Dahlhoff (2004), "How Is Manifest Branding Strategy Related to the Intangible Value of a Corporation?" *Journal of Marketing*, 68(4), 126–141.

Rubera, G. and C. Droge (2013), "Technology versus Design Innovation's Effects on Sales and Tobin's Q: The Moderating Role of Branding Strategy," *The Journal of Product Innovation Management*, 448(30), 3.

Strebinger, A. (2004), "Strategic Brand Concept and Brand Architecture Strategy: A Proposed Model," *Advances in Consumer Research*, 31, 656–661.

Sullivan, M. (1990), "Measuring Image Spillovers in Umbrella-branded Products," *Journal of Business*, 63(3), 309–329.

Van Osselaer, S. M. J. and J. W. Alba (2003), "Locus of Equity and Brand Extension," *Journal of Consumer Research*, 29(4), 539–550.

Völckner, F. and H. Sattler (2006), "Drivers of Brand Extension Success," *Journal of Marketing*, 70(1), 18–34.

Zook, C. (2004), *Beyond the Core*, Bain Company Inc. Boston, Massachussetts: Harvard Business School Press.

Chapter 2

A Strategic Approach to Grow Profits: Defining, Measuring, and Maximizing Customer Value

V. Kumar and Bharath Rajan

INTRODUCTION

This chapter defines and provides ways of measuring customer value (CV). We identify the major constituents of CV—customer lifetime value (CLV), customer brand value (CBV), and customer referral value (CRV)—and explain their inter-linkages in collectively driving up the customer value for the firm. In the subsequent sections, we delve deeper into the three components of CV. For each component, we provide the definition, the methodology of computing it, the related strategies of maximizing it, and the implementation of the strategies.

CUSTOMER VALUE: DEFINITION AND MEASUREMENT

How can we define customer value? The concept of customer value can be defined as (Kumar and Reinartz, 2006):

> The economic value of the customer relationship to the firm—expressed on the basis of contribution margin or net profit.

A case in point is the Connecticut-based grocery retailer, Stew Leonard's. It is estimated that an average customer at Stew Leonard's spends around $100 a week, shops around 50 weeks a year, and remains in the area for around 10 years. Therefore, in terms of customer value, Stew Leonard's is looking at around $50,000 from each of its customers (Hill and Alexander, 2000). Based on this, one can estimate the loss it would incur if a customer were to leave it unsatisfied. It would be a loss of $50,000! Stew Leonard's has realized this and has entrenched customer satisfaction into its company policy, which reads—"Rule #1: The Customer is Always Right; Rule #2: If the Customer is Ever Wrong, Re-Read Rule #1."[1] Therefore, it is clear that by identifying customers' value, a company can define and adopt effective CRM practices from their value perspective.

Need for Measuring Customer Value

A company can measure and optimize its marketing efforts by incorporating the concept of customer value at the core of its decision-making process. What can it do after measuring customer value?

The answer lies in managing customer value. Customer value management (CVM) rests on the concept of allocating resources differently to different customers, based on the value they bring to an organization. A CVM approach enables companies to redesign customer relationship management (CRM) programs that focus on enhancing customer value. Specifically, a CVM approach to CRM can provide guidelines to managers on questions such as:

1. Under what circumstances is it prudent for a company to nurture and cultivate customer loyalty?
2. How can we ensure profitable customer loyalty?
3. How can we ascertain the future profitability of a customer?
4. What strategies can we adopt to maximize customer value?

Furthermore, CVM enables companies to focus on managing individual customer value as the basis for managing customer

---

[1] See "Company Story" on Stew Leonard's website (http://www.stewleonards.com/html/about.cfm [accessed November 2, 2009]).

relationships, as against managing products or marketing campaigns. The benefits derived from such an approach are significant for companies. Some of the key ones that accrue include (a) a tighter control over costs, (b) significant increases in revenues, (c) a substantial rise in profits, (d) enhanced return on investment (ROI), (e) acquisition and retention of profitable customers, and (f) realignment of marketing resources to maximize customer value.

However, before managing customers, companies need to gain a thorough understanding of how they can compute the value contribution of each customer to them.

How to Measure Customer Value

While there are 50+ important metrics that every executive should know (Farris, Bendle, Pfeifer, and Reibstein, 2006), in this section we review only a few that are relevant. The ultimate focus of this chapter is on the three metrics that every manager should master—CLV, CBV, and CRV. These metrics can be categorized into traditional marketing metrics, primary customer-based metrics and strategic customer-based value metrics.

Traditional marketing metrics: Market share and sales growth are popular traditional marketing metrics that are normally computed for the geographical area a particular market covers. Market share refers to the share of a company's sales in relation to the sales of all others in the industry—across all customers. Sales growth compares the increase or decrease in sales volume or value during a given period to sales volume or value in the previous period. This metric is measured in percentage terms and indicates the degree of improvement in the company's sales performance between two or more time periods.

These metrics were developed when individual customer data was difficult or impossible to obtain and therefore did not provide a customer-level insight into the market. Traditionally, managerial rewards and incentives have been based on these metrics. With the availability of customer-level data, a new set of metrics have emerged—primary customer-based metrics.

Primary customer-based metrics: These metrics can be grouped into three categories that measure three important marketing functions—customer acquisition, customer activity and customer win-back.

Customer acquisition measures include the acquisition rate and cost. The acquisition rate refers to the proportion of prospects converted to customers. It is calculated by dividing the fraction of prospects acquired by the total number of prospects targeted. Acquisition cost refers to acquisition campaign spending divided by the number of acquired prospects.

Customer activity measurements include average inter-purchase time (AIT), retention and defection rates, and P(Alive). The average inter-purchase time is the average time between purchases, measured in terms of time (days, weeks, months, etc.). It is computed by taking the inverse of the number of purchase instances per period. Retention rate refers to the average likelihood that a customer purchases from a particular firm in a period (t), given that this customer has made purchases in the previous period (t–1). Defection rate refers to the average likelihood that a customer defects from the focal company during a period (t), given that the customer was making purchases up to period (t–1). In simple terms, defection rate is 1 minus the retention rate. P(Alive) measures the probability of the customer being active in time t. These metrics help managers track customers' activities from after they have been acquired until they cease to be customers.

Customer win-back measures the proportion of acquired customers in a particular period that a company has lost in an earlier period. This indicates either successful communication of an important change in its product offering or service or a change in the customers' needs. This requires constant monitoring to keep track of lost customers and identification of customers when they re-enter the customer base at a later time.

These metrics were developed, since managers were sensitive about balancing acquisition and customer-retention activities. However, these metrics do not reveal the total value a customer can provide to a company. This set of metrics is being increasingly replaced by other customer-based value metrics that are strategic in nature.

Strategic customer-based value metrics: There are three key metrics in this category—share of wallet (SOW), recency-frequency-monetary value (RFM), and past customer value (PCV). For a detailed discussion on these metrics, see Kumar (2008).

SOW refers to the degree to which a customer meets his/her needs in the category with a focal brand or company. RFM is a composite score of recency, frequency, and monetary value. Recency measures the time since a customer last placed an order with the company. Frequency measures how often a customer purchases from the organization during a particular period. Monetary value refers to the value of purchases made by a customer in an average transaction. PCV refers to the value of a customer, determined by his/her profit contribution in the past, after adjusting for the time value of money. This metric is a more refined one as compared to SOW for computing the relative worth of individual customers.

In essence, these metrics are backward-looking and lack the ability to look ahead into the future and predict the value a customer is likely to bring to an organization.

Introducing Forward-looking Metrics—CLV, CBV, and CRV

As mentioned earlier, there are three constituents of customer value—CLV, CBV, and CRV. It is essential to understand these constituents in order to measure customer value. So, what are they?

CLV refers to the net present value of future cash flows from a customer. In other words, this metric tracks the future purchase behavior of a customer and computes his/her value in present day terms. Since the metric tracks future contributions to profit, it is a forward-looking one, and an ideal choice based on which customer relationships can be managed.

CBV refers to the differential effect of an individual's brand preference (as exhibited by his/her knowledge about the brand, attitude to it, intention to purchase it, and attachment to it) on his/her response to its marketing. When this metric is related to the CLV metric, it provides new avenues for managers to implement communication strategies that encourage positive growth in both the metrics.

CRV refers to a customer's expected future referral value to an organization. The CRV metric enables managers to measure and manage each customer, based on his/her ability to generate indirect profit to the company, through savings in acquisition costs and acquisition of new customers via referrals.

These metrics overcome the drawbacks posed by the backward-looking metrics listed earlier and help companies accurately measure customers' behavior and manage their profitably. How do these three metrics fall into the broader realm of customer value?

Inter-linkages between CLV, CBV, and CRV

Not all customers are created equal. They differ in their economic value to a company and in their expectations from it. Therefore, attraction, retention and nurturing of customers and target groups are integral to an effective CRM system. These three activities can be performed either on the transaction behavior of customers, on their value contribution to a brand or on a their word of mouth (WOM) publicity. As mentioned earlier, there are three major constituents of CV. Figure 2.1 provides the constituents and their linkages.

When companies implement these linkages, not only do they see an increase in their customer value, but they also identify effective business practices that form the basis for a sustainable and hard-to-imitate competitive advantage for them. Now let us look into each of these constituents in detail.

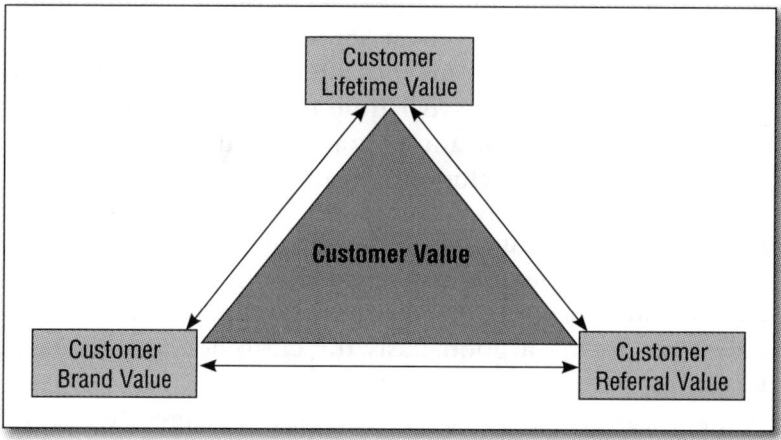

Figure 2.1 Inter-linkages between CLV, CBV, and CRV

CONCEPT OF CLV

The challenge for a company today is to develop an optimal blend of differential levels of treatments such that over every customer's lifetime, the profits earned by the organization are maximized. This necessitates the use of CLV as the primary tool to design and implement its marketing initiatives.

Defining CLV

We define CLV as follows:

> The sum of cumulated future cash flows—discounted using the weighted average cost of capital (WACC)—of a customer over their entire lifetime with the company.

Based on the value provided by customers, a company can optimally allocate resources among them to generate a maximum return. The CLV framework also serves as the base from which a company selects customers, sells the next best product/service to customers, and decides on its customer-specific communication strategies. In essence, CLV can be considered as the metric that guides companies' allocation of resources for their ongoing marketing activities in adopting a customer-centric approach.

When computing the lifetime value of a customer, the definition of "lifetime" is critical. In the purest sense, CLV implies measuring of a customer's value over his/her lifetime. We compute the CLV of a customer over a three-year time period for most applications. There are several important reasons for this "restricted lifetime" consideration. These include:

1. In many product categories, there are significant changes in the life-cycles of products. Considering a future revenue stream from a product that has changed its stage in the life-cycle may not be a good basis for customer management decisions.
2. In many cases, the needs of customers change after three years. In such situations, computation of CLV may not yield valuable insights about a customer's profitability.

3. It is estimated that nearly 80% of profit from customers comes in three years (Gupta and Lehmann, 2005).
4. Since we discount future cash flows, any contributions discounted beyond a three-year window would yield a small value—one that would be of little use to managerial decision-making.
5. For longer time periods, the predictive accuracy of the models we use tends to decline.

However, there are exceptions to this three-year measurement period. For instance, the auto industry has a different purchase pattern from other industries. In this industry, we suggest 20 years in the future for at least three purchases to take place. Therefore, the lifetime period for automobile customers is 20 years. Similarly, the insurance industry takes up to 7 years to recover its acquisition costs. Therefore, we suggest the lifetime period for insurance customers to be between 7 and 10 years. Therefore, how is CLV calculated?

Computing CLV

As noted earlier, CLV is calculated as the sum of the cumulated cash flows of a customer over his/her entire lifetime with a company. It is important to note that the customer's buying behavior can be viewed in two different settings—contractual and non-contractual. A contractual setting is one where customers are bound by a contract, for example, a mobile phone subscription. In a non-contractual setting, customers are not bound by a contract, for example, grocery store purchases. In a contractual setting, a company receives fixed monthly revenue through the subscription, but this is not so in a non-contractual setting. Therefore, these differences need to be included while computing CLV. To cover both the situations, CLV can be expressed in the following form:

$$CLV_i = \sum_{t=1}^{T} \frac{\text{Base GC}}{(1+r)^t} + \sum_{t=1}^{T} \frac{\hat{p}(\text{Buy}_{it}=1)*\hat{GC}_{it}}{(1+r)^t} - \frac{\hat{MC}_{it}}{(1+r)^t}$$

Equation (1)

where

CLV_i = lifetime value for customer i

$\hat{p}(Buy_{it})$ = predicted probability that customer i will purchase in time period t

$\hat{GC}_{it}$ = predicted gross contribution margin provided by customer i in time period t

$\hat{MC}_{it}$ = predicted marketing costs directed toward customer i in time period t

t = index for time periods; such as months, quarters, years, etc.

T = marks the end of the calibration or observation time frame

r = monthly discount factor

Base GC = predicted base monthly gross contribution margin

As is evident from the formula given above, it can be applied in both the contractual and non-contractual settings. Now, let us look how it works in each of the settings.

In a contractual setting, the first term $\left(\sum_{t=1}^{T} \frac{\text{Base GC}}{(1+r)^t} \right)$ corresponds to the constant gross contribution a customer is going to make to a company. This could be either on a monthly, quarterly or annual basis. The second term $\left(\sum_{t=1}^{T} \frac{\hat{p}(Buy_{it}=1)*\hat{GC}_{it}}{(1+r)^t} \right)$ corresponds to the predicted net present value of future purchases made by the customer during a particular period. The third term, $\left(\frac{\hat{MC}_{it}}{(1+r)^t} \right)$ corresponds to the net present value of future purchases made by the customer during a particular period. The final value of these three components would yield the CLV in a contractual setting.

In a non-contractual setting, the first term $\left(\sum_{t=1}^{T} \frac{\text{Base GC}}{(1+r)^t} \right)$ would not be valid, since there is no constant flow of base income from a customer on a periodic basis. In short, there is no assured income from subscriptions. As in the previous case, the second term $\left(\sum_{t=1}^{T} \frac{\hat{p}(Buy_{it}=1)*\hat{GC}_{it}}{(1+r)^t} \right)$ corresponds to the predicted net present value of future purchases by the customer at a particular time period. The third term $\left(\dfrac{\hat{MC}_{it}}{(1+r)^t}\right)$ corresponds to the net present value of future purchases attributed to the customer at a particular time period. The final value of these three components would yield the CLV in a non-contractual setting.

As noted earlier, Stew Leonard's pegs its CLV at $50,000 over the 10-year lifetime of its average customer. This is a simplistic way of calculating CLV. Here, Stew Leonard's assumes that its customers shop once a week and spend around $100 for the next 10 years. After reviewing the CLV computation equation above, you will notice that this is a non-contractual setting and therefore does not have a constant/base revenue stream. Furthermore, the company has not factored in marketing costs and its discounting rate. However, Stew Leonard's current value gives it an idea about how the profit potential its customer base holds and the benefits that would accrue if it were to leverage this. Therefore, performing a "true" CLV analysis gives the company an accurate picture about which customer segments are profitable and how it should manage customer segments based on the value they provide to it.

Computation of CLV explained thus far is used to compute it at the individual customer level. When an aggregate CLV is required, we can sum the lifetime values of all the customers (for information on other approaches to compute aggregate CLV, see Kumar [2008]). This value is referred to as the customer equity (CE) of a company (Gupta, Lehmann, and Stuart, 2004) and is calculated as follows:

$$CE = \sum_{i=1}^{I} \sum_{t=1}^{T} GC_{it} \left(\frac{1}{1+d}\right)^t \qquad \text{Equation (2)}$$

CE = customer equity of the customer base (sum of individual lifetime values),
GC_{it} = average gross contribution margin of customer i in time period t, (after taking into account marketing costs)
d = discount rate,
i = customer index,

t = time period,
T = the number of time periods for which CE is being estimated.

Information on the average gross contribution margin (GC) and the duration (T) are derived either from managerial judgment or from actual purchase data. The discount rate (d) is a function of the cost of the capital of the company and can be obtained from its financial accounting function. Based on this, its average CLV can be calculated by dividing its CE by the number of customers. Now that we know what CLV is and how it is computed, it would be interesting to know what drives it.

Drivers of CLV

For effective implementation of customer management strategies, we need to know what the drivers of CLV are. These can be thought of as the main factors that affect the lifetime value of a customer. These drivers determine the nature of the relationship between a company and a customer, and help it estimate the level of profitability and the CLV of each customer. The drivers of CLV can be broadly classified into two categories:

1. *Exchange characteristics:* Exchange characteristics broadly include all the variables that affect and influence the customer-organization relationship, such as the customer-spending level, cross-buying behavior, purchase frequency, product returns, the marketing contacts made by the company and its loyalty instruments. Exchange characteristics are predominantly the same for most of the cases in the business-to-business (B2B) and business-to-customer (B2C) scenario.
2. *Customer characteristics:* Customer characteristics differ in the case of B2B and B2C companies. In case of a B2B enterprise, customer characteristics include variables such as type of industry, level of annual revenue, and location of the business. In the case of a B2C company, customer characteristics include variables such as age, gender, income, and the physical location of the customers.

Having learned how to measure CLV and its drivers, we need to know how to maximize CLV in order to reap the full benefits of the metric. The next section discusses the popular CLV-based customer management strategy that helps companies maximize CLV and the respective implications of adopting recommended strategies.

Strategies and Implications of Maximizing CLV

A powerful metric such as CLV enables companies to address marketing issues with greater accuracy. This metric also help them develop important CRM strategies that will help them cultivate profitable relationships with their customers. Figure 2.2 illustrates strategies known as the "Wheel-of-Fortune."

Customer Selection

The strategy: As evident from Figure 2.2, it all starts with selecting the right customers, based on their value potential, as opposed to other strategic customer-based value metrics such as RFM, PCV, and SOW.

Managing Loyalty and Profitability Simultaneously

The strategy: In an effort to cultivate and nurture profitable customer loyalty, it is essential that companies manage loyalty and profitability simultaneously. To implement this strategy, they should segment customers, based on their loyalty and profitability to the firm. Loyalty can be measured using the various metrics discussed in the previous sections.

With this strategy in place, companies can aim to (a) build and enhance behavioral loyalty by focusing on each customer's purchase behavior and his/her respective contribution to the companies' profit, (b) cultivate attitudinal loyalty by studying customers' attitudes to a company through customer feedback and focus groups, and (c) link loyalty to profitability by using the CLV metric and ensure a successful loyalty program. This would help companies identify high-value customers and spend their limited marketing resources on them.

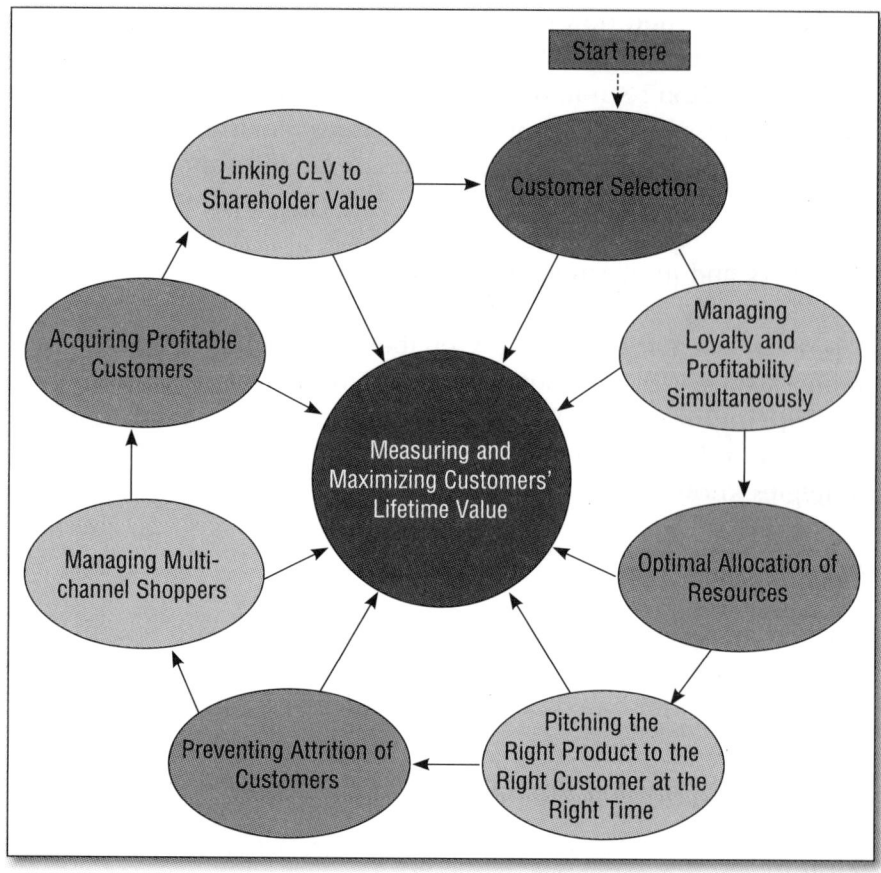

Source: Adapted and updated from Kumar, 2008.

Figure 2.2 The Wheel of Fortune

Optimal Allocation of Resources

The strategy: Many companies continue to spend their resources on a large number of unprofitable customers. They either invest in those who are easy to acquire, but are not necessarily profitable or try to increase the retention rate of all their customers, thereby wasting their limited resources.

Implementation of this strategy involves three important steps. First, managers have to identify the most profitable customers and those who are most responsive to marketing efforts. Second, managers need to determine the right mix of different channel contacts for each customer. This can be determined by the responsiveness of customers to each available marketing channel of a company and how cost-effective these channels are. Third, managers have to decide how frequently a customer should be contacted and what the inter-contact time should be. It is also important for managers to consider the factors affecting their up-selling and cross-selling efforts. Along with these efforts, they should also monitor customers' purchase frequency, their interpurchase time and their individual profit contribution in determining the frequency of marketing initiatives that can maximize CLV.

Pitching the Right Product to the Right Customer at the Right Time

The strategy: Managers are interested to know when a customer is likely to purchase the next product. This strategy helps them accurately predict customers' purchase sequences and thereby tailor sales messages that can pitch the right product to the right customer at the right time.

In order to predict the purchase sequence of each customer, this strategy requires three important pieces of customer purchase information: (a) in which product category the customer is likely to make a purchase, (b) at what intervals and at time period the customer will make a purchase, and (c) how much is the customer likely to spend on the purchase or what is the likely profit contribution going to be.

Preventing Customer Attrition

The strategy: Recent research indicates that a company has a 60%–70% chance of successfully repeat-selling to an active customer, a 20%–40% chance of successfully repeat-selling to a lost customer, and only a 15%–20% chance of successfully closing a sale on a brand new customer (Thomas, Blattberg, and Fox, 2004). This finding clearly shows the importance of preventing customer attrition or churn. This strategy involves calculating the probability of defection for each customer. After calculating the likelihood of defection, companies can make informed decisions about intervention offers that would make customers stay with them for a longer period. Typically, the questions that can be answered after calculating customers' probability of quitting include: (a) Should we intervene? (b) With which customers should we intervene? (c) When should we intervene? (d) Through which channel should we intervene? and (e) What should we offer?

Managing Multichannel Shoppers

The strategy: Multichannel shoppers initiate more contacts with companies, stay with them for a longer duration, make purchases more frequently, and are more receptive to contacts through multiple communication channels.

When this strategy was implemented in a B2B company, it was found that as a customer shops across more channels (from one channel to four channels), he/she (a) spends more on the company, (b) spends a higher proportion on a focal company (rather than its competitor), (c) has a higher past profitability (which is correlated with its future profitability) and (d) has a higher likelihood of buying in the future (Kumar and Venkatesan, 2005).

Acquiring Profitable Customers

The strategy: Using CLV, this strategy optimizes the acquisition/retention cost of customers and links such efforts to a company's overall profitability. It helps companies decide which customers are worth acquiring/retaining and which dormant customers should be pursued to return to the company. An important aid to this strategy is the customer profile analysis. Based on profile analyses, companies can precisely target specific customer segments that match their customer base and channels that match their customers' preferences.

Linking Customer Equity and Shareholder Value

The strategy: Customer equity represents the sum of the lifetime values of all customers of companies. This implies that when they maximize their individual CLV, it should result in maximizing their customer equity. If their cash flow is primarily generated from customers, an increase in the CE (or cash flow) from customers should relate to an increase in the MC (or the stock price of the firm, Kumar and Shah, 2008). Maximizing its CLV and CE jointly enhances the shareholder value of a company. In other words, computation of customer equity indicates how much an enterprise is worth at a point of time, and therefore, serves as a link between its CLV and shareholder value.

CONCEPT OF CUSTOMER BRAND VALUE

A company can strengthen its brand by ascertaining and increasing the value a customer provides to it. This value is referred to as CBV. CLV can help companies manage their customer relationships profitably. By establishing a link between CBV and CLV, they can strengthen their brands and build profitable relationships simultaneously. This section provides an effective approach to determine CBV and also designs an approach that will link CLV and CBV in order to ensure simultaneous growth in companies' brand and customer equity.

Defining and Measuring Customers' Brand Value

The concept of CBV, as defined earlier, refers to the differential effect of a customer's brand preference on his/her response to the marketing of a brand. It is comprised of eight constructs (Kumar, Luo and Rao):

1. *Brand knowledge*, which constitutes a customer's awareness of a brand (brand awareness), and his/her image of it (brand image)
2. *Brand attitude*, which is made up of a customer's trust in a brand (brand trust), and his/her emotional response to it (brand affect)

3. *Brand behavior intention*, which is made up of a customer's intention to purchase a brand (purchase intention)
4. *Brand behavior*, which constitutes a customer's repeat-buying behavior (brand loyalty), relationship with other customers buying the brand (brand advocacy), and his/her willingness to pay a price premium for it over other brands (brand price premium behavior)

Figure 2.3 illustrates these constructs:

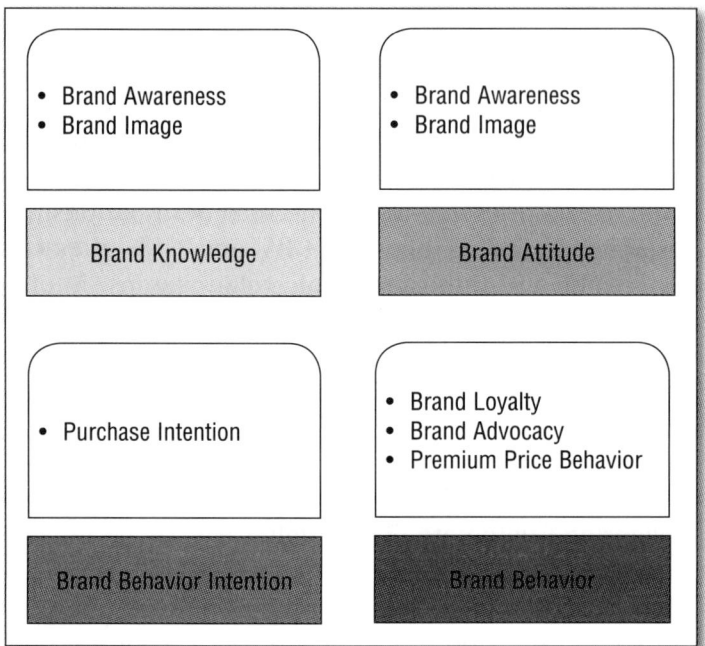

Figure 2.3 Components of CBV

A company can expect to maximize its profitability when the brand purchase behavior of customers is linked to their lifetime value. This linkage is performed by using four key customer behavior outcomes. They are:

1. The level of marketing costs incurred on a customer
2. The intensity or frequency of a customer's purchases

3. The profit or margin contribution by the customer
4. The number of referrals he/she makes about the brand to other customers

With these eight constructs and key behavior outcomes, we can measure a customer's brand value. This is typically calculated on a range of 0 to 10 for these eight constructs. For instance, Customer A may rank highly on the constructs that make up brand knowledge, brand attitude and brand behavior intention, but may rank low on brand behavior. A sample output of such a scenario is depicted in Figure 2.4.

This figure clearly indicates that the company will have to influence and improve Customer A's purchase behavior relating to the brand. This would be true if Customer A is a high-value customer (as estimated on the basis of CLV). However, if Customer A is a low-value customer, the company should evaluate whether he/she is worth pursuing to influence and improve his/her purchase behavior. This brings us to the next question, how do we link CBV and CLV?

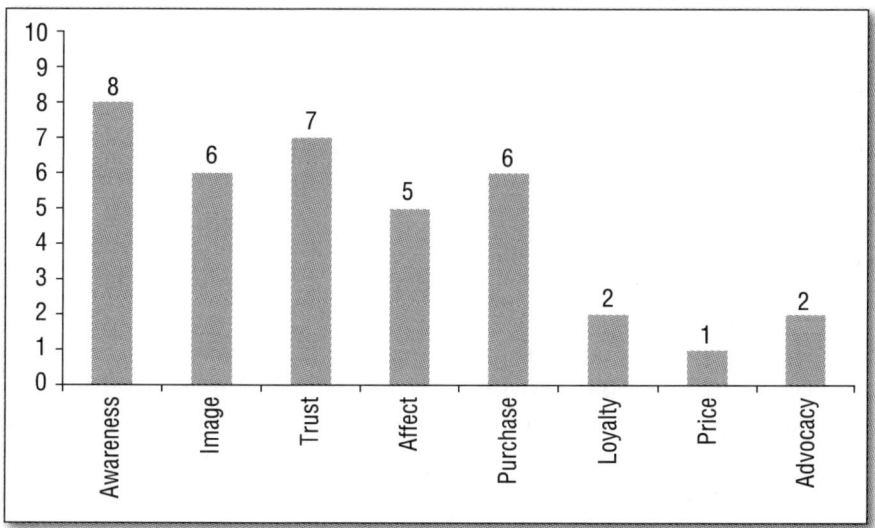

Figure 2.4 Sample Output of Customer A's Observed Brand Value

Linking Customers' Brand Value to Their Lifetime Value

A survey with questions pertaining to the eight constructs can yield information required to compute a company's CBV. Once this information is available, the next step is to estimate how these components affect each other by using sophisticated estimation techniques. The components of CBV are obtained by using a 10-point scale from a sample of customers. CLV is also computed for the same customers at this time. The following set of equations map the interaction between these components:

Internal linkage between the various components of CBV:

Brand Attitude = function of
(Brand Knowledge)   Equation (3)

Brand Behavior Intention = function of
(Brand Attitude)   Equation (4)

Brand Behavior = function of
(Brand Behavior Intention)   Equation (5)

Linkage between CBV and CLV:

CLV = function of (Brand Behavior)   Equation (6)

These equations demonstrate the dynamic process of transferring a customer's brand knowledge (brand awareness and brand image) to his/her brand attitude (brand trust and brand effect), brand purchase intention, and brand behavior (brand loyalty, premium price behavior and brand advocacy), then ultimately his/her lifetime value to a company.

Seemingly unrelated regressions (SURs) is the statistical estimation technique that can be used to achieve this is. By doing so, companies can obtain coefficients from the system of equations. Furthermore, they can use a genetic algorithm approach to achieve the optimal level of CBV that would maximize CLV under given budgetary constraints.

Now, let us look at how this link can be implemented between CBV and CLV.

Implementing the Link between Customers' Brand Value and Lifetime Value

There are seven steps in the implementation procedure that need to be implemented to successfully operationalize the link. These include:

1. In the first step, the CLV of customers is calculated at the individual level.
2. Then the customers are ranked in order, based on their CLV—from high to low.
3. Then the customers are segmented into 10 deciles, with Decile 1 including the most valuable customers and Decile 10 the least valuable ones.
4. From this decile chart, a small percentage (for example, 10%) of customers can be taken from each decile and information obtained about the components of their brand value.
5. Using this information, the components of CBV to CLV can be linked and the importance or weight of each component of their brand value obtained. Let us continue with the example of Customer A that was reviewed earlier. Let us assume that Customer A is a high-value customer for the company and has a CLV score of $10,000. From Figure 2.3, we saw how Customer A performed on all the eight constructs. Therefore, Customer A's brand behavior attribute needs to be influenced to maximize its CBV and CLV.
6. After measuring the individual attributes of Customer A's brand value, we need to optimize the various factors of its brand value to maximize his CLV. Based on Customer A's CLV score and marketing budgets, we can send targeted messages to him/her. Since Customer A has performed poorly on his/her brand behavior attribute, an invitation can be sent to him/her to join the company's loyalty program. Let us assume that the cost involved in this exercise is $500. After such optimization, the company will have to measure the brand value components of Customer A. Figure 2.5 details the optimized brand value of Customer A.
7. After the components of brand value have been optimized, the company can translate these optimized values to create

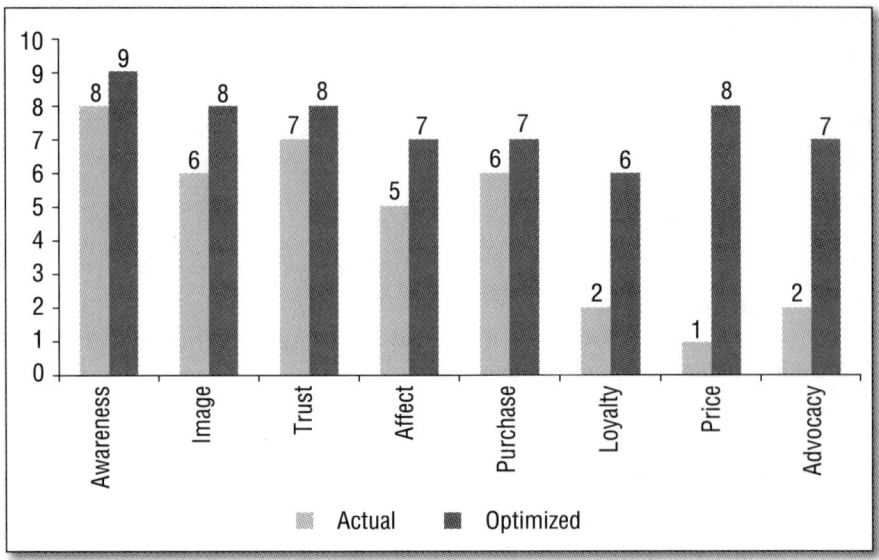

Figure 2.5 Optimized Brand Value of Customer

brand management strategies. For instance, from Figure 2.4 we can see that Customer A's brand value increases with respect to the brand behavior attribute. After this optimized brand value is available to us, we can measure Customer A's CLV again. After implementing new brand management strategies, let us assume that the company's CLV is now $15,000. It then sends out an invitation for Bob to join its loyalty program to build his brand loyalty. Therefore, we can conclude that Customer A's CLV has improved greatly, and this increase was directly driven by the company increasing its brand value.

An ROI of 10% was calculated by considering the $5,000 increase in the company's CLV (at $500). This not only demonstrates the effectiveness of its CBV and CLV strategies, but also directly leads to its maximizing its profits. Now that we have learned about CBV and its link to CLV, let us see the managerial implications of adopting this approach.

Managerial Implications of Linking Customers' Brand Value to Their Lifetime Value

There are three key implications of linking CBV to CLV. They include:

Monitoring the overall performance of CBV: This linkage can help companies monitor the overall performance of their CBV. They can sample a group of existing and potential customers and measure their individual brand values. Then they can identify the weak components in individual brand values and come up with different strategies to improve or positively influence these.

Managing brand at the segment level: To manage a brand at a segment level, companies segment customers based on their CBV and CLV. This yields a matrix with four cells, which are similar to the "Managing Loyalty and Profitability Simultaneously" strategy of CLV. Here, we segment high CLV-high CBV customers as "True Loyalists," high CLV-low CBV customers as "Acquaintances," low CLV-high CBV as "Poor Patrons," and low CLV-low CBV customers as "Strangers."

Managing brand at the individual level: We saw in the "Managing Loyalty and Profitability Simultaneously" strategy of CLV that "cultivating attitudinal and behavioral loyalty is important to ensure profitability." Therefore, firms should manage brand at the individual level to make sure that the brand message appeals to a particular segment of customers.

CONCEPT OF CUSTOMER REFERRAL VALUE

It is clear that customers not only contribute value to a company through their own transactions (direct profits), but also have an impact on the transactions of other customers by word-of-mouth publicity and referrals (indirect profits) by helping the organization acquire new customers at lower costs. Therefore, we need a metric such as CRV to determine the value of a customer's ability to spread word-of-mouth publicity about a brand and make referrals.

Defining and Measuring Customers' Referral Value

Calculating CRV is more complex than computing lifetime value. Consider a customer, Jane, for whom we will compute the referral value. First, we need to calculate the average number of successful referrals she is likely to make after we offer her an incentive to do so through a marketing campaign. We need to look at Jane's past behavior for a period longer than a month to get adequate variance in the number of referrals she has made for proper statistical modeling and predictive accuracy. The period varies from industry to industry.

Then we estimate when our marketing campaign is likely to make an impact on Jane generating referrals. In research studies, referrals made by customers after a referral-incentive marketing campaign can be attributed to the promotion for around a year.

We can then determine how many of the referrals would have become customers of the company in any case even if Jane had not recommended it. If a new customer (let us call him John) would not have joined without Jane's referral (referred to as a type-one referral), then her referral value should include the value of John's business. However, if John would have become a customer without Jane's referral (referred to as a type-two referral), then Jane's CRV should include only the savings in acquisition costs for John, since no direct marketing effort was needed to net him. This information can be obtained through surveys by asking a simple question, for example: "How likely is it that you would have purchased our product/service without a referral in the next 12 months?"

After collecting this information, we can compute Jane's referral value as the present value of her type-one referrals plus the present value of her type-two referrals. Therefore, if we assume that if John would not have become a customer had Jane not referred him, then Jane's type-one referral of John is essentially the same as his lifetime customer value—the present value of the difference between John's contribution to the company's margin and the cost of marketing for him, projected over a year. Consequently, the value of type-two customers is the present value of a company's savings in acquisition costs. As in the case of all cost-revenue analyses, if the cost involved in acquiring type-two referrals exceeds that of alternative acquisition methods, type-two customers can be a liability for a company. Therefore, the CRV formula can be expressed as follows:

A Strategic Approach to Grow Profits

$$CRV_i = \sum_{t=1}^{T}\sum_{y=1}^{n1}\frac{(A_{ty} - a_{ty} - M_{ty} + ACQ1_{ty})}{(1+r)^t} + \sum_{t=1}^{T}\sum_{y=n1}^{n2}\frac{(ACQ2_{ty})}{(1+r)^t}$$

Equation (7)

where

- T = the number of periods that will be predicted into the future (for example, quarters or years)
- A_{ty} = the gross margin contributed by customer y who would not have otherwise bought the product
- a_{ty} = the cost of the referral for customer y
- 1 to n1 = the number of customers who would not have joined without the referral
- n2 – n1 = the number of customers who would have joined any way
- M_{ty} = marketing costs for retaining referred customers
- $ACQ1_{ty}$ = savings in acquisition cost for customers who would not have joined without the referral
- $ACQ2_{ty}$ = savings in acquisition cost for customers who would have joined any way

In simple terms, Equation (7) can also be expressed as follows:

$$CRV_i = \frac{\text{Value of customers who joined because of referral}}{\text{Discount rate}} + \frac{\text{Value of customers who would have joined any way}}{\text{Discount rate}}$$

Equation (8)

Having seen the concept and measurement of CRV, let us actually compute the CRV of a customer of a hypothetical financial services company.

Computing Customers' Referral Value

There are four steps involved in computation of CRV. These include:

Step 1: In the first step, we determine whether customers would have bought the brand anyway. As evident from Table 2.1, Tom

Table 2.1 Tom's Referral Behavior in a Financial Services Company (Semi-annual Data)

Number of referrals per period (n_2)	4
Marketing cost per period (M_{ty})	$18
Average gross margin (A_{ty})	$98
Cost of referral (a_{ty})	$40
Acquisition cost savings ($ACQ1_{ty}$ and $ACQ2_{ty}$)	$5
Number of referrals that would have joined any way ($n_2 - n_1$)	2
Yearly discount rate (r)	15%

refers four customers per period (six months) and of these, two would have joined anyway. So in this case, n1 is two and n2 is four. For the purpose of illustration, we only consider here the value of those customers who were directly referred by Tom and made purchases. This approach can also be extended to include the value brought in by customers who were indirectly referred by Tom, wherever applicable.

Step 2: In the second step, we predict the future value of each referred customer. This is based on his/her gross margin per period ($98), marketing cost per period ($18), acquisition cost savings ($5), cost of referral ($40), and discount rate (15% annually).

Step 3: In the third step, we predict the number of referrals generated. The number of referrals predicted for Tom is four per period. Because we are measuring CRV for one year, Tom will therefore generate a total of eight referrals.

Step 4: In the final step, we predict the timing of customer referrals. Since Tom refers four customers per period, in terms of timing this means that these customers are referred in the first half of the year and four are referred in the second half.

Applying these steps for the data we have for Tom, we get the following:

For Period 1:

$$CRV_1 = \sum_{y=1}^{n1} \frac{(A_{1y} - a_{1y} - M_{1y} + ACQ1_{1y})}{(1+r)^l} + \sum_{y=n1+1}^{n2} \frac{(ACQ2_{1y})}{(1+r)^l}$$

Equation (9)

$$\text{CRV}_1 = \sum_{y=1}^{2} \frac{(\$98 - \$40 - \$18 + \$5)}{(1+0.075)^1} + \sum_{y=3}^{4} \frac{(\$5)}{(1+0.075)^1} \approx \$93$$

For Period 2:

$$\text{CRV}_2 = \sum_{y=1}^{n1} \frac{(A_{2y} - M_{2y})}{(1+r)^2} + \sum_{y=1}^{n1} \frac{(A_{2y} - a_{2y} - M_{2y} + ACQ1_{2y})}{(1+r)^2}$$
$$+ \sum_{y=n1+1}^{n2} \frac{(ACQ2_{2y})}{(1+r)^2}$$

Equation (10)

$$\text{CRV}_2 = \sum_{y=1}^{2} \frac{(\$98 - \$18)}{(1+0.075)^2} + \sum_{y=1}^{2} \frac{(\$98 - \$40 - \$18 + \$5)}{(1+0.075)^2}$$
$$+ \sum_{y=3}^{4} \frac{(\$5)}{(1+0.075)^2} \approx 225$$

Total CRV = $\text{CRV}_1 + \text{CRV}_2 \approx 318$

Therefore, the total CRV for Tom for one year is the sum of CRV_1 and CRV_2, which is around $318. As the results indicate, the impact increases as time progresses. The main reason for this is the growth of the customer base due to referrals in each period. In Period 1, there were only four new customers, whereas in Period 2 there were six customers in the value of the CRV (four new customers and two customers from Period 1 who only bought due to the referral).

As already mentioned, because this is a conservative estimate of the value of customer referrals (only direct referrals are used in the CRV), it does not give a true picture in terms of the number of new customers who have been acquired by the company and what their total value is worth to it. If we want to see how many new customers came on board over these two periods (stemming from the original customer and the value of these new customers), we need to look at both the direct and the indirect referrals (for more information on direct and indirect referrals see Kumar et al. [2013]). If each of the customers who were referred during a specific period also made referrals in subsequent periods, we would see an exponential growth in the total number of new customers who were acquired in the two periods as well as the total CRV for these customers. Given that CRV also considers the net present value brought in by a customer, one might wonder how CRV is linked with CLV. The following section provides the linkage.

Linking Customers' Referral Value to Their Lifetime Value

A recent marketing study found that customers who score high on CRV are not the most valuable ones, as determined by their CLV. This study used the transaction and referral behavior data of a telecommunications company to investigate the link between CLV and CRV. The findings of the study are depicted in Table 2.2 (Kumar, Petersen and Leone, 2007).

As evident from Table 2.2, the top 30% of the customers ranked on the basis of CLV (Deciles 1, 2 and 3) have no overlap with the top 30% of customers based on CRV (deciles 5, 6, and 7). This finding gives managers important insights on customer management.

Table 2.2 Customer Deciles of CLV and CRV for a Telecommunications Company

Deciles (ranked by CLV)	CLV ($) (1 year)	CRV ($) (1 year)
1	1,933	40
2	1,067	52
3	633	90
4	360	750
5	313	930
6	230	1,020
7	190	870
8	160	96
9	137	65
10	120	46

Source: Adapted from Kumar, Petersen, and Leone (2007).

Companies have now taken up referral programs to acquire new customers and reward existing ones for their positive WOM. For instance, companies such as AT&T and DIRECTV have introduced a value-oriented referral incentive program that rewards both the referral and the referring customer. Figures 2.6 and 2.7 provide examples of these companies' campaigns.

AT&T rewards both referral as well as the referring customer $25 whenever a referral activates a new, qualifying AT&T wireless service. The referring customer gets a $25 AT&T gift card, which he/she can exchange for the company's products/services. DIRECTV gives $100 to both the referral and the referring customer. These incentives seem to be in proportion to the typical value brought in by each customer in the respective referral groups. Therefore, managers need to understand that customers who score highly on the CLV measure are not the same who do so on the CRV measure. Furthermore, companies should measure both CLV and CRV to implement marketing campaigns that focus on customers based on both the dimensions. A marketing campaign that focuses on both the metrics will allow companies to increase the profitability of each customer as well as cash-in on the power of positive WOM. Now, let us look at how the link between CRV and CLV can be implemented.

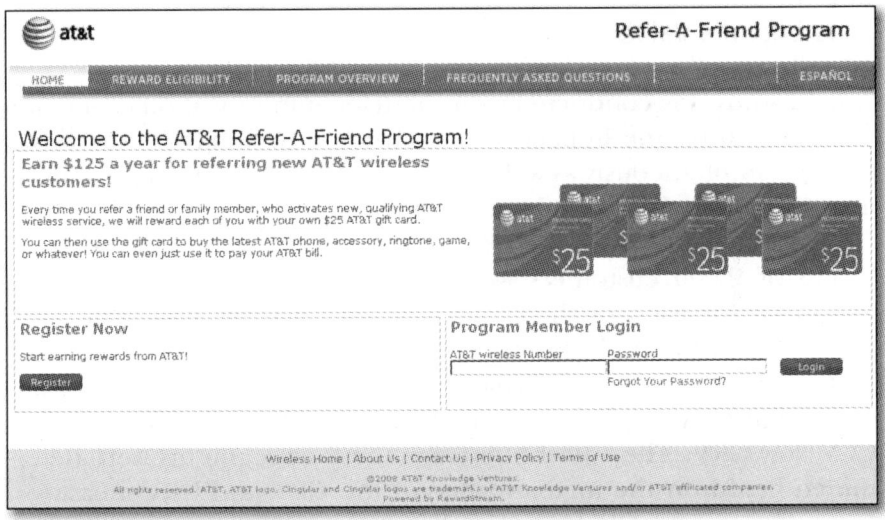

Source: http://www.att.com/

Figure 2.6 Sample Referral Program from AT&T

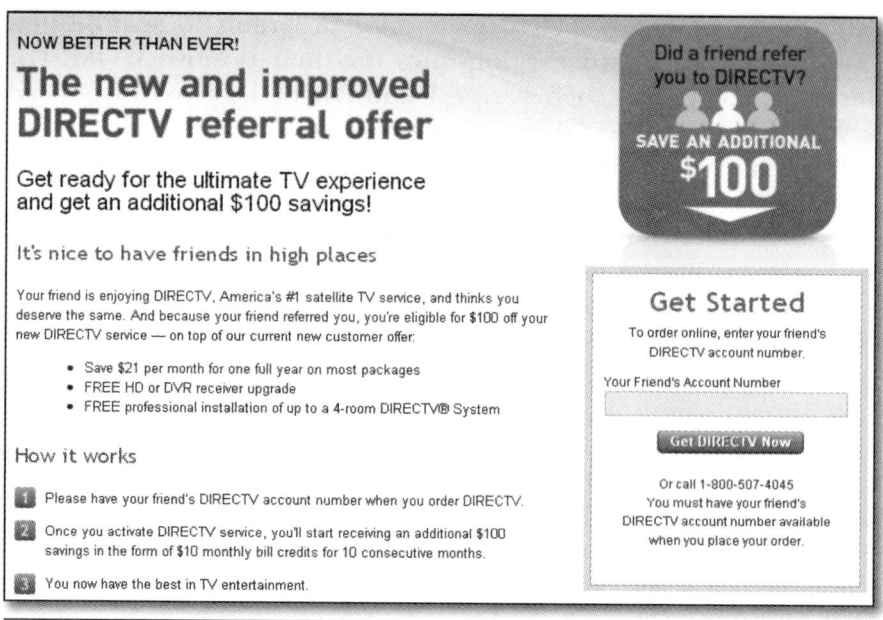

Source: http://www.directv.com/

Figure 2.7 Sample Referral Program from DIRECTV

Implementing the Link between Customers' Referral Value and Their Lifetime Value

A field study was conducted with the telecommunications company to demonstrate the impact of measuring and managing these two metrics simultaneously as well as the benefits of measuring and managing CLV and CRV simultaneously.

For the purpose of the field study, a test group and a control group of 9,900 customers were considered. CLV and CRV were measured for each of the groups. Based on these two values, the customers in the both groups were divided into four cells of a 2X2 matrix. The cells were segmented on the following basis—high CLV/high CRV, high CLV/low CRV, low CLV/high CRV, and low CLV/low CRV. The cutoff points for the four segments were determined based on the median value of the CLV and CRV measures. Figure 2.8 summarizes these results.

Out of the sample of 9,900 customers, the "Misers" and "Champions" segments had 2,079 customers each, and the

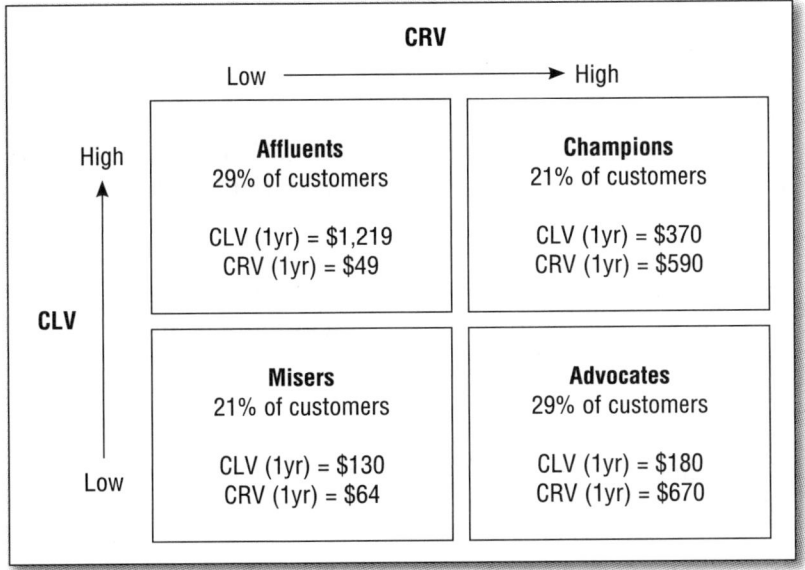

Source: Adapted from Kumar, Petersen, and Leone (2007).

Figure 2.8 CLV–CRV Matrix of a Telecommunications Company

"Affluents" and "Advocates" segments 2,871 customers each. These findings validate those depicted in Table 2.2—that high CLV and high CRV customers are two distinct sets of customers. The results of this measurement of CLV and CRV indicate that there are distinct sets of customers found in the four different cells, based on the large differences in the values for CLV and CRV across the cells. Furthermore, it should be noted that there is a significant difference between customers who are high on the CLV measure and those who are high on the CRV measure. Now, let us consider each of the cells separately.

The "Affluents" or high CLV/low CRV customers purchase a large number of products and services, but they do not refer many new customers to buy products and services. The "Misers" or low CLV/low CRV customers do not either purchase much or refer many new customers. Their low purchase behavior may be due to frequent brand switching, their small SOW or they may be waiting to find out from others whether the product is worth purchasing.

The "Advocates" or low CLV/high CRV customers do not exhibit a high purchase behavior. However, they are actively involved in talking about the product to other customers and encourage them to buy it. Finally, and true to their name, the "Champions" or high CLV/high CRV customers are more likely to buy more products/services from a company and talk more about these to other customers.

Given the vast differences between the four cells, the customers in each of the cells should be evaluated differently with respect to their total value to a company and then approached with different types of marketing offers to derive the greatest overall value from them. Based on the segment level differences, customized marketing campaigns were developed for these segments (Table 2.3) that generated impressive results (Table 2.4).

Managerial Implications of Linking Customer Referral Value to Their Lifetime Value

Now the question is how will managers know which campaign they should choose—a campaign for CLV or a campaign for CRV? With adequate information on the objective of the campaign, the stage of the product in its life cycle, the potential number of prospects in the pool, and the nature of competition in the market, managers can decide on the nature of a campaign that will drive the company's revenue and profit.

A CLV campaign would be most appropriate in a situation where the goal is to get users to buy more in a specific category or across more categories. Typically, such campaigns take place in competitive markets where it is tough to acquire new customers or in niche ones where the prospect pool is limited. On the other hand, a CRV campaign would be most appropriate in a situation where the aim is to acquire more customers/prospects through current customers. This is because the current customers may already be spending the bulk of their budget on the company's products and programs to increase cross-selling or up-selling would not yield much success. Of course, the caveat in selecting customers for CRV campaigns is to be cognizant of the fact that high-CLV customers are not those who make the most referrals. The study demonstrates the importance of measuring the value of a customer's own transactions and the value of their impact on those of other customers, and not one or the other in isolation.

Table 2.3 Campaign for "Misers," "Advocates," and "Affluents" for a Telecommunications Company

Campaign for "Misers"	Campaign for "Affluents"	Campaign for "Advocates"
Targeted with bundled offers for one or more products	Targeted with emphasis on the referral incentive for them and referred customers	Sent personalized direct mail communication including offers that bundle one or more products
Personalized communication sent via direct mail and followed up with another direct mail within a two-week period	Contacted through direct mail communication, followed by another one within two weeks	Follow up communication sent through direct mail within two weeks
Telephone assistance provided to customers on queries regarding additional services and the value of obtaining these	Emphasis laid on a $20 incentive for the referral and referring customer for signing up for products and/or services	A sample of such customers contacted via telephone to answer queries regarding additional services and the value of subscribing to multiple products/services
The value of making referrals was highlighted for these customers and a $20 incentive was offered to each of them for making a referral.		

CONCLUSION

The goal of strategic CRM is to track, monitor and re-align interactions between a company and its customers in a manner that facilitates maximization of the value of customers to it. The three key providers of CV include (a) CLV, (b) CBV, and (c) CRV.

The strategies developed must be able to provide a value proposition to customers, a business case for their investment in CRM, and an enterprise transformation plan that will prepare and re-align the organization to better suit its CRM initiatives.

Table 2.4 Campaign Results for "Misers," "Advocates," and "Affluents"

Segment	Total Segment Size		% of Customers That Migrated to			Average Customer Value Before Campaign		Average Customer Value Increase After Campaign		
	Before Campaign	After Campaign	Affluents	Champions	Advocates	1-yr CLV	1-yr CRV	Affluents	Champions	Advocates
Misers	21%	9%	4%	4%	4%	$130	$64	CLV ↑ to $370 (a 185% increase)	CLV ↑ to $310 (a 138% increase) CRV ↑ to $274 (a 328% increase)	CLV ↑ to $334 (a 422% increase)
Affluents	29%	25%	-	4%	-	$1,219	$49	-	CLV ↔ at $1,219 CRV ↑ to $239 (a 388% increase)	-
Advocates	29%	24%	-	5%	-	$180	$670	-	CLV ↑ to $290 (a 61% increase) CRV ↔ at $670	-

Source: Adapted from Kumar, Petersen, and Leone, 2007.

REFERENCES

Farris, Paul W., Neil T. Bendle, Philip E. Pfeifer, and David J. Reibstein (2006), *Marketing Metrics: 50+ Metrics Every Executive Should Master.* NJ: Wharton School Publishing.

Gupta, S. and D. R. Lehmann (2005), *Managing Customers as Investments: The Strategic Value of Customers in the Long Run.* NJ: Wharton School Publishing.

Gupta, S., D. R. Lehmann, and J. A. Stuart (2004), "Valuing Customers," *Journal of Marketing Research*, 23(2), 89-100.

Hill, N. and J. Alexander (2000), *Handbook of Customer Satisfaction and Loyalty Measurement* (2nd ed). Hampshire, England: Gower Publishing Company.

Kumar, V. (2008), *Customer Lifetime Value—The Path to Profitability*, Foundations and Trends in Marketing, Hanover: now Publishing Inc.

——— (2008), *Managing Customers for Profit.* NJ: Wharton School Publishing.

Kumar, V. and Denish Shah (2008), "Expanding the Role of Marketing: From Customer Equity to Market Capitalization," *Journal of Marketing*, 73(6), 119–136.

Kumar, V. and R. Venkatesan (2005), "Who Are the Multichannel Shoppers and How Do They Perform?: Correlates of Multichannel Shopping Behavior," *Journal of Interactive Marketing*, 19 (Spring), 44–62.

Kumar, V., Vikram Bhaskaran, Rohan Mirchandani, and Milap Shah (2013), "Creating a Measurable Social Media Marketing Strategy: Increasing the Value and ROI of Intangibles and Tangibles for Hokey Pokey," *Marketing Science*, 32(2), 194–212.

Kumar, V. and Werner J. Reinartz (2006), *Customer Relationship Management: A Databased Approach.* New York: John Wiley and Sons.

Kumar, V., Anita (Man) Luo, and Vithala R. Rao (2015), "Linking an Individual's Brand Value to the CLV: An Integrated Framework," Working Paper, Georgia State University.

Kumar, V., J. Andrew Petersen, and Robert P. Leone (2007), "How Valuable Is Word of Mouth?," *Harvard Business Review*, October, 139–146.

Thomas, J. S., R. C. Blattberg, and E. Fox (2004), "Recapturing Lost Customers," *Journal of Marketing Research*, 41(1), 31–45.

Chapter 3
Branding in Retail

Lluis Martinez-Ribes

Retail branded goods have gained an impressive market share in recent years. At the same time, more and more companies want to retail.

UNDERSTANDING THE CONTEXT

Senior managers are not those who know more, but those who know how to better understand the context and "read the other players' hand." As a result, their decisions are better contextualized, and therefore, tend to be more effective.

So let's first get an aerial view of the field in which companies compete, the market economy in which they try to gain customers' sustained preference. Therefore, the aim of marketing is to be the customer's sustained preferred choice.

One of the most widely used methods to attract customers is to reduce prices. If several competitors follow this strategy, a price war starts. Many retail sectors experience such a situation. Another route to face this challenge is to use the power of the brand. Every brand has a more or less desirable meaning, values, and expectations depending on how it is perceived by the customer. If a branded solution is appealing to a customer, he/she is more predisposed to pay slightly (or a lot) more to have the benefit of enjoying it.

Branding is important since it is not only the most valuable asset of a company, but it also affects its profit and loss account, since it is the only way in which it can get customers pay more for a given product. A mere 1% increase in the sales price of a product may lead to a significant rise in its net profit, and this can be easily calculated on a spreadsheet. Consequently, brands have a huge impact on companies' finances.

However, realizing that a brand is a gross margin enhancer only offers temporary relief to managers until they start worrying about how they will communicate its values to their target audience. At this point, they find out that today, media is not only more expensive, but also more fragmented, and sometimes ineffective when companies are trying to reach specific audiences.

In fact, although we are supposed to be living in the "Information Society," perhaps we are actually—based on the subject we are addressing—in an "Attention Deficit Society." Efficient management of an advertising budget is a challenge, and the productivity and effectiveness of a communication budget is not always clear. However, this limitation does not seem to greatly affect retail branded goods in a multitude of product or service categories, which continue to grow in the majority of markets around the world.

Marketing's raison d'être is to be the customers' sustained and preferred choice in order to obtain sustained competitiveness (and not only short-term profits).

FACTS ABOUT RETAIL BRANDED GOODS

Facts

Retail branded products grow almost everywhere in many product categories. There are several reliable information sources that demonstrate the growth of retail branded goods almost everywhere. Here we present a few of those that can be the key to the analysis. Ipsos MORI conducted research for the PLMA (Private Label Manufacturers Association), "polling more than 3,000 shoppers in France, Germany and Great Britain, [and] found that the consumer's connection to retailer brands extends far beyond the issues of price, economic conditions and retail format."[1]

Looking at the AC Nielsen report, "The power of private label 2005," which reviewed 38 countries on Fast Moving Consumer Goods (FMCG), can be highlighted:

---

[1] See PLMA website (www.plmainternational.com).

1. Europe is the most developed private label region worldwide with an aggregated private label share in value sales of 23% in 2005.
2. Almost every household purchased private label products in 2005.
3. On a global basis, private label brands were priced 31% lower than manufacturers' brands and even 40% lower in emerging markets.
4. A contributing factor to the growth of private labels, particularly in Europe, has been the growth of Hard Discounters, which mainly sell private label products, for example, Aldi, whose products account for 95% of the company's sales.

If we look at Planet Retail's reports:

1. "Some US retailers show their scepticism, given the US consumer's strong affinity for brands, regarding the long-term success of private label," said Delhaize's CEO, Pierre-Olivier Beckers. He added, "I think US consumers continue to be interested in brands, but I do see private labels growing from 18% or 20% to 25% in their penetration in the US."
2. While some retail companies choose to name their premium private labels after their store names, others have created new brands as a way of generating excitement and a feeling of exclusivity. Examples of these include Archer Farms, Central Market, 365, and Kirkland Signature.

Many questions appear after such data.

1. Is Mr Beckers going to be right?
2. Could the private label business become as big in the USA as it is in Switzerland?

If we now look at the current situation through IRI report (2013) on private label, balancing quality and value, and Symphony IRI Group (2011) retail private label in Europe, current and emerging trends, this is the update:

1. Europe has maintained its position as the most developed private label region worldwide with an aggregated private label share in value sales of 30% (2013).

2. Switzerland (53%), Spain (51%), Portugal (45%), the UK (45%), Germany (44%) and Belgium (41%) are the six countries with the highest private label shares in Europe (2013).
3. The private label share in the USA accounts for 18.5% (2013).
4. Overall, the price of private labels is on an average 29.9% less per unit than of suppliers' brands across Europe, while in the USA, this gap is around 13% (2013).
5. More premium private labels are being introduced with higher prices and margins across a number of categories. In fact, in some of these, the private label product is the most expensive and innovative (2011).
6. Consequently, the price gap has narrowed, but more slowly in food and beverages than in non-food categories (2013).
7. Shoppers have switched to private labels because they are convinced that the quality of many products is as good as national brands (2013).
8. According to 82% of US consumers, the quality of private labels is the same or better, as compared to national brand alternatives (IRI MarketPulse survey, 2013).
9. In Europe, private label products are now available in 9 out of every 10 FMCG categories (2011).

As we see, Mr Beckers was right. US retail companies tend to focus on growth, while European ones are more centred on attracting customers with savings.

However, the scenario keeps changing in Europe and the USA and some queries come to the fore:

1. Should suppliers be worried?
2. Should retail companies without their own branded goods be also worried?
3. If so, which could be the strategies to counterattack?

So let's go into the depths.

THE ORIGINS AND THE EVOLUTION

According to Henry van Ruymbeke, who quotes the French Fédération des enterprises du Commerce et de la Distribution, the first historic retail brand was Sainsbury in 1869. By 1901, Casino, an important retail chain with own production facilities, was using its brand on some of its manufactured products. In 1928 Monoprix, a retail company with large format shops (4000 m2) began selling its brand of a basic assortment of limited high-quality products at a very low-price. In 1931, Printemps decided to launch a new chain, "Prisunic," with own branded products.

However, the real boom in retail branded products occurred in France in the mid-1970s. Continent launched a few generic products with white packaging known as "white products." These were fairly inexpensive because the customer was "not paying for the brand."

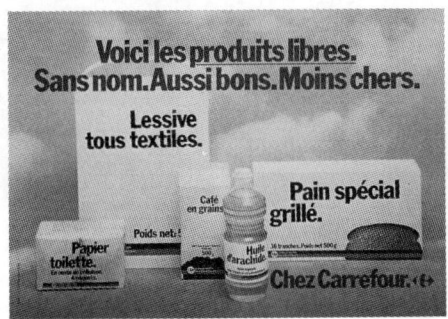

Courtesy: Carrefour.

In 1976, Continent's competitor Carrefour launched its so-called "free products," which it positioned as "Without a brand. Just as good, less expensive," without advertising or a special package design, but with the symbol of freedom—the seagull. Carrefour's packaging also had a white background. Perhaps that is why many people in Europe still use the colloquial term "white brand" when referring to retail brands

In 1977, Eroski, a key Spanish retail company, launched its products, which were also dressed in white. In 1985, Carrefour added its own name to the "Free Products" denomination, and in 1992, the company launched a bio assortment under its own brand. From 1996 to 1999 many French distribution chains launched segmented product categories, with different brand names such as Reflets de France (Promodès), Escapades Gourmandes (Carrefour), Savoir des Saveurs (Système U).

Courtesy: Carrefour.

In 2005, Carrefour split its own branded assortment into three subcategories—the cheapest (*first price*), mainstream, and premium (*Sélection and Reflets de France*). The company also launched its own fair trade brand, Agir, committed itself to social values and began permitting its customers to make purchases that promoted sustainable development. Since this time, retail companies have developed their brands and focussed these on different strategic directions.

STAGES IN RETAIL BRANDING

The European evolution may give some clues about the different stages of retail firm's branded goods.

The best-known description of retail brands was written by Laaksonen and Reynolds (1994). According to them, there are four generations of branded goods under the control of retail companies. This approach is used as a basis for further enrichment and continuous development.

Generics or "no-name" products: These are commodities or basic goods whose price sensitivity is high. They are usually made in a limited quality, packed in a simple way, and sold at a low price, since these are the reasons why consumers purchase them.

This initial stage in the evolution of retail brands made a comeback during the global economic crisis in 2008–2009, boosted by customers' awareness of sustainability. Therefore, we forecast the growth of easy-to-refill products, although these will be branded ones in the current scenario.

Private label products: These usually do not carry retail companies' names. Therefore, if customers do not like them, the reputation of the retail company that made them is not directly affected. Their quality is also rather poor and their price much lower than the supplier's leader brand products.

Own branded products: Their name is the same as that of the chain. Their quality has obviously been improved, since the chain's reputation is at stake. Their positioning tended to be of a cheap imitation of the leader supplier's brand. In some countries, this stage is still the dominant one.

Retail branded products: At this last stage, products are sold under a brand name with a meaning, which is provided or decided by the retail company. The price may or may not be cheaper than that of the reference supplier's brand. These may be real brands, and their meaning is not necessarily based on a given price position:

1. These include retail cobranded goods that add another brand to complement their position, for example, Tesco Fair Trade, whose products are purchased from developing countries according to fair trade regulations.
2. Some retail companies develop portfolios of segmented retail brands, each with a different positioning. Tesco was among the first to do so. Now many other companies follow a similar path. For example, Eroski has the "Eroski" brand as its mainstream one, "Eroski Natur" for fully assured fresh food (meat, fruit, vegetables, etc.), "Eroski Seleqtia" as its gourmet sub-brand, "Eroski sin gluten" as its gluten-free sub-brand, etc.
3. Since a retail brand is a real brand, it can become an umbrella when a company diversifies and markets new categories of its original products. Many retail companies are now offering new branded product categories that are far from their core business, for example, Carrefour's travel agency, Carrefour Financial Services, Carrefour Insurance, etc. These sub-brands complement the message communicated by the Carrefour brand with new dimensions without damaging its brand DNA.

4. It may be implied that the following step in the evolution of retail branded goods can be segmented sub-brands within branded new categories, probably resulting in a combination of the two previous options given earlier.

> Price position is not a unique dimension retail companies can use when branding their own products.

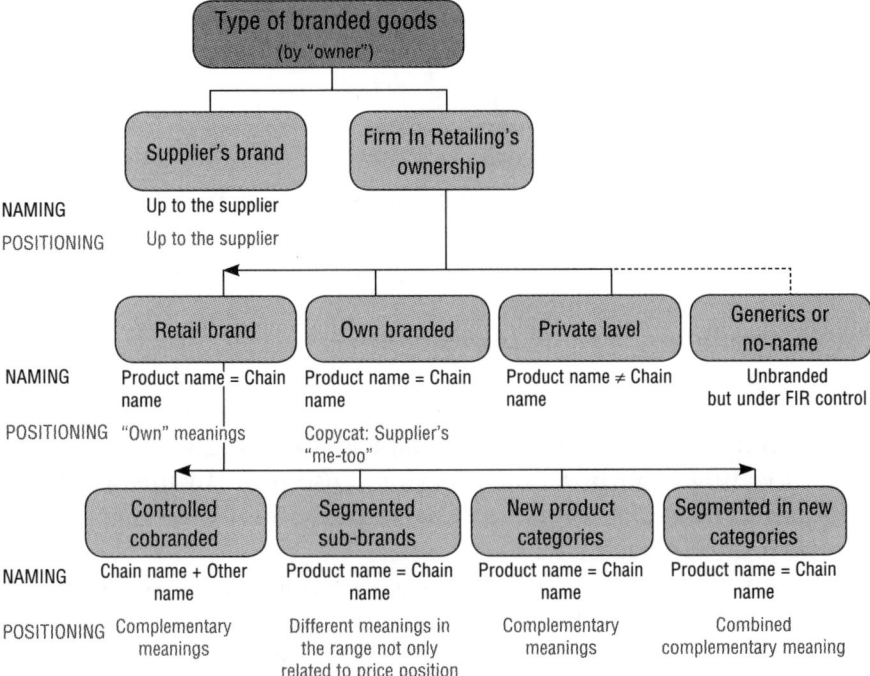

FROM RETAIL BRANDED GOODS ONWARD

Increasingly, more retail companies are beginning to understand that in order to transform their retail branded goods from cheap commodities to real brands, they will have to learn how to manage the meaning of their brands, and discover new routes that diverge from the traditional price-positioning dimensions.

Once such routes are discovered, it will be easy for organizations to begin branding the real "retail product"[2]: every retail formula and every chain in the portfolio of a retail company.

Some examples of branded retail formats in a retail company:

1. Tesco:
    - Tesco (superstores)
    - Tesco Metro
    - Tesco Extra
    - Tesco Express
    - www.tesco.com
    - Tesco groceries (app)

2. El Corte Inglés:
    - El Corte Ingles (department stores)
    - Supercor (supermarkets)
    - Viajes El Corte Ingles
    - www.elcorteingles.es
    - eBooks El Corte Ingles (app)

In fact, portfolio management of its chain is the key for any retail company. To brand every chain is not just giving it a name, but allocating a purpose, meaning or sense to it. In this way retail companies manage shopper's expectations about what may or may not be found in each chain.

When a retail company reaches this point, it is aware of the need to put in place brand architecture, not only at the branded goods level, but also at the chain level. Obviously, those levels must be strongly connected to the meaning of the company's corporate brand.

Therefore, a retail company's brand can be displayed at three levels. Each level supports the others, and at the same time, each receives the support of the others. Technically speaking, the source of inspiration for any brand strategy at the product and the chain levels should be a company's retail corporate brand values.

---

[2] It's important to realize that the retail firms main product is the shop. What any firm in retailing really wants to "sell" is shop: come to my shop, instead of going the competitor's one.

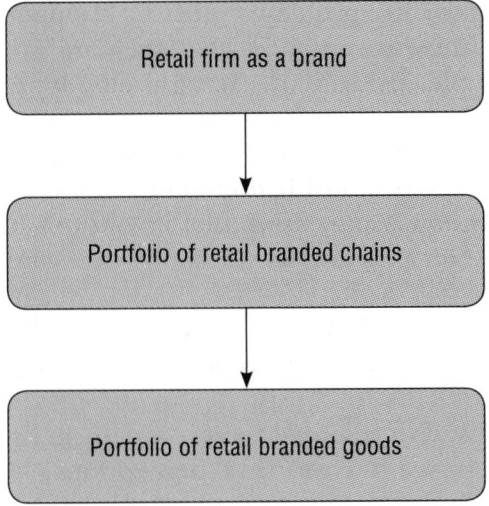

McKinsey & Co. confirms that "when everything has the same brand name, it's easier to get better economic results" (Henderson and Mihas, 2000).

A retail company may have a brand architecture, where any level supports the others.

FUTURE CHALLENGES FOR RETAIL COMPANIES' BRANDS

When branding, some challenges might arise for retail firms, especially while expanding into new markets (Burt and Sparks, 2000). Their brand meaning could be misunderstood due to cultural differences, so retail firms have been experiencing more troubles than large suppliers when exporting their products (i.e. their chains) outside their domestic markets.

Other challenges for retail firms may relate to the percentage of their own brands compared to their total turnover. If this proportion is low, the impact of the brands is limited. If this proportion is 100%, meaning that all the products are the company's own brands, these will not have any problems meeting shoppers' expectations, since they will know in advance what they are going to find at a store. For example, IKEA, Zara, Mango, etc., have 100% branded retail products.

However, a company is in a precarious situation when the proportion of its own brand is dominant, but still less than 100%. In this case, customers may think that its options have been drastically reduced. Managing target customers' expectations is therefore the key.

A third challenge facing a company may lie in the diverse meanings of messages under its retail brand architecture. Avoiding complexity and maintain consistency in the meaning of messages relating to its brands is essential for a company in its quest to reduce the risk of dissonance in customers' perceptions.

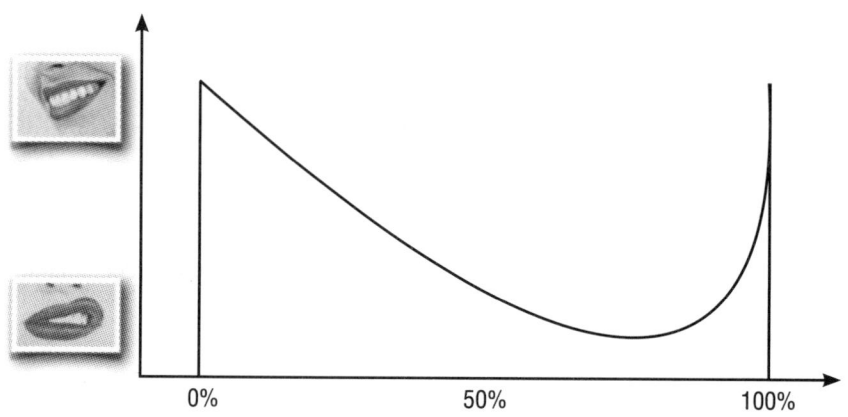

Possible customer expectations trend according to % of retail firm brand presence

SO WHAT IS IT?

Different terms have been used to convey the same message.

Some authors and organizations using the term "private label" include:

- The claim made by the now extinct *Private Label magazine,* founded in 1979—"The publication for store brand leaders" (privatelebelmag.com)
- Nielsen's—"The power of the private label (July 2003) and IRI's—"Private label report" (2013)
- Nirmalya Kumar and Jan-Benedict Steenkamp—"Private label strategy" (Harvard Business School Press, 2007)
- Raj Sethuraman—"Private-label marketing strategies in packaged goods: management beliefs and research insights," MSI Reports, Working Paper series, Issue 2, 2006 (In the document, he also uses the term "store brand" as an equivalent.)
- Saatchi & Saatchi X and POPAI—"The global association for marketing at-retail: Private label research," June 2007.
- Private label Manufacturers Association—its corporate name

In general, it seems the term "private label" is more used in the USA than in Europe.

Some organizations use the terms "retailer brand" or "retail brand":

- These terms are common in Europe, and are the most frequently used nowadays in France ("marque de la distribution") and Spain ("marca de la distribución").
- McKinsey & Co. uses it (Henderson and Mihas, 2000).

After having seen the historic transformation these terms have witnessed around the world, it is obvious that a new approach is needed now, especially if we want to inspire future managerial implications.

It is reasonable to say that a "retail brand" is:

- A legal registered brand
- Applied to products, services, shops, store chains and even to retail companies at their corporate level
- Applied to an organization whose positioning is controlled by a retail company

Some important missing elements need to be highlighted in this definition:

- Retail brands can be real brands or simple labels, just like any supplier's brand. The richness of their positioning is not part of their definition. This relates to the level of managerial skills applied to the branding process.
- A company's positioning does not necessarily need to be linked to a cheaper priced product. It can be associated with other values such as trust, involvement, an easier life, gourmet tastes, hedonism, novelty, ethics, freshness, fashion, mood enhancement, etc.
- It applies not only to the grocery domain, but also to any retail sector (anything that can be sold directly to the public), for example, fashion, furniture, opticians, financial services, travel agencies, computers, insurance, bars, hotels, sport clubs and airlines. Even Public Administration can brand its services when delivering these to the citizens. A retail brand is usually owned by a retail organization, but it may be that some products that are branded with the supplier's brand can be slightly modified to be only sold by a given retail chain. For example, imagine the Sony TV model XX45 being sold exclusively by the "Wonderful Buy" chain. In this fictitious case, the brand is Sony, but the model is controlled by the retail company so that its gross margin can be better defended.

There is a potential variation of this case: it can also be cobranded.

- Retail branded goods can also be sold outside retailers' premises. For example, if a brand becomes prestigious and famous, it can also be sold externally, for example, Laura Ahsley's towels at Eroski's supermarkets. Another example is La Bruixa d'Or[3] (golden witch), the leader in the Spanish lottery ticket market. It sells lottery tickets, not only in its small 40 m2 shops and on its website, but sometimes third parties

---

[3] La Bruixa d'Or is the retail firm leader in the Spanish lottery sector. It accounts for 8% market share, although it only has one 40 m2 shop, located in a 2,000 inhabitants town, in the mountains, the Pyrenees, and later on launched a web site (www.labruixador.es) which sells almost everywhere in the world. This is a wonderful example of how an independent retail firm, owned by Xavier Gabriel, created a brand and become leader, even tough its location is simply horrible.

websites as well, to resell tickets. Interestingly, these lottery tickets are sold at an official price of €20, which is printed on one side of the ticket by the official Spanish Lottery Agency. However, on the website of a third party seller, the price was €22.32 because the demand for such retail branded lottery tickets is high, and customers are willing to pay more than the official price for them. This is an example of how branded retail goods can be more expensive than supplier's ones.
- In fact, retail branding is about who is writing the script and who is creating the meaning or the sense of the item, and then delivering it through a powerful five-senses medium (a shop).

> A retail branded product is one that is usually sold in a "commercial" space (a shop) where the five senses are used.

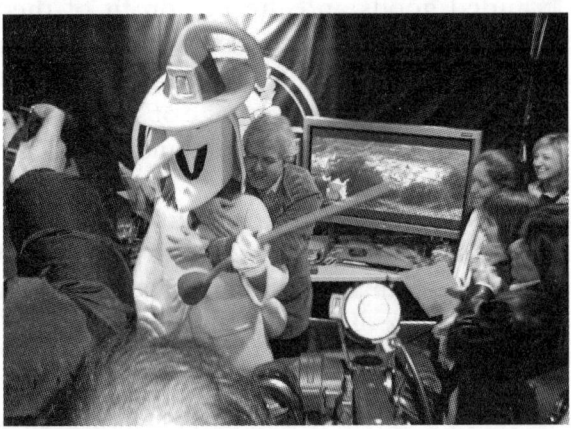

Courtesy: Xavier Gabriel Lliset.

WHAT MAKES RETAIL BRANDS SO POWERFUL?

Since retail firms—business-to-customer (B2C) companies—sell directly to private customers, they enjoy a "natural" set of benefits such as:

- They have complete control of their "selling machines"—their shops. They decide what they want to sell, the retail price

as well as the way in which they want to manage their relationship with customers and suppliers.
- They display their branded products in the way that suits their image, they can place these on the best shelves (if we are talking about standard FMCG products), and they can add anything these products may need, for example, light, proper fixtures, information, etc.
- They have direct knowledge of customers, especially if they use customer cards[4] to track the latter's purchasing behavior. Therefore, retail organizations have a huge potential to generate segmented or customized offers to their customers, usually by using a mass-customized approach. They may not be product-specialists, but they can easily become customer-experts.
- Improved economic performance: There is a direct correlation between the percentage of sales which correspond to retail branded goods and the net profit of the chain[5]. The wider the presence of a retail brand, the higher its net profit.

Retail firms can take special advantage of some "natural" competitive benefits when branding. Instead of considering shops as places where they install "in-store advertising," the stores can be transformed to five-senses communication media. This communication is based on semiotics (signs, color, textures, rhythm, light, sound, fragrances, etc.). Even human smiles are crucial here. According to Amancio Ortega, founder of Inditex (of the Zara chain),

> "The shop is the best way to create a brand" (Cinco días, June 25, 2007).

A shop may be a 25-minute commercial, more convincing than standard ones, since all human senses are simultaneously stimulated,

---

[4] Instead of talking of "loyalty card" it's much better to say "customer cards" or "customer identification cards," because their main purpose is to link a customer behavior to a given identified customer. In this way the retail firm owns an incredibly rich database, linking products, people, time, place, and his/her sensitivities (to price, novelty, brand, time, etc.), and other behavioral patterns.

[5] AT Kearney report, using Nielsen European data, 1980–1992.

turning it into a multi-sensorial experience. When the impact on the five senses is properly aligned, an advertisement's persuasion capacity is much higher, and control over delivery of the meaning of a brand is almost 100%.

Allowing customers to participate in the shopping experience is one of the best methods of co-creating brand sense. Although it may be argued that a company is losing control over its brand, it should be remembered that the meaning of the greatest brands is emotionally owned by customers.

The shopping experience is an essential part of the main retail product and this is an "overt consumption,"[6] since shoppers can see each other at a store, using the brand. This behavioral side of the purchasing process is key, since brand image is created through marketing communications, but ultimately through consumers' experience (Thomas, 2005).

If a retail company thinks about this possibility, for example, Apple stores in Genius bars, customers may not only interact with staff, but also with their peers and may influence and be influenced by others, as in social media. In this way, the retail branded experience becomes co-owned.

This indicates that the "web 2.0" concept may be too restrictive, since its philosophy may also be valid offline.

When a person is in front of a shelf is already a "customer," since he/she has already "bought" a product in the shop, it means that the person has chosen this store among others. Therefore, if the customer has trusted the chain, there is a strong possibility that he/she will transfer this trust to the chain's branded products.

By putting the chain name on the products, the retail firm shows a deeper commitment to customers, so it can gain their trust easily. And trust is an essential part of branding (Castaldo, 2006).

Through the shopping experience, a company can create or develop solid customer's attitudes. "Attitudes formed from direct behaviour or experience are more accessible than attitudes based on information or indirect forms of behaviour" (Fazio and Zanna, 1981, cited in Keller, 1993). A shop may be an "imagination shuttle." This is extremely useful to boost sales, especially for products relating

---

[6] "Overt consumption of brands is found when a brand is used in a way where other consumers can see the usage of the brand" (Thomas, 2005).

to personal expression (fashion, furniture, home decoration, wine, accessories, etc.). Therefore, to sum up, a retail company's source of power in branding is not only rooted in its preferential display. Its strategic advantage is the communicative nature of its stores, which blend consumers' emotion and conscious reflection.

By combining all these features, it is clear that a shop is not only a wonderful brand communication medium, but also a place where a brand is fully lived and experienced by customers. Therefore, if a store is perceived as the brand, it may also be viewed as a "retail brand temple" as well.

> The most important product that any retail company is "selling" is the shop (and everything inside it).
> If the customer does not go into the shop, the company will not make any sales.

IMPACT ON SUPPLIERS

Almost all suppliers are concerned about the increasing market share being gained by products branded by their "dear business customers." These products grow because they have privileges at the point-of-sale—a secure place in companies' products portfolios as well as in their shops, and they enjoy a better shelf location. Sometimes they are only cheap versions (copies) of suppliers' most innovative products.

There are trade associations such as the Spanish Promarca, whose mission is to protect and develop the brands of its associates (prestigious suppliers), who are concerned by the ground gained by such brands. According to the former president of Promarca, Ramon Tais, "retailers can't innovate, just copy, and attract customers due to the price."[7] Therefore, it is clear that suppliers view retail business customers as tough competitors. This creates a paradox, since they look at the latter with both love and hate at the same time.

---

[7] Una hora con Amancio Ortega (An Hour with Amancio Ortega), Cinco Días (Five Days), October 25, 2005.

SUPPLIER'S RESPONSES

There are many ways in which suppliers can counter-attack. All of these have been reviewed in academic papers and in many practitioners' conferences.

- By offering better quality products, since this is the main reason why customers may prefer their brands
- By increasing advertising budgets and implementing more efficient advertising campaigns, integrated with other communication media (buzz, blogs, or even paying for a better shelf space, etc,).
- By rationalizing brand and category portfolios, for example, many international suppliers such as Unilever have reduced their brand portfolios, dropping their less efficient brands, categories, and items, in order to allocate an increased advertising budget for the remaining brands.
- By managing the price gap between suppliers' and retailers' brands, for example, in any brand, there is a point when even loyal customers will switch to a competitor's brand, which may be a retail one. Therefore, this "disloyalty" price gap needs to be filled up, but the side effect is that this could shrink a company's gross margin. Nevertheless, there are cases in which a competitor' new product can challenge cheaper branded retail goods.
- By collaborating with retail companies and manufacturing branded retail products (either with a company's own products or in a dedicated manner, one can more easily enhance one's portfolio to achieve increased manufacturing productivity. The most radical position adopted by a company is to build a completely new business model by becoming a dedicated supplier.
- The best way in which suppliers can face the challenge relating to retail branded goods is by fostering innovation In products. According to N. Kumar and J-B Steenkamp (2007), "[m]anagers, academics, and consultants, they all agree that the single best approach to combating private labels is to offer innovative new products."

Apart from such traditional options, there are others that claim that the challenge should be faced from a different angle. According to Marcos de Quinto, Coca-Cola's CEO in Spain:

> Retailers may also innovate, and on top they know the customers, and they may have a better presence (of their branded products) on the shop shelves. Manufacturers only have the brand.
>
> Manufacturers innovation doesn't last for long. Quality and functionality are simply a basis. Only emotional differentiation is a valid route.
>
> We are in a paradoxical world: retailers are at the same time business customers and competitors. (AECOC Congress, 2006)

Mercadona, the Spanish retail chain, is a relevant example of what Coca-Cola's CEO, Marcos de Quito, was referring to. The chain launched an easy-to-use shoe polisher, risk-free from self-staining while using it. The product has been a success and was awarded the prize for the best packaging design at the Spanish packaging contest "Liderpack 08."

Can one now doubt the fact that retail brands can also be innovators?

As the example given above anticipates, manufacturers' actions on threats from retail brands are short-term remedies, but are far from being a complete solution to the problem.

The following part of this chapter explores Quinto's challenge in depth.

THE CRUCIAL MISUNDERSTANDING

It is not clear why brands should be split into two groups:

1. Manufacturers' brands
2. Retail firms' brands

The following includes criteria used to sort out brands in companies. It is an arbitrary method.
Can you imagine sorting out brands by the following?

- North/South origin
- Big/Small logo size
- Long/Short names

We think that classifying brands, based on the type of company, may reveal a prejudice emanating from a serious misunderstanding, for example, that "manufacturer" and "retailer" are different types of companies. Many decades ago, these terms were technically correct, since there were companies whose only business was to develop products, brand them, sell these to third party business customers (retailers), and to promote them, usually through strong advertising campaigns. These were manufacturers.

During that period, there were also some other companies, whose role was only to resell the products supplied by the manufacturers in an very operative manner without adding anything more than some services, including proximity to customers. These were retailers.

Later, although rather slowly, retailers understood that they could play a more proactive role and began changing some rules of the game—they undertook activities,[8] which had been previously performed by suppliers. One such example was the initial generation of labeled retail goods.

In the last few decades, some of these companies who were in direct contact with their end customers gained a clear picture of shoppers' interests, needs, reactions and their shopping behavior. They could even conduct an outstanding segmentation, for example, Tesco, which is famous for this capability.

Once the different customer segments became known to companies, it become fairly easy for them to give the right briefing to product specialists in order to develop new products, including innovative ones. One example was Tesco's low-fat and low-cholesterol branded eggs.[9] This was an innovation led by a retailer. But Tesco is not alone in this. Decathlon, a well-known French retail company selling sports goods, has an R&D department, which was developed in 2002 and has won many design and innovation awards.[10] And last but not the least, Mercadona's aerosol shoe polish perfectly describes how a retailer can interpret customers' tastes and needs as well as (or even better than) a supplier.

Consequently, it is clear that what is really important is to innovate. And every company needs to do this, no matter whether it is a manufacturer or a retailer.

The scenario has also changed for supplier firms, which have discovered that the sources of value may not always be at the origin

---

[8] The author calls them "micro-functions." These small activities are the basic molecules for channel innovation, especially if some of these are reallocated to a different channel player.

[9] Launched in October 2004. For more information look at http://www.tescocorporate.com/page.aspx?pointerid=F1EEFE5A25354F69A2A08FDB84F17BC3

[10] To check Decathlon's innovation commitment see http://oia.oxylane.com/edition-2013-video/winner

of the value chain, but are usually at the end—being in touch with end customers. Therefore, many manufacturers decided to undertake activities usually engaged exclusively by retail companies. Some started opening showrooms to present their complete product portfolios in an appealing manner: offering a monobrand experiential knowledge place, whose aim was to influence end customers and boost their preference for their brand. These showrooms were like a 3-D catalog, where purchasing was not accepted in order to avoid irritating business customers. Later, some suppliers decided to undertake hitherto vetoed activities such as selling directly to customers, and they entered the world of retailing.

There are many examples of companies that now retail (B2C), which were suppliers in the past (B2B). Included among these is Zara, which grew and became a key global player when it decided to develop its own retail chain, and changed its strategy from business-to-business (B2B) to B2C. Another example is Nestlè, the first food company in the world, which launched Nespresso, a very successful and profitable brand it conceived for development in retailing. Now Nespresso has attractive shops, where customers are delighted with the enriching shopping experience. Nespresso shops know all their customers (by name, email, phone, address, purchasing habits, tastes, sensitivity to new varieties and seasonal promotions, etc.). Therefore, for Nespresso, it was easy to engage in a one-to-one marketing activity. Nespresso shops have individual input data, and they can also activate individual response actions if they wish to. It is however important to notice that its parent company Nestlè not only ignores end-customer data, but has no control on how its products (for example, Nescafe) are being sold in third-party shops.

BREAKING OF A PARADIGM

Both types of companies (let's use for a moment the traditional vocabulary "manufacturers" and "retailers") are currently the same—simply companies. They are both completely free to undertake activities. By doing so, they engage in an activity that is somewhat like the "Lego," where a company can devise a new business model by putting some pieces together, and most importantly, create a product with a "sense." This sense is the brand.

Nowadays almost any firm[11] can, among other activities:

- Choose its customers
- Understand their insights
- Devise innovative solutions and brand these
- Advertise the solutions (even by using five-senses shops)
- Sell to the public (by retailing)

Reallocation of activities or micro-functions breaks the old and static roles of manufacturer and retailer, and these traditional names become not only useless, but even a source of misunderstanding when a company is trying to interpret the reality or innovate. Therefore, the best way to categorize companies (when analyzing retail branded goods) is not by looking at the beginning of their value chains (whether or not they have factories), but by focusing on their end products.

We strongly suggest this new way of clustering companies:

- Firms-In-Retailing (FIR)
- Firms that are not in retailing—suppliers

Firms engaged in retailing include B2C businesses, while the suppliers' business model is B2B.

To be in retailing is to be in direct contact with the end customer, and this is what really makes the difference.

CONCLUSION

When thinking about brand positioning, what comes to many people's minds is *price positioning*. Moreover, we have become used to relegating retail brands to the cheap side of the spectrum.

---

[11] This sentence is valid for any firm selling products or services that target the public.

IS THIS PRECONCEPTION STILL WORKING TODAY?

If we look at commercial life today without prejudice, we realize that companies retailing brands may no longer be selling cheap ones, but may also have other positioning dimensions such as in the case of any supplier. More so, as they sell directly to consumers, they may know the latter's needs and opinions better, so they may be more innovative and devise improved solutions. Some retail brands can also be found on third-party premises, in addition to their own shops, as in the case of any supplier's brand.

So What?

Simply put, it makes no sense to distinguish between retail brands and supplier's brands. They both are the same—there are good or bad brands, and elicit a certain awareness level and position in customers' minds.

Moreover, brands in retailing have key privileges due to their being in direct contact with customers. The most important of these is that a shopping trip could be a 25–45-minute five-senses commercial, through which customers' imaginations can be activated and the brand's meaning co-created. In this way, the store becomes a multi-sensory and live corporate brand experience.

The branding process in retailing is like creating a "matryoshka" —the meaning of the brand must be the same along all its layers, including that of the product, the shelf, the shop area, the store, the chain, the FIR, and even the shopping center or city area where the store is located.

If all the layers are well-aligned and consistent with the same brand sense, the shop becomes the best branding machine a manager can dream of. Think of how a precious Tiffany diamond would look in a supermarket shopping bag!

A branded retail product is sold in a highly efficient commercial initiative, endowed with the power of the five senses, and goes directly to the limbic system in a customer's brain. The controversy on retail branding is not about "what" it is, but about "who" is writing the *brand score* and then communicating it directly to the public by a five-senses medium, without any interface in-between.

Therefore, the real nature of the challenge in retail branding is not the choice between retail and supplier's brands. The real issue is related to companies' channel-related strategic decisions:

> To be or not to be in retailing.

That is the question.

	Supplier's Brand Brand owned by the supplier	Brand in Reatailing Brand owned by the Firm Retailing (FIR)
Price positioning	"The cheap one" is not the most common position for big brands, but it may be, as well as other options.	"Cheaper than ..."may be one option, but there are many others, not always price driven.
Research & Development	This is an important task for the most innovative brands.	This may be an important task for some Firms In Retailing: the most innovative ones.
Distribution channel	Usually sold through third party firms	Usually sold within own shops, but may also be sold through third party firms
Marketing communication	Multimedia platforms (TV, Internet, ...) are some of the best convincing tools, but with 2 senses.	On top of the media used by suppliers, they can rely on the shop itself as a five-senses commercial.
In conclusion	Both may be great or awful brands. The difference: the retail branded product is sold within a living five-senses corporate brand experience.	

REFERENCES

Burt, S. L. and L. Sparks (2002), *Corporate branding, retailing and retail internationalisation. Corporate reputation review*, 5, 194–212.

Castaldo, Sandro (2006), *Trust in market relationships*. MA, USA: Edward Elgar Publishing, Inc.

Évolution du marché européen dels Marques Distributeurs et des Premiers Prix, Conference in Tunis, April 3, 2007, quoting the French Fédération des entreprises du Commerce et de la Distribution. Retrieved from http//:www.fcd.asso.fr

Keller, K. L. (1993), "Conceptualizing, measuring and managing customer-based brand equity," *Journal of Marketing*, 57(1), 1–22.

Laaksonen, H. and J. Reynolds (1994), "Own brands in food retailing across Europe", *Journal of Brand Management*, 2(1), 37–46.

Henderson, Terilyn A. and Elizabeth A. Mihas, Building retail brands. *The McKinsey Quarterly*, 2000 (3).

Thomas, Greg (2005), *Brand Hijack: When Unintended Segments Desire Your Brand*. Zyman Institute of Brand Science. Retrieved from http://www.marketingprofs.com/6/thomas1.asp

Una hora con Amancio Ortega, Cinco días, June 25, 2007.

Section II
Brand Building

Chapter 4

Brand Identity: Brand Naming Process and Brand Linguistics in the International Context

Bernd Schmitt and Shi Zhang

Do not fear being born into a bad life. A far worse fear is being given a bad name.
—Chinese saying

BRAND NAMING: A COMPLEX PROCESS

Organizations invest substantial resources in creating brand names that would result in positive brand identities (Schmitt and Pan, 1994). As part of the naming process, they often engage multiple parties such as naming agencies and corporate identity consultants, advertising and communications agencies, as well as trademark lawyers, market research firms, and linguists. In selecting the names, these organizations take into account various factors ranging from brand and image factors to competitive, legal and linguistics considerations.

Consider, for example, the detailed management process Microsoft undertook to coin the name for its search engine "Bing." As *Business Week* reported, "[i]t took six months and dozens of experts to settle on the name. Brand naming is serious business in an age when goods must have global appeal and when an unfortunate choice can turn a promising product into a punch line" (*Business Week,* 2009). Interbrand, a corporate identity consulting firm Microsoft hired to develop a preliminary name list, assigned eight people to brainstorm names relating to "speed" and "relevance." The consultants generated 2,000 initial names. Next, 2 trademark lawyers and 20 linguists examined the remaining 600 choices. The experts ultimately submitted approximately 50 names to Microsoft, which picked 8 that were tested in focus groups and underwent more trademark screening.

The brand-naming efforts and process are particularly challenging and complicated in the international context, especially if the target markets use structurally different languages. In East Asia, where we conducted our studies, there are numerous languages with radically different phonological, grammatical and semantic structures (for example, Chinese, Thai, Indian, and Indonesian, among others), and even those that are structurally similar may differ significantly in their script (for example, Chinese, Japanese, and Korean), or use different scripts at the same time (for example, Japanese, and Korean). In addition, in these markets, there are consumers that may not know English as well as others that know the language and may be linguistically adapt in processing an English brand name.

The success of a name will ultimately depend on how a company's current and potential consumers perceive corporate, brand and product names (Keller, 1998; Keller, Heckler, and Houston, 1998; Pan and Schmitt, 1994; Schmitt and Pan, 1994). Therefore, name creation in an international context needs to be grounded in a conceptual understanding of how consumers process and respond to names.

THE CONSUMER'S PERSPECTIVE

The question of what constitutes a good brand name for a consumer arises, in particular, in international business. The key issue is how an established brand name can be translated into a foreign language so that consumers in a new and foreign market can evaluate it positively. Strictly speaking, it is not appropriate to speak of "name translations," which often comprise one-to-one correspondence of a linguistic item between two languages. Instead, brand names in one language need to be adapted to the unique linguistic structures of another. This task is complicated when the writing system used in the local language in the new country is different from that was used for the original name. This is a situation that arises, for example, when a US company enters the Chinese market.

One way of approaching the adaptation issue is to use the two key criteria of sound and meaning, that is, the name used in the new market should sound like the original name (for consistency) and refer in its meaning to product characteristics (for identification purposes) (Aaker, 1991; Keller, 1998; Schmitt and Simonson, 1997; Zhang and Schmitt, 2001). Some companies have admirably translated names, for example, the name for Coca Cola in Chinese. While the Chinese name is written in Chinese characters (known as logographs), the name (*ke kou ke le*) sounds very similar to the English name, and the meaning of the characters used to represent the name ("tastes good and makes you happy") refers to the product category and the brand's positioning. Another excellent example is the name of the cosmetics company Avon, *ai fang*, meaning "love-fragrance," which sounds similar to the English name and expresses the meaning of the product. Other companies have settled for a pure "sound translation" of the original name, for example, a name with a similar sound but with no reference to the meaning of the product (for example, Ford and Winston). Others have translated names by meaningfully referring to the product category without considering the original sound (for example, Clinique's Chinese name, *qian bi*, means "pretty and transparent green," but it does not sound like Clinique). Finally there are examples of companies that have created entirely new names. For example, name of the former accounting firm Coopers and Lybrand was translated to *yong dao*, a compound word meaning "eternal way," which is unrelated to the product category and dissimilar from the sound of the original English name.

In this chapter we examine conceptually and empirically four kinds of translations. We first present a conceptual analysis of writing systems and types of translations between the systems. Focusing on the most general and complex translation type—translation from a phonographic into a logographic writing system (for example, English into Chinese)—we then discuss and develop hypotheses on consumers' processing and evaluation judgment of translations of such brand names. Finally, we present some empirical studies of translations of names we have conducted over the years that address the question of names that are best liked by consumers.

In our consumer-focused research, we have not only conceptually and empirically addressed translation of brand name-related issues, but also the broader question of how language affects linguistic mental representation and information processing (Hunt and Agnoli, 1991; Lucy, 1992; Schmitt and Zhang, 1998). We have demonstrated the importance as well as relevance of linguistic factors on consumers' judgment and evaluations (O'Shaughnessy and Holbrook, 1988; Mick, 1986; Luna and Peracchio, 2001).

INTERNATIONAL BRAND LINGUISTICS: A CONCEPTUAL ANALYSIS

There are two major types of writing systems, which include various scripts that represent the different languages spoken around the world. These include (1) the phonographic writing system comprising the alphabetic script used to represent, for example, English, French, Spanish, and German; the Cyrillic system used to represent most Slavic languages, and the Japanese *hiragana* and *katakana*; (2) the logographic writing system including complex and simplified Chinese characters, Korean *hanza* and Japanese *kanji*. While phonographic writing systems represent the sound components of the spoken language either as letters or syllabic symbols, logographic writing systems represent words and concepts in the form of "sign" symbols (Akmajian, Demers, Farmer, and Harnish, 1992, p. 467). As a result, in phonographic systems there is close correspondence between speech and writing because the written word is a more or less direct representation of the components of the spoken word. Words are written according to how they sound. In these systems, only 20 to 60 symbols are needed to represent the phonemes of a given language, and therefore, newly coined words can be easily represented in writing. However, in logographic systems, the correspondence between speech and writing is largely conventional, resulting in the need for many different symbols. For example, in Chinese, roughly 5,000 logographs are needed to represent common concepts. New characters are difficult to create, since there are no unambiguous rules for representing the sound of a new word or inventing new characters. Therefore, when new words or new names emerge, they are represented by a combination of existing symbols that have already acquired certain meanings rather than by inventing new logographs. This feature of the Chinese language provides both challenges and opportunities for translations of foreign names into Chinese while selecting names for products.

Based on an understanding of the characteristics of phonographic and logographic writing systems, three types of situations for name translations can be distinguished in an international context. Within the same script, translations of names are between languages that use the same script in the same writing system, for example, an English brand name in German, a French brand name in Spanish, a Russian brand name in Bulgarian, or a Cantonese brand name in Mandarin. Literate individuals are familiar with the script and may have even have acquired knowledge of the original language of the brand as a second language (as is the case, for example, in many European countries with respect to English). Thus, symbol-to-symbol matching using the original (for example, English) brand name without significant modification usually provides an easy and acceptable solution. The only concern with this type of translation may be how phonetic accuracy can be guaranteed, and at the same time, negative semantic associations avoided. These associations may include existing negative meanings of the name in the foreign language (for example, in the case of Ford's "Fiera," which means "ugly old woman" in Spanish) or negative meanings resulting from mispronunciation of the original name (for example, in the case of Clairol's "Mist Stick," which is mispronounced as "Miststück," which means "manure" in German). Even seemingly meaningless names in one language (such as Toyota's MR2) may result in negative associations in another due to the fact that they result in a homophone with a distinct meaning (for example, "merde" in French, which has a very negative meaning).

Even in scripts within the same writing system, there are translations of names between different scripts within the phonographic system (for example, an English name in Russian or a Spanish name in Arabic) and the logographic system (for example, a Chinese name represented in Japanese *kanji*). Between scripts, translations are more complicated than translations of names within the same script. Different scripts follow different rules for mapping elementary units of speech (for example, phonemes) to elementary units of writing (for example, letters or syllabic symbols). For example, some such as Arabic primarily represent consonants and not vowels, and still others such as *hiragana* and *katakana* in Japanese represent consonants and vowels jointly. The key concern is still the same as with translations within the same script—optimization of symbol-to-symbol matches while guaranteeing phonetic accuracy and avoiding negative semantic associations.

The third type of name translations between phonographic and logographic—between writing systems (for example, from English to Chinese)—are even more difficult. This type of translation includes all the complexities discussed in relation to phonetic accuracy being guaranteed and negative associations avoided. In addition, translations are adaptations of creative names rather than symbol-to-symbol matching translations (mentioned earlier in the case of Coca-Cola, Ford, Coopers & Lybrand, and Clinique, and in many other instances including Kodak, Colgate, Dell, Fluor, Revlon, and Goldman Sachs (Seligman, 1986). In the case of English names based on existing words, for example, United Airlines and General Electric, translation is a simple process, which involves use of the corresponding lexical items in Chinese, and therefore, is not considered in this study.

Let us consider how the issue mentioned above may apply to Jamba Juice, a California-based company that sells smoothies and other fresh fruit drinks. A translation or adaptation option used in the Chinese market by foreign companies is to create an entirely new name—one that does not resemble the English name in sound or meaning (as in the case of Coopers & Lybrand). In the case of Jamba Juice, such a name may refer to general characteristics such as "quality" or "innovation," without relating in any specific way to the product category of fruit juice and without sounding like the English name. Another naming option is sound-based translation (for example, "Jiang ba"), in which the Chinese name will sound very similar to the English one, but will not refer to the product category (as in the case of Ford). A third option is meaning-based translation (for example, "Zha guo zhi"), which makes sure that the Chinese name semantically conveys core product or brand attributes such as "blended fruits" and "freshness," even though it does not sound like Jamba Juice (as in the Clinique approach). A final, difficult and (logically) rare option (relative to sound or meaning) is to have sound-based and meaning-based translation at the same time (as in the case of Coca-Cola). This can be accomplished by using the translation "Jian-bao," a name that sounds like Jamba and consists of two Chinese characters that mean "healthy" and "fit," referring to characteristics that are commonly associated with fresh fruit juice.

As the example of the Jamba Juice illustrates, translations from a phonographic-to-logographic writing system can be analyzed along two dimensions—relatedness in sound and in meaning. Depending on whether sound-based translations are closely related to the sound of the original name and whether meaning-based translations are related to the key characteristics of a product, they fall into one of the four categories according to a 2×2 scheme. These include (1) names that are similar in sound to the original ones and are related in meaning to the characteristics of the product category, (2) names that are similar in sound to the original ones, but are not related in meaning to the characteristics of the product category, (3) names that not similar in sound to the original one, but are related in meaning to the characteristics of the product category, and (4) names that are neither similar in sound nor related in meaning to the characteristics of the product category. Evaluation of these four types of translations of names requires an understanding of how consumers (for example, Chinese customers) process sound- and meaning-based translations of the original (for example, English) names.

CONSUMER INFORMATION PROCESSING: DIFFERENCES BETWEEN PHONOGRAPHIC AND LOGOGRAPHIC SYSTEMS

Prior psychological research (Nguy, Allard, and Bryden, 1980; Perfetti, Bell, and Delaney, 1988; Perfetti and Zhang, 1991) has shown that in phonographic systems, such as English, the primary mental code for verbal information, as in the case of brand names, is phonological—a phenomenon known as "phonemic coding." In contrast, in logographic systems, such as Chinese, phonemic coding is used much less (Hung and Tzeng, 1981; Zhou and Marslen-Wilson, 1999). In these writing systems, written information, such as characters, is encoded visually and the meaning is directly extracted from these characters. This is a process that is referred to as a higher degree of visual-semantic processing. This process is common because of the structural characteristics of the logographic system—the presence of thousands of meaningful characters, loose orthographic-phonemic correspondence, and the lack of word boundaries that necessitate a contextual semantic analysis (Tavassoli, 1999).

Evidence of phonemic vs visual-semantic encoding can be provided by examining individuals' name recall as well as their recall of temporal information and associations. Schmitt, Pan, and Tavassoli (1994) used a cue for phonemic encoding (by speaking out a word aloud) or visual-semantic encoding (by writing down a word) as part of a memory related experiment. As expected, it was found that Chinese speakers were more likely to recall a name when they were asked to do so it by writing it down. In contrast, English speakers were more likely to recall a name by saying it out aloud rather than by writing it down. In another set of experiments on consumers on words and brand names, Tavassoli (1999) proposed that a higher degree of phonemic encoding should result in better encoding of temporal information, whereas visual-semantic encoding and processing should result in better memory in the case of inter-item associative information. As expected, English speakers displayed their superior memory for temporal information and the Chinese were found to be better at processing inter-item associative information.

We applied the concept of differential encoding and processing, based on such language triggers, in the context of translation of brand names. In one of our studies (Zhang and Schmitt, 2001), we asked native Chinese respondents to judge so-called "dual names"—brand names represented in English and a Chinese translation, a format that is frequently used in China. The Chinese translation of a name was either sound- or meaning-based. Moreover, in prime phonemic or visual-semantic processing, the dual name format was displayed by emphasizing the component of the English or Chinese name (by showing one above the other in a larger typeface). In the case of meaning-based translations, there was no difference in the attitude to brand names in the two emphasis conditions. However, when respondents were shown a sound-based translation without a meaningful component, the preferred emphasis was on English, presumably because the English emphasis triggered phonemic processing.

To sum up, prior brand-naming research, including our own, provided support for differential encoding and processing, based on language triggers. However, most of the supporting evidence was somewhat indirect. For example, proxy manipulations such as "saying out loud" or "writing down a word" or proxy measures such as studying memory for temporal versus visual-associative information were employed. The Zhang and Schmitt (2001) name-translation study did not also completely manipulate the components of sound and meaning. We did not test along the dimension of sound and meaning in a complete 2 (sound—similar to the original English name or not similar to the original name) by 2 (meaning—related to the original name or not related to the original name) scheme. Such a scheme and experimental test would be very important because it would include an essential baseline condition—a Chinese name without any sound or meaning in reference to the English name—against which the potential additional relation effects of the created Chinese name to the original English name can be compared. In sum, the previous work resulted in an incomplete conceptual analysis and empirical test of dual brand naming and did not provide direct process-related evidence for differential phonemic vs visual-semantic processing. This may explain, for example, the lack of effect observed in meaning-based translations.

THE CRITICAL TEST: SOUND AND MEANING IN A 2 × 2 SCHEME

In the study we report next, we will present a critical comprehensive test. We will manipulate the dimensions of sound and meaning by using the 2 by 2 scheme we have described earlier. Consumers were shown four types of stimuli—names with a similar sound/related meaning, not with a similar sound/related meaning, with a similar sound/not related meaning, and not with a similar sound/unrelated meaning. Brand-naming studies in the international context are complex and complicated to run. Because this study has not been published previously, we will describe this in detail so that the reader can judge the stimuli, manipulations, and empirical analyses that we have conducted and get a sense of the linguistic intricacies involved in such research.

What results did we expect from our study? We based our predictions on the conceptualization discussed earlier that makes differential predictions regarding exposure to phonographic and logographic systems. If the phonetic writing system in English triggers phonetic processing, while Chinese logographs trigger visual-semantic processing, we should then expect respondents in the English emphasis condition to judge brand names primarily on the basis of sound (irrespective of meaning) and respondents in the Chinese emphasis condition judge the same names, primarily based on meaning (irrespective of sound).

The participants in our study included 240 college students from Shanghai. To control for cultural confounds, we used native speakers of Chinese (Mandarin), who had adequate knowledge of and skills in English (studying English for five years in college and graduate schools), in different language emphases conditions (Chinese vs English). Participants with similar characteristics took all the pre-tests. They were randomly assigned conditions by receiving different questionnaire booklets. They were given dual names across five product categories (for example, boxing gloves, supermarket store, soap bar, pen, and seasoning), according to a between-subjects design of 2 (sound component of the name—whether it was similar to the original name or not) × 2 (meaning component of the name—whether it was related to the product or not) × 2 (language emphasis—English or Chinese).

To make this study comparable with our earlier one (Zhang and Schmitt, 2001), we also included a priming condition using language emphasis. Here, language emphasis was manipulated in various ways—via verbal instruction (for example, participants were told that the Chinese or that the English name was the target of emphasis), via the position of the name (English above vs English below the Chinese name), and by presenting the emphasized name (English or Chinese) in large and bold typeface.

We have mentioned earlier that naming studies in the international context are complex and require careful testing of stimuli. Therefore, to select the stimuli, we conducted quantitative pre-tests on focus groups. In the focus group, four native speakers of English generated fictitious English brand names for a variety of consumer products. Several names for each product were selected, based on linguistic criteria (for example, syllabic structure, and vowel and consonant combinations) of word formation. Then 22 native speakers of English provided ratings on a list of fictitious English brand names, judging how familiar each name was to them (1 = not at all familiar; 7 = very familiar), and to what degree each name was seen as a likely brand name (1 = not at all likely; 7 = very likely). Those that were perceived to have similar familiarity and high likelihood brand name ratings were then used as original English names for Chinese translations.

Next, four types of Chinese translation names were created by a group of bilingual speakers skilled in the field of translation, based on the English names, and differences were resolved through discussions (pair wise inter-rater agreement>.92). A translated Chinese name is defined as being similar in phonetic translation if the individual characters making up the Chinese translation sound like a part or parts of the original English name. Similarly, a translation is defined to be related in semantic translation if the individual characters making up the Chinese translation suggest meanings related to the product.

Table 4.1 demonstrates the stimuli used in Study 1. As shown in Table 4.1, column 3, the first type of Chinese names was created to relate in sound to the original name and had the relevant product-category meaning. The second type was related in phonetic translation, but not in semantic translation (see Table 4.1, column 4). The third type was not related in phonetic translation, but related in semantic translation (see Table 4.1, column 5). Finally, the fourth type was not related in either phonetic or semantic translations (see Table 4.1, column 6).

Four types of Chinese names were tested with 80 college-going native speakers of Chinese (20 per cell) in Shanghai, based on familiarity and likely brand names. Participants in the pre-test were randomly assigned to each of the four conditions (the four types of names). They were asked to indicate their familiarity with each

Table 4.1 Stimuli Brand Names for Study 1

Products	English Names	Chinese Names 1: Sound: similar Meaning: related	Chinese Names 2: Sound: similar Meaning: not related	Chinese Names 3: Sound: note similar Meaning: related	Chinese Names 4: Sound: not similar Meaning: not related
1. Boxing gloves	Dethlon	De(2)shi(4)yong(3) 得势勇	Di(2)shi(4)long(2) 迪师隆	Wei(1)feng(1) 威风	Dan(1)hui(4) 丹汇
2. Seasoning	Voada	Wei(4)da(2) 味达	Fu(2)de(2) 佛得	Hao(3)cai(4)lu(3) 好菜侣	Xian(2)hong(2) 贤虹
3. Soap bar	Daylan	Da(2)run(4) 达润	De(2)luo(2) 德罗	Jie(2)ling(2) 洁灵	Rui(4)yin(1) 锐音
4. Pen	Vinbro	Wen(2)bo(2) 文博	Wei(1)bo(1) 维波	Cui(4)si(2) 萃思	Li(4)jue(2) 利觉
5. Superstore	Petons	Bei(4)du(1) 贝都	Pai(4)teng(2) 派腾	Gui(1)man(3)le(4) 归满乐	Hao(3)tai(4) 好泰

De(2)shi(4)yong(3) meaning "gaining force and courage," wei(4)da(2) meaning "flavor satisfactory," da(2)run(4) meaning "resulting in moist and smoothness," wen(2)bo(2) meaning "literary and knowledgeable," bei(4)du(1) meaning " a place/capital with precious items."
Di(2)shi(4)long(2) meaning "enlightening, teaching, and thriving," fu(2)de(2) meaning "Buddhism and acquisition," de(2)luo(2) meaning "merit and net," wei(2)bo(1) meaning "to maintain waves," pai(4)teng(2) meaning " dispatch and jump."
Wei(1)feng(1) meaning "power," hao(3)cai(4)lu(3) meaning "accompanying good dishes," jie(2)ling(2) meaning "clean and effective," cui(4)si(1) meaning "gathering thoughts," gui(1)man(3)le(4) meaning "going back in satisfaction and happiness."
Dan(1)hui(4) meaning "redness comes together," xian(2)hong(2) meaning "a worthy rainbow," rui(4)yin(1) meaning "sharp sound," li(4)jue(2) "keen senses," hao(3)tai(4) meaning "good and peaceful."

Chinese translation on a seven-point scale (1 for not at all familiar and 7 for very familiar) and the extent to which they thought the translation was a likely brand name (1 for not at all likely and 7 for very likely). Based on the test results, 20 names (5 names for each type) were selected for the main study, as shown in Table 4.1. There were no significant differences between the selected names regarding familiarity or likely brand names in each condition as well as between conditions (all p's > .25).

In the actual experiment, the participants were told that the study related to brand-naming, and that they would be shown a number of dual names (the original English name and the Chinese name). On the stimulus page, information on the product category was provided first, followed by the dual name in a rectangular frame. At the bottom of the page were three seven-point evaluation items (good/bad, unsatisfactory/satisfactory, and dislike/like). Each subject evaluated five dual names. The order of the stimulus name presentation was held constant for different conditions.

To analyze the data, an brand name evaluation index was formulated by averaging the evaluation items (Cronbach alpha = 0.93). A $2 \times 2 \times 2$ ANOVA revealed a three-way interaction, $F (1,232) = 3.47$, $p = .05$. We had expected that when English was emphasized, the participants would focus more on processing of sound, and when Chinese was emphasized, they would focus more on the processing of meaning.

As indicated in Figure 4.1a and b, our hypothesis was confirmed. When Chinese was emphasized, names that were related in meaning were evaluated more favorably than those that were not, regardless of whether the sound of the name was similar or unsimilar to the original English name (Ms = 4.86 vs 3.52, $t (58) = 5.68$, $p < .0001$; Ms = 4.58 vs 3.51, $t (58) = 4.57$, $p < .0001$). In contrast, when English was emphasized, names that were similar in sound to the original name were evaluated more favorably than those that were unsimilar in sound, regardless of whether the meaning of the name was related or unrelated to the product (Ms = 4.75 vs 3.86, $t (58) = 3.95$, $p < .001$; Ms = 4.83 vs 3.48, $t (58) = 6.07$, $p<.0001$).

The ANOVA we conducted also revealed the main effect of sound, $F (1,232) = 32.07$, $p < .0001$ and the main effect of meaning, $F (1,232) = 32.05$, $p < .0001$, suggesting that names that were similar in sound were more favorably evaluated than those that

(a) Chinese Emphasis

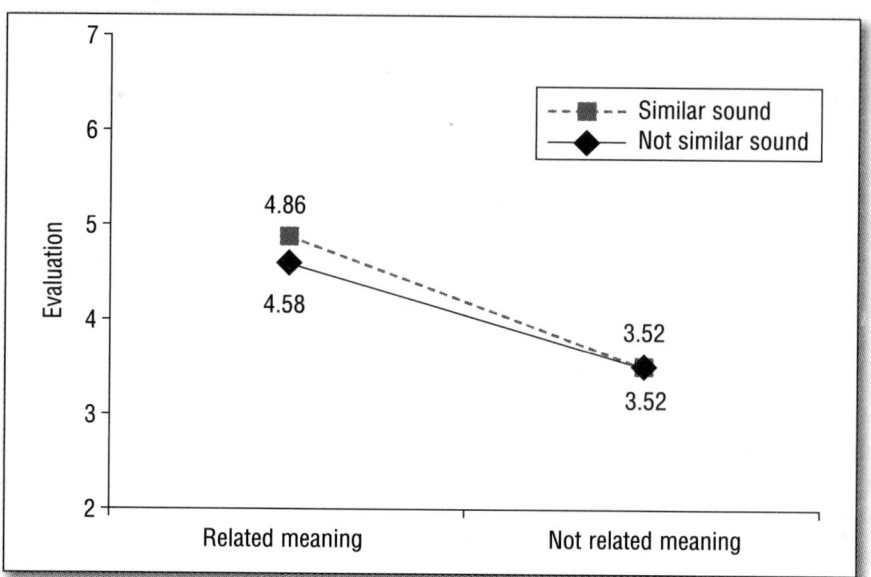

(b) English Emphasis

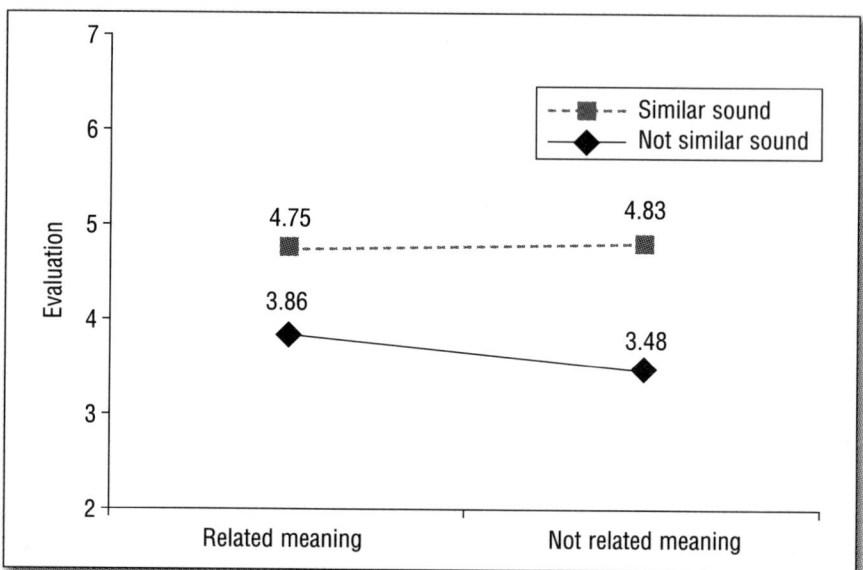

Figure 4.1 Brand Name Evaluation as a Function of Name Emphasis, Sound, and Meaning in Study 1

were not similar in sound to the original name, and that names that were related in their meaning received more favorable evaluations than those that did not relate in their meaning to the product. There was also two-way interaction between emphasis and sound, $F (1,232) = 19.97$, $p < .0001$, which revealed that names that were similar in sound to the original English name were judged significantly better than those that were not when English was emphasized (Ms = 4.79 vs. 3.67, $p < .0001$), but not when the emphasis was on Chinese (Ms = 4.18 vs 4.04, $t < 1$). Finally, there was two-way interaction between emphasis and meaning, $F (1,232) = 22.59$, $p < .0001$. This revealed that names that were related in their meaning to the product were judged significantly better than those that were not when Chinese was emphasized (Ms = 4.72 vs 3.51, $p < .0001$), but not when the emphasis was on English (Ms = 4.22 vs 4.31, $t < 1$).

The results of this study strongly supported our hypothesis for language-based differential processing and evaluation of sound- and meaning-based translation. Chinese respondents engaged in differential processing of dual names by placing more weight on the sound dimension over the meaning dimension when English was emphasized, but more weight on the meaning dimension over the sound dimension when the emphasis was on Chinese. These differential weight assignments provided direct evidence, which indicated differential encoding and processing of phonographic and logographic writing systems. Thereby, we demonstrated that relevant linguistic factors related to brand names significantly influenced their evaluation.

BRANDS IN THE MARKETPLACE

All the previous studies that we discussed were conducted in laboratory settings with fictitious brand names. Thus, prior research was strong in internal validity but weak in ecological validity. But what actually happens in the market place? For example, could we observe the sound and meaning components that we identified in our laboratory studies in the actual marketplace?

To address this question, we conducted a study in Shanghai. (The study is thus far unpublished, but is available with us as a working paper.) We analyzed over 100 translations of major brands in several product categories, focusing primarily on consumer businesses (for example, bottled water, beer, candy, cosmetics, detergents, ice-cream, soft drinks, home appliances, etc.), but also included some brand names from highly visible industrial (for example, airplanes) and services businesses (for example, accounting houses and banks). We coded the data in terms of the degree of desirability of the translation of a name on sound and meaning as well as for language-related emphasis. This was subsequently evaluated by a team of language specialists.

To analyze the data, we conducted simple regression analyses. Separate models were run with overall evaluation as the dependent measure, desirability ratings of sound and desirability of meaning being the two predictor variables for dual names that were judged to emphasize Chinese, English, or both. For names emphasizing on Chinese, we expected the regression coefficient for desirability of meaning (but not for desirability of sound) to be significantly positive. Conversely, for names emphasizing on English, we expected the regression coefficient for desirability of sound (but not for desirability of meaning) to be significantly positive. Finally, for names emphasizing both Chinese and English equally, we expected the coefficients for desirability of sound and meaning to be both significantly positive.

Starting with names that equally emphasized on Chinese and English, we discovered that the regression model was of significant importance. As expected, the coefficients for desirability of sound and of meaning were significant. For names that emphasized on Chinese, the regression model was also significant. Consistent with the prediction, the coefficient for desirability of meaning, but not of sound, was significantly positive. For names that emphasized on English, the regression model was again significant. However, both the coefficient for desirability of sound and of meaning was significantly positive.

Data collected on brand names from the market largely confirmed the results obtained in earlier experimental studies. Relative to controlled experiments, the wide range of product categories and brands used from an actual market may have contributed to large variances, giving rise to slightly different results from the experiment. Nevertheless, out of the six expected signs of the coefficients relating the characteristics of the componental name to the overall evaluation of names, five were fully supported, providing substantial validation of the positive results of the experiment.

LANGUAGE PROFICIENCY

Another limitation of prior studies related to person-related factors. These were treated in a typical experimental manner as an error variance. However, not all consumers are equal in their language skills, and some seem to know a language much better than others. Therefore, we asked whether we could observe the differential effect on Chinese speakers, especially young consumers, who are more or less proficient in English. To find out, we conducted an experiment that focused on dual English-Chinese brand names and included language proficiency as a key individual difference variable (Zhang and Schmitt, 2004). As in some earlier studies, we also asked again whether it mattered which language was highlighted or emphasized, and therefore, included an emphasis on language as another variable in the experiment.

To measure language proficiency, we gave our participants the widely used College English Test (CET). Those who achieved levels 5–6 (equivalent to a score of 550 or above in TOEFL) were classified as being highly proficient in English and those who were rated between levels 1–2 (equivalent to a score of 500 or below) were classified as having low proficiency in English.

As in the study conducted earlier, four types of Chinese names were constructed through extensive linguistic pre-testing according to a 2×2 scheme of sound (related/similar vs unrelated/dissimilar) and meaning (related/similar vs unrelated/dissimilar) and evaluated by 368 Chinese respondents. What should we expect from our study? First let us consider highly proficient Chinese-English speakers processing dual English-Chinese names. They should activate phonological and semantic representations of both the languages and thereafter attend to the sound-relations and meaning-relations of the names. Less proficient bilingual speakers should primarily activate phonological and semantic representations of the dominant Chinese language. Since Chinese primarily focuses on visual-semantic and processing, and English seems to be based on Chinese semantic mediation, processing of dual names and evaluations should be largely based on meaning. Consequently, less proficient speakers should rely more on meaning than sound relatedness in evaluating brand names. Finally, contextual cues such as emphasis on language should direct respondents to place weight on sound and meaning differentially. Since highly proficient speakers access both phonological and semantic representations of Chinese and English, their emphasis on language should cue either phonological or semantic representations, and consequently the relation of "sound" or "meaning" between English and Chinese names. This cuing effect should be less pronounced for less proficient individuals because they are more likely to access phonological and semantic representations of Chinese.

We found strong support for our hypotheses in a significant three-way interaction on language proficiency by emphasis and by meaning, and a three-way interaction on language proficiency by emphasis and by sound. The results of the experiment indicated that highly proficient Chinese-English speakers activated both lexical-semantic and phonological representations of the dominant (Chinese) and non-dominant (English) languages. Less proficient speakers, in contrast, primarily activated representations of Chinese.

CREATING POSITIVE BRAND IDENTITIES THROUGH PROPER NAMING

To summarize, brand-naming is one of the most important aspects of branding. It is central to gaining a complete understanding of the concept of brand identity and brand equity. For a long time, much anecdotal evidence has existed on the beneficial or disastrous effects of good and bad brand meanings as well as good and bad-sounding brand names (Ricks, 1999). Yet, until recently, there was very little empirical research conducted, which focused more broadly on isolating the key determinants of good and bad name translations.

The results of our research reported in this chapter demonstrates that of all the methods available for translation or adaption of brand names, no one method is consistently preferable for creating a positive brand identity. Instead, preferences are contingent upon three factors—(1) immediate and environment-based linguistic cues, (2) long-term, memory-based linguistic cues, and (3) person-specific characteristics such as language proficiency. Therefore, when marketers take brand-naming decisions, which often require a significant amount of time and resources, they should pay close attention to the name, the naming context and a consumer's linguistic abilities.

Although the basic principles of brand-naming in the international context have been revealed in this study, there is still additional research to be done. We need to examine brand names, not only in terms of their strategic relevance in creating names that are consistent in sound and in terms of their meanings that relate to product features. We should also assess them in terms of their "good" or "bad" sound imagery (for example, some words sound more beautiful, appealing or powerful than others) and in terms of "good" or "bad" word connotations and associations. This is a critical task, especially in the case of Asian languages and Asia, on which we have focused in this research because of their unique phonetic, structural, and semantic characteristics.

REFERENCES

Aaker, David (1991), *Managing Brand Equity*. New York: Free Press.
Akmajian, Adrian, Richard A. Demers, Ann K. Farmer, and Robert M. Harnish (1992), *Linguistics: An Introduction to Language and Communication*. MA, USA: MIT Press.
Business Week (2009), The Dubbing of Bing, June 4, 2009.
Hung, Daisy L. and Ovid J. L. Tzeng (1981), "Orthographic Variations and Visual Information Processing," *Psychological Bulletin*, 90(3), 377–414.
Hunt, Earl and Franca Agnoli (1991), "The Whorfian Hypothesis: A Cognitive Psychology Perspective," *Psychological Review*, 98(3), 377–389.
Keller, Kevin Lane (1998), *Strategic Brand Management: Building, Measuring And Managing Brand Equity*, NJ: Prentice Hall.
Keller, Kevin Lane, Susan Heckler and Michael Houston (1998), "The Effects of Brand Name Suggestiveness On Advertising Recall," *Journal of Marketing*, 62(1), 48–57.
Lucy, John A. (1992), *Language Diversity And Thought: A Reformulation of The Linguistic Relativity Hypothesis*. New York: Cambridge University Press.
Luna, David and Laura Peracchio (2001), "Moderators of Language Effects in Advertising to Bilinguals: A Psycholinguistic Approach," *Journal of Consumer Research*, 28(2), 284–294.

Mick, David Glen (1986), "Consumer Research and Semiotics: Exploring the Morphology of Signs, Symbols, and Significance," *Journal of Consumer Research*, 13(2), 196–213.
Nguy, Timothy, F. A. Allard, and M.P. Bryden (1980), "Laterality Effects For Chinese Characters: Differences Between Pictorial and Nonpictorial Characters," *Canadian Journal of Psychology*, 34(3), 270–273.
O'Shaughnessy, John and Morris B. Holbrook (1988), "Understanding Consumer Behavior: The Linguistic Turn in Marketing Research," *Journal of the Market Research Society*, 30(2), 197–223.
Pan, Yigang and Bernd H. Schmitt (1994), "What's in a Name? An Empirical Comparison of Chinese and Western Brand Names," *Asian Journal of Marketing*, 4, 7–16.
Perfetti, Charles A., Laura Bell and Suzanne Delaney (1988), "Automatic Phonetic Activation in Silent Word Reading: Evidence from Backward Masking," *Journal of Memory and Language*, 27(1), 59–70.
Perfetti, Charles A. and Sulan Zhang (1991), "Phonological Processes in Reading Chinese Characters," *Journal of Experimental Psychology: Learning, Memory, And Cognition*, 17(4), 633–643.
Ricks, David A. (1999), *Blunders in International Business* (3rd ed.) MA, USA: Blackwell.
Schmitt, H. Bernd and Alex Simonson (1997), *Marketing Aesthetics: The Strategic Management of Brands, identity and Image*. New York: The Free Press.
Schmitt, Bernd H. and Yigang Pan (1994), "Managing Corporate and Brand Identities in the Asia-Pacific Region," *California Management Review*, 36(4), 32–48.
Schmitt, Bernd H., Yigang Pan, and Nader Tavassoli (1994), "Language and Consumer Memory: The Impact of Linguistic Differences Between Chinese and English," *Journal of Consumer Research*, 21(3), 419–431.
Schmitt, Bernd H. and Shi Zhang (1998), "Language Structure and Categorization: A Study of Classifiers in Consumer Cognition, Judgment and Choice," *Journal of Consumer Research*, 25 (September), 108–121.
Seligman, Scott D. (1986), "Translating Your Trademark into Chinese," *China Business Review*, 13(6), 14–16.
Tavassoli, Nader T. (1999), "Temporal and Associative Memory in Chinese and English," *Journal of Consumer Research*, 26(2), 170–181.
Tavassoli, Nader T. and Jin Han (2001), "Scripted Thought: Processing Korean Hancha and Hangul in a Multimedia Context," *Journal of Consumer Research*, 28(3), 482–493.
Zhang, Shi and Bernd H. Schmitt (2001), "Creating Local Brands in Multilingual International Markets," *Journal of Marketing Research*, 38(August), 313–325
—— (2004), "Activating Sound or Meaning: The Role of Language Proficiency in Bilingual Consumer Environments," *Journal of Consumer Research*, 30(June): 220–228
Zhou, Xiaolin and William Marslen-Wilson (1999), "Phonology, Orthography, and Semantic Activation in Reading Chinese," *Journal of Memory and Language*, 41(4), 579–606.

Chapter 5

The Six-station Model of Corporate Identity: Developing and Assessing the Model

Jean Yannis Suvatjis and Leslie de Chernatony

INTRODUCTION

The quest to understand corporate identity better has been one of increasing concern to managers and management scientists alike. This chapter addresses the issue of corporate identity modeling. At the beginning, an overview of corporate identity is presented, followed by a brief critique of existing corporate identity models. Then the "six-station corporate identity model," which is grounded in the literature, is introduced. Thereafter, qualitative and quantitative research conducted to assess the model's usefulness and managerial applicability is presented and discussed. Finally, the model in vivo is presented. The "six-station corporate identity model" introduced below can help companies build and manage their corporate identities more effectively than they have done before.

AN OVERVIEW OF CORPORATE IDENTITY

Corporate identity is an important concept because it demonstrates corporate ethos, aims and values, and presents a sense of individuality that can help to differentiate an organization from its competitors

(Hatch and Schultz, 1997). According to Zinkhan et. al. (2001: 154), corporate identity represents "the ways a company chooses to identity itself to all the public" (Zinkhan, Jaiskankur, Jaju, and Hayes, 2001). As Baker and Balmer noted more simply, although far more generally, corporate identity is "what an organization is" (Baker and Balmer, 1997). Corporate identity can be viewed as a vehicle by which a company's character is conveyed to different audiences Erikson (1960). It reflects a sense of its "essential character," since every organization has its own personality, uniqueness and individuality (Bernstein, 1984).

Effective corporate identity management can build understanding and commitment among an organization's various stakeholders. It helps a company attract and retain customers and employees, achieve strategic alliances, gain support from financial stakeholders and generate a sense of direction and purpose (Hatch and Schultz, 1997). Senior managers attach considerable importance to corporate identity modeling and regard it as a strategic marketing strategy (Balmer, 1994).

All prior existing models have contributed to developing the concept of corporate identity. However, they have failed to agree on a corporate identity construct with common and acceptable components. Our work introduces and explains a new corporate identity construct.

NEED FOR A NEW CORPORATE IDENTITY MODEL

The discipline perceived a strong need for a new corporate identity model, which motivated an intense research program, which is briefly described below.

The first review of corporate identity literature involved exploring traditional and new areas of general, marketing and brand management, advertising, communication, corporate symbolism and corporate visual identity systems, organizational behavior, interpersonal relationship psychology, digital technology, corporate image, and reputation studies. Expression of corporate identity is a dynamic process, evolving as the organizational context changes (Gioia, 1998). It requires effective management through the use of an appropriate model.

A second thorough review of literature explored the area of business and corporate identity modeling to assess the limitations of existing models and consider the need for a new one. Ten model criteria emerged that were deemed important for a robust model. These included visual clarity, ease of interpretation, logical sequence, adjustment and adaptability, production of synergies, employee operationalization, ease of memorizing, effectiveness, modularity and proactivity, and facilitated the construction of a sound model. These criteria were applied to the modeling process to introduce a clear, workable, useful and valid visual model. This model encompassed all the dimensions that were needed in the corporate identity construct according to the literature review.

The goal of constructing the model was, first of all, to create one that would include all the acceptable, meaningful and salient aspects of corporate identity. Second, the model needed to incorporate only those components/variables that were directly related to and accepted by the corporate identity context used by most researchers. Addressing and interpreting each component/variable, individually and in terms of their interrelationships, can facilitate an understanding of the model, especially for organizations that are willing to investigate, evaluate and adapt it and that may implement it as a strategy to formulate and manage their corporate identities. Third, in developing a corporate identity model, all endogenous and exogenous forces needed to be considered, which have an impact on corporate identity and its incorporated variables to reveal practical managerial applications. Fourth, the model had to be assessed empirically qualitatively and quantitatively by corporate identity consultants and business managers to determine its scientific value, usefulness and managerial applicability.

Ten Criteria of a Good Model

Our new corporate identity model was based on the following 10 selected criteria, and incorporated only those components/variables that were directly related to and accepted by the corporate identity context postulated by most researchers.

1. *Visual clarity:* All corporate identity models were visually congested, resulting in the representation of an unclear visual

model. To provide visual clarity, the six-station model proposed in the next section clearly displays the relationships between internal and external factors.

2. *Ease of interpretation:* Corporate identity models were difficult to interpret even after thorough examination and review. Since simplicity is a key element of successful models, our model was developed to enable interpretation with a minimum of effort.

3. *Logical sequence:* Most models fail to explain clearly or chart navigation. The six-station model was built to reflect a clear sequential logic in its presentation of the stations, which relate to each other through the movement processes depicted by the triangles and stations. For example, top management, with an appropriate leadership pattern, defines a company's mission, vision, and values. This stimulates the next station to create powerful corporate brands by using an effective corporate strategy that can be implemented with the input of the marketing department.

4. 4. *Adjustment and adaptability:* The structure of the model easily lends itself to adjustment and adaptation, since it enables a user to take all the parameters into account and focus on a particular area when necessary. For example, if an advertising campaign is unsuccessful, the user of the model can examine the interrelated areas that affect advertising and attempt to remedy the problem.

5. *Production of synergies:* This model was constructed to include awareness of interactivity and cooperation between the various elements represented by each station. It also incorporates interactivity between the audience (receiver) of the corporate identity message and its sender (the organization). This is reflected in each station's open relationship with the organizational culture and what is external to it. In this way, the model acknowledges that effective communication of corporate identity requires multi-level synergies.

6. *Employee operationalization:* The proposed model was designed to take into account the important role played by employees in putting the theoretical aspects of the model into practice.

7. *Ease of memorizing:* The model facilitates memorization, since it does not have any tangential lines or complicated loops

and relays, unlike previous ones. Its pictorial presentation, together with the topology of its elements, makes it easier to assimilate, and thus to recall.
8. *Efficiency and effectiveness:* This model helps to highlight possible areas of inefficiency in a company. These can be broken down into two parts—*managerial inefficiency*, which relates to the exclusive responsibilities of management, and *regulatory inefficiency*, which relates to the traditional, legal, and administrative environment in which companies operate (Gathon and Pestieau, 1995). The model helps to prevent managerial inefficiency, since it incorporates factors relating to management, and its use will help to solve problems by enhancing leadership and management capabilities. It also takes into account areas that are outside the business activities of an organization, but may affect it, and is therefore useful in areas beyond its control.
9. *Modularity:* Previous corporate identity models did not consider modularity, whereas ours does. It takes into account the interface that occurs when an organization transmits signals to the external environment. Thus, both the company and the market can readjust their behavior if feedback is unfavorable.
10. *Proactivity:* This criterion was used to keep the model open to change. Proactivity was considered an important element, which would indicate that a company determines its behavior by analyzing the interaction between its executives' value systems, its stakeholders' interests and existing societal issues.

EXPLANATION OF THE SIX-STATION CORPORATE IDENTITY MODEL

Corporate identity is the reflected microcosm of an organization's macrocosm. It is structured by a chain of related elements that converge to consolidate a corporate identity as the organization's representative image for external and internal consumption. For example, one can conceive of IBM's total corporate identity as "Big

Blue," which is its logo and effectively communicates its image, attitude, style of communication, and corporate history, all of which exemplify its business model, way of working and corporate view of life.

The structure of the six-station model is depicted in Figure 5.1 as the new corporate identity mix.

1. *Head Station:* Top management, mission/vision/values, leadership
2. *Strategy Station:* Brands/products and services, corporate strategy, marketing
3. *Creativity Station:* Visual identity, corporate visual identity systems, advertising
4. *Communication Station:* External and internal communication, digital communication (Internet)
5. *Human Power Station:* Stakeholders, organization's staff and group dynamism
6. *Critical Triplet Station:* Reputation, corporate image and personality

Architecture, Topology, and Mechanisms of the Model

The six-station corporate identity model is comprehensive and clearly defines the corporate identity formation process. It can be easily adapted to the local or global needs of an organization.

The model has two stages—the right the left stage. This is indicated by the different shades of the areas on the right and left in the central circle. The model depicts the presence and developmental transformation of three types of cultures. The projected culture, which an organization desires to project as its ideal, which is perceived and interpreted by consumers, and is depicted by the outer circle. The homogeneous organizational culture depicted within the perforated circle is manifested as a moderately strong or desirable culture in which an organizational consensus is attempted. There is an effort to make espoused values consistent with formal practices, which ideally would be consistent with informal beliefs, norms, and attitudes. In the best possible case, members would share the same cultural values and thereby promote a shared sense of loyalty and

The Six-station Model of Corporate Identity 125

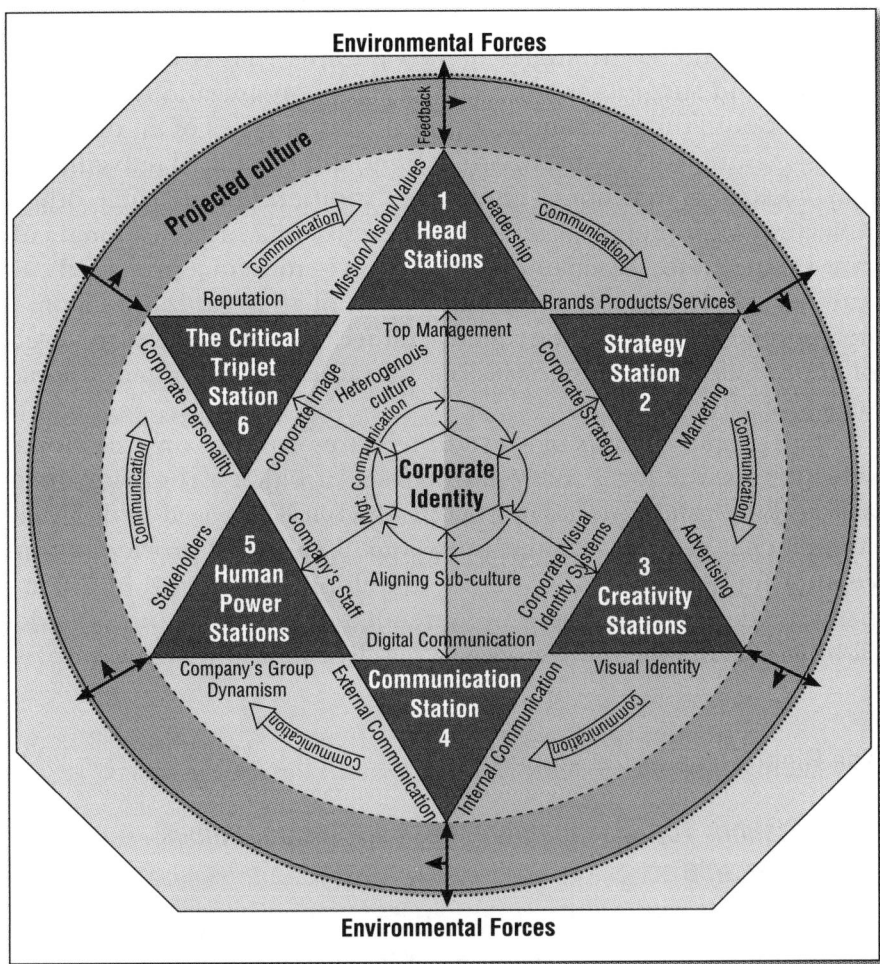

Figure 5.1 The Six-station Corporate Identity Model

commitment. This culture projects the characteristics of the integrative organizational culture described by Martin and Meyerson (1988) and what Schein depicts as its "deeper culture," which is related to a group's values and comprises goals and concerns that form its sense of what it "ought to be" (Schein, 1985). These notions about acceptable norms, values and behavior should work in such a manner that they expose the "dominant values of the organization" (Deal and Kennedy, 1982).

Finally, the heterogeneous culture within the polygonal area enclosed by the six triangles depicts an area that is not culturally uniform and suggests that instead of being organization-wide, consensus should only be sought within the boundaries of an organization's existing sub-culture. At this level, differentiated sub-cultures may coexist in harmony, conflict or indifference to each other, reflecting Martin and Meyerson's differentiating organizational culture (Martin and Meyerson, 1988). The evolution of a projected culture occurs after the successful transition of an organization from a heterogeneous to a homogeneous culture, provided adequate levels of cooperation and understanding prevail within its organizational structure.

This model consists of six stations, three types of organizational sub-cultures, the local (national) market in which a company operates and the international market in which it is exposed to different stimuli, changes and business intrusions. The model provides a conceptual framework in the identity development process of a company can be analyzed, and is not intended to be a mechanical model of what is in reality a continuous, synergistic and non-linear process.

The Right Stage of the Model

Head Station: Top Management, Mission, Vision, Values, and Leadership

The model can be broken down in terms of its stages or spheres to illustrate the internal relations of its adjacent components. The right stage of the model is composed of corporate stations 1, 2, and 3. The station 1 is the head station in which, under the leadership of senior management, with the company's vision, mission, and values as well as its objectives are set for it efficient operation. The role of its top executives is critical here, since their contribution, attitudes, values, policies, and degree of leadership will have an enormous effect on it continuing existence in the market and future longevity.

Top executives are assigned the most important role in this station in that they "kindle" the system through their effective leadership. Management's definition of a clear company vision, mission and objectives, managed by capable executives and managers through a facilitative management style, will help it transition from the first station to the second station (strategy).

Strategy Station: Corporate Brands and Strategy, and Marketing

This station's major function is formulation of a corporate strategy. This involves selection of certain branding strategies related to products and services, always in conjunction with and under the direction and cooperation of a company's marketing department. Strategy is set by a general consensus among top executives and managers as well as by other tactical strategies designed for each of the company's different strategic units under its marketing umbrella. All strategic activities of such a nature are marketing-oriented, with related functions dealing mainly with a study of the market, consumers' tastes and demands, product development and other prerequisites that precede final decisions on corporate branding. The strategy station and its mechanisms need to align cooperation among team members, and only then extend these synergies to station 3, the "creativity" station.

Creativity Station: Visual Identity, CVIS, and Advertising

This station incorporates necessary corporate creativity functions, and their evolution and interrelation with corporate advertising. The creative station is informed by feedback from the two previous stations regarding the company's strategic intent and decision-making. It explores and creates a "visual essence," not only to label and symbolize it and its products, but also to visualize its objectives, vision, mission, values, and tangible and intangible products. This station is also concerned with the organization's already formulated corporate strategies, human attitudes and behavior, physical premises, corporate objects and tools. It finally presents the total and distinct visual representation of the organization.

This station employs the concept of the traditional theory of visual identity. It is recommended that adaptation of visual symbolism is considered by a company stage by stage and is executed in two phases. First, visual artefacts and symbols need to be selected to represent it and its products after careful examination and research into its traditional symbolism, so that these are indicative of the organization's nature, products, beliefs, attitudes, management's philosophy, and employees, as well as its social and business behavior. Completion of this stage requires an evaluation of the effectiveness and efficiency of the selected "visual" representations and their effect on the organization.

After positive feedback has been received regarding the effectiveness of the selected artefacts, logos, colors, shapes, and slogans, the second phase should be introduced. This will require adaptation of unique integrated systems of total visual representation, known as corporate visual identity systems.

It is useful, appropriate and effective to take into account the evolution of the corporate visual identity system concept, not only as a tool for developing a company's representation of itself, but as an alternative to the more ambitious and unique visual identity representations common in local and international markets. Finally, in this station, visual representation of a company has been considered as a part of its organizational culture with all its related artefacts, including its logo, trademark, slogan, and color, which comprise its total emblematic apparatus. On completion of all the processes in the three stations of the model's right stage, it will be seen that the first and most critical strategic decisions and activities are within the company's control. All the parameters in these three stations contain elements that are designed, directed, executed, modified and initiated under the care, supervision and direct control of an organization's top management and are affected by its technocratic nature and idiosyncrasies.

Left Stage of the Model

Communication Station: Corporate External, Internal, and Digital Communication

In the left stage of the model, the fourth station is known as the communication station, since it operates as a two-way channel performing communication-related tasks is a company's internal and external environment. It pertains to communication of all the organizations formulated messages, different types of business communication and related communications activities to the market with the aid of the traditional print medium as well as electronic and digital means of marketing communication.

The concept of communication concerns the entire organization, especially its stakeholders and employees, who are significantly affected by the flow of communication and the modes used by the company. It is affected both formally and informally, since its management and organizational communication play a significant role in the organization.

Human Power Station: Stakeholders, Staff, and Group Dynamics

This is the "human corporate power station," the most important component of a company's corporate ecology and deals with the human factor, which has conscious or unconscious attributes in the formation of corporate identity. Internal and external stakeholders' roles, attitudes, values, ethics, actions, and interests are transmitters of information about a company to the outside world. In this model, an organization's employees include all the people working in it, especially those at the lower levels (production line and factory staff). The company's personnel may also have dual status as both internal and external stakeholders or either one.

It is believed that lower level staff members can greatly affect a company's corporate identity because they usually outnumber the rest of its employees, and consequently, have more direct and immediate contact with its customers. They communicate daily with their own constituencies, either as consumers or as the company's employees; they do not hesitate to discuss the prevailing environment within their organization, comment on it favorably or unfavourably, and make a concerted effort to convey their message with respect to their own benefits (compensation, working conditions, etc.).

Human behavior always tends to initiate conflicts, since group dynamics can produce multiple conflicts within organizations. An unavoidable phenomenon, conflict within and among groups can create a major obstacle in the process of their forming a corporate identity. The fewer conflicts in this station, the fewer disturbances are caused in a company's entire model, contributing to a more stable and solid process for the formulation of corporate identity.

Critical Triplet Station: Corporate Reputation, Personality, and Image

In this station, establishment of a company's corporate personality, reputation, and image is ultimately left to consumers' judgement. This is probably the most crucial station in the model, since it defines consumers' perceptions of the company and fulfils the goal of "relationship marketing." The components of this station constitute the company's critical "reaching out" to consumers.

This is the first station to be negatively affected when consumers convey signs of dissatisfaction and are discontent with the company. If *corporate perishability* occurs due to a company's heterogeneous sub-culture, misalignment of human behavior, and lack of clear communication will weaken relay of the system. The resulting blockage of the required circular flow of synergies will be due to the broken flow of successive synergies that should be maintained as a full-time and continuous corporate practice.

ASSESSING THE SIX-STATION CORPORATE IDENTITY MODEL

A dual research technique, including qualitative and quantitative methods for triangulation purposes, was used to investigate the model's applicability.

Triangulating findings enable precise and reliable results and explanations (Mingers, 2001). The goal of mixed method-based research is not to replace either of these approaches, but to draw from their strengths and minimize their weaknesses in a single cross-study research effort.

Qualitative Findings of the Research and Discussion

In-depth and semi-structured interviews were conducted with 28 corporate identity consultants and business managers. This sample was selected from the records of reputed companies in the manufacturing, commerce, industry, and services sectors, and the interviewees included CEOs, general managers, corporate identity managers, marketing managers, advertising managers, and human resources managers.

Content analysis revealed that the model was regarded as useful and having managerial applicability, although business managers would prefer additional training and guidance on how to use it. Finally, the model was perceived as being representative of corporate identity and clearly depicting it as a concept. The respondents felt that it presented many components of corporate identity in an interlinked and holistic manner.

The respondents accepted that the six stations of the model, with their elements, reflect the fundamentals of corporate identity. The consultants and business managers did not express any concerns about the model being inadequate.

The applicability of this model was examined to first define its degree of appropriateness as far as the concept of corporate identity was concerned; secondly, to identify how receptive business stakeholders are to it, and thirdly, how it is perceived by managers and employees. The comments received from the sample group presented a wide range of opinions. For example, according to a CEO, "[t]aking for granted that it is a valid model and fits with reality, it appears to be a model rather easily put into practice." A creative director was of the opinion that "the model, despite its unavoidable complexity, can be easily put into practice," while a public relations manager declared that "the model appears to be workable, although in reality the interrelations and interactions between all the factors depicted in the diagram are in most cases much more complex and require intensive work."

Corporate identity consultants highlighted the necessity of managers facilitating applicability, adoption and implementation of the model. Business managers and executives thought it would be easier to apply the model if guidelines and specific explanations were supplied. According to a financial manager, the "model requires more explanations and guidelines for exploring its components. More specifically, the model requires the help of all company departments, that is, interaction, in order to be applied in a holistic manner. Only then will it be applicable. So explanations and the assistance and guidance of experienced people will make it applicable."

Quantitative Research Findings and Discussion

The quantitative phase was based on a sample of 105 corporate identity consultants, academics and business managers who participated in the study.

The quantitative research design was based on tests conducted on individuals who had a stake in determining what corporate identity means and how corporations go about achieving a positive corporate identity. This group included consultants specializing in corporate identity and corporate executives. Research included two phases. In the first phase, respondents were presented with the six-station model. Thereafter, they completed a self-administered questionnaire regarding the applicability of the model. The questionnaire was developed from previous research conducted by Kennedy (1997), Stuart (1998), and Greyser 1999, and was based on feedback obtained from the qualitative research stage. A five-point scale (1: strongly disagree to 5: strongly agree) was used.

A pilot study was undertaken with 15 business executives and corporate identity consultants who suggested well-justified changes to refine the questionnaire. This led to a pool of 86 items that describe the variables in the model.

In order to identify whether the six-station model reflected respondents' perceptions of its appropriateness to facilitate the creation and management of corporate identity, and them understand the structure of the variables suggested by the interviewees, a principal component analysis with varimax rotation was performed on the quantitative data.

Based on a statistical analysis, six factors were derived from the responses to the sample, and a response-based model was constructed that matched the structure of the theoretical six-station model. The extrapolated factors were identified and were found compatible with the stations and their elements.

The first factor encapsulated a synthesis of three elements—corporate image, personality and reputation. It was determined that external forces affect and shape a company's reputation. Corporate image is the result of an aggregate process by which the public evaluates an organization. The resulting image is the overall impression the public have of it. Corporate personality interacts with all the other corporate identity variables.

The second factor introduced the elements of corporate brands, strategies and marketing functions. This factor expressed the "strategic synergy" required between corporate strategies and brands, and the marketing function in formulating the overall course of a company's corporate strategy.

The third factor included issues relating primarily to a company's mission, vision and values as well as its concept of leadership, in order to emphasize the importance of its top management's role. All these elements reveal an interlinked relationship and a synergistic task function. The bonding between these communicates the interdependence of the elements.

The fourth factor indicated that the model demonstrated the relation between digital and other forms of communication, and that the internet could be important to a business in developing its corporate identity. More specifically, it indicated that digital communication is to a large extent replacing and supporting the external communication element, since digital communication, and specifically the internet in its various forms, can replace a substantial part of the functions and properties of external communication. On the other hand, traditional communication forms, including all of a company's marketing functions, are media for conducting and initiating its external and internal communication.

The fifth factor emphasized the importance of symbolism of visual identity and corporate visual identity systems that highlight the direct interrelation between these elements. The evolution of the traditional concept of corporate symbolism in the advancement and implementation of corporate visual identity systems was conveyed in this factor.

The sixth factor indicated the physical presence and participation of a company's employees in the model. Their direct involvement is acknowledged in this model because nothing functions without the intervention of the human factor, which is evident in different roles and performs various activities in this model.

The integrative nature of these six factors reflects most of the fundamentals of the corporate identity concept. The literature supports the structure of the six-station model. Birkigt and Stadler (1988), Schmidt (1995), and Balmer and Soenen (1997/8) had introduced models that included some parameters, which were identical to those in the sixstation corporate identity model. Other corporate identity models also exhibit similarities with the six-station model (for example, Abratt, 1989; Dowling, 1986; Stuart, 1998; Markwick and Fill, 1997), and include similar parameters, but in a more expansive manner.

THE MODEL SYNOPTICALLY IN VIVO

Audits, questionnaires and interviews are the main tools for investigating an organization's corporate identity under the umbrella of the newly introduced corporate identity station model. This model initiates the creation and management of corporate identity with the tools mentioned next.

At the first stage, the MV^2 audit, interviews with top management are mandatory and relate to the company's emerging corporate identity from the viewpoint of its top management. Auditing the organization's "mission, vision, and values" is important as the first step in investigating its corporate identity.

The second stage, situ analysis, focuses on a situation analysis of the company's current corporate identity status, and will enable it to assess the external and internal factors that affect its corporate identity. A problem and opportunity analysis will locate and identify all crucial points, and simultaneously help it turn problems into opportunities.

The third stage of the investigation will require a corporate segmentation audit, the C-Seg audit. The company's market segmentation strategy will be re-evaluated, and its customer lists and relationship marketing examined further. The concept of relationship marketing should be adopted by companies to upgrade their relationship with consumers and thereby enhance their market dominance and appeal.

The fourth stage requires a corporate strategy audit in which corporate brands and the role of marketing in an organization need to be aligned and considered in its entirety. A company's corporate positioning should be examined and evaluated by a product portfolio audit. After evaluation of data, it should the required improvements to its overall marketing strategy. It is also extremely important for the company to evaluate its past and more recent performance.

The fifth stage encompasses auditing efforts (exoteric and esoteric visual audits—E2VA), which focuses on corporate symbolism. In this field, auditing has to do with an evaluation of the contribution of visual symbolism, the impact of corporate visual identity systems, if adopted, and the active role of advertising. The process of enhancing presentation of visual identity needs to be a gradual and refining process in conformity with existing national and global trends.

A company's symbols, logos and artefacts should be evaluated through a visual identity audit analysis, and enhancement only proposed if these are judged to be a valuable contribution to its self-image and philosophy.

A tailor-made audit on a company's corporate visual identity system, if adopted by it, will evaluate all aspects, such as different national traditions and idiosyncrasies, cultural philosophies and even religious affiliations. Enhancement will be only proposed on the basis of these. All of the company's selected artefacts, logos, colors, shapes, and slogans should be adapted to people's perspectives, philosophies and ways of life.

The role of advertising should be evaluated through a media analysis audit to assess all types of media communications (internal and external) employed to convey a company's messages effectively.

This approach should lay the foundation for a new or enhanced universal corporate identity that will be applicable to any stakeholder. A strong corporate identity depends on a clear understanding an organization's character and its corporate values. A company only acquires an identity after its values combine to form its image. By acquiring a good reputation, it gains a competitive advantage over its rivals in the market.

The sixth stage will be devoted to an MIA audit, a "mystery identity audit" program focusing on evaluating a company's corporate reputation and corporate personality, including an analysis of its stakeholders.

All the findings can be accumulated and triangulated together to construct an integrated corporate SWOT matrix (the Corp SWOT matrix). This matrix should include all the findings from the audit and interviews conducted in the six stages mentioned earlier, which unveil corporate identity.

The integrated corporate identity SWOT matrix should clarify the organization's corporate status and identify routes for it to embark on a new or enhanced way of managing its corporate identity.

CONTRIBUTION TO THE THEORY OF CORPORATE IDENTITY

The six-station model advances knowledge of corporate identity modeling in a number of ways.

First, the model overcomes some of the limitations of previous models in terms of visual clarity. It clearly and comprehensibly represents the parameters of corporate identity. The circular representation of the model clarifies some of the confusion encountered in previous models. This has been achieved by the conceptual and diagrammatic interrelation of the various elements of corporate identity

Second, the introduction of 10 criteria attempts to counteract some of the limitations of previous models by rectifying certain omissions.

Third, through its circular process, the model clearly represents the causes and effects of the various parameters involved in establishment of corporate identity.

Fourth, the openness of the model facilitates an understanding of the interrelationship between the internal and external parameters of corporate identity.

The following points outline the model's contribution to knowledge, and more specifically, to the entire business spectrum.

The model redefines the structure, scope and processes of the corporate identity concept in its formation and management process, and introduces a new corporate identity mix that is derived through the model framework.

It enables a holistic management approach that entails the maintenance of a synergistic effect, based on cooperation between and synchronization of predefined and interdependent corporate identity variables.

Precise implementation of the model minimizes possible gaps by addressing a mechanism that promotes corporate identity internally and externally, and helps stakeholders realize the positive results in the management process of corporate identity.

The data was considered representative, unique, useful, valuable, and appropriate due to the participation of different managers from diverse business areas, from companies with varying statuses (national, international and multinational) of various cultural and educational levels, and philosophical perspectives,. The interview guide that accompanied the interview process and the self-administered questionnaire can also be used as tools to increase an understanding of the model and initiate the task of dealing appropriately with the subject of corporate identity.

IMPLICATION FOR MARKETING MANAGEMENT

Although research on corporate identity modeling has been conducted by academics and practitioners, substantial effort will be required to promote its evolution and recognition of its significance in the corporate world. The concept of corporate identity is often overlooked and tends to receive more attention when alarming events in the corporate world necessitate the implementation of "corporate remedies." The managerial implications of this research address the following important issues related to corporate identity and its modeling.

Clear Goals, Objectives, and Expected Results

The idea of managing corporate identity requires a strong understanding of exactly what the goals are and what behavioral and non-behavioral synergies are needed. Working toward creating and managing corporate identity is comparable to a manager trying to achieve high efficiency, and optimizing efforts and outcomes.

Managers need to be aware of the organizational attributes that are desirable and valued by internal and external stakeholders and accordingly strive to meet desirable organizational requirements.

The six-station model incorporates all these aspects and enables management to proceed with confidence in implementing the model.

Synergy-oriented Environment

The new model demands concentration on creation of synergies within an organization. This model of corporate identity requires the implementation of an integrated system of mutually activated synergies to confront the endogenous and exogenous forces that adversely affect the corporate identity concept.

The model suggests that centralized management is needed to ensure that it functions efficiently. One possible benefit to be derived from a centralized approach is increased control over the conduct of internal and external stakeholders. It also provides all the stakeholders, including members of the organization, the opportunity to make relevant contributions as well as a wide range of innovative recommendations and meaningful suggestions. Finally, the model supports the notion that identity is perceived as a constantly evolving process, which is reproduced and transformed by every interaction between an organization and its stakeholders.

Development of Relationship with Stakeholders

The implementation of the six-station model is a feasible approach to the creation and management corporate identity and generating value and trust in a company.

First, a company communicating its corporate identity is akin to its developing an exchange relationship with all stakeholders. The model demonstrates how organizations should transmit all their attributes, values and characteristics. This also clarifies what they expect their stakeholders to appreciate. Therefore, the management of a company should have a long-term commitment to achieving excellence in its operations in order to preserve and grow positive relationships through its management of corporate identity.

Second, management should observe and monitor individual employees' contribution to management of corporate identity.

Enthusiastic and positive employee behavior in the market results effectively conveys an organization's goals and values. Such conduct indicates employees' satisfaction and is a signal that they act instinctively in ways that benefit the organization.

Third, the six-station model calls for initiation and adaptation of an empowerment program among all internal stakeholders and employees. Empowerment promotes and communicates satisfied and pleasant behavior, excellent customer service, a quick response to needs and problems, productive employee-generated ideas, and cooperative and interactive employees.

Open and Interactive Approach to Communication

The aim of the six-station model is to communicate a series of consistent and favorable corporate attributes to stakeholders as well as to collect comprehensive data through an organization's multi-stage interactions with its stakeholders.

This model offers a company an overall and flexible but well-defined approach to management of corporate identity, which is not only suited to the rapidly changing environment in which it operates, but also in the behavioral context in which its stakeholders form relationships, initiate responses and establish behavioral patterns that affect its corporate identity.

Corporate Identity and Performance

It is strongly felt that effective management of all model parameters will have a positive effect on an organization's corporate identity status. However, further research is required to assess the total impact.

Need for Appropriate Application/Implementation of Model

Managers need to be able to relate to the model so that they feel comfortable dealing with it, but also to be sure that it suits their corporate environment and business case. Managers who fail to select an appropriate corporate identity model to deal with their own business reality are doomed to be unsuccessful in managing corporate identity issues effectively.

Elaboration of variables to produce manageable data is a key goal in applying the model successfully. Every variable is structured to present and maintain its own complexity, framework, idiosyncrasy, and contribution to the corporate identity model.

Management should balance and properly manage all variables involved in the formation and management of corporate identity by identifying the best way of measuring these and by defining their contribution to the context of corporate identity. It is up to management to define an evaluation system, based on a continuous monitoring of the variables related to corporate identity, and define the impact of each separately as well as all of all of these as a whole.

Implementation of the six-station corporate identity model enables companies to examine each variable separately in order to examine its impact on their corporate identity.

CONCLUSION

We have introduced the six-station corporate identity model along with explanations and justifications. It depicts corporate identity management as a circular process, which designates and thereafter links the sequential synergies and effects produced within each station, and thereby connects all the stations to each other.

The stations are strategically located so that each depicts specific benefits that can be transmitted to the next station. This process produces synergies that contribute to the overall process of establishment of a corporate identity.

Findings from the qualitative and quantitative research conducted provide evidence that this is a sound model, which is managerially acceptable and manageable within the corporate identity context. The model provides a conceptual framework for analyzing the identity development process and is not intended as a mechanical model, but a continuous, synergistic and non-linear process. However, developments at later stages do not always depend exclusively on causes arising from the previous stage.

It is believed that by postulating a corporate identity model that meets key criteria for robustness and by demonstrating its managerial applicability, researchers will be stimulated to consider how refinements can be made to corporate identity models by initiating and implementing closer dialogue between researchers and practitioners.

APPENDIX

Synoptic Presentation of the Quantitative Analysis

The quantitative phase was based on a sample of 105 corporate identity consultants, academics and business managers who participated in the study.

The design of the quantitative research was based on testing of individuals with a stake in determining what corporate identity means and how corporations go about achieving a positive corporate identity. This group comprised consultants specializing in corporate identity and corporate executives.

The research included two phases. First, respondents were presented with the six-station model. Second, they completed a self-administered questionnaire regarding the applicability of the model. The questions in the questionnaire were developed from previous research conducted by Kennedy (1977), Stuart (1998), and Greyser (1999), and feedback received at the qualitative research stage.

A five-point scale (1: strongly disagree to 5: strongly agree) was used. A pilot study was undertaken with 15 business executives and corporate identity consultants who suggested well-justified changes to refine the questionnaire. This resulted in a pool of 86 items that describe the variables in the model. Alpha coefficients were calculated for the total number of items as well as for those of each of the six stations whose values exceeded 0.60 (86 items: alpha = 0.97, 12 general items: alpha = 0.89, 19 items of station 1: alpha = 0.89, 15 items of station 2: alpha = 0.86, 9 items of station 3: alpha = 0.86, 8 items of station 4: alpha = 0.79, 8 items of station 5: alpha = 0.84, 15 items of station 6: alpha = 0.91).

Nunally (1967) argues that at the early stages of the basic research, reliabilities of 0.50 to 0.60 are adequate. In this study, the alpha coefficients of each of the scale components were calculated. Since all of the alpha coefficients exceeded 0.60, the instrument was deemed suitable for further testing.

A principal component analysis with varimax rotation was performed on the quantitative data to identify whether the six-station model reflected respondents' perception of it as appropriate for facilitating the creation and management of corporate identity as well as to enable an understanding of the structure of the variables (provided by the interviewees). Bartlett's test of sphericity (5.663, sig. 0.0000) and the Kaiser Meyer Olkin test (0.611) indicated that the data was suitable for this analysis.

It was to be expected that the large number of variables (74) and multi-dimensionality of the data would produce a large number of factors. The number of variables involved in factor analysis was reduced, based on the results, and after taking the responses to the 105 questionnaires into consideration.

We specifically excluded the variables that demonstrated loadings of less than 0.55 and/or cross loadings factors, that is, loadings of relatively similar value in more than one factor. Following this procedure, we progressively reduced the number of variables from the initial set of 74 to a final set of 21.

Factor analysis performed on the final set of 21 variables revealed a set of 6 factors. All loadings, except one, demonstrated values of more than 0.60. See Table 5A.1.

Table 5A.1 Rotated Factor Matrix: Sorted Form of Variables Loadings

Variables	Factor 1	
v80_s6e2	The model shows that corporate image is the result of an aggregate process by which the public evaluates a company.	0.881
v81_s6e2	It emphasizes that corporate image is the overall impression made on the public about the company.	0.799
v75_s6e1	It includes consideration of outside forces affecting the organization's reputation.	0.752
v82_s6e2	The model emphasizes the importance of the company's entire workforce in the creation of its corporate image.	0.731

(Table 5A.1 Contd)

(Table 5A.1 Contd)

Variables	Factor 1	
v84_s6e3	It includes consideration of the importance of the company's corporate personality.	0.688
v85_s6e3	The interaction between corporate personality and other corporate identity variables is clear in the model.	0.611
	Factor 2	
v35_s2e1	The model emphasizes the relevance of developing a branding strategy as part of a corporate strategy.	0.743
v37_s2e1	The relationship between corporate strategy and marketing products/services is clearly represented in the model.	0.738
v34_s2e1	The model shows that brands should be linked to a company's vision, values and corporate culture.	0.693
v36_s2e1	It shows that brands contribute to the perception of a company's identity.	0.664
v46_s2e3	It points out that its marketing strategy is part of a company's corporate strategy.	0.598
	Factor 3	
v20_s1e1	The model emphasizes that a company's vision should be evaluated regularly.	0.748
v41_s2e2	It highlights the fat that a company's values should be fundamental to its corporate success.	0.743
v22_s1e1	It emphasizes the relationship between corporate identity and leadership.	0.742
v14_s1e1	It reflects all variables that are relevant to a corporation's mission.	0.625
	Factor 4	
v62_s4e3	The model takes into consequence that the internet may be important to a business in developing its corporate identity.	0.861
v63_s4e3	It demonstrates the relations between digital and other forms of communication.	0.856
	Factor 5	
v50_s3e2	The model shows that a company should standardize its corporate visual identity systems to project its identity.	0.842

(Table 5A.1 Contd)

(Table 5A.1 Contd)

Variables	Factor 5	
v51_s3e2	It stresses that a company must always use corporate visual identity systems to broaden its communications mix.	0.807
	Factor 6	
v70_s5e3	The importance of stakeholders in a company's corporate identity is shown in the model.	0.851
v71_s5e3	The model shows that a company's employees and stakeholders should interact regularly.	0.609

Extraction method: Principal component analysis. Rotation method: Varimax with Kaiser normalization.
a) Rotation converged in six iterations

As this is a standard procedure followed by other researchers such as Stuart (1998), Simoes, Dibb, and Fisk (2001), and Sabiote and Roman (2005), only those extracted factors accounting for a notable percentage of total variance are reported.

The six factors given below explain 68.16% of the total variance. Apart from the first factor, which explains 32.16% of the total variance, the contribution of the remaining 5 factors ranges from 9.9% to 4.9%. See Table 5A.2.

Table 5A.2 Total Variance Explained

	Initial Eigenvalues			Rotation Sums of Squared Loadings		
Factor	Eigenvalue	% of Variance	Cumulative %	Total	% of Variance	Cumulative %
1	6.756	32.169	32.169	3.962	18.865	18.865
2	2.082	9.912	42.081	2.825	13.453	32.318
3	1.841	8.768	50.849	2.386	11.361	43.679
4	1.410	6.713	57.562	1.839	8.759	52.439
5	1.187	5.651	63.213	1.745	8.310	60.748
6	1.039	4.946	68.159	1.556	7.411	68.159

Total number of variables: 21
Extraction method: Principal component analysis

Based on the statistical analysis, six factors were derived from the responses in the sample to construct a response-based model that matched the structure of the theoretical six-station model initially introduced. These factors (Table 5.1) identified and revealed their compatibility with the stations and their elements in the six-station model.

The critical triplet factor consists of corporate reputation, image and personality. The strategy factor comprises corporate brands and strategy, and marketing. The head factor includes a company's mission, vision, values leadership, and indirectly, its top management. The communication factor includes traditional channels of communication along with digital communication. The creativity factor comprises visual symbolism and corporate visual identity systems. The human factor includes employees and stakeholders.

Identification of the factors and confirmatory factor analysis was undertaken to test whether the model fits the data. More specifically, we used the same set of data (n = 105), only including the 21 variables that shape the six factors earlier. A number of fit statistics were estimated to test how well the six factor model fits the data. The fit indices, Tucker-Lewis Index (TLI) = 0.97, Comparative Fit Index (CFI) = 0.98, and Bollen Fit Index (IFI) = 0.98, showed acceptable levels of fit. All indices in values higher of more than 0.95 indicated that the model fit the data. The root mean square error of approximation (RMSEA) indicated a low value of 0.03, which is acceptable. Lastly, the "chi square" criterion, which tests the hypothesis that the model is consistent with the pattern of co-variation among the observed variables, showed a non-significant value ($X2(174) = 192.73$, $p = 0.157$), which supports the null hypothesis. See Table 5A.3.

Table 5A.3 Confirmatory Factor Analysis

Factor/Variable	Factor Description	Factor Loadings
Critical Triplet		
v80_s6e2	The model shows that corporate image is the result of an aggregate process by which the public evaluates a company.	0.835

(Table 5A.3 Contd)

(Table 5A.3 Contd)

Factor/ Variable	Factor Description	Factor Loadings
v81_s6e2	It emphasizes that the corporate image is the overall impression made on the public about the company.	0.849
v75_s6e1	It includes a consideration of outside forces affecting the organization's reputation.	0.697
v82_s6e2	The model emphasizes the importance of the company's workforce in the creation of its corporate image.	0.792
v84_s6e3	It recommends consideration of the importance of corporate personality.	0.690
v85_s6e3	The interaction between corporate personality and other corporate identity variables is clear in the model.	0.682
Strategy		
v35_s2e1	The model emphasizes the relevance of developing a branding strategy as part of a corporate strategy.	0.717
v37_s2e1	The relationship between corporate strategy and marketing product/services is clearly represented in the model.	0.682
v34_s2e1	The model shows that brands should be linked to a company's vision, values and corporate culture.	0.624
v36_s2e1	It shows that brands contribute to the perception of a company's identity.	0.631
v46_s2e3	It points out that marketing strategy is part of corporate strategy.	0.679
Head		
v20_s1e1	The model emphasizes that a company's vision should be evaluated regularly.	0.718
v41_s2e2	It highlights the fact that a company's values should be fundamental to its corporate success.	0.545
v22_s1e1	It emphasizes the relationship between a company's corporate identity and leadership.	0.827
v14_s1e1	The model reflects all variables that are relevant for the mission of a corporation.	0.405
Communication		
v62_s4e3	The model takes into consequence that the internet may be important for a business to develop its corporate identity.	0.734
v63_s4e3	It demonstrates the relations between digital and other forms of communication.	0.901

(Table 5A.3 Contd)

(Table 5A.3 Contd)

Factor/ Variable	Factor Description	Factor Loadings
Creativity		
v50_s3e2	That a company should effectively use Corporate Visual Identity Systems standardization to project its identity is evident in the model.	0.834
v51_s3e2	The model stresses that a company must always use corporate visual identity systems to widen its communications mix.	0.783
Human		
v70_s5e3	The importance of stakeholders to a company's corporate identity is evident in the model.	0.576
v71_s5e3	The model shows that a company's employees and stakeholders should interact regularly.	0.780

Model Summary Statistics: $X^2(174) = 192.731$, $p = 0.157$, TLI = 0.97, CFI = 0.98, IFI = 0.98, RMSEA = 0.03. All factor loadings are significant at $p<0.05$.

REFERENCES

Abratt, R. (1989), "A New Approach to the Corporate Image Management Process," *Journal of Marketing Management*, 5(1), 63–76.

Baker, M. J. and J. M.T. Balmer (1997), "Visual Identity: Trappings or Substance," *European Journal of Marketing*, 31(5/6), 366–379.

Balmer, J. M. T. (1994), "The BBC's Corporate Identity: Myth, Paradox and Reality," *Journal of General Management*, 19(3), 33–47.

Balmer, J. M. T. and G. B. Soenen (1997/8), "Operationalizing the Concept of Corporate Identity: Articulating the Corporate Identity Mix and the Corporate Identity Management Mix," *Working Paper Series*, International Centre for Corporate Identity Studies.

Bernstein, D. (1984), *Company Image and Reality: A Critique of Corporate Communication*, London: Cassel Ltd.

Birkigt, K. and M. M. Stadler (1988), "Corporate identity, Grundlagen, Funktionen. Fallspiellen," Verlag Moderne Industrie, Landberg am Lech.

Deal, T. and A. Kennedy (1982), *Corporate Cultures: The Rites and Rituals of Corporate Life*. Reading, MA: Addison-Wesley.

Dowling, G. R. (1986), "Managing your Corporate Images," *Industrial Marketing Management*, 15(2),109–115.

Erikson, E. H. (1960), "The Problem of Ego Identity," In Maurice M. Stein, Arthur J. Vidich, and David Manning White (Eds), *Identity and Anxiety*.

Gathon. H. J. and Pestieau, P. (1995), "Decomposing efficiency into its managerial and its regulatory components: the case of the European railways," *European Journal of Operational Research*, 80(3), 500–507.

Gioia, D. A. (1998), "From Individual to Organizational Identity," In Whetten and Godfrey (Eds), *Identity in Organizations: Building Theory through Conversations*, Thousands Oaks, CA: SAGE Publications, pp. 17–33.

Greyser, A. S. (1999), "Advancing and enhancing corporate reputation," *Corporate Communications: An International Journal*, 4(4), 177–181.

Hatch, M. J. and M. Schultz (1997), "Relations between Organizational Culture, Identity and Image," *European Journal of Marketing*, 31(5/6), 356–365.

Kennedy, S. H. (1977), "Nurturing Corporate Images," *European Journal of Marketing*, 11(3), 120–164.

Markwick, N. and C. Fill (1997), "Towards a framework for managing corporate identity," *European Journal of Marketing*, 31(5/6), 396–410.

Martin, J. and D. Meyerson (1988), "Organizational culture and the denial, channeling and acknowledgement of ambiguity," In L. Pondy, R. Boland, Jr., R. J. and Thomas, H. (Eds), *Managing ambiguity and Change*, New York, NY John Wiley & Sons.

Mingers, J. (2001), "Combining IS Research Methods: Towards a Pluralist Methodology," *Information Systems Research*, 12(3), 244–259.

Schein, E. H. (1985), *Organizational Culture and Leadership*. 2nd ed., San Francisco, CA. Jossey-Bass.

Schmidt, K. (1995), *The quest for identity: Corporate identity, strategies, methods and examples*, London: Cassell.

Simoes, C. and S. Dibb (2001), "Rethinking the Brand Concept: New Brand Orientation," *Corporate Communications: An International Journal*, 6(4), 217–224.

Stuart, H. (1998), "Exploring the Corporate Identity/Corporate Image Interface: An Empirical Study of an Accountancy Firm," *Journal of Communication Management*, 2(4), 357–373.

Zinkhan, G. M., Jaiskankur, Anumpam Jaju, and Linda Hayes. (2001), "CorporateImage: A Conceptual Framework for Strategic Planning," In Greg Marshall and Stephen Grove (Eds), *Enhancing Knowledge Development in Marketing*, Vol. 12, Chicago: American Marketing.

Chapter 6

Brand Development Processes and Planning

Kevin Lane Keller

OVERVIEW

Great brands are no accident. They are a result of thoughtful and imaginative planning. An individual or organization launching a new product needs to carefully and creatively craft brand strategies and tactics to maximize the probability of its being a success. Before developing optimal brand-related plans for a new product, you need to take four crucial steps: (1) conduct a pre-launch brand audit, (2) codify your brand positioning, (3) decide on the brand's elements and (4) organize the internal branding effort. In the following pages, we will highlight core concepts with illustrative examples and practical guidelines for each step.

INTRODUCTION

Building a great brand is the dream of any marketer launching a new product or service, creating a new organization, or introducing a new venture. Today's challenging and unforgiving marketplace, however, makes brand-building for new products extremely difficult. A fickle public, intense competition, demanding retailers, constrained resources, and impatient investors combine to put unparalleled pressure on marketers to skillfully design and execute branding programs for new products and services.

To address this challenge, we will consider some of the crucial steps that brand marketers must take in developing and launching new brands. Our assumption is that a promising new product or service has been developed that has an inherent appeal for at least a group of target market consumers. The challenge then is to craft a brand strategy that maximizes the potential marketing value of the product or service.

To reach this goal, we suggest the following four key steps to successfully develop an optimal brand identity and position of a new product or service:

1. Conducting a pre-launch brand audit
2. Codifying brand positioning
3. Deciding on brand elements
4. Organizing internal branding effort

In each case, we highlight core concepts, illustrative examples and practical guidelines. The remaining chapters in this section provide insights into how brand strategies and plans can be effectively and tactically implemented.

BRAND AUDITS

Marketers need to learn what consumers know about relevant brands and products so that their companies can make informed strategic positioning decisions for new products or services. To do this, they should first conduct a pre-launch brand audit to profile consumer brand knowledge structures. A pre-launch *brand audit* is a research exercise that gives direction and substance to initial branding efforts. Although brand audits are often conducted to assess the health of an existing brand, a pre-launch brand audit can be useful to identify and refine the potential sources of equity for a new product or service and how it should be positioned and branded.

Brand audits consist of an internal company examination, called a *brand inventory*, and an external marketplace examination, called a *brand exploratory*. The brand inventories and exploratories that make up pre-launch brand audits, however, differ from those typically conducted after the launch when there is more focus on the merits of the positioning strategy and the effectiveness of marketing programs and activities to achieve this positioning. A pre-launch brand audit, on the other hand, is used to set a strategic focus and direction for a brand. It helps marketers craft their initial positioning strategies and launch introductory marketing programs and activities.

A pre-launch brand inventory attempts to collect impressions about brands and products from marketers and other key employees within an organization. Surfacing beliefs and potential misconceptions can be important while developing a viable brand positioning and branding strategy. As part of the brand inventory, competitive brands need to be profiled in as much detail as possible in terms of their branding and marketing efforts. Additionally, consumer and category dynamics in terms of attitudes, beliefs, and behaviors must be surfaced at the product level.

Pre-launch brand exploratory involves research that is directed at understanding what consumers think and feel about existing brands and what they may think and feel about the new brand to suggest potential sources of brand equity. It digs deeply into the minds of consumers, and taps their perceptions and beliefs to profile the competitive brand landscape, and thus, where the new product or service may best fit in. A good pre-launch brand exploratory identifies potential opportunities and challenges for the brand. As a result of this strategic analysis, a marketing program can be put into place to increase the odds of success of the brand launch. Pre-launch brand exploratory typically involves qualitative and quantitative research.

QUALITATIVE BRAND AUDIT RESEARCH

A pre-launch brand audit is designed to discover how customers shop, use products and services and what they think of various brands. To allow a broad range of issues to be covered and certain issues to be pursued in greater depth, brand exploratory often employs qualitative research techniques (Gardner and Levy, 1955) (see summary in Table 6.1).

Table 6.1 Summary of Qualitative Techniques

Free association	Day/Behavior reconstruction
Adjective ratings and checklists	Photo/Written journal
Confessional interviews	Participatory design
Projective techniques	Consumer-led problem solving
Photo sorts	Real-life experimenting
Archetypal research	Collaging and Drawing
Bubble drawings	Consumer shadowing
Story telling	Consumer–Product interaction
Personification exercises	Video observation
Role playing	Metaphor elicitation

In Table 6.1, the tasks at the top of the left hand list (for example, free associations) ask very specific questions whose answers may be easy to interpret. The tasks at the bottom of the list (for example, personification exercises and role playing) include potentially much richer questions, but ones that are much more difficult to interpret. Tasks at the top of the right hand list (for example, day/behavior reconstruction, and collaging and drawing) are elaborate exercises that consumers undertake on their own, and may be either specific or broadly directed. Tasks at the bottom of the right hand list (for example, consumer shadowing and video observation) involve direct observation of consumers as they engage in different kinds of behavior.

The more specific the question, the narrower the range of information given by the respondent (Levy, 1985). When the stimulus information in a question is open-ended and responses are free or less constrained, the information provided tends to be greater. The more abstract and symbolic the research technique employed, however, the more important it is to follow up with probes and other questions that explicitly reveal the motivation and reasons for consumers' responses.

Ideally, qualitative research conducted as part of brand exploratory should vary in its direction and depth as well as in the diversity of the techniques involved. Regardless of the techniques actually employed, the challenge facing qualitative research is to provide an accurate interpretation—going beyond what consumers explicitly state to determine what they implicitly mean. Good qualitative research should yield insights and hypotheses on how the consumer market is functioning and what the nature of the new brand should be.

QUANTITATIVE RESEARCH

Qualitative research is suggestive, but a more definitive assessment of optimal brand strategies and positioning often requires a quantitative phase of research. Guidelines for the quantitative phase of an exploratory are relatively straightforward. All potentially salient associations identified at the qualitative research phase should be assessed according to their possible strength, favorability, and uniqueness. Typically, it is necessary to conduct similar types of research for competitors to better understand their sources of brand equity and how these compare with the target brand. Different internal management personnel can be part of the planning and positioning process (for example, brand, marketing research, and production managers) as well as relevant outside marketing partners (for example, representatives of ad agencies).

As a first cut, open-ended measures can be employed that tap into the strength, favorability, and uniqueness of associations for competitive brands, as follows:

1. What are the strongest associations you have of the brand? What comes to mind when you think of the brand? (Strength)
2. What is good about the brand? What do you like about the brand? What is bad about the brand? What do you dislike about the brand? (Favorability)
3. What is unique about the brand? What characteristics or features does the brand share with other brands? (Uniqueness)

To provide more specific insights, belief associations for each competitive brand could be rated on scales according to their strength, favorability, and uniqueness, as Table 6.2 illustrates with Lipton Iced Tea.

Table 6.2 Example of Brand Association Ratings in Terms of Strength, Favorability, and Uniqueness

1. To what extent do you feel the following product characteristics are descriptive of Lipton Iced Tea (where 1 = strongly disagree and 7 = strongly agree)?
   _____ convenient
   _____ refreshing and thirst-quenching
   _____ real and natural
   _____ good-tasting
   _____ contemporary and relevant
   _____ used by young professionals

2. How important is it for iced tea to have the following product characteristics (where 1 = very unimportant and 7 = very important)?
   _____ convenient
   _____ refreshing and thirst-quenching
   _____ real and natural
   _____ good-tasting
   _____ contemporary and relevant
   _____ used by young professionals

3. How unique is Lipton Iced Tea in terms of the following product characteristics (where 1 = not at all unique and 7 = highly unique)?
   _____ convenient
   _____ refreshing and thirst-quenching
   _____ real and natural
   _____ good-tasting
   _____ contemporary and relevant
   _____ used by young professionals

Any potentially relevant association can and should be measured, including performance-related attributes and benefits such as (where appropriate) primary characteristics and supplementary features; product reliability and durability; service effectiveness, efficiency, and empathy; style and design; and price, as well as imagery-related attributes and benefits related to users' profiles; purchase and usage situations; brand personality and values, and history, heritage, and experiences. It may also be productive to explore various judgments, and particularly feelings, along these lines. Please note that indirect tests can also be conducted to assess the derived importance and favorability of these brand associations (for example, through multivariate regression techniques).

BRAND POSITIONING

A pre-launch provides crucial input on the brand positioning effort. Brand positioning is the act of designing a company's new offering and image to occupy a distinctive place in the minds of its target market. Positioning a new brand requires that similarities and differences between other existing brands be defined and communicated (Keller et al., 2002).

As described below, there are four key components in superior competitive brand positioning: (1) a competitive frame of reference in terms of the target market and nature of competition, (2) points of difference in terms of strong, favorable, and unique brand associations, (3) points of parity in terms of brand associations that negate any potential weaknesses of the brand or potential points of difference among competitors, and (4) a brand mantra that summarizes the essence of the brand and key points of difference in three to five words.

KEY COMPONENTS OF BRAND POSITIONING

The *competitive frame of reference* specifies the other brands with which a brand competes, and therefore, which brands should be the focus of analyses and study. A good starting point in defining a competitive frame of reference for brand positioning is to determine the products or sets of products with which a brand competes and which function as close substitutes. For a brand with explicit growth intentions to enter new markets, a broader or maybe even more aspirational competitive frame may be required to reflect possible future competitors. The appropriate frame of reference typically emerges from a good brand audit.

Points-of-difference are attributes or benefits that consumers strongly associate with a brand, positively evaluate, and believe they cannot find in a competitive brand to the same extent. Examples in the automobile market include Volvo (safety), Toyota (quality and dependability), and Mercedes-Benz (quality and prestige). There are three key criteria that determine whether or not a brand association can truly function as a point-of-difference:

- *Desirable for consumer:* Brand association must be seen as important and personally relevant to consumers as well as believable and credible.
- *Deliverable by company:* A company should have the internal resources and commitment to be able to feasibly and profitably create and maintain brand association in the minds of consumers. Ideally, brand association should be pre-emptive, defensible, and difficult to attack.
- *Differentiation from competitors:* Finally, brand association must be seen by consumers as being distinctive and superior compared to the company's relevant competitors.

Points-of-parity, on the other hand, are associations that are not necessarily unique to a brand, but may in fact be shared with other brands. These types of associations have two basic forms: category and competitive. *Category points-of-parity* are associations that consumers view as essential for a legitimate and credible offering within a certain product or service category. In other words, they represent necessary—but not adequate—conditions for brand choice.

Competitive points-of-parity are associations designed to negate the potential competitive weaknesses of a brand. One type of competitive point-of-parity is designed to negate competitors' points-of-difference—areas where other brands are perceived more favorably. Another type of competitive point-of-parity reflects the fact that to some consumers "if you are good at one thing, you must be bad at something else." In the minds of consumers, inverse product relationships are pervasive across many categories. For example, it may be difficult for consumers to see a brand as "inexpensive" and at the same time assert that it is "of the highest quality." Thus, a point-of-difference in one area may necessaraily result in the need to establish a point-of-parity in another area.

Regardless of the particular type of competitive point-of-parity, if a brand can "break even" in the eyes of consumers in areas where it is weak or where competitors are trying to find an advantage, *and* can demonstrate its plus points in other areas, it should be in a strong—and perhaps unbeatable—competitive position.

OTHER CONSIDERATIONS

Some other considerations are important for developing brand positioning.

- *Good brand positioning has a "foot in the present" and a "foot in the future."* It needs to be somewhat aspirational so that the brand has room to grow and improve, but it must also reflect the realities of the current situation and state of affairs.
- *Both points-of-parity and points-of-difference need to be well-positioned.* Too often, marketers only concentrate on areas of strength and ignore crucial areas where a brand is potentially disadvantaged. A strong brand typically has three to five points-of-difference and two to four points-of-parity. Even though these numbers may be smaller at a launch to permit a greater focus, both points-of-parity and points-of-difference are needed to establish a successful brand position.
- *Points-of-parity are not points-of-equality; there is a zone or range of indifference or tolerance.* For a brand to achieve point-of-parity on a particular attribute or benefit, an adequate number of consumers must believe that it is "good enough" on that dimension. The brand does *not* literally have to be seen as being equal to its competitors, but consumers must feel that it does well enough on particular attributes or benefits. If they do, they may be willing to base their evaluation and decisions on other factors that are potentially more favorable and valuable to the brand
- *Points-of-parity may need to be the focus of marketing communications and other marketing activities, since the points-of-difference may be a "given."* In other words, the key to positioning is often not so much achieving a point-of-difference as achieving points-of-parity.
- *It is important a duality exists in positioning of a brand such that there are rational and emotional components.* In other words, good positioning contains points-of-difference and points-of-parity that appeal both to the "head" and the "heart."

ILLUSTRATIVE EXAMPLE

A good example of effective competitive brand positioning is Accenture (Keller, 2008). Accenture saw its differentiator as its dual ability to provide innovative ideas—grounded in business processes as well as IT—and execute these effectively. Some of Accenture's competitors, including McKinsey, were seen as being highly specialized at developing strategy, whereas its other competitors such as IBM were seen as being highly skilled at implementing technology. Given that clients felt that both strategy *and* implementation were important, Accenture wanted to be seen as excelling at both.

Figure 6.1 depicts a competitive positioning map that summarizes Accenture's "best of both worlds" strategy. Although Accenture was not seen as being quite as strategic and visionary as McKinsey, it was considered to be close to the latter. Accenture was seen as being much superior to McKinsey on technology and its execution. The reverse was true with respect to IBM. Although Accenture was not seen as being quite as strong as IBM on technology and execution, it was considered to be close to the latter and was seen as being much more superior on its strategy and vision.

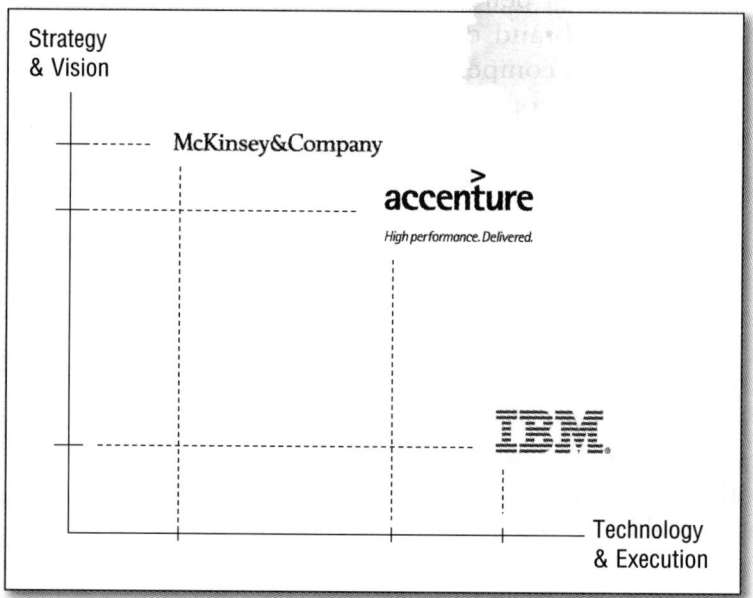

Figure 6.1 Accenture's Competitive Positioning Map

	McKinsey	IBM
Strategy & Vision	POP	POD
Technology & Execution	POD	POP

Figure 6.2 Accenture Straddle Positioning

Accenture's "straddle positioning" strategy was designed to simultaneously achieve key points-of-difference and points-of-parity with respect to two crucially important issues clients faced, as summarized in Figure 6.2.

BRAND MANTRAS

To provide further focus on the intent of the brand positioning and how firms would like consumers to think about the brand, it is often useful to define a brand mantra for a new product (Keller, 1999). A brand mantra relates to branding concepts such as the "brand essence" or "core brand promise." It is the articulation of the intended "heart and soul" of a brand. Brand mantras are short, three- to five-word phrases that capture the irrefutable essence or spirit of brand positioning.

Brand mantras can be powerful devices. Every time a consumer or customer encounters a brand—in any way, shape, or form—his or her knowledge about it may change, and and consequently, the equity of the brand is affected. Given that a large number of employees, either directly or indirectly, come into contact with customers in a way that may affect their knowledge of a brand, it is important that their words and actions consistently reinforce and support the brand meaning. A brand mantra should summarize the crucial, salient and top-of-the-mind considerations of a brand.

What is a good brand mantra? McDonald's brand philosophy of "Food, Folks, and Fun" succienctly captures the company's brand essence and core brand promise. Brand mantras must economically communicate what a brand is and what it is not. Nike is a brand with a keen sense of what it represents to consumers. The company has a rich set of associations with consumers. These revolve around such considerations as its innovative product designs, sponsorships of top athletes, award-winning advertising, competitive drive, and irreverent attitude. Internally, marketers of Nike have adopted the three-word brand mantra of "authentic athletic performance" to guide their marketing efforts. Thus, in Nike's viewpoint, its entire marketing program—products and how they are sold—must reflect the key brand values conveyed by its brand mantra.

Please note that brand mantras are designed with internal purposes in mind. A brand slogan is an external translation that attempts to creatively engage consumers. Therefore, although Nike's internal mantra is "authentic athletic performance," its external slogan is "Just Do It." The following are the three key criteria for a good brand mantra.

- *Communicate:* A good brand mantra should define the category (or categories) of business for a brand and set its boundaries. It should also clarify what is unique about the brand.
- *Simplify:* A strong brand mantra should be memorable. As a result, it should be short, crisp, and vivid in its meaning.
- *Inspire:* An effective brand mantra should stake out ground that is meaningful and relevant to as many of an organization's employees as possible.

Please note that brand mantras are typically designed to capture a brand's points-of-difference—what is unique about it. Other aspects of brand positionins, especially its points-of-parity, may also be important and need to be reinforced in other ways.

PULLING IT ALL TOGETHER

It is helpful to have a simple one-page overview of all the different components that make up brand positioning. Figure 6.3 display a "bullseye model," which summarizes the main brand positioning concepts reviewed here. In the center circle are the key points-of-parity, points-of-difference, and brand mantra. The next outward

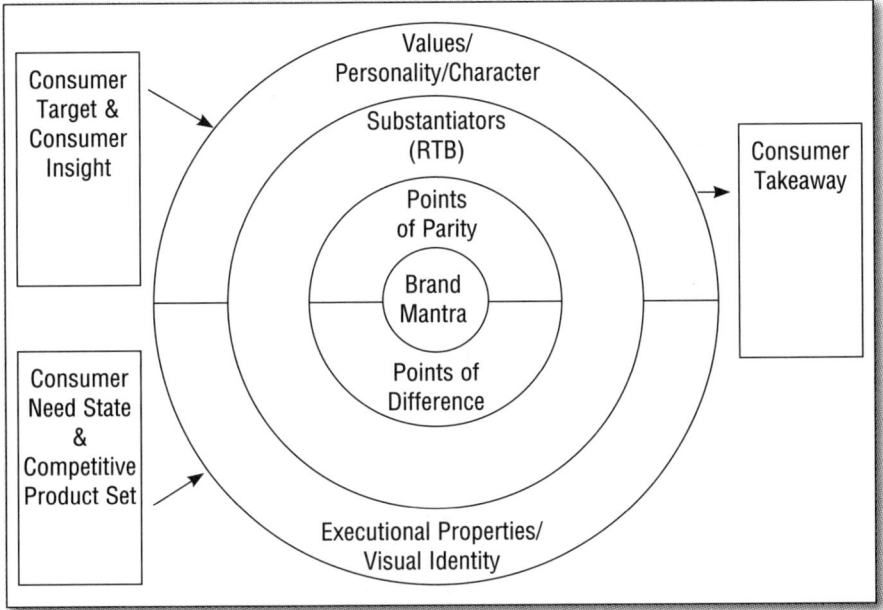

Figure 6.3 Brand Positioning Worksheet

circle includes the substantiators or reasons-to-believe that support the key concepts. These are attributes or other information that help to justify points-of-parity and points-of-difference to consumers. Finally, the outer circle ring contains two categories of information that add more texture and insight on brand positioning, for example, values, personality, and character are means to capture some of the crucial intangibles embodied in the brand; executional properties and visual identity are ways in which important aspects of brand identity are categorized.

Although the contents of the four circles or rings constitute the core components of brand positioning, it is also helpful to provide some contextual information in order to facilitate interpretation and comprehension. The two boxes leading into the positioning bullseye summarize some of the important output from a brand audit in terms of the competitive frame of reference, including consumer target and insights, consumer need states, and the competitive product set. The box emanating from the positioning bullseye captures the desired consumer takeaway. Figure 6.4 displays a hypothetical brand positioning bullseye for Starbucks.

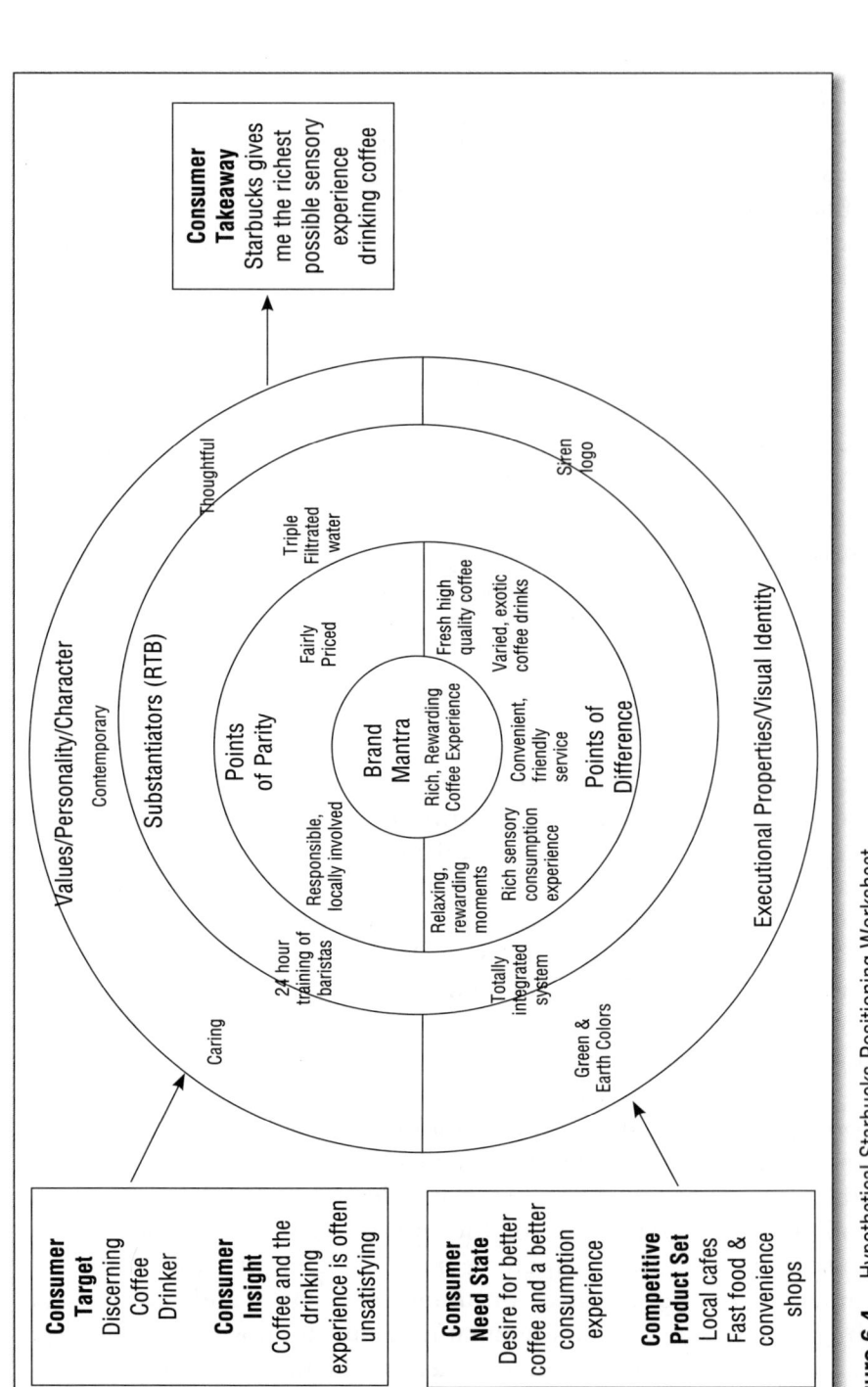

Figure 6.4. Hypothetical Starbucks Positioning Worksheet

BRAND ELEMENTS

Actual branding of a company's new product can only begin once its initial brand positioning is determined. First, a new product or service must be branded in terms of the brand elements, which include trademarkable visual or verbal information that serves to identify and differentiate a product or service. The most common brand elements include brand names, logos, symbols, URLs, characters, packaging, and slogans.

A number of options exist and a number of criteria are relevant for choosing brand elements (Keller, 2005). Brand elements can be selected to build as much brand equity as possible, independent of decisions made about a product or service and how it is marketed. For example, brand elements can be chosen to enhance brand awareness or facilitate the formation of strong, favorable, and unique brand associations that can serve as points-of-difference.

In a cluttered and competitive marketplace, the brand elements that make up a brand may have to undertake more and more of the selling function. In a time-compressed marketing world, the fact that a brand name can be noticed and its meaning registered or activated in memory within just a few seconds can be a tremendous asset. Creating a powerful set of brand elements with inherent marketing value in directly creating brand awareness and image, as well as their serving as a solid foundation to link associations, can give a company a strong competitive advantage.

For example, apart from its catchy name, Snapple has other valuable brand elements that have helped it build its brand equity, for example, its unique wide-mouth bottles with colorful graphics and catchy names of flavor such as *Bali Blast, Mango Madness,* or *Amazing Grape*; slogans such as "Made from the Best Stuff on Earth" and "The Best Stuff Is in Here"; and Wendy, its down-to-earth, friendly receptionist, who served as an advertising spokesperson and brand character for the brand.

The best test of the brand-building contribution of brand elements is what consumers would think about the product or service *if* they only knew its brand name, associated logo, etc. A brand element that makes a positive contribution to brand equity, for example, would be one where consumers assumed or inferred certain valued associations or responses. For example, based on its name alone, a consumer might expect ColorStay lipsticks to be long-lasting, SnackWell to be healthful snack foods, and Beautyrest mattresses to provide a comfortable sleep.

Because different elements have different advantages, a subset or even all of the possible brand elements should be employed. Most strong brands employ multiple brand elements. Nike has the distinctive "swoosh" logo, its empowering "Just Do It" slogan, and the mythological "Nike" name, based on the winged goddess of victory.

CRITERIA FOR CHOOSING BRAND ELEMENTS

There are six criteria for choosing brand elements (see Table 6.3), and specific choice-related considerations in each case. The first three (memorable, meaningful, and likable) can be characterized as "brand-building" in terms of how brand equity can be built through

Table 6.3 Brand Element Choice Criteria

1.	**Memorable** Easily recognized Easily recalled
2.	**Meaningful** Descriptive Persuasive
3.	**Likeability** Fun and interesting Rich visual and verbal imagery Aesthetic
4.	**Protectable** Legal Competitive
5.	**Adaptable** Flexible Updateable
6.	**Transferable** Within and across product categories Across geographical boundaries and cultures

the judicious choice of a brand element. The latter three (protectable, adaptable, and transferable) are more "defensive" in nature and are concerned with how the brand equity in a brand element can be leveraged and preserved in an environment where there are different opportunities and constraints.

- *Memorability:* How easily is the brand element recalled? How easily is it recognized? Is this true in the case of purchase as well as consumption? Short brand names such as *Tide, Crest,* and *Puffs* can help.
- *Meaningfulness:* To what extent is the brand element credible and suggestive of its corresponding category? Does it suggest something about a product ingredient or the the type of consumer who might use it? Consider the inherent meaning in names such as *DieHard* auto batteries, *Mop & Glo* floor wax, and *Lean Cuisine* low-calorie frozen entrees.
- *Likeability:* How aesthetically appealing do consumers find the brand element? Is it inherently likable, both visually andverbally as well as in other ways? Concrete brand names such as *Sunkist, Spic and Span,* and *Firebird* evoke significant imagery.
- *Transferability:* Can the brand element be used to introduce new products in the same or different categories? To what extent does the brand element add to its brand equity across geographic boundaries and market segments? Volkswagen nameed its new SUV *Touareg* after a tribe of colorful Saharan nomads. Unfortunately, historically, Touareg were also notorious slave-owners, which created a negative press backlash in the USA.
- *Adaptability:* How adaptable and updatable is the brand element? Betty Crocker has had over eight makeovers through the years, and although she is more than 88 years old, she does not look a day over 35!
- *Protectability:* How legally and competitively protectible is the brand element? Can it be easily copied? It is important that names that have become synonymous with product categories such as *Kleenex, Kitty Litter, Jell-O, Scotch Tape, Xerox,* and *Fiberglass* retain their trademark rights and not become generic.

DEVELOPING BRAND ELEMENTS

In creating a brand, marketers have many choices over the brand elements they select to identify with their products. Because various brand elements have different strengths and weaknesses, it is important to "mix and match" them to maximize their collective contribution to brand equity. Brand elements are "mixed" by selecting different brand elements to achieve different objectives. Brand elements are "matched" by designing some brand elements to mutually reinforce and share some meaning.

Brand names are not the only important brand element. Often, the less concrete the brand benefits the more important it is that brand elements capture the brand's intangible characteristics. Many insurance companies use symbols of strength (the Rock of Gibraltar for Prudential and the stag for Hartford), security (the "good hands" of Allstate, Traveller's umbrella, and the hard hat of Fireman's Fund), or a combination of the two (the castle in the case of Fortis).

Brand elements can play a number of brand-building roles. If consumers do not search for comprehensive information on products before making their product-related decisions, brand elements should be easily recognized and recalled because they are inherently descriptive and persuasive. Memorable or meaningful brand elements can reduce the burden on marketing communications to build awareness and link brand associations. The different associations that arise from the likeability and appeal of brand elements may also play a critical role in the equity of brands. Keebler's elves stress on the quality of home style baking, and the sense of magic and fun depicted in their line of cookies. Geico's *Gecko Lizard* has helped to create a friendly brand identity for a challenger brand in the crowded auto insurance category.

Slogans are powerful, but sometimes overlooked brand elements. Like brand names, slogans are an extremely efficient, "shorthand" means of building brand equity. They can function as useful "hooks" or "handles" to help consumers grasp the characteristics of a brand and what makes it special. Slogans are an indispensable means of summarizing and translating the intent of a marketing program. Think of the inherent brand meaning in slogans such as

"Like a Good Neighbor, State Farm Is There," "Nothing Runs Like a Deere," "Help Is Just around the Corner: True Value Hardware," and "The Citi Never Sleeps."

FUTURE CONSIDERATIONS

In designing a brand in the 21st century, brand elements will increasingly involve verbal and visual elements that creatively and dramatically help to build brand equity. Meaningful brands with creative potential will benefit from multiple sensory presentations. Brands have long used auditory branding devices, for example, the three-note Nabisco jingle, the percolating Maxwell House jingle, and the NBC jingle. Movie studios have always been able to take advantage of their cinematic exposure to use sight, sound, and motion to present their brands (for example, Universal's spinning globe, Paramount's mountain peak, and MGM's roaring lion).

With increased technical abilities and improved special effects, especially online options, marketers will now be able to create brand elements that come to life and capture consumers' attention. This will give them an edge, given their need to communicate and sell their brands in markets. Thus, static images of brands will be supplemented by multidimensional forms that play an important role in audio and video presentations of brands. A 21st century brand will consider how to take advantage of different media to customize its brand presentation so that (1) each brand element more effectively contributes to brand equity through its enhanced image and awareness of the brand, (2) brand elements more effectively reinforce each other to become more consistent and cohesive.

INTERNAL BRANDING

Once marketers have a good understanding of brand audit of the current brand knowledge structures of their target consumers and arrive at a brand positioning and branding strategy for new products or services, their attention can shift to how they can effectively launch new brands in the market. Additional research may however be required to test the viability of alternative tactical programs to achieve their positioning. There may be a number of possible marketing programs or activities that exist at least on the surface, and may be able to achieve the same goals. However, additional research may be useful to assess their relative effectiveness and efficiency.

Before launching any new programs or activities in the marketplace, there are however several steps that must be taken within an organization to improve the odds of the success of any marketing program. Internal branding has become a top priority for many companies. As part of these efforts, a brand equity management system must be put into place. A brand equity management system is defined as a set of organizational processes designed to improve an understanding and use of the brand equity concept within a company.

Three major activities should be undertaken in an organization to implement a brand equity management system. These include creating brand equity charters, assembling brand equity reports, and defining brand equity responsibilities. The following subsections discuss each of these in turn.

BRAND EQUITY CHARTER

The first step in establishing a brand equity management system is to formalize a company's viewpoint on brands and brand equity in general and a particular new product brand in particular into a document, the *brand equity charter*, which provides relevant guidelines to marketing managers within a company as well as to key marketing partners outside it (for example, ad agency personnel). This book should do the following:

- Define the company's view of the brand equity concept and explain why it is important.
- Describe the scope of the brand in terms of associated products and the specific manner by which they will be branded and marketed.

- Specify the desired equity for the brand in terms of points-of-parity and points-of-difference, and the brand mantra.
- Explain how brand equity is measured in terms of a tracking study and the resulting brand equity report (as described later).
- Suggest how brand equity should be managed in terms of some general strategic guidelines (for examply, by stressing on clarity, relevance, distinctiveness, innovativeness, and consistency in marketing programs).
- Outline how marketing programs should be devised in terms of some specific tactical guidelines (for example, marketing communications and brand extension criteria).
- Specify the proper treatment of the brand in terms of trademark usage, packaging, and communications.

Although parts of the brand equity charter may not change much in subsequent years, it should nevertheless be reviewed and updated (as appropirate) on an annual basis to provide decision-makers with current brand profiles and identify new opportunities and potential risk of brand. As additional new products or product extensions are introduced under a brand, marketing programs are changed, and other marketing initiatives are implemented, they should be reflected adequately in the brand equity charter. Many of the in-depth insights that emerge from brand audits are from the brand charter.

Brand Equity Report

The second step in establishing a successful brand equity management system is to compile the results of tracking surveys and other relevant performance measures for a brand into a brand equity report or scorecard, to be distributed to management on a regular basis (monthly, quarterly, or annually). A brand equity report attempts to effectively integrate a number of different measures and inputs such that a holistic understanding is possible (Rubinson and Pfeiffer, 2005).

Brand-tracking studies as well as brand audits can provide a huge reservoir of information on how to best build and measure brand equity. Nevertheless, the potential value of these research efforts will not be realized unless proper internal structures and procedures are put into place within organizations to capitalize on the usefulness of the brand equity concept and the information collected with respect to it. Although a brand equity management system does not ensure that "good" decisions are always taken about a brand, it should increase the likelihood that they do, and if nothing else, at least decrease the likelihood of "bad" decisions.

A brand equity report should provide descriptive information on *what* is happening with a brand as well as diagnostic information on *why* this is happening. It should include all relevant internal and external measures of the brand's performance, and sources and outcomes of brand equity (Ambler, 2004). In particular, one section of the report should summarize consumers' perceptions of a brand's key attributes or benefit associations, preferences, and reported behavior, as revealed by the tracking study. Another section of the report should include descriptive market-level information such as the following:

- Product shipments and movement through channels of distribution
- Retail category trends
- Relevant cost breakdowns
- Price and discount schedules where appropriate
- Sales and market share information broken down by relevant factors (for example, geographic region, type of retail account or customer)
- Profit assessments

These measures can be compared to various frames of reference—performance in last month/quarter/year—and color-coded green, yellow, or red, depending on whether the trends are positive, neutral, or negative, respectively (Clark and Ambler, 2001; Ambler and Clark, 2004; Clark et al., 2005).

Management can assemble a summary set of all relevant internal and external measures in a *marketing dashboard* for synthesis and interpretation (LaPointe, 2005). Marketing dashboards are like instrument panels in cars that display visual real-time indicators to ensure the proper functioning of vehicles. They are only as good as the information on which they are based, but sophisticated visualization tools are helping to bring data alive to improve an understanding and analysis of these (Zabin, 2006).

As an input to their marketing dashboards, companies should include two key market-based scorecards that reflect performance and provide possible early warning signals.

- *A customer-performance scorecard* records how well a company performs year after year on customer-based measures, as those shown in Table 6.4. Management should set norms for each measure and take action when results go out of bounds.
- *A stakeholder-performance scorecard* tracks the satisfaction of various constituencies that have a critical interest in and impact on a company's performance, including on its employees, suppliers, banks, distributors, retailers, and stockholders. Management should take action when one or more groups register increased or above-normal levels of dissatisfaction (Kaplan and Norton, 1996).

Table 6.4 Sample Customer-performance Scorecard Measures

- Percentage of new customers to average number of customers
- Percentage of lost customers to average number of customers
- Percentage of win-back customers to average number of customers
- Percentage of customers falling into very dissatisfied, dissatisfied, neutral, satisfied, and very satisfied categories
- Percentage of customers who indicate they will repurchase the product
- Percentage of customers who say they will recommend the product to others
- Percentage of target market customers who have brand awareness or recall
- Percentage of customers who indicate that the company's product is the most preferred in its category
- Percentage of customers who correctly identify the brand's intended positioning and differentiation
- Average perception of company's product quality relative to its main competitor's
- Average perception of company's service quality relative to its key competitor's

Brand Equity Responsibilities

To develop a brand equity management system that will maximize long-term brand equity, organizational responsibilities and processes with respect to a brand must be clearly defined. Brands need constant and consistent nurturing to grow. There must be discipline, commitment, and investment in brand building.

To provide central coordination, a position entitled Vice President or Director of Strategic Brand Management (or Brand Equity Management) can be established within an organization. The person in this position should be responsible for overseeing implementation of the brand equity charter and brand equity reports to make sure, as much as possible, that product and marketing actions across divisions and geographic boundaries are performed in a way that reflects the spirit of the brand equity charter and the substance of the brand equity report to maximize the long-term equity of the brand. The natural place to house such oversight duties and responsibilities is in a corporate marketing group with a senior management reporting relationship within it.

Scott Bedbury, who helped to direct the Nike and Starbucks brands during some of their most successful years, is emphatic about the need for "top-down brand leadership" (Bedbury, 2002). He advocates the appointment of a Chief Brand Officer (CBO) who reports directly to the CEO of the company and whose role encompasses the following:

- *His/Hers is an omnipresent conscience whose job is to champion and protect the brand—the way it looks and feels—both inside and outside the company.* The CBO recognizes that the brand is the sum total of everything a company does and strives to ensure that all the employees understand it and its values, and creates "brand disciples" in the process.
- *He/She is an architect and not only helps to build the brand but also plans, anticipates, researches, probes, listens, and informs.* Working with senior leadership, the CBO envisions not just what works best for the brand at that particular point of time, but also what can help to drive it forward in the future.
- *The CBO determines and protects the voice of the brand over time with a long-term (two to three years) perspective.* He/She can be

accountable for brand-critical and company-wide activities such as advertising, positioning, corporate design, corporate communications, and consumer or market insights.

Bedbury also advocates periodic brand development reviews (full-day meetings quarterly or even half-day meetings monthly) for brands in difficult circumstances. As part of a brand development review, he suggests the following topics and activities (Bedbury, 2002):

- *Review of brand-sensitive material:* For example, brand strength monitors or tracking studies, brand audits, and focus groups, as well as less formal personal observations or "gut feelings" should all be reviewed.
- *Review of the status of key brand initiatives:* Because brand initiatives entail strategic thrusts to either strengthen a weakness in a brand or exploit an opportunity to grow it in a new direction, customers' perceptions may change and therefore need to be assessed.
- *Review of brand-sensitive projects:* This involves, for example, evaluation of advertising campaigns, corporate communications, sales meeting agendas, and important human resource programs (recruitment, training, and retention, which profoundly affects an organization's ability to embrace and project its brand values).
- *Review of new product and distribution strategies with respect to core brand values:* For example, projects that can be evaluated include licensing a brand to penetrate new markets, forming joint ventures to develop new products or brands, and expanding distribution to nontraditional platforms such as large-scale discount retailers.
- *Resolution of brand positioning conflicts:* Any inconsistencies in positioning across channels, business units, or markets must be identified and resolved.

In a general sense, the marketing function must be organized within the firm in a way that optimizes brand equity (Hulbert et al., 1998). Many companies are therefore attempting to redesign their marketing organizations to better reflect the challenges faced by their brands. At the same time, because of changing job requirements and duties, traditional marketing departments are disappearing from a number of companies that are exploring other ways of conducting their marketing functions through business groups, multidisciplinary teams, and so on. The goal of these new organizational schemes is to improve organizations' internal coordination and efficiency as well as their external focus on retailers and consumers. However, although these are laudable goals, clearly one of the challenges facing these new designs is to ensure that the equity of brands is preserved and nurtured, and not neglected due to a lack of oversight.

CONCLUSION

This chapter has concentrated on the of the crucial steps brand marketers must take while branding new products or services. Assuming that a promising new product or service has been developed, we have outlined the following four key steps for successfully developing its optimal brand positioning and strategy:

- *Conducting a pre-launch brand audit:* A good pre-launch brand audit consists of research both within the company (brand inventory) and outside it with consumers (brand exploratory).
- *Codifying brand positioning:* Brand positioning involves defining points-of-parity and points-of-difference for a brand—areas where a brand breaks even and areas where it demonstrates its superiority—as well as a brand mantra—a short three to five word experession that captures the essence of a brand.
- *Deciding on brand elements:* Brand elements are trademarkeable information such as brand names, logos, symbols, characters, packaging, signage, slogans, and URLs. Brand elements need to be "mixed" and matched" so that they collectively help to appropriately reflect brand positioning, and build and protect brand equity.
- *Organizing internal branding effort:* A brand equity management system is defined as a set of organizational processes that are designed to improve an understanding and use of the brand

equity concept within a company. A brand equity management system within an organization helps to improve the likelihood of the success of its external marketing programs and activities. A brand equity management system requires that three major activities should be undertaken. These include creating brand equity charters, assembling brand equity reports, and defining brand equity responsibilities.

Accomplishing these four steps helps a company ensure that it puts in place a brand strategy, which maximizes the potential value of its new product or service.

REFERENCES

Ambler, Tim (2004), *Marketing and the Bottom Line* (2nd ed.). Great Britain: Financial Times Prentice Hall. Available at http://www.amazon.com/Marketing-Bottom-Line-Tim-Ambler/dp/0273661949/ref=sr_1_1?ie=UTF8&qid=1438744317&sr=8-1&keywords=Marketing+and+the+Bottom+Line (accessed July 27, 2009).

Ambler, Tim and Bruce Clark (2004), "What Will Matter Most to Marketers Three Years From Now?," paper presented at Marketing Science Institute Conference, *Does Marketing Measure Up? Performance Metrics: Practices and Impacts*, June 21–22, 2004, London, United Kingdom.

Bedbury, Scott (2002), *A New Brand World*. New York: Viking Press.

Clark, Bruce H. and Tim Ambler (2001), "Marketing Performance Measurement: Evolution of Research and Practice," *International Journal of Business Performance Management*, 3(2/3/4), 231–244

Clark, Bruce H., Andrew Abela, and Tim Ambler (2005), "Organizational Motivation, Opportunity and Ability to Measure Marketing Performance," *Journal of Strategic Marketing*, 13(4), December, 241–259.

Gardner Burleigh B. and Sidney J. Levy (1955), "The Product and the Brand," *Harvard Business Review* (March–April), 33–39.

Hulbert, J. M., P. Berthon, and L. F. Pitt (1998), "Brand Management Prognostications," *Sloan Management Review* (Winter), 53–65.

Kaplan, Robert S. and David P. Norton (1996), *The Balanced Scorecard*. Boston: Harvard Business School Press.

Keller, Kevin Lane (1999), "Brand Mantras: Rationale, Criteria, and Examples," *Journal of Marketing Management*, 15(1–3), 43–51.

——— (2005), "Branding Short-Cuts," *Marketing Management*, September/October, 14, 18–23.

——— (2008), "Accenture: Rebranding a Global Brand," In *Best Practice Cases in Branding* (3rd ed.), Upper Saddle River, NJ: Prentice-Hall.

Keller, Kevin Lane, Brian Sternthal, and Alice Tybout (2002), "Three Questions You Need to Ask About Your Brand," *Harvard Business Review*, September, 80(9), 80–89.

LaPointe, Patrick (2005), *Marketing by the Dashboard Light—How to Get More Insight, Foresight, and Accountability from Your Marketing Investments*, www.marketingNPV.com.

Levy, Sidney J. (1985), "Dreams, Fairy Tales, Animals, and Cars," *Psychology and Marketing* 2(2), 67–81.

Rubinson, Joel and Markus Pfeiffer (2005), "Brand Key Performance Indicators as a Force for Brand Equity Management, *Journal of Advertising Research*, 45(2), 187–197.

Zabin, Jeff (2006), "Marketing Dashboards: The Visual Display of Marketing Data," *Chief Marketer*, June 26.

Chapter 7
Managing the Brand Experience

Bernd Schmitt

INTRODUCTION

Marketing practitioners worldwide have come to realize that understanding how consumers experience brands, and in turn, how to provide appealing brand experiences to them is critical for differentiating brands in the competitive environment (Schmitt, 1999). The brand experience has come to the foreground in both developed economies and fast- growing emerging economies, for example, in Asia and Latin America (Zarantonello, Jedidi, and Schmitt, 2013).

Numerous trade writings have appeared that present useful frameworks, concepts, and tools for managing experiences (Pine and Gilmore, 1999; Schmitt, 1999 and 2003; Shaw and Ivens, 2002; Smith and Wheeler, 2002; Chattopadhyay and Laborie, 2005). In their book, *The Experience Economy,* Pine and Gilmore (1999) have argued that economies went through different stages of economic value creation, starting with commodities, then consumer goods, and then services. The most recent way of economic value creation according to the authors occurs by "staging experiences." It is questionable whether even the most highly developed economies (such as the USA, countries in Europe, Japan, Hong Kong and Singapore, or South Korea and Taiwan) should be dubbed "experience economies," given that more than two-thirds of their GDP is typically created through services and only a minor part through the type of staged experiences described by Pine and Gilmore (1999), such as theme restaurants or forms of entertainment. However, there is no doubt that in the 21st century, products and services, and even some commodities (for example, coffee) will be increasingly branded and marketed by using experiences in both developed and emerging markets. Thus, I feel it is more accurate to use the terms "experiential marketing" or "brand experience" rather than describing this movement in economic terms (Schmitt, 1999 and 2012).

In academic branding literature, several concepts have been developed regarding emotions, the self and relationships—including brand personality, brand relationships, brand community, brand trust, brand attachment, brand engagement, and brand love (Aaker, 1997; McAlexander, Schouten, and Koenig, 2002; Delgado-Ballester, Munuera-Alemán, and Yagüe-Guillén, 2003; Thomson, MacInnis, and Park, 2005; Carroll and Ahuvia, 2006). These concepts are closely related to experiential marketing and brand experience. Most importantly, the concept of brand experience has entered the marketing field. Academic researchers have defined the concept, designed a scale to measure the brand experience, and shown that the brand experience impacts a variety of response variables (Brakus, Schmitt, and Zarantonello, 2009; Zarantonello and Schmitt, 2010 and 2013; Schmitt, 2011; Raffelt, Schmitt, and Meyer, 2013; Schmitt, 2013).

The experiential turn in marketing is a recent phenomenon. Branding and marketing were done differently in the last century. During this period, marketers were not particularly concerned about the experiences their brands provided to customers. Instead, marketing approaches focused on functional features and the performance characteristics of products, such as hardware and memory in electronics products, gas mileage in a car, durability in a major appliance, or cleaning power in a detergent.

Traditional marketers viewed customers as rational decision-makers who weighed these features and benefits against one another and carefully selected products with the highest overall utility. This was marketing during the industrial and consumer age. Similarly, the dominant paradigm in academic consumer research viewed the consumer as a kind of information processor that made comparisons and generated decisions—a very rational creature who would systematically consider alternatives, weigh pros and cons, and make appropriate judgments (Bettman, 1979). Marketers subscribing to this approach looked at their consumers as engineers might; they treated them as analytical and rational decision-makers. Applied to branding, the rational approach stressed the importance of choice models and perceptual maps, and advertising as the key persuasion tool because through advertising marketers could present—and tweak—product features and benefits easily to consumers.

The experiential approach to marketing and branding differs significantly from the traditional analytical and rational "features-and-benefits" approach. In this chapter, which is both academic and applied in its focus, I will first describe the concept of brand experience and its dimensions and then show how these concepts and dimensions have been validated in research. Next, I will present a project-based management framework for managing experiences and discuss organizational and measurement issues related to experience. I will conclude with the key characteristics of experiential branding and then show how the brand experience concept can be used to address several perennial marketing issues.

THE CONCEPT OF BRAND EXPERIENCE

An experience is essentially a private event that occurs in response to some kind of stimulus. Experiences are usually not self-generated but induced; experiences are "of" or "about" something external to the subject (Schmitt, 1999). Brand experience, in particular, has been defined as "subjective, internal consumer responses (sensations, feelings, and cognitions) as well as behavioral responses evoked by brand-related stimuli that are part of a brand's design and identity, packaging, communications and environments" (Brakus, Schmitt, and Zarantonello, 2009).

Consumer and marketing research have shown that brand experiences occur in many settings and marketing contexts. Brand experiences occur when consumers search, examine and evaluate products, when they shop for them and receive service, and when they consume them (Holbrook, 2000; Arnould, Price, and Zinkhan, 2002; Hoch, 2002; Brakus, Schmitt, and Zhang, 2008). In stores, experiences result from a consumer's interaction with a store's physical environment—its so-called "store atmosphere"—and its staff and sales people (Hui and Bateson, 1991; Boulding et al., 1993; Jones, 1999; Kerin, Jain, and Howard, 2002; Grace and O'Cass, 2004; Arnold et al., 2005;; Ofir and Simonson, 2007). And, of course, experiences occur when consumers use products and services. Consumption experiences include feelings and hedonic dimensions. For example, Holbrook (2000) and Hirschman (1982) identified many relevant emotions in consumption experiences—love, hate, fear, joy, boredom, anxiety, pride, anger, lust, and guilt. They argued that there are also other important responses involved in consumers' experiences, such as, for example, fun, play, and aesthetic responses. Their pioneering work changed the study of customer value. Much of interpretive research on consumption experiences, following Holbrook and Hirschman (1982), focused on hedonic goals that occur during and after the consumption of, for example, jazz, movies, museums, river rafting, baseball, and sky-diving (Arnould and Price, 1993; Celsi, Rose, and Leigh, 1993; Holt, 1995; Joy and Sherry, 2003).

The experience a brand provides to its customers extends far beyond the realm of advertising (Rust and Oliver, 1994). Public relations, events, and online communications, and, of course, social media are increasingly important (Ries and Ries, 2004; Chase et al., 2006; Zarantonello and Schmitt, 2013). In fact, in some cases, advertising may be irrelevant for building brand experiences, and may not even be used. Google is such an example. Its brand value has been built without advertising. Starbucks has primarily built its brand through the in-store experience. Facebook, Twitter, Skype, and many leading new media brands have also been built without the use of the traditional medium of advertising.

DIMENSIONS OF BRAND EXPERIENCES

When marketers manage and create brand experiences for their customers, they need to be aware of the various dimensions of brand experiences. Across a wide variety of disciplines, from philosophy to psychology to management, a rather consistent set of experience dimensions, which one can also apply to brands, has been proposed.

Philosopher John Dewey viewed experience as the intertwining of human beings and their environments (Dewey, 1922 and 1925). He argued that knowledge (which he considered to be classifying, analyzing and reasoning about things) is only one part of our understanding of the world. He proposed that in addition to cognitive or intellectual experiences resulting from knowledge, there are three other experiences including perceiving (through the senses), feeling, and doing. Moreover, he felt that human beings are fundamentally connected with other people, and that during these connections and interactions, relational experiences may take place.

Following Dewey, Dubé, and LeBel's (2003) well-known four "pleasure dimensions"—intellectual, emotional, social, and physical pleasures: Psychologists and cognitive scientists have investigated similar "mental modules" (Pinker, 1997; Fodor, 1998). For example, Pinker (1997) identified four mental modules that correspond closely to the experiences postulated by Dewey—sensory perception, feelings and emotions, creativity and reasoning, and social relations. However, Pinker did not distinguish a separate "doing" or "physical" module; instead, he considered bodily experiences as well as motor actions and behaviors as part of a "sensory-motor module," similar to Lakoff and Johnson's (1999) concept of embodied cognition.

In their applied management writings, Pine and Gilmore (1999) focused on "staged experiences" in retail environments and events. They distinguished four types of staged experiences: aesthetic, educational, entertaining, and escapist experiences. Again, the similarity and overlap with some of the dimensions of experience proposed by the authors mentioned earlier is noteworthy.

Finally, in my first major publication on experiential marketing (Schmitt, 1999), I proposed five general experience dimensions, and referred to them as "sense," "feel," "think," "act," and "relate." These five experiences are closely related to Dewey's categorization, Pinker's mental modules, Pine and Gilmore's dimensions, and Dubé and LeBel's pleasure construct, but have been adjusted to fit the marketing and branding context. The "sense" experience includes aesthetics and sensory qualities ; the "feel" experience includes moods and emotions; the "think" experience includes convergent/analytical and divergent/imaginative thinking; "act" refers to motor actions and behavioral experiences, and "relate" refers to social experiences such as those relating to a reference group.

Deciding on which experience dimension a brand should focus on is a key management decision in brand experience management. Let me therefore discuss each dimension in more detail and provide practical examples of each, focusing on some marketing, branding, and advertising campaigns that have become classics (for further details, see Schmitt, 1999).

The "sense" experience results from stimulation of the different individual senses—sight, sound, touch, smell, and taste—or frequently, the experience is multi-sensory. "Sense" closely relates to marketing of designs—how to create a unique experience by arousing interest through design (Schmitt and Simonson, 1997). For example, consumer electronics brands use a multi-sensory approach in the designs of their products—from the color scheme of a product line to the "user experience" in the sound and touch elements when consumers interact with the device. In the automotive industry, sight, sound, touch, and smell are key considerations when designing the interior of a car. Small differences in smell and taste can make or break a refined food product (for example, wine or chocolates), or determine whether the brand is a mass-market or up-market one. As a result, the presentation and packaging of many "luxury" chocolates is extravagant, for example, pure glossy white, with gold or silver embossed lettering; with red cloth ribbons, or unique patterns for each chocolate.

"Feel" experiences appeal to customers' inner feelings and emotions, with the objective of creating effective experiences that range from mild moods linked to a brand to strong emotions. Most feelings—whether they are simple moods or strong emotions—occur during consumption of a brand. The importance of emotions has been discussed earlier. The impact of mild moods, on the other hand, should not be underestimated. Positive moods not only make customers feel good, they also affect their decision-making and creativity (Russ, 1998). Standard so-called emotional advertising (for example, smiling faces) is often not effective because it does not target feelings during consumption. An example of a successful "feel" branding campaign is Estee Lauder's campaign for its fragrance, "Clinique Happy," which has become a classic in the industry (Elliott, 1997). Ad videos at the point of purchase communicated the name's message, showing the product's sunny orange packaging and the jumping, smiling figure of the model Kylie Bax. Moreover, Clinique produced a limited-edition CD of "happy" songs that were played at brand islands in department stores. These songs included Judy Garland's "Get Happy" and the Turtles' "Happy Together."

"Think" experiences appeal to the intellect and have the objective of creating cognitive, problem-solving experiences that engage customers creatively. As I have emphasized earlier (Schmitt, 1999), this can be done through surprise, intrigue, and provocation. Such campaigns are common in the case of new technology products. But "think" marketing is not restricted to high-tech products. This type of experiential marketing has also been used in product designing, retailing and communications in many other industries. For example, in its classic, now terminated campaign in the 1980s and 1990s into the 2000s, Benetton, the Italian casual-wear retail brand, presented images that alluded to race, war and disease (for example,, a black horse mounting a white horse, the bloodstained T-shirt of a soldier killed in action, or a dying AIDS patient) to shake up customers and get them to think about societal issues.

The "act" experience refers to bodily reactions, individual actions and behaviors, and general lifestyles. It requires a close understanding of how consumers view their bodies, their clothing, and their appearance as well as how they like to live. Nike's classic "Just Do It" campaign is an example of "act" branding. Frequently depicting famous athletes in action, the campaign has transformed the brand experience by appealing to the need to identify with celebrity role models, and thereby enticing the customer to action.

"Relate" experiences include aspects of other experiences, in particular "feel" (Brakus, Schmitt, and Zarantonello, 2009). However, "relate" expands beyond the individual's personal and private feelings, thereby relating him/her to something outside his/her present state. "Relate" experiences appeal to the individual's desire for self-improvement (for example, a future "ideal self" that he/she wants to relate to). These experiences appeal to the need to be perceived positively by others (for example, one's peers, girlfriends, boyfriends or spouses; family and colleagues). They relate the person to a broader social system (a subculture, a country, etc.), and establish strong brand relations and communities. "Relate" campaigns have been used in a number of industries, ranging from cosmetics, personal care and lingerie (to create fantasies about the other sex) to national image improvement programs. The motorcycle brand Harley-Davidson, by now a commonplace example in marketing textbooks, is a "relate" brand. From the physical experience of riding a Harley-Davidson to the psychological devotion the product demands, it transcends the consumption experience, which is a way of life among bikers. Individual users become members of a brand community (Muniz and O'Guinn, 2001)

It is important to note that experiential appeals rarely result in only one type of experience. Many brand managers therefore strive to use experiential hybrids that combine two or more experiences at the same time in order to broaden the experiential appeal. Ideally, marketers should strategically strive to create holistically integrated experiences that have, at the same time, all five experience dimensions.

Finally, the experience dimensions are evoked by various brand-related stimuli (for example, colors, shapes, typefaces, designs, slogans, mascots, and brand characters). Brakus, Schmitt, and Zarantonello (2009) noted that there is no one-to-one correspondence such that a certain stimulus type only triggers a certain experience dimension. For example, while colors, shapes, typefaces, and designs usually result in a sensory experience, they may also lead to emotions (for example, red for Coca-Cola) or in intellectual experiences (for example, when designs use complex patterns). Similarly, slogans, mascots and brand characters, while they may result in imaginative thoughts, may also trigger emotions (for example, "Bibendum," the Michelin Man) or stimulate actions (for example, Nike's "Just Do It").

CONSUMERS' CONCEPTIONS OF BRAND EXPERIENCE

Do consumers have a conception of brand experience, that is, when experiences occur and what triggers them? Do they think in terms of the type of experience dimensions discussed earlier? When they talk about their experiences with brands, how do they describe these?

To address these questions, my co-authors and I conducted qualitative research (Brakus, Schmitt and Zarantonello, 2009). We asked young adults (MBA students) in the USA to describe their experiences with brands of their choice. The participants were instructed to select brands that provide them with strong experiences and to describe these. They gave descriptions of many brands, for example, Abercrombie and Fitch, Apple/iPod, Body Shop, BMW, Disney, Google, Nike, Starbucks, and W Hotel. They also selected and described weak experiential brand, for example, Aeropostale, Dell, Hilton, Macy's, Microsoft, Reebok, Visa, and Wal-Mart.

The results of the survey empirically confirmed many of the tenets of experiential branding described earlier. First, all the consumers in the study had a concept of brand experience. Second, they reported brand experiences that occurred when they shopped and consumed brands. Third, they viewed brand experiences as being evoked by brand-related stimuli that are part of a brand's visual identity, packaging, communications and environment.

Most importantly, the participants gave descriptions that could easily be mapped on to the experiential types and dimensions discussed earlier. They described sensations (for example, "touch and feel," "appeal to different senses," and "smells nice and is visually warm"), feelings (for example, "fun," "refreshed," "inspired," and "nostalgia," "in a good mood"), convergent and divergent thoughts (for example, "the brand intrigues me," "I think of topics like animal testing, purity and wellness," "reminds me to use my imagination," and "makes me think about precious things in life"), and behaviors and lifestyles (for example, "enjoy playing with all the products," "I change the way I organize and interact with information," "I want to work out," and "It's a place I want to go to"). The respondents also mentioned the socio-cultural context of branded experiences (for example, "It's like a membership in an exclusive, country-clubish community," "I am part of a 'smarter' community," and "I feel like an athlete").

Weak experiential brands, in contrast, were described in terms of their functionality, price and promotions. About Wal-Mart, respondents were of the opinion that "it focuses on prices as low as price can be; their retail stores are incredibly basic." They said that "Visa is not about experience. It promotes being accepted everywhere. It is about convenience and reliability, and less about how I as a customer feel about the brand." For them, Aeropostale, the clothing brand, stood for "little more than cheap clothing."

The brand experience concepts and models that I have mentioned earlier may be viewed as conceptualization and analytical frameworks of a *customer-based brand-experience* model, similar to Keller's customer-based brand equity models (Keller, 1993 and 2003). They are useful for academic research and in part in business practice. However, managers who focus on experiences need a step-by-step process to manage the brand experience. They should also have a project management approach to experiences. The following is a simple project-based framework I have developed. It includes research, development of strategy, and various implementation phases.

A PROJECT-BASED FRAMEWORK

In my book, *Customer Experience Management*, I presented the CEM framework, which is a project-based framework for managing experiences (Schmitt, 2003). The original CEM framework had five steps. For the purpose of this article, which focuses specifically on brand experiences, we can simplify the framework into three basic steps:

1. Analyzing the experiential world of the customer
2. Building the experience platform
3. Designing the brand experience

Step 1 ("Analyzing the experiential world of the customer") is an *analytic* step. Step 2 ("Building the experiential platform") is a *strategic* step. Step 3 ("Designing the brand experience") is an *implementation step*.

Analyzing the Experiential World of the Customer

The first step in the CEM framework requires original insight into a consumer's world and his/her perception of a brand. The research and analysis at step 1—referred to as "customer insight"—is conducted from a broad perspective by analyzing and researching not only the brand, but also the consumption and usage patterns of customers and the socio-cultural context that affects their experiential needs. For example, in the beauty and cosmetics industry, socio-cultural analysis may include trends such as "wellness," "spiritualism," or "coolness" that affect consumers' lifestyles, and, ultimately, their perception of skin care products and cosmetics.

In the case of business-to-business (B2B) brands, managers analyze the business environment, including business requirements and desired solutions that may have an impact on the brand experience of a business customer. For example, trends in the business environment (such as outsourcing, cross-functional integration, or globalization) may affect an enterprise resource software brand such as SAP or Oracle.

Customer-insight research can include focus groups, surveys and interviews, but is frequently supplemented by ethnographic and interpretive research techniques, and "big data" today.

Building the Experience Platform

The second step, the experience platform, includes the formulation of a core experience concept that can be used as a guiding principle for subsequent implementation. An experience platform is different from a positioning statement or perceptual map. It includes a dynamic, multi-sensory and multi-dimensional depiction of the desired experience (referred to as "experiential positioning") and a specification of the experiential value a customer can expect from the product (the "experiential value promise")—for example, in terms of the experience dimensions discussed earlier. The experiential platform culminates in an overall implementation theme that can be used to coordinate subsequent marketing and communication efforts and future innovation.

To be useful, the platform must be simple and crisp; it may be an intriguing concept or idea (for example, "energy" for a beauty brand, or "authenticity" for a car brand), or it may be captured in a phrase or brand line. Frequently, it is also expressed visually (for example, on a visual board) or via a brief "brand video." The concept must resonate with consumers and be in line with the brand's values and personality (D. Aaker, 1996; J. Aaker, 1997).

Designing the Brand Experience

Finally, the experience platform must be implemented so that it results in a brand experience. Designing the brand experience includes, among other things, selection of experiential features that can serve as a jumping-off point for an experience. Experiential features may have some functionality, but their main purpose is to create an experience. That is why we find Asian herbs in fruit juices or green tea in cosmetics nowadays.

The experience also includes an appealing "look and feel" in the visual identity, packaging, on websites as well as in environments or stores). Experiential messages and imagery in advertising and collaterals, as well as online, complete the brand experience. Finally, in service businesses, dynamic customer interface, that is, face-to-face exchanges and contact points (for example, via call centers) are important for designing the right experience.

Many organizations outsource designing of the brand experience. It thereby becomes the domain of corporate identity and design forms, graphic and interior designers as well as media and advertising agencies. Agencies communicate with each other to guarantee consistency and integration. In addition, more and more organizations are appointing "customer experience" or "brand experience" managers who make sure that integration takes place. For new brands, the task of designing a brand experience requires creativity to differentiate the brand in unusual ways in the market. Outside-industry benchmarking can also be a useful tool to create innovative solutions.

Before a company embarks on a brand experience project, it needs to be clear about its objective. This is critical in any business project, including a CEM venture. Moreover, it is also critical not to lose track of the objective as the project progresses. Two characteristics differentiate good objectives from bad ones. First, an objective should be measurable, and measurement criteria need to be specified (for example, for an experience, project criteria could be satisfaction scores; loyalty increases by a certain percentage point, premium pricing above a threshold, a certain number of new customers; increased trial by certain percentage, or return on investment). Second, a simple empirical model should be built that lays out how the quantitative objective is to be reached via the experience project.

Brand experience projects in major companies usually last for 6 to 12 months. After an experience project is completed, the experience should be managed on a continuous basis. It needs to be upgraded and updated. Ideally, the experience philosophy needs to be "institutionalized." This requires alignment of organizational structures and processes, and most importantly, of people and systems.

ALIGNING A CORPORATION: PEOPLE AND SYSTEMS

To deliver an attractive brand experience over time requires organizational alignment (Labovitz and Rosansky, 1997). Management ensures that employees understand the importance of experience management and how their own behavior can affect the brand experience. Alignment is especially important in service businesses where employees directly interface with customers.

As part of hiring procedures, human resource managers need to find a way of assessing whether applicants will be committed to focusing on the customer experience. Do they enjoy people? Do they understand the importance of the customer experience? Are they willing to expend the energy it takes to provide a memorable brand experience for their customers? Once a company has recruited employees with experiential skills and attitudes, it is important to train them on the job so that they deliver the right experience to customers. Employees need to be made aware of the importance of their role in the brand experience context and be empowered to enhance the customer experience. They should be encouraged to consider the customer's point of view whenever possible.

Companies have realized that hiring and training is usually not enough. Many of them now offer their employees meaningful incentives to motivate them, and reward them financially when they deliver the right experience. In such companies, employee behavior is measured against performance standards that focus on the customer experience with the brand. Employees receive feedback based on how they perform on this standard.

Finally, companies have begun to focus on the employee experience (Heska, 2009). For a positive employee experience with a brand, work needs to be challenging and rewarding. When employees feel bored or oppressed, or that their input does not matter, management cannot expect them to deliver a good experience to their customers. In other words, a desirable employee experience with a brand is imperative for delivering a desirable customer experience. As a result, managing the employee experience has become an important topic in human resource management. Like analyzing the experiential world of customers, it is critical from a human resource perspective to study the experiential world of employees and develop an experience platform for them from this analysis.

Alignment is not only about people, but also systems, especially databases and computer systems involving customers. The details in a database often tell customers about a company's priorities—internal operations or customer experience. For example, what information do your front-line employees have available when they interact with customers? Does this information help them serve customers better? Is the information up-to-date? Finally, should there be room in databases for storing special information ? For example, a database should include information that enables a company to celebrate special anniversaries of customers for being loyal to a brand.

To sum up, systems should record information customers care about so that brands provide a special experience for them. Of course, databases are also an internal record-keeping device for companies, but to provide differentiation, databases need to be experience-focused.

MEASURING BRAND EXPERIENCES

There are various scales and measurement tools available for measuring various aspects of the brand experience. In academic consumer behavior literature, for example, there are numerous scales that measure specific experiential dimensions.

The Visual Product Aesthetics Scale (Bloch, Brunel, and Arnold, 2003) measures sensory experiences, in particular, individual differences in skill and sensitivity in visual design. With the scale, it is possible to examine how much a consumer values design, responds to it, and in general, evaluates design with skill. Scale items include, for example, "I enjoy seeing displays of products that have a superior design," "Being able to see subtle differences in product designs is one skill I have developed over time," or "When I see a product that has a really great design, I feel a strong urge to buy it" (Bloch, Brune, l and Arnold, 2003).

There are numerous scales that measure feelings (Izard, 1978), ranging from simple measures of mood to measures of strong emotions. Of particular interest in the experiential context are scales that measure strong emotions because they can result in strong "feel" experiences. For example, Thomson, MacInnis and Park (2005) designed a scale that measures brand attachment, the emotional bond that consumers have with a brand, which goes beyond simple liking. The scale has three sub-dimensions—connection, affection, and passion, out of which passion, in particular, may result in a strong "feel" experience.

There are also scales that focus on the other experience dimensions. In relation to "think" experiences, the well-known "Need for Cognition Scale" may be of particular interest (Cacioppo and Petty, 1982). Items include, "I would prefer complex to simple problems," or "The notion of thinking abstractly appeals to me." Finally, for "act" experiences, there are multiple lifestyle scales (such as VALS), and for "relate," there are measures, developed in the fields of social psychology and sociology, which address issues of groups and social roles (Olson, 2005).

While these scales focus on specific experiential dimensions, my co-researchers and I have developed a scale that measures at once all experiential dimensions (Brakus, Schmitt, and Zarantonello, 2009). Because the scale is short and easy to administer, it is the most efficient way of measuring brand experiences.

Scale development of the Brand Experience Scale was extensive and required multiple studies to construct a reliable and valid scale. It measures brand experience as a whole with four experience dimensions—sense, feel, think, and act. As part of scale development, "relate" was subsumed under "feel."

The scale includes of a 12-item scale, and is short, simple and easy to administer. Psychometrically, it is internally consistent and has been tested with multiple samples. It has also successfully passed the standard reliability and validity tests, and demonstrated its test-retest reliability and criterion validity. Moreover, the scale displays "discriminant" validity from some of the most widely used branding measures and scales, including brand evaluation, involvement, and attachment; customer delight and brand personality. Most important, the scale can predict consumer satisfaction and loyalty (see also Chang and Chieng, 2006).

The scale is not only useful in academic research, but also in marketing. As marketers engage in projects to understand and improve the experience their brands provide to their customers, they can use the scale for assessment, planning and tracking purposes.

In management practice, the brand experience may also be related quantitatively to customer equity (Rust, Zeithaml, and Zemon, 2000). This can be done via regression analyses or structural equation modeling to measure the effect of individual experience components and integratio, on customer equity. Regression weights can indicate the degree of importance of each experience component as well as of integration in the business. Additional analyses could focus on the subcomponents of customer equity, related to acquisition and retention of, or add-on selling to customers.

USING BRAND EXPERIENCE TO ADDRESS OTHER MARKETING ISSUES

In this chapter, I have presented concepts, frameworks and tools to manage brand experiences. Yet, the concept and tools of brand experience can also be useful in addressing other marketing issues because, brand experience is an important construct whenever an organization faces a customer-focused issue. Therefore, brand experience can contribute to and solve a wide range of marketing issues that relate to customers, and provide a fresh and new perspective on these issues. I will now elaborate on how the concepts and tools of brand experience management can also be useful for addressing customer-focused marketing issues.

Segmentation and Targeting

Understanding brand experiences is very useful for segmentation and targeting. Most segmentation in business is not done from the customer's point of view, but from the perspective of products (for example, by segmenting by features, price or distribution channel). Similarly, companies often believe that their targeting decisions are sound as long as their analysts have engaged in massive data mining to search for structures in geographically and demographically prepared data sets. Given their huge computing power and data mining capabilities, this temptation is strong. However, adequate segmentation and targeting decisions should be supplemented by customer insight—by understanding the experiential world of customers and segmentation, based on the their current or desired experience with a brand.

Positioning

Another key strategic issue faced by companies is how they should position their corporate and individual product brands in a competitive market. To achieve this, many organizations perform brand-architecture analyses and design commission perceptual maps, which are based on similar data and analyzed using multi-dimensional scaling techniques. The maps are usually based on verbal input and frequently do not represent customers' daily experiences. Dimensions are often generic (for example, "high price—low price," "high quality—low quality," or" strong image—weak image"). Even when labeling is a bit more specific (for instance, "fresh—processed" for a food product, or "more durable—faster setting" for an industrial adhesive), we often lack an understanding of what exactly these terms mean to a customer, what is their value, and how they are supposed to affect packaging, advertising, service, and innovations. The alternative from the perspective of experience is the introduction of a customer-relevant new concept or dimension. Moreover, a creative and innovative implementation theme can be used to execute the new positioning. Both the concept and the theme can be developed, based on customer insight, and relate to the experience platform discussed earlier.

Service Management

Providing high quality service is on every company's priority list. However, much of service management is not experience-focused and therefore can harm the brand experience. Moreover, service management is based on prior assumptions made about customers' preferences about service and universal service procedures, for example, customers want to be treated in an intimate and personalized manner, or they prefer self-service. As a result, most service systems are either personnel- or technology-intensive, but not customer-focused. As mentioned earlier, to create a desirable brand experience through service, people and technologies need to be brought together to deliver outstanding, memorable and unique service experiences.

Innovation Management

Innovation is often viewed narrowly as residing in the R&D department and being focused on technical innovation. From a brand experience perspective, however, technical innovation in product features is only part of the story; there is also brand and marketing innovation, especially when a brand is experienced in new ways. One needs to remember that customers value innovation, but not just features-and-benefits-oriented technical innovation. Minor improvements in product design can be a major brand experience innovation. A brand extension that changes the product form slightly can be a breakthrough innovation if it makes a customers' lives easier. Even innovation in communications can be viewed as an innovation. Consider Dove's "Campaign for Real Beauty," which transformed aspirational communications into inspirational messages. Managers often overlook such innovation opportunities because they are not focused on the brand experience. Therefore, many issues that are framed as innovation-related challenges relate, in fact, to the better understanding of the brand experience.

CONCLUSION

With marketing practitioners in developed and emerging markets focusing on the brand experience, there is an increasing need for them to lay emphasis on concepts and frameworks as well as the overall approach to experiences (elaborated on in this chapter).

Brand experience management is a unified way of thinking and offers a comprehensive framework for addressing the research-, strategy-, and implementation-related issues of a brand.

Moreover, brand experience management is both *analytical and creative* in its use of novel concepts, unique tools and unusual research techniques for creating customer insights. Finally, brand experience management is focused *both externally and internally*. While the foremost concern is clearly the external, that is, the customer experience, brand experience management also relates to the internal customer, that is, the employee, and his/her experience with a brand. There is a simple reason for this concern. How employees feel and experience a brand and various company initiatives is critical for it to deliver the right brand experience to its customers.

REFERENCES

Aaker, David (1996), *Building Strong Brands*. New York: The Free Press.
Aaker, Jennifer L. (1997), "Dimension of Brand Personality," *Journal of Marketing Research*, 34(3), 347–356.
Arnold, Mark J., Kristy E. Reynolds, Nicole Ponder, and Jason E. Lueg (2005), "Customer Delight in a Retail Context: Investigating Delightful and Terrible Shopping Experiences," *Journal of Business Research*, 58(8), 1132–1145.
Arnold, Mark and George L. Zinkhan (2002), *Consumers* (2nd ed.). New York: McGraw-Hill/Irvin.
Bettman, James (1979), *An Information Processing Theory of Choice*, Addison-Wesley.
Bloch, Peter H., Frédéric F. Brunel, and Todd J. Arnold (2003), "Individual Differences in the Centrality of Visual Product Aesthetics: Concept and Measurement," *Journal of Consumer Research*, 29 (March), 551–565.
Brakus, J. Joško, Bernd H. Schmitt, and Lia Zarantonello (2009), "Brand Experience: What Is It? How Do We Measure It? And Does It Affect Loyalty?" *Journal of Marketing*, 73(3), 52–68.

Boulding, William, Ajav Kalra, Richard Staelin and Valarie Zeithaml (1993), "A Dynamic Process Model of Service Quality: From Expectations to Behavioral Intentions," *Journal of Marketing Research*, 30(1), 7–27.

Brakus, J. Joško, Bernd H. Schmitt, and Shi Zhang (2008), "Experiential Attributes and Consumer Judgments." In Bernd H. Schmitt and David Rogers (Eds), *Handbook on Brand and Experience Management*. Northampton, MA: Edward Elgar.

Brakus, J.J., Schmitt, B. and Zarantonello, L. (2009). "Brand Experience: What Is It? How Is It Measured? Does It Affect Loyalty?" *Journal of Marketing*, 73(3), 52–68.

Cacioppo, John T. and Richard E. Petty (1982), "The Need for Cognition," *Journal of Personality and Social Psychology*, 42(1), 116–31.

Carroll, Barbara A. and Aaron Ahuvia (2006), "Some Antecedents and Outcomes of Brand Love," *Marketing Letters*, 17(2), 79–89.

Celsi, Richard L., Randall L. Rose, and Thomas Leigh (1993), "An Exploration of High-Risk Leisure Consumption through Skydiving," *Journal of Consumer Research*, 20(June), 1–23.

Chattopadhyay, Amitava and Jean-Louis Laborie (2005), "Managing Brand Experience: the Market Contact Audit™," *Journal of Advertising Research*, 45(1), 9–16.

Close, Angeline G., R. Zachary Finney, Russell Z. Lacey, and Julie Z. Sneath (2006), "Engaging the Consumer through Event Marketing: Linking Attendees with the Sponsor, Community, and Brand," *Journal of Advertising Research*, 46(4), 420–433.

Delgado-Ballester, Elena, Jose L. Munuera-Alemán, and María J. Yagüe-Guillén (2003), "Development and Validation of a Brand Trust Scale," *International Journal of Market Research*, 45(1), 35–53.

Dewey, John (1922), *Human Nature and Conduct*, New York: The Modern Library,

——— (1925), *Experience and Nature* (revised edition). New York: Dover.

Dubé, Laurette and Jordan L. LeBel (2003), "The Content and Structure of Laypeople's Concept of Pleasure," *Cognition and Emotion*, 17(2), 263–295.

Elliott, Staurt (19970, "Clinique Is Introducing Scent in Bid for Share of Premium Market," *The New York Times*, September 30, Section D, p. 6.

Fodor, Jerry (1998), *In Critical Condition: Polemic Essays on Cognitive Science and the Philosophy of Mind*, Cambridge, MA: Bradford Books, MIT Press.

Grace, Debra and Aron O'Cass (2004), "Examining Service Experiences and Post-Consumption Evaluations," *Journal of Services Marketing*, 18(6), 450–461.

Heska, Linda (2009). *Enhancing the Employee Experience*. Germany: VDM Verlag.

Hoch, Stephen J. (2002), "Product Experience Is Seductive," *Journal of Consumer Research*, 29(December), 448–454.

Holbrook, Morris B. (2000), "The Millennial Consumer in the Texts of Our Times: Experience and Entertainment," *Journal of Macromarketing*, 20(2), 178–192.

Elizabeth C. Hirschman (1982), "The Experiential Aspects of Consumption: Consumer Fantasies, Feelings, and Fun," *Journal of Consumer Research*, 9(September), 132–140.

Holt, Douglas B. (1995), "How Consumers Consume: A Typology of Consumption Practices," *Journal of Consumer Research*, 22(June), 1–16.

Hui, Michael K. and John E. G. Bateson (1991), "Perceived Control and the Effects of Crowding and Consumer Choice on the Service Experience," *Journal of Consumer Research*, 18(September), 174–184.
Izard, Carroll E. (1978), *Human Emotions* (2nd ed.). New York: Plenum.
Jones, Monique A. (1999), "Entertaining Shopping Experiences: An Exploratory Investigation," *Journal of Retailing and Consumer Services*, 6(3), 129–139.
Joy, Annamma and John F. Sherry Jr. (2003), "Speaking of Art as Embodied Imagination: A Multisensory Approach to Understanding Aesthetic Experience," *Journal of Consumer Research*, 20(September), 259–282.
Keller, Kevin (1993), "Conceptualizing, Measuring, and Managing Customer-based Brand Equity," *Journal of Marketing*, 57(1), 1–22.
Keller, Kevin Lane (2003), *Strategic Brand Management: Building, Measuring, and Managing Brand Equity* (2nd ed.). Upper Saddle River, NJ: Pearson Education.
Kempf, Deanna S. and Robert E. Smith (1998), "Consumer Processing of Product Trial and the Influence of Prior Advertising: A Structural Modeling Approach," *Journal of Marketing Research*, 35(3), 325–338.
Kerin, Roger A., Ambuj Jain, and Daniel J. Howard (1992), "Store Shopping Experience and Consumer Price-Quality-Value Perceptions," *Journal of Retailing*, 68(4), 376–397.
Lakoff, George and Mark Johnson (1999), *Philosophy in the Flesh: The Embodied Mind and Its Challenge to Western Thought*. New York: Basic Books.
McAlexander, James H., John W. Schouten, and Harold F. Koenig (2002), "Building Brand Community." *Journal of Marketing*, 66 (1), 38–54.
Muniz, Albert M. Jr. and Thomas C. O'Guinn (2001), "Brand Community," *Journal of Consumer Research*, 27(March), 412–432.
Ofir, Chezy and Itamar Simonson (2007), "The Effect of Stating Expectations on Consumer Satisfaction and Shopping Experience." *Journal of Marketing Research*, 44(1), 164–174.
Olson, Peter (2005), *Consumer Behavior and Marketing Strategy*. Chicago: McGraw-Hill.
Pine, Joseph B. II and James H. Gilmore (1999), *The Experience Economy: Work Is Theatre and Every Business a Stage*. Cambridge, MA: Harvard Business School Press.
Pinker, Steven (1997), *How The Mind Works*. New York: Norton.
Raffelt, Ursula, Bernd Schmitt, and Anton Meyer (2013), Marketing Function and Form: How Functionalist and Experiential Architectures Affect Corporate Brand Personality, *International Journal of Research in Marketing (IJRM)*, 30(3), 201–210.
Ries, Al and Laura Ries (2004), *The Fall of Advertising and the Rise of PR*. New York: Harper Collins Publishing.
Russ, Sandra (1998), *Affect, Creative Experience and Psychological Adjustment*, Philadelphia: Routledge.
Rust, Roland T. and Richard W. Oliver (1994), "The Death of Advertising," *Journal of Advertising*, 23(4), 72–77.
Rust, Roland T., Valerie A. Zeithaml and Katherine N. Lemon (2000), *Driving Customer Equity: How Customer Lifetime Value is Reshaping Corporate Strategy*. New York: The Free Press.

Schmitt, Bernd H. (1999), *Experiential Marketing: How to Get Customers to Sense, Feel, Think, Act, Relate to Your Company and Brands*. New York: The Free Press.
—— (2003), *Customer Experience Management*. New York: Wiley.
—— 2012), "The Consumer Psychology of Brands." *Journal of Consumer Psychology*, 22, 7–17.
—— (2013), "The Consumer Psychology of Customer-Brand Relationships: Extending the AA Relationships Model." *Journal of Consumer Psychology.* 23(2), 249–252.
Schmitt, Bernd H. and Alex Simonson (1997), *Marketing Aesthetics: The Strategic Management of Brands*. New York: The Free Press.
Schmitt, Bernd (2011). *Experience Marketing: Concepts, Frameworks and Consumer Insights*. Now Publishers Inc.
Shaw, Colin and John Ivens (2002), *Building Great Customer Experiences*. New York: Palgrave Macmillan.
Smith, Shaun and Joe Wheeler (2002), *Managing the Customer Experience: Turning Customers into Advocates*. Upper Saddle River, NJ: Financial Times Prentice Hall.
Sprott, David, Sandor Czellar, and Eric Spangenberg (2009), "The Importance of a General Measure of Brand Engagement on Market Behavior: Development and Validation of a Scale." *Journal of Marketing Research*, 46(1), 92–104.
Thomson, Matthew, Deborah J. MacInnis, and C. Whan Park (2005), "The Ties That Bind: Measuring the Strength of Consumers' Emotional Attachments to Brands." *Journal of Consumer Psychology*, 15(1), 77–91.
Zarantonello L., K. Jedidi, and B. H. Schmitt (2013), "Functional and Experiential Routes to Persuasion: An Analysis of Advertising in Emerging vs. Developed Markets." *International Journal of Research in Marketing—Special Issue on Marketing in Emerging Markets*, 30(1), 46–56.
Zarantonello, L. and B. H. Schmitt (2013), The Impact of Event Marketing on Brand Equity: The Mediating Roles of Brand Experience and Brand Attitude, *International Journal of Advertising*, 32(2), 255–280.
Zarantonello, L. and B. Schmitt (2010), Using the brand experience scale to profile consumers and predict consumer behavior, *Journal of Brand Management*, 17(7), 532–540.

Chapter 8

Rethinking Brand Development in an Interactive Marketplace

Don E. Schultz

INTRODUCTION

New evidence, developed at Northwestern University, has raised some concerns about the ongoing viability of the brand development and management process using currently available brand management tools. We question whether the methods and approaches brand managers have used for the past 50 or more years to build hugely successful brands are still relevant in today's digitally driven, increasingly decentralized, and highly interactive marketplace. This is a new marketplace in which customers and consumers are increasingly gaining knowledge about brands, how they work, the benefits they are supposed to provide them, and so on, that is, the entire repertoire of brand value in nontraditional ways. Therefore, we question whether existing tools are as relevant as they were in the "golden age" of branding, which seems to have taken place in the latter half of the 20th century.

RESEARCH FOR THIS CHAPTER

In 2011, using US respondent responses to a large-scale, longitudinal, ongoing online data set, developed by Prosper International[1],

---
[1] www.goprosper.com

a Net Promoter Score-type measurement system was developed to determine the importance of brand preferences. It was believed brand preferences would lead to the creation of strong brand connections (Schultz and Block, 2011) and therefore value to brand managers.

Starting with "Retail Store Brand" preference and using consumer-reported "Brand Preference" scores, it was possible to identify consumers who had a stronger preference for the "Store" than the "Manufacturer" brand, along with those who had "No Brand Preference (NBP)" in the category. Store and Brand scores were then compared. It was found that NBP for Manufacturer Brands in almost every category was much higher than for Retail Store brands. This was interpreted to mean that stores were more important than manufacturer brands in most consumers' decisions. We then further analyzed two product categories: ready-to-eat cereals and savory snacks (Schultz and Block, 2012). What was most interesting was that consumers' reported NBP in the breakfast cereals category was approximately 30%, outdistancing the preference for the leading category brand Cheerios at 12.7%. There was a similar finding in the savory snacks category, where the NBP was 36.7%, outstripping the leading brand, Lay's, which generated only 15.8% preference. This was a disturbing finding, given brand managers' reliance on the basic concept of building and maintaining brand preference in the marketplace to generate continuing sales.

The research framework was expanded substantially based on reception by the academy of the initial study. Using the same research methodology, but a greatly expanded data set (of over 1 million online consumer responses gathered over a 10-year period in the USA), it was found that brand preference was declining in almost all of the more than 1,500 brands of consumer package goods used in the study. A summary of the findings is given in Table 8.1.

As already shown, these findings raise the issue of a continuing decline in consumers' preferences for both store and manufacturer brands over time. This challenges acceptance and adherence of brand managers to one of the cornerstones of most branding methodologies, that is, consumer brand preference. If brand preference for consumer package goods of brands is declining, (and this seems to have been the case) over the past decade then today's brand managers' belief that brand preference is a pre-cursor to and generally leads to brand purchases seems flawed. If this is true, then many,

Table 8.1 Market Performance of Stores and Products

	Stores*	Products**
Share Leading Brand	26.52	15.89
AGR Leading Brand	0.54	−1.68
Share No Preference	25.66	50.22
AGR No Preference	1.21	1.38
Competitive Index	0.097	0.061
Net Promoter Score	19.48	−9.07

*Preferred store where product purchased
**73 product categories averaged over 10 years

Source: Schultz and Block, 2013.

if not most, brand management concepts need to be re-examined. Simply put, if consumer brand preference is declining significantly, being replaced by NBP, many consumer package good brands are likely will face major challenges going forward (Schultz and Block, 2013).

More importantly, if consumer brand preference has been declining for some time, as data seems to indicate, a logical conclusion would be that the brands and branding tools used over the past decade and currently in use are either no longer effective or their use is not appropriate. Whatever the case, the current brand management toolbox does not seem to fit today's brand management needs and certainly not tomorrow's.

A summary of the Schultz and Block extended study is shown in Table 8.2.

Seventy three consumer product categories were analyzed in the extended study. These are summarized in Table 8.2 and aggregated into quintiles, that is, 20 brands per group. The calculation shown is for the top brands, that is, the Leading Brand Share is a summary of all the product categories. (Actually, the brand listed at the top is the brand with the greatest preference in that product category as rated by consumers' responses). The next column is the average growth or decline rate (AGR) during the 10-year study on the brands in this category. The next column is the consumers' stated brand preference for the Store Brand (i.e., preference by reporting consumers for the store where the brand was purchased). This is followed by the AGR (growth or decline over the 10-year study period).

Table 8.2 Top Leading Brand Categories Characteristics

Category	Leading Brand	Number of Brands	Comp. Index	NPS	Monthly Freq.
Bleach	Clorox	10	0.215	2.03	0.74
Glass Cleaners	Windex	12	0.230	2.70	0.49
Razors	Gillette	7	0.140	−13.88	0.48
Aluminum Foils	Reynolds	15	0.150	−5.50	0.70
Facial Tissue	Kleenex	12	0.120	−5.46	0.70
Dish Detergents	Dawn	17	0.122	4.01	0.83
Toothpaste	Crest	17	0.143	10.09	0.59
Baby Shampoo	Johnson & Johnson	14	0.123	22.17	0.56
Insect Repellent	OFF!	10	0.083	−27.49	
Tooth Brushes	Oral B	12	0.091	−0.46	0.51
Sports Drink	Gatorade	7	0.054	−33.35	0.92
Laundry Detergent	Tide	24	0.104	15.76	1.04
Food Storage Bags	Ziploc	8	0.103	−13.75	0.79
Toilet Tissue	Charmin	14	0.077	12.68	0.77

Source: Schultz and Block, 2013.

The next column features consumers' NBP in the category, followed by the AGR for NBP. The findings clearly indicate that manufacturer brand preference is declining, store brand preference is essentially flat and consumers' NBP has grown considerably during the study period. Therefore, the claim made that consumer package goods brands in the USA face a bleak future unless substantial changes are made seems substantiated.

There are a number of factors that may explain the dramatic decline in consumers' preference for fast-moving consumer goods (FMCG) manufacturer brands. These range from the US economic decline, which began in 2008, to changes in consumers' reported media consumption and a reported increase in their use of digital and social media, all of which occurred during this time period. The primary factor that seems to explain the decline in manufacturer brand preference, i.e., it has a strong correlation with NBP growth (in the order of .8 to .9), was consumers' reported use of digital and social media. While this data did not enable the calculations of causality, the changes in increased consumer NBP and the amount of time devoted to the use of digital and social media was extremely high. Therefore, we believe the decline in consumers' use of mass media, a format which generally generates widespread consumer knowledge about a brand, and the switch to digital and social media, which fragments and separates the market and marketplace, may have been a major factor. The research report and suppositions flowing out of the findings have raised some interesting questions about brand management in the age of interactivity.

To further explain the findings, additional research was undertaken. The authors of this research contacted two other research organizations that had conducted similar forms of consumer brand research and have longitudinal data covering the initial study period in the USA—BAV Consulting[2] and Brand Keys[3]. Both agreed to cooperate in an additional study that would combine the three sets of data. BAV has developed and maintains a global data-set of more than 40,000 consumer responses per year relating to brands and branding. The data covers more than 20 previous years.[4] Brand Keys, through its Consumer Engagement Studies Index[5], has captured more than 30,000 consumer responses each year over the past 13 years as the base for its study.

To confirm the findings of initial brand study, data was combined and analyzed from the three sources. To make the comparison viable, the data-set was limited to three product categories and a triangulation study was conducted. The three product categories studied included cosmetics, over-the-counter allergy medications, and ready-to-eat cereals. When viewed over the same 10-year period, all showed a similar decline in consumer brand preference, that is, there was growing consumer choice of NBP in the category. Thus, the initial Schultz and Block (2011) study findings were confirmed. The time-line comparisons of the findings is best understood through a set of graphics developed from the BAV dataset.[6]

[2] www.bavconsulting.com
[3] www.brandkeys.com
[4] BAV.com, 2013.
[5] Brandkeys.com, 2013.
[6] To confirm the findings of their initial study, Schultz and Block added a third associate, Viswanathan, who helped to combine and analyze data from the three studies.

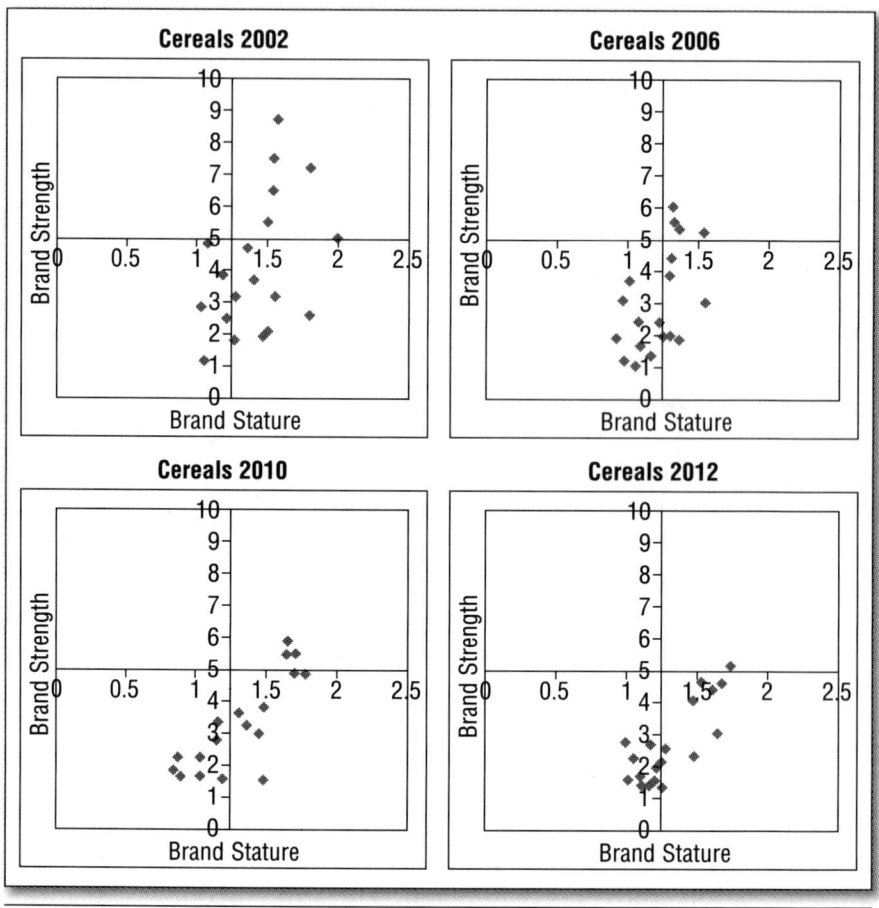

Source: Schultz, Block, and Viswanathan, 2014.

Figure 8.1 Positioning Map for Cereal Brands Using BAV Measures of Brand Stature and Brand Strength

Figure 8.1 illustrates the brand plots on the two axes of Brand Strength and Brand Stature, BAV's key preference and consideration measures. The plots of the initial data for the ready-to-eat cereals category are for the measurement periods 2002, 2006, 2010, and 2012. Figure 8.2 provides the same information on the cosmetics category and Figure 8.3 on allergy medications.

Without going into great detail about each of these category studies, it is clear from the graphics that brands in each of these categories are declining in consumer-perceived brand differentiation,

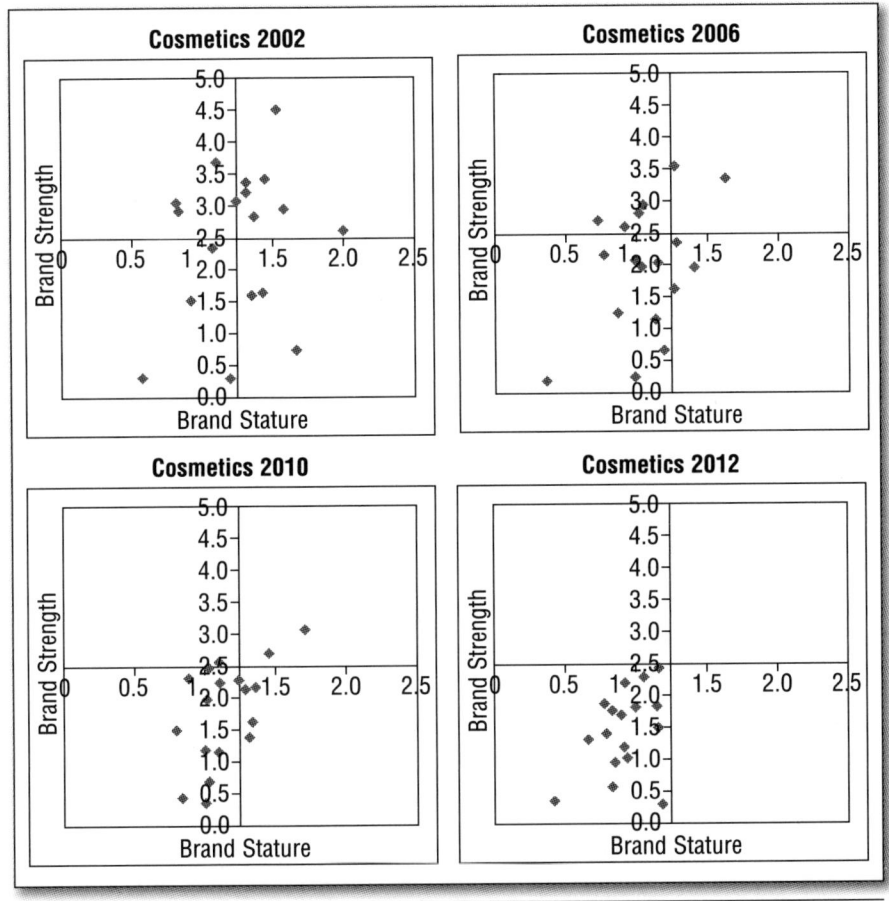

Source: Schultz, Block, and Viswanathan, 2014.

Figure 8.2 Positioning Map for Cosmetics Brands Using BAV Measures of Brand Stature and Brand Strength

thus partially explaining the rise in NBP. Whereas in 2002, individual brands were fairly well separated into the four BAV quadrants in all three product examples. By 2012, most of these had migrated to the lower lef t-hand quadrant of the plot. This clearly indicates that consumers see less and less differentiation between the individual brands in all three of these categories, which implies increased similarity and commoditization. Since the primary purpose of a brand is to differentiate itself from its competitors, clearly this has not been happening during the decade over which this study was

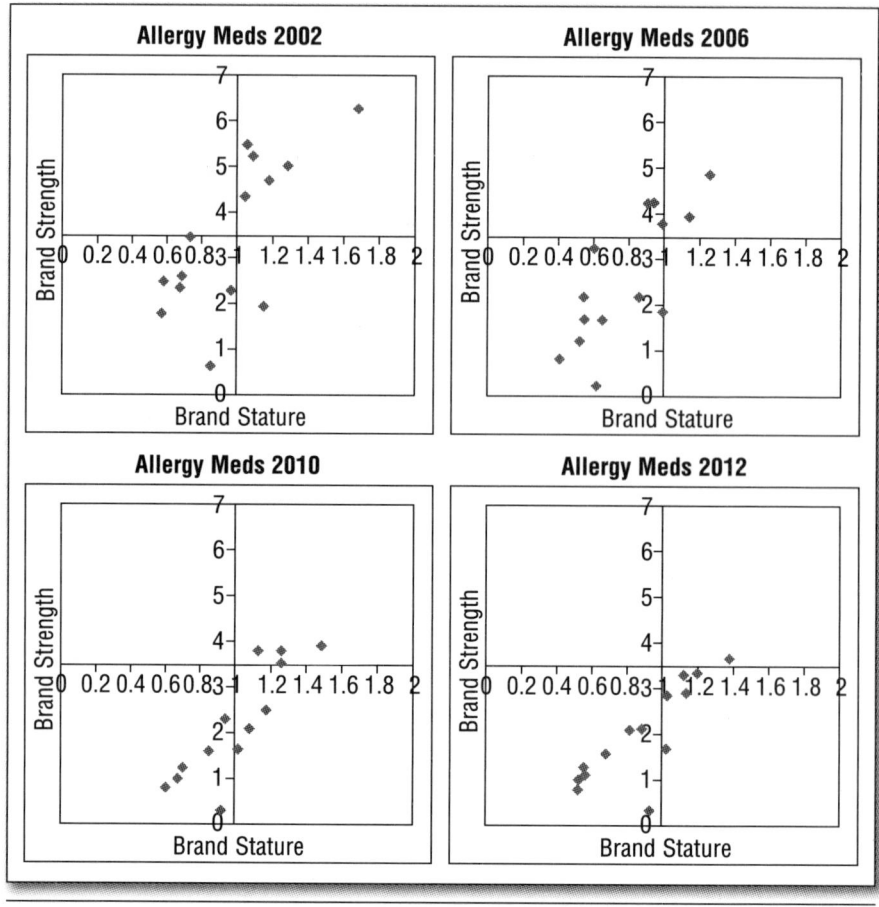

Source: Schultz, Block, and Viswanathan, 2014.

Figure 8.3 Positioning Map for OTC Allergy Brands Using BAV Measures of Brand Stature and Brand Strength

constructed. This is not to say that brand sales, share or even distribution declined. Instead, it means that consumers see less and less difference between the brands in the categories in which they compete. Thus, if the brands are perceived to be the same, declining consumer brand preference is the natural and likely ongoing result. It is this type of consumer response to questions about their brand preference that leads to the belief that current brand management techniques and approaches are no longer working in the marketplace, at least in the USA. Therefore, it is our belief that a new set of brand-building and management tools are needed now and in the future. The next section suggests a new brand research agenda that may help to uncover some new approaches.

RESEARCH AGENDA FOR REINVENTING BRAND MANAGEMENT IN AN INTERACTIVE MARKETPLACE

There are a multitude of reasons why brand management needs to be re-thought in today's interactive marketplace. In a recent article (Schultz, Malthouse, and Pick, 2012), a major new approach and system, built on what is known as a "CN^2" (customer networked and negotiated approach) methodology, was presented. The view was that the current (and future) marketplace has become a set of interlocking and interacting networks, all of which put more power in the hands of the buyer and reduce the marketer's traditional control of a brand and branding system. This shift in the control of the marketplace makes it possible for buyers to better negotiate with sellers, further shifting the emphasis away from ongoing brand loyalty to instantly negotiated agreements between various parties. Thus, while brands may still provide recognition and acceptance value for the seller, the ability to generate premium prices in the marketplace is likely to become increasingly difficult. Consequently, going forward, brands will need to adopt new and different approaches to succeed in this "shared value" marketplace. In this CN^2 situation, the marketer is essentially cast as a "responder to" not a "leader of" sales and marketing activities, and while the CN^2 marketplace is still developing, this clearly illustrates the impact of the shift of power that is currently taking place in it and the impact this is having on brands and branding.

There are also a number of other factors that will require attention. Each makes an impact on how brands are developed, managed and maintained, going forward. Some of these factors include globalization of various marketplaces and the growth of local and regional brands (Kapferer, 2012), the rise in consumers' access to information available through mobile and online data-sets that provide instantaneous access to the unlimited amounts of marketplace information now available through search engines, and so on (Labrecque et al., 2013), the increased amount of consumer/ customer data-sharing brought about by social media (Larson and Watson, 2011), the growth in the use of brand consortia and their data and experiencing capability (Kapferer, 2012), and the development of new media forms that bring instant fame to products and services that traditionally required months or even years to build and establish (Scott, 2013). All these factors and others are contributing to what we believe today is a malaise in brand thinking and management. The problem this creates that brand managers seemingly continue to rely on what they know and have done in the past, and they generally do not venture into new and what may well prove to be rewarding areas. Simply because these areas are as yet uncharted. That creates major challenges for the development of new brand and branding approaches.

In this section, we suggest six new areas of brand research that need to be developed to either match up with or replace some of the traditional concepts that may have served their time. The following recommendations are listed in no specific order, since all are considered vital to the growth and future of the entire concept of brands and branding.

A shift to behavioral data: In the past, most brand thinking and management were based on the belief that brands existed primarily in the mind of the customer or buyer. Therefore, using various psychological approaches, brands were studied from the view of the consumer or customer to uncover what was felt to be the decisions that were occurring in the human brain. Many of these concepts relied on research, based on small sets of gathered data, commonly using college students as the research sample which were then projected to larger populations. Therefore, most brand thinking and management continued to try to unlock the "black box" of human decision-making through an understanding of the attitudes, feelings, intents, and so on, that consumers use to manage their views of brands and branding. Thus, traditional brand research focused on how consumers capture, store away and use brand information they receive from various sources. This resulted in a codified system of consumer analysis and projection to others (Kapferer, 2012). Today, massive amounts of behavioral data are available almost instantly to a brand manager through search engines that are capable of accessing various data-sets. Much of this data is based, not on what consumers indicate they will or may do, but on behavioral data that provides real-world and real-time information on what customers and consumers actually did, have done, or are currently doing. Consequently, we emphasize that the focus on brand research should be more on understanding why customers and consumers did what they did, rather than on trying to estimate or guess what they might do in the future. Customers being creatures of habit, it is often more useful to gather details of their observable behavior and then try to explain those rather than trying to predict what they might do in the future, based on what they say. This does not, however, mean that traditional attitudinal data has no value. But, it does indicate that attitudinal and qualitative data should be used quite differently in the future, primarily to explain, not predict consumers' future behaviors.

Longitudinal analysis: Far too much current brand research and analysis is and has been based on one-time, non-replicated, and experimental research. Thus, the brand manager has snapshots of points in time of what is or might be happening to a brand rather than a longitudinal view of what is or has happened over time. While some of this longitudinal data is available in the form of ongoing consumer user panels, even this type of data is limited in its view. The increasing availability of big data shows that there are now large samples of multiple consumer/customers' responses which will only increase over time. However, nothing can substitute for the observation of consumers' behavior under different conditions based on varying sets of events and conditions. These are what are needed to explain why such behavior occurred. The development of new analytical capabilities should make this type of research increasingly viable and cost-effective.

Today, the major challenges are the lack of tools and techniques available to the brand manager and the shortage of suitable analytic people talent, which will hopefully be resolved at some point. This new type of data will also require retraining of brand managers. This will require a major commitment of time and energy by both the brand manager and the brand owner. However, in spite of these challenges, we believe that longitudinal data is the only viable method to truly understand how consumers and brands act, interact and relate to each other over time in the marketplace.

Networked systems: Clearly, we live in a networked world—everything is or can be easily connected to almost everything else. In our attempt to understand this world in which we live, much research has sought to identify or develop direct connections between various elements that have been done through linear connections, i.e., A leading to B, which leads to C, and so on. These approaches fit the linear statistical tools that have been available to researchers. From there, they have built models or drawn conclusions about how things or elements are different or alike. We are learning that most consumer-brand interactions are not linear, but multidimensional (see Recommendation D), that means that they are generally non-linear. Part of this reductionist approach to brands and branding, i.e., reducing our concepts or factors to two dimensions so they can be explained in a textbook or illustrated in a PowerPoint slide, has obscured the rich diversity and relationships among factors, which is what brands are all about. Consequently, in an attempt to create easily understandable direct connections, and hopefully, at some point, causality, we have lost sight of the real meaning of a brand for a consumer—the connection between a buyer and a seller, intermediaries and recommenders, market mavens, brand followers, along with history and experience, and a host of other individuals factors that encourage or discourage consumers to buy, use a brand, or recommend it to others. Unilateral western models have also often limited our capacity to think and manage brands in networked systems. They appear to have often limited or discouraged development of the richness that really make up most brands. For example, McDonalds is clearly more than hamburgers, the Golden Arches and Ronald McDonald. It is a rich mixture of food, fun, fantasy, and a host of other factors, all of which are connected and interact with each other over and over again to create brand value for both the consumer/customer and the company.

One of the major challenges facing brand marketers today is that much of our current brand thinking has been developed and evolved in western cultures, that means they focus primarily on the brand relationships of individual consumers and pay scant attention to those of the communal society. However, individualistic societies make up only about 20% of the world's population (Castells, 2011). The balance of societies is communal, which generally means that there are networks within networks within even more networks—all the connections that make societies and cultures possible. In communal societies, networks of friends, family, the tribe, and other groups constitute much of consumer and customer brand decision-making. Therefore, to understand and succeed in an increasingly global market, where cultures and societies dominate, brand managers need to throw off linear and one-way systems that have bound brand thinking for the past century. It is critical for brands and brand managers to engage and embrace the networked world in which we all live. However, networks are not the common language of marketing, communication, or even branding. Therefore, new models and approaches are needed.

Multi-dimensional models: Similar to and perhaps a part of the preceding discussion on networks and networked brand information is that of viewing brands and branding as multi-dimensional factors, models, and systems that are dynamic and ever-changing. We do not live in a two-, three-, or even four-dimensional world. As many oriental cultures believe, "everything is somehow connected to everything else" and that creates multi-level factors that we are only now beginning to understand. Brands, like the world around us, are multi-dimensional, that is, they have depth and breadth, length, scope and density, and so on. And, they change and evolve continuously. What the brand is today or was yesterday is less important than what it might be tomorrow or the next day. Therefore, we need new views of how consumers use and rely on brands to live their lives. Clearly, there are brands that have explored their meanings and connections to consumers, the marketplace and global systems in great depth and scope. Brands such as Legos, Nike, and some others immediately come to mind. Too often, brands are seen as just a bunch of pieces and parts that can be gathered up and pasted on a brand information sheet because that's the way brand experts discuss and manage them. Brand managers need to think beyond only what a brand represents to a customer today. They need to think of tomorrow and beyond. What role does a brand play in society, in the countries in which it is available, and among various levels of customers and advocates that keep it viable? We need to explore brands and branding as a social as well as a commercial venture—how they contribute value not just to customers but to employees, stakeholders, the financial community, the environment, and a host of other ancillary factors that are too often ignored in today's fast-paced marketplace. Indeed, a case could be made that brand managers need to be as much social managers as business managers, going forward. However, all of this will require new and more innovative approaches than have been used in the past. Clearly, we need to cross interdisciplinary lines in the commercial and academic fields to fully understand the scope and value of a brand. This is not an easy task in a world of specialization, but if we are to truly manage brands, these connections are vital.

Financial focus: Having made a case for a broader view of brand, longitudinally, multi-dimensionally and socially, the brand manager cannot forget that the brand is and must serve as a basic resource and income producer, and create financial value for the brand-owner. The numerous brand-valuation estimates developed by external consultants and analysts continue to demonstrate the increasing value of brands to brand-owning organizations. More than 500 US-based brands now have a financial value of more than US$1 billion today.[7] Having said that, there are some new views, approaches, and methodologies that are clearly needed to manage brands. As an intangible asset, a brand or brands often get scant attention from the senior management of a company or its board of directors, all of whom are too often focused on managing the organization's tangible assets. New forms and methods of illustrating the financial value of a brand need to be developed to demonstrate the ongoing returns brands can bring to the company. Part of the difficulty in accomplishing this is the current focus on attitudinal measures of brand value. While these may be important to a brand's customers and even to the brand manager, most senior managers, lacking training in psychology and consumer behavior, tend to ignore current attitudinal measures used by brand managers. Knowing that "brand awareness increased by 2% over the past six months" has little or no meaning or value to senior managers when brand expenditures are being considered. The inability to connect attitudinal brand measurement systems to financial ones is and has been a major gap in effectively managing a brand at a senior level. One way of solving this problem is by finding ways to combine attitudinal and behavioral data (as mentioned earlier). That can lead to senior managers considering customers as creators of income flows for the brand

---

[7] Brandfinance.com, 2014.

rather than simply as short-term expenses for the company. Thus, investments and returns are based on a much sounder footing when ways are developed that combine attitudinal and behavioral data to illustrate that a group of customers actually constitutes an income flow back to the organization. This issue partly arises due to the inability of the brand manager to separate short-term (usually during the company's fiscal year) returns from a brand to long-term returns (three to five years) on that same brand. That would give managers a more relevant view of the value of the brand to the company. As noted earlier, for some time, Kapferer has been stressing that organizational brand value is the key element in the management of a brand by an organization. Our increasing knowledge and understanding of such concepts as "customer lifetime value (Rust et al., 2001)" can help along with this or other approaches. Extensions, expansions and adaptations of Kapferer's (Kapferer, 2012) concepts, along with those of Steenkamp (1997), may provide a more relevant view of the brand as an organization's income-driver, both nationally and globally, and illustrate the actual income-producing potential that brands have for their organizations.

Connections to and inclusion of other organizations in brand and branding development: Over the years, too much of our brand and branding research has focused on management and application of brand concepts to consumer package goods (CPG) or FMCG brands to the detriment of other brand-owners such as retailers, not-for-profit players, services, business-to-business, and so on. And because CPG brands have focused so heavily on media advertising or other forms of highly visible consumer-focused activities to build acceptance and volume returns in the marketplace, in many instances, other brand-owners or managers have assumed that branding is largely about advertising and promotion. This has meant that large budgets and heavy spending were required to build or maintain a brand. Consequently, as new media forms developed, many brand managers assumed that substantial spending was or would be required in these areas as well to either maintain or grow brands. This seems to be particularly true when it comes to major national or international events such as the Olympics, the Super Bowl, the World Cup, and so on. Yet, the marketplace is full of successful brands that have been developed with limited budgets, with Red Bull being a prime example (Rasmussen, 2009). From a strictly national brand, the organization has grown to be a global powerhouse. Today's most common brands, including Amazon, Nike, Facebook, Twitter, and so on, where brands seek global attention have grown in different ways, many by providing matchless customer service and through users' recommendations rather than by major media brand- promotion activities. Yet, the "big brand spenders" seem get the bulk of media attention. This results in too many organizations believing that branding is simply an advertising game that is beyond their means. However, not all brands operate, perform, or have the volume or financial requirements of Coca-Cola, Budweiser, or Kentucky Fried Chicken. More effort is needed to understand how brands can be built and maintained using new forms of communication such as the internet, digital and social media, and so on. Unfortunately, all the hype on social media does not seem to help brand-building, as is evident in the research previously cited in this chapter. In addition, there should be a particular focus on how retailers, online marketers and their intermediaries can build and maintain brands. Moreover, it must be borne in mind that not every brand developed will be a global one. Consequently, additional research is needed on how local and regional brands can be developed and maintained. If, as most of us believe, brands are the future of all marketing activities, it is vital for brand managers to expand their horizons. This may mean a greater focus on building more personal and individual brands in the future. However, this may seem a major challenge for brands and brand managers. All the ancillary elements that make brands and branding so important today, and what will make them increasingly important in the future will only continue to grow—that's what makes the challenge seem so daunting.

In this section, it has only been possible to skim the surface of brand- and branding-related research and what will be required in the future. The approaches presented, however, seem to be the most relevant, given our current knowledge and understanding. Additional complexities will doubtless develop as we move forward, but unless and until some of the issues described in this section are addressed effectively, it is likely that brand preference will continue to decline and brand managers will continue to use tools that are either no longer relevant or lack the focus and emphasis needed in today's marketplace.

A FINAL NOTE

The references that follow are and can be a rich resource for today's brand manager. Only by knowing the underlying concepts on which today's brand logic has been built can a brand manager understand the elements that are still relevant and those that need to be reconsidered. However, as the old saying goes, "Don't throw out the baby with the bathwater." Brands and branding are (and will continue to be) critical for successful management of all forms of commerce. However, although brands have a rich history and a wealth of useful and helpful concepts some need to be reconsidered in light of the many changes that have occurred in the marketplace over the past decade. It is our belief that a brand manager who is able to make this transition, from yesterday to today, and then look ahead to tomorrow, will be the one who will succeed. Do remember, however, one cannot drive a car by staring at the rear view mirror! We need to open our minds and look to the future—and not just dwell in the past.

REFERENCES

Aaker, David A. (1991), *Managing Brand Equity*. New York: Free Press.

―― (1996), *Building Strong Brands*, New York: Free Press.

Brandfinance.com (2014), http://brandirectory.com/league_tables/table/global-500-2014http://www.brandfinance.com/images/upload/brand_finance_us500_press_release_embargoed_03172014_final.pdf (accessed September 9, 2015).

Brandkeys.com (2013), http://brandkeys.com/syndicated-studies/customer-loyalty-engagement-index/ (accessed September 9, 2015).

Castells, M. (2011), *The Power of Identity: The Information Age: Economy, Society, and Culture*, Vol. 2. West Sussex: John Wiley & Sons.

Kapferer, Jean Noel (1992), *Strategic Brand Management*. London: Kogan Page.

―― (2012), *The New Strategic Brand Management: Advanced Insights and Strategic Thinking*. London: Kogan Page Publishers.

Kumar, V. and W. Reinartz (2012), *Strategic Customer Relationship Management Today*, In *Customer Relationship Management* (pp. 3–20). Berlin Heidelberg: Springer.

Labrecque, L. I., C. Mathwick, T. P. Novak, and C. F. Hofacker (2013), "Consumer Power: Evolution in the Digital Age," *Journal of Interactive Marketing*, 27(4), 257–269.

Larson, K. and R. T. Watson (2011), The Value of Social Media: Toward Measuring Social Media Strategies. In Proceedings of ICIS, Thirty Second International Conference on Information Systems, Shanghai, 2011.

Prosper Business Development (2012), http://www.goprosper.com/ (accessed September 9, 2015).

Rasmussen (2009), http://www.rasmussen.edu/degrees/business/blog/guerrilla-marketing-campaigns/ (accessed September 9, 2015).

Schultz, Don E. and Martin Block (2003), "Moving Marketing Communication Measurement Inside, Special World Marketing Association Edition," *Singapore Nanyang Business Review*, 2(1).

Schultz, Don E. and Martin Block (2011), "Understanding Customer Brand Engagement Behaviors in Today's Interactive Marketplace," *Micro & Macro Marketing*, (2), 227–244.

Schultz, Don E. and Block, M. (2013), "Killing Brands… softly," *Journal of Brand Strategy*, 2(3), 284–299.

Schultz, Don E. and Schultz, Heidi (2004), *Brand Babble: Sense and Nonsense about Branding*. Mason: South-Western /Thompson Learning.

Schultz, D on E., Martin P. Block and Vijay Viswanathan (2014), "Brand Preference being Challenged," *Journal of Brand Management*, advance online publication, March 28, 2014.

Schultz, Don E., E. Malthouse, and Doreen Pick (2012), "From CM to CRM to CN2: A Research Agenda for the Marketing Communications Transition" *Advances in Advertising Research* (Vol. III) European Advertising Academy, 421–432. Mason, Ohio: South-Western.

Scott, W. D. (1903), *The Psychology of Advertising in Theory and Practice*. New York: Kessinger Publishing, LLC.

Scott, D. M. (2013), *The New Rules of Marketing and PR: How to Use Social Media, Online Video, Mobile Applications, Blogs, News Releases, and Viral Marketing to Reach Buyers Directly*. New York: John Wiley & Sons.

Steenkamp, J. B. E. and M. G. Dekimpe (1997), The Increasing Power of Store Brands: Building Loyalty and Market Share," *Long Range Planning*, 30(6), 917–930.

Steenkamp, J. B. E., D. L. Alden, and R. Batra (1999), "Brand Positioning Through Advertising in Asia, North America, and Europe: The Role of Global Consumer Culture," *Journal of Marketing*, 63(1).

Steenkamp, J. B. E., R. Batra, V. Ramaswamy, D. L. Alden, and S. Ramachander (2000), Effects of Brand Local and nonlocal Origin on Consumer Attitudes in Developing Countries," *Journal of Consumer Psychology*, 9(2), 83–95.

Steenkamp, J. B. E. and N. Kumar (2007*)*, *Private Label Strategy: How to Meet the Store Brand Challenge*. USA: Harvard Business Press.

Chapter 9

Luxury Brands

Vanessa M. Patrick and Henrik Hagtvedt

INTRODUCTION: LUXURY AS THE "PROMISE OF PLEASURE"

Luxury branding is a topic of growing importance for marketing practitioners and academics alike. In affluent societies, and increasingly in poor ones, luxury has an allure beyond mere practical necessities. Indeed, some would argue that the luxury industry epitomizes the phrase "marketing is everything" (Beverland, 2004), and in this sense, it should represent a unique area of interest for research in marketing. The global market for luxury products and services is estimated to reach US$100 billion in 2008 (Merrill Lynch/Capgemini, 2005; Unity Marketing, 2006). Notably, this estimate depends entirely on how luxury is defined. For instance, a report from Research and Markets (2006) estimated the total US luxury market to have reached US$1,002.2 billion in 2005, up 11.6% from US$898 billion in 2004. This underscores one of the important prerequisites for effectively managing a luxury brand—that of understanding how luxury is conceptualized and what it represents to consumers.

Traditionally, underlying the consumption of luxury goods was the principle of rarity (Veblen, 1899). It was thought of as a privilege restricted to the wealthy and the powerful, and it was tied to specific activities and product categories. However, along with a broad increase in wealth and sophistication in Western societies, luxury is increasingly being coveted as a source of pleasure to which the average consumer can aspire. This trend is exemplified by a recent ad for Pegasus, a line of bathroom fittings by Home Depot. The as has a headline that says "Luxury is only for the privileged? What gave you that idea?" Silverstein and Fiske (2003) identify a new type of luxury goods for consumers who are responsible for democratizing the luxury market. These middle-market consumers selectively trade-up to "higher levels of quality, taste and aspiration." Indeed, luxury brands have helped the middle-class attain the perception of prosperity (Schwartz, 2002).

At the same time, the concept of luxury is stretching beyond its traditional boundaries. In other words, the range of goods considered as luxury products is expanding. Today, the promise of a good life and the ultimate experience of luxurious living is made to mass market consumers by products in virtually every category. Typical luxury categories such as furs, watches, and jewelry are being replaced by luxury home appliances, fine dining, bath soap, and travel. Indeed, according to Danziger (2005), old luxury was defined by product category while new luxury is independent of product category, but is all about the experience. Consequently, the "luxury fever" (Frank, 1999) that has purportedly swept the nation does not pertain to the pursuit of furs, diamonds, and cars, but of traditionally functional products such as grills, washing machines, and lawn-mowers.

The broad relevance of luxury branding is becoming increasingly evident with the emergence of the "new luxury" phenomenon. However, while there are some notable exceptions (for example, Park Milberg and Lawson, 1991; Vigneron and Johnson, 2004), the concept of luxury, marketing of luxury brands, and directions for effective management of luxury brands have for the most part been ignored in extant literature. The central aim of this chapter is to present current knowledge in regard to luxury branding and address some of the key gaps in existing knowledge that pertains to (1) conceptualization of luxury brands, (2) consumers of luxury brands and how they relate to and processes information about these, (3) identification of the benefits and risks inherent in managing luxury brands, and (4) effective management of such brands in the 21st century.

CHANGING FACE OF THE LUXURY MARKET AND EMERGENCE OF NEW LUXURY

Comparing New Luxury with Old Luxury

Silverstein and Fiske (2003, p. 1) discuss "new luxury" as a recent socio-economic trend in which middle-market consumers trade up to "products and services which possess higher levels of quality, taste, and aspiration than [other] goods in the [same] category but are not so expensive as to be out of reach." Thus, the new luxury market is not restricted to conventional luxury goods such as diamonds, furs, and expensive cars (referred to by Silverstein and Fiske as "old luxury"), but may include products at the top of their category from sandwiches (for example, Panera Bread) to body washes (for example, Bath and Body Works). According to Silverstein and Fiske, new luxury products are premium goods that connect with consumers at an emotional level.

The emergence of new luxury in virtually every product category and the democratization of luxury (Tsai, 2005), making the luxury experience accessible to more consumers, is viewed by many observers as a radical transformation of the luxury market. However, if the terms "old luxury" and "new luxury" are to facilitate understanding and discussion of this transformation, rather than confuse the issue of what luxury really is, the relationship between the two concepts should be clarified. The latter concept is differentiated from the former in that it is not restricted to specific product categories. Furthermore, the aspect of conspicuous consumption is less important for the latter concept, giving way to a more complete focus on experience, affect, and hedonism. Notwithstanding this trend in the marketplace, old luxury clearly exists alongside new luxury. Moreover, consumers' perceptions of old luxury inform their perceptions of new luxury, and the clear distinction between the two concepts is somewhat arbitrary. However, this distinction may nevertheless be useful for brand management in the current marketplace. While the old luxury market focused on the status and prestige of a brand, the new luxury market focuses on the pleasure and emotional connection the consumer has with a brand. In the old luxury market, brand management entailed managing the attributes, features, and image of a brand to convey the perception of luxury to consumers. Brand management of new luxury products also entails this practice, but only to the extent that it facilitates or enhances the perception of the promise of pleasure represented by the luxury items.

What constitutes "luxury" today reflects the changing nature of consumers' needs, specifically the evolution of utilitarian or basic needs to hedonistic or higher order ones. Many consumers no longer struggle to meet the basic needs for survival, security, and basic comfort, but strive to enhance their pleasure and broaden their life experiences. As the face of the luxury market rapidly changes, the issue of how luxury brands can and should be strategically and dynamically managed to connect with consumers on the emotional level, ensuring that they derive pleasure from the brand experience at each encounter, becomes an important issue for marketers and academic researchers.

Democratization of Luxury

Democratization of luxury is based on several concurrent trends. First, the buying power of the average consumer is increasing. This is true both because of rising levels of wealth and increasing availability of credit. Second, the concept of luxury is expanding to embrace a wide variety of product categories. Third, brands are stretching to embrace different levels of luxury within the same product category. Not only have cars such as Rolls Royce and Bentley been joined by new and more easily accessible luxury vehicles such as Lexus and Acura, but different models are being introduced within the same brand. Luxury cars that cost US$35,000 or more have now introduced models that will sell for US$10,000 less, while attempting to maintain a luxury experience. The trend toward "semi-luxury" cars is underway with luxury brands such as Mercedes, BMW, and Audi becoming increasingly accessible to the mass-market consumer.

A fourth trend is visibility and availability of luxury. It has only been a decade since Godiva sold exclusively at Neiman Marcus and a few other upscale stores. Today, it attracts consumers across the spectrum and can be found in 2,500 outlets, including Dillard's department stores and Hallmark card stores. Similarly, fashion brands such as Gucci or Chanel were once restricted to haute couture that were sold at select locations to a select clientele, and flashy advertising was shunned as a vulgar practice (Thomas, 2007). Today, fashion brands are accessible at a wide variety of outlets, and their high visibility is assured with the huge amount of funds poured into advertising on a regular basis. Furthermore, the range of fashion brands, which began as a few and select ones, has expanded to not only embrace a multitude of high-end brands, but also ones that are slotted at various price points and levels of prestige.

The Luxury Market Today: Managing Luxury Brands in a Recession

Democratization of luxury is, however, also affected by other processes. For instance, recessions such as the one that is ongoing at the time of writing, arguably exerts an influence on consumers' response to luxury brands. According to "The Survey of Affluence and Wealth in America," conducted by the American Express Publishing and Harrison Group (April 29, 2009), 52% of the USA's wealthiest households believe they could lose everything because of current economic volatility. Furthermore, 76% of Americans take pride in their newfound, more frugal shopping habits and in their ability to make careful and reasoned purchase-related decisions. According to Cara David, Co-Director of the study, "This new resourcefulness means, however, that as the recession ebbs, merchants cannot expect a return to the sort of 'retail gluttony' that has characterized the last 10 years. Instead, consumers will continue to apply their newfound skills in comparative pricing, needs identification, budget-based and values-based shopping. Brands will have to get in line with the spirit of this 'rational exuberance': the tendency to take pleasure in saying 'no'." Given historical evidence, however, this conclusion should be tempered by an additional observation—that consumers' memory is often limited. However, it is true that habits learned under dire circumstances sometimes continue even after the circumstances have long since changed. For instance, one might make the observation that some consumers who experienced lean times during World War II still appear to exhibit certain frugal tendencies stemming from the cataclysm. In general, however, there is little evidence to show that consumers are so much in touch with history that they will retain the frugal habits they acquired during the current recession. Past recessions have not had a lasting effect.

There may be periodic changes in the specific types of luxuries consumers seek, and there may also be changes in what they consider luxuries versus necessities. For instance, Pew Research Center reports (April 23, 2009) that many products viewed by Americans as necessities in 2006 were viewed by the same consumers as luxuries they could do without in 2009. However, luxury satisfies a fundamental human drive for pleasure, and it seems unlikely that consumers will continue to avoid spending on them, even long after lean times have passed. In fact, even during lean times, consumers have the need to indulge in luxuries. In the survey discussed earlier on affluence and wealth, 57% of the respondents reported that "a few luxuries are important in tough times." Thus, the best strategy during a recession may not be to throw the luxury brand image out and attempt to replace it with a value-for-money brand image in response to consumers' frugal shopping habits. Instead, it may benefit managers to pay close attention to the types of luxuries consumers are still buying and make temporary adjustments in their offerings and marketing communications to be in synch with the economic and psychological climate of the times. For instance, if conspicuous consumption becomes unfashionable, then companies could emphasize the luxury products that can be consumed in private. If consumers become wary of making large purchases of luxury products, companies can find a way to divide such purchases into smaller portions. In this manner, the irreparable erosion of a favorable luxury brand image can be avoided with such tactical adjustments, rather than companies having to resort to making major strategy changes.

ALLURING LAP OF LUXURY: A REVIEW OF EXTANT LITERATURE ON LUXURY BRANDS

What Is a Luxury Brand?

Luxury is defined by the Merriam-Webster Dictionary as "a condition of abundance or great ease and comfort" or "something adding to pleasure or comfort but not absolutely necessary." This definition underscores the overlap between the concept of luxury and the concept of hedonistic consumption (Hirschman and Holbrook 1982). In the same vein, Vigneron and Johnson (2004) cite Kapferer's (1997) description of luxury products as those providing extra pleasure and flattering all the senses at once. They emphasize that psychological benefits, rather than functional ones, are the main factor distinguishing luxury products from non-luxury products. Luxury products have also been defined as those "whose ratio of functionality to price is low, while the ratio of intangible and situational utility to price is high" (Nueno and Quelch, 1998, p. 61).

In this chapter, we present a consumer-focused definition of luxury brands that is reflective of current market trends and the emergence of new luxury. We conceptualize a luxury brand as one that is at the top of its category in terms of its "premiumness" and connects with consumers on an emotional level, providing pleasure as a central benefit (Hagtvedt and Patrick, 2009). We suggest that the formulation of a luxury brand captures the prerequisite of premiumness, but also emphasizes the delivery of emotional benefits that constitute the primary benefit obtained by a consumer.

What Are the Associations of Luxury Brands?

Extant research has investigated different aspects of brands that signal luxury to consumers. Although this research has largely examined what may be considered most relevant for "old luxury," some of these brand associations remain important for "new luxury" as well, although empirical research is needed to determine which ones these are. For instance, Phau and Prendergast (2000) suggest that luxury brands are those that imply exclusivity, have a strong brand identity and high brand awareness, and are perceived to be of high quality.

Other research systematically investigates the multi-dimensional nature of the concept of a luxury brand and suggests how these dimensions should be managed to create lasting luxury brand value. Vigneron and Johnson (2004) propose that five key dimensions must be established or monitored to create a lasting luxury brand—perceived quality, conspicuousness, uniqueness, extended self, and hedonism. The first of these dimensions refers to the expectation that luxury brands should offer superior performance. While an important source of revenue expansion for companies is increased purchase intent induced by increased perceptions of quality (Rust, Moorman, and Dickson, 2002), luxury also implies premium pricing that could deter some consumers who may prefer a value-for-money proposition that connotes more quality per dollar spent. For the next three dimensions of luxury, a high price is, in fact, desirable. Indeed, luxury products are often purchased simply because they cost more, without offering additional direct utility over their cheaper counterparts (Dubois and Duquesne, 1993). The concept of conspicuous consumption suggests that consumers purchase luxury products because of their social signaling effect. Such consumers achieve an enhanced level of status or prestige, which sets them apart from others (Veblen, 1899). Perceived uniqueness or scarcity of a product adds to this social signaling effect, and companies sometimes incorporate this into their brand strategies. For instance, Ferrari made a commitment not to produce more than 4,300 vehicles, despite the fact that there was a more than a two-year waiting list for its cars; Christian Dior sued supermarkets for carrying its products, fearing that their easy availability could hurt its exclusive image (cited in Amaldoss and Jain, 2005). The underlying assumption here is that luxury brands may serve to classify or distinguish consumers in relation to others. Consumers may also integrate the symbolic meaning of these brands into their own identity (Holt, 1995). Belk's (1988) concept of extended self suggests that possessions may form part of a consumer's identity, and the construction of one's self thus seems to be a factor in consumption of luxury products (Vigneron and Johnson, 2004).

The last dimension, perceived hedonism, refers to sensory gratification, as opposed to the social context, of consumption of luxury brands. The hedonistic aspect of such consumption therefore refers to the intrinsic pleasure and emotional reward derived from the consumption experience itself (Hirschman and Holbrook, 1982). This notion is in line with Silverstein and Fiske's (2003) "new luxury," i.e., of premium goods that connect with consumers on an emotional level. In regard to brand extensions, it seems reasonable that the hedonistic aspect of consumption of luxury brands could make a favorable impact on consumers' evaluations, even in the absence of the social context inherent in the previous three dimensions. After all, pleasure is not only a fundamental human drive (Higgins, 1997), but it is universally applicable such that a consumer may be delighted and feel sensory and emotional gratification through consumption of virtually any product category. Furthermore, although the rarity principle underlying conspicuous consumption (Dubois and Paternault, 1995) may be counteracted by too many brand extensions, there is no evident reason why consumers would be averse to sensory and emotional gratification in abundance.

Who Is the Luxury Brand Consumer?

A *New York Times* article (Steinhauer, 2005) reports the observation made by Mark Fiorilli, a manager at a local Godiva store, about the difficulty of making assumptions about customers due to the diversity of those who purchase from the Godiva store. One customer is the traditional luxury consumer wearing designer clothes and a huge diamond ring, while another could be someone living off a disability check, looking for a special treat. The key is to identify consumers who pursue the promise of pleasure given by a luxury brand. These are not necessarily consumers who have large incomes and whose appearance signals status.

Traditionally, the luxury consumer was identified by the simple metric of income, but with the democratization of the luxury market (Silverstein and Fiske, 2003), such a consumer is identified in terms of income security and disposability. Paco Underhill, author of *Why We Buy: The Science of Shopping* (2000), describes a shift in the way the luxury consumer may be identified in relation to the current downturn of the economy. He goes on to describe three segments—one group comprising consumers who have lost their jobs and are cutting back on extras such as spa appointments and pet grooming services; the second group including consumers who are in a relatively secure position, but are sensitive to the downturn in the economy via the experiences of their friends, family, and colleagues, and the third group is relatively untouched by the downturn and consists of those who have stable incomes and an adequate cushion that protects them from the ups and downs of the recession. Consistent with this observation, social class or income status no longer defines the luxury consumer. With rising incomes and flattening prices, cars in driveways and handbags on the arm do not signal luxury like they used to. Not only do middle-class families enjoy such luxuries, but wealthy consumers might shop at Nordstrom for clothes, but buy wine from Costco and towels from Target.

Perhaps an area in which the classic luxury consumer can still be identified is in consumption of luxury services and experiences, which are often consumed in private or in an intimate setting with friends and family. Such services and experiences may constitute a new badge for high-end consumption. According to Steinhauer (2005), the true high-end luxury consumer has a personal chef, a home manager, travels on exotic vacations, rents islands, and goes in for costly and frequent cosmetic procedures.

Another luxury consumer is the type exemplified by retired couples who have a lifetime of savings to live on and a few good years left to do so. Consumers like this do not want things. They want to garner experiences, for example, by renting a villa on the Amalfi coast, watching the sunset over the Gobi Desert, or looking at Mount Everest glistening in the moonlight. These are experiences most people could only dream of earlier, but for those consumers with disposable incomes and no responsibilities, namely, the retired rich, such experiences are increasingly within their reach.

Drivers of Consumer Choice of Luxury Brands

Although research on luxury branding from the consumer's perspective is still at an early stage, some extant literature sheds light on motivations that drive consumers to choose luxury products and on conditions that facilitate choice of a luxury brand option. Early research, motivated by economic theory, has analyzed the consumption choices of affluent consumers (Dubois and Duquesne, 1993; Dubois and Laurent, 1993; Veblen, 1899), the role of snobbery and conspicuousness in consumption choices (Leibenstein, 1950), and the economic and political factors that drive luxury purchases (Vigneron and Johnson, 1999). Other research has investigated characteristics that predispose consumers to consume luxury brands. Bearden and Etzel (1982) indicate that for consumers who are susceptible to interpersonal influence, approval from their reference group is a strong motivator for their choice of luxury brands. Dubois and Laurent (1994) suggest that individuals with high hedonistic and perfectionist motives are more likely to purchase luxury products. Feelings of guilt, on the other hand, dissuade consumers from making such purchases (Kivetz and Simonson 2002). Wong and Ahuvia (1998) illustrate that Asians and Westerners differ in their motivations to purchase status goods and luxury brands, suggesting that cultural differences are important in driving consumption of luxury brands. They assert that since East Asian culture is based on an interpersonal construal of self, Asians (vs Westerners) tend to be influenced by group norms and goals, leading to a preference for public and visible possessions that communicate financial achievement. This fits well with what Thomas (2007) describes as the Japanese obsession with luxury goods. She reports that analysts estimate that 20% of luxury goods are purchased in Japan and another 30% are purchased by Japanese traveling abroad. By this calculation, Japanese consumers represent around half of the consumers in global luxury goods market. It should be noted that Thomas appears to be speaking exclusively of fashion items such as leather handbags and does not seem to acknowledge that other types of luxury goods exist. Nonetheless, half of the global market for such fashion items is substantial, to say the least. Conversely, Asians appear less likely than Westerners to display materialistic behavior based on personal tastes, traits, or goals. In a similar vein, Tsai (2005) discusses the differences between socially oriented and personally oriented consumers in terms of the luxury market, and also makes recommendations for enhancing the purchase value of luxury brands for personally oriented consumers.

There are scattered research findings that illuminate some situational factors driving choices of luxury brands. Mandel, Petrova, and Cialdini (2006) demonstrate that when a depicted media personality is perceived to be similar and the media depiction is one of success (vs failure), consumers tend to have increased expectations of their own future wealth along with a preference for luxury brands. Chartrand, Huber, Shiv, and Tanner (2008) demonstrate that primed exposure to a premium/luxury concept (for example, walking past Nordstrom) activates a prestige-related goal and results in an increased propensity to choose a luxury product (for example, the choice of an expensive pair of socks). Kivetz and Simonson (2002) illustrate that when making a choice between a hedonic experience (for example, going on a cruise) and a utilitarian one (for example, saving for college), feelings of guilt often result in consumers choosing the latter. Interestingly, however, these researchers show that knowledge about such feelings of guilt results in individuals "precommitting" to luxury over necessities. The researchers demonstrate that people prefer rewards, which are more effective than cash as an incentive for participating in a lottery, and underscore the appeal of luxury and its power to influence consumer behavior.

Dubois and Paternault (1995) emphasize how the appeal of luxury can change in a cycle of aspiration and consumption. They suggest that the luxury concept has "dream value." The paradox of luxury marketing is revealed through a regression analysis, which demonstrates that in the case of luxury brands, awareness feeds the dream of owning the brands, but purchase makes the dream come true, and thereby contributes to its destruction.

In our research, we provided consumers with consumption goals that are either consistent or inconsistent with a luxury (vs value) brand concept (unpublished data). As expected, consumer goals interacted with brand concept such that a brand was evaluated more favorably when there was congruency between its concept and consumers' goals. However, when evaluating brand extensions, participants did not seem to take these goals into consideration, thus revealing the same pattern of luxury demonstrated in previous studies. In other words, it would seem that consumers are able to distinguish different consumption opportunities from each other, such that conflicting goals for one consumption opportunity need not adversely affect an evaluation of other consumption opportunities, even though the products are under the same brand umbrella.

Several marketers have successfully segmented the market, based on consumers' goals, for example, the same consumer may shop at Banana Republic for a business suit, but buy flip-flops from Old Navy. Silverstein and Fiske (2003) discuss the success of Sara Lee's segmentation strategy for the Coach brand. Appealing to three consumer segments with different goals to shop in different locations from high-end boutiques to outlet stores, Coach has increased its sales from US$500 million to US$1.7 billion with a gross margin of 76.5%.

FUTURE AREAS OF RESEARCH ON LUXURY BRANDS

In this chapter, we have summarized much of extant literature on luxury brands. However, there much remains to be further clarified to increase the current understanding of how such brands influence consumers' behavior and how they can be most effectively managed (Patrick and Hagtvedt, 2009). Some of those areas are outlined in the following:

Aesthetics, Hedonism, and Psychological Benefits

Consumers are willing to pay money to receive certain benefits, and the greater or more numerous the benefits, the more they are willing to pay. This is a common assumption in marketing thought. It is therefore not surprising that luxury brands have been able to command a premium price for providing the benefits of status, conspicuousness, and exclusivity, in addition to those such as high quality and functionality. In fact, while consumers view premium prices as indicators of high quality (Quelch, 1987; Arghavan and Zaichkowsky, 2000; O'Cass and Frost, 2002), it is also true that luxury products can be purchased just because they cost more without providing additional direct utility over their cheaper counterparts (Dubois and Duquesne, 1993). However, such observations do not adequately illuminate all the psychological benefits that distinguish luxury products from non-luxury ones and counterfeits (Arghavan and Zaichkowsky, 2000). Future research should investigate benefits apart from the ones currently discussed in the literature. For instance, luxury experiences may provide temporary relief from a dreary routine, they may ignite romantic feelings, or they may awaken feelings of wonder that is tied to a sense of aesthetics. Perhaps they may even spark a spirit of aspiration or adventure because the experience of luxury goes beyond the merely sufficient and may remind consumers of the possibility to do more than just satisfy basic needs.

The notion of luxury for its own sake should also be highlighted. Scant research has been conducted or even proposed in this regard, but a growing stream of research in arts and aesthetics may shed some light on this notion. Dissanayake (1995) discusses art in relation to the concept of "making special" or "artifying," which is tied to ritualistic behavior. Humans are thought to have a drive, developed through the process of evolution, to make and experience the extraordinary, and this is what underlies our impulse for artistic creation and consumption. Although Dissanayake focuses on the benefits of art in terms of groups and a sense of community, others have emphasized the quest for the extraordinary in terms of individuals (Dutton, 2009). A parallel notion for creation and consumption of luxury does not seem unreasonable, and Kapferer (1997) even refers to luxury as art applied to functional items. In a related vein, Hagtvedt and Patrick (2008) discuss the luxury-related perceptions inherent in the concept of art, noting that both are tied to a special kind of quest for excellence. This does not however imply that luxury is the most salient or important aspect of art, but that an underlying drive that gives rise to both these expressions of human ingenuity stems from the same source, i.e., the desire to experience the extraordinary (Patrick and Hagtvedt, 2009).

This drive to experience the extraordinary lends intrinsic value to artworks. In fact, extant literature asserts that artworks, in the pure sense of the word, are valued in and for themselves, and that any utilitarian value is incidental to their status as art objects (Hagtvedt and Patrick, 2008; Hirschman, 1983). An oft asserted characteristic of aesthetic experiences in general is that they must be intrinsically motivated (Averill, Stanat, and More, 1998). Following this argument, the notion of intrinsic value also pertains to the concept of luxury. Several streams of research, such as those pertaining to arts, aesthetics, design, and hedonic products, are clearly relevant for enhancing an understanding of luxury brands. Consequently, research on these could benefit from the development of an overarching framework that captures the commonalities between these related areas.

Consumers' Processing of the Luxury Brand Concept

Very little research explicitly investigates processing of luxury brand concepts (Patrick and Hagtvedt, 2009). However, an emerging stream of literature that investigates consumers' responses to hedonistic products may serve as a starting point. Indeed, Hagtvedt and Patrick (2009) demonstrate that a central role is played by the hedonistic potential in consumers' responses to luxury brands. Such products are associated with emotions and pleasure (Hirschman and Holbrook, 1982), and extant research suggests that these have a different set of criteria by which they are evaluated (c.f. Yeung and Wyer, 2004 and 2005) and a different set of consumption goals compared to functional products (Pham, 1998). Luxury brands are also likely to be evaluated on a different set of criteria than are other brands. In line with our conceptualization of luxury, the extent to which such a brand is able to meet affective expectations is likely to influence its evaluation, even more than its performance along a series of attributes (c.f. Patrick, MacInnis, and Park, 2007). Furthermore, Hagtvedt and Patrick (2009) demonstrate that the prospect of re-experiencing emotional gratification—the "promise of pleasure"—is also a key driver of consumers' responses to extensions of luxury brands. Other research suggests that while functional products satisfy, hedonistic products delight (Chitturi, Raghunathan, and Mahajan, 2008). The role of specific emotions such as delight in consumers' processing of luxury brands remains an interesting avenue for future research.

Luxury brands also constitute a unique context in which some key findings in the attachment literature can be examined (Thomson, MacInnis, and Park, 2005). However, further understanding is needed on how processing of the luxury brand concept can influence brand loyalty. Influences such as this may also be moderated by individual or cross-cultural differences between consumers. For instance, holistic processing prevalent in Eastern societies versus analytic processing in Western societies have recently been investigated (Monga and John, 2007). Future research may investigate these and other cross-cultural and individual differences in consumers' processing of the luxury brand concept.

Benefits and Risks of Luxury Brands

Based on this, the hedonistic properties associated with luxury brands represent benefits that merit further investigation. For instance, these benefits not only entail a luxury brand being inherently desirable, but also that its extensions can be judged on a less strictly rational basis than other brand extensions; that consumers' attachment may be easier to achieve with such brands, and so on (see also Park, Milberg, and Lawson, 1991). The promise of pleasure, which is central in the emerging conceptualization of luxury, also suggests that the feelings-as-information approach (Schwarz and Clore, 1983) may be useful for an investigation of consumers' responses to luxury branding (Hagtvedt and Patrick, 2009). The centrality of pleasure and emotional gratification therefore also has implications for management of a luxury brand portfolio. For instance, whether a luxury brand should line extend within its category or extend across categories, and the overall impact of its concept on marketing-related criteria such as market share and shareholder value (Park and Eisingerich, 2008) are important questions for future investigation. A monetary valuation of the emotional benefits delivered by a luxury brand could also be the focus of future research.

Along with the benefits, there are specific risks inherent in the concept of luxury brands. For instance, commitment to the concept of a luxury brand entails the provision of brand-related cues that are consistent with the concept. Cues such as premium pricing and exclusive distribution may be considered consistent with this concept (Silverstein and Fiske, 2003; Amaldoss and Jain, 2005). Although such factors may themselves bring about certain benefits, such as the increased margins associated with premium pricing, they may also not be advantageous. For example, both premium pricing and exclusive distribution tend to be incompatible with mass marketing. Furthermore, extant research demonstrates that the consistency of cues has a particularly strong influence on consumers' evaluations of luxury brands and their extensions (Hagtvedt and Patrick, 2009). In fact, even positive experiences, such as consumers coming across a good deal, may ultimately lead to his/her less positive response to a luxury brand. Given that the centrality of emotions may lead to a less rational basis for consumers' responses to luxury brands, this also introduces challenges in maintenance of a positive image of a luxury brand. A less rational basis for consumers' evaluations may give an edge to a manager who is astute enough to take advantage of this, but it also represents a risk, since it is arguably more difficult to systematically develop marketing strategies when one cannot rely on the predictable, rational behavior of consumers.

SUMMARY

In this chapter, we have discussed current trends in democratization of luxury and the broadened scope of luxury brands. While "old luxury" is exemplified by conventional luxury goods such as diamonds, furs, and expensive cars, "new luxury" may include any premium products that connect with consumers on an emotional level. We also emphasize the central role of pleasure in luxury brands. While aspects such as prestige, conspicuous consumption, and quality are discussed in extant literature, the "promise of pleasure" is also beginning to receive significant attention.

After a brief discussion of the current trends, we look at extant literature on conceptualization of a luxury brand, its correlates, its consumers, and drivers of consumers' choice in luxury brands. We then identify future areas of research for luxury brands, including aesthetics, hedonism, psychological benefits, consumers' processing of the concept of luxury brands, and their benefits and risks.

REFERENCES

Amaldoss, Wilfred and Sanjay Jain (2005), "Conspicuous Consumption and Sophisticated Thinking," *Management Science*, 51(October), 1449–1466.

Arghavan, Nia and Judy L. Zaichkowsky (2000), "Do Counterfeits Devalue the Ownership of Luxury Brands?" *Journal of Product and Brand Management*, 9(7), 485–497.

Averill, James R., Petra Stanat, and Thomas A. More (1998), "Aesthetics and the Environment," *Review of General Psychology*, 2(2), 153–174.

Bearden, William O. and Michael J. Etzel (1982), "Reference Group Influence on Product and Brand Purchase Decisions," *Journal of Consumer Research*, 9(September), 183–194.

Belk, Russell W. (1988), "Possessions and the Extended Self," *Journal of Consumer Research*, 15(September), 139–168.

Beverland, Michael (2004), "Uncovering 'Theories-in-use': Building Luxury Wine Brands," *European Journal of Marketing*, 38(3/4), 446–466.

Chartrand, Tanya L., Joel Huber, Baba Shiv, and Robin J. Tanner (2008), "Nonconscious Goals and Consumer Choice," *Journal of Consumer Research*, 35(2), 189–201.

Chitturi, Ravindra, Rajagopal Raghunathan, and Vijay Mahajan (2008), "Delight by Design: The Role of Hedonic Versus Utilitarian Benefits," *Journal of Marketing*, 72(May), 48–63.

Danziger, Pamela N. (2005), *Let Them Eat Cake; Marketing Luxury to the Masses—as well as the Classes*. Chicago, IL: Dearborn Trade Publishing.

Dissanayake, Ellen (1995), *Homo Aestheticus: Where Art Comes From and Why*. Seattle: University of Washington Press.

Dubois, Bernard and Patrick Duquesne (1993), "The Market for Luxury Goods: Income Versus Culture," *European Journal of Marketing*, 27(1), 35–44.

Dubois, Bernard and Gilles Laurent (1994), "Attitudes Toward the Concept of Luxury: An Exploratory Analysis," in *Asia-Pacific Advances in Consumer Research*, 1(2), 273–278.

Dubois, Bernard and Claire Paternault (1995), "Observations: Understanding the World of International Luxury Brands: The 'Dream Formula'," *Journal of Advertising Research*, 35(4), 69–76.

Dutton, Denis (2009), *The Art Instinct*. New York: Bloomsbury Press.

Frank, Robert H. (1999), *Luxury Fever*. New York: The Free Press.

Hagtvedt, Henrik and Vanessa M. Patrick (2008), "Art Infusion: The Influence of Visual Art on the Perception and Evaluation of Consumer Products," *Journal of Marketing Research*, 45(June), 379–389.

Hagtvedt, Henrik and Vanessa M. Patrick (2009), "The Broad Embrace of Luxury: Hedonic Potential as a Driver of Brand Extendibility," *Journal of Consumer Psychology*, 19.

Higgins, E. Tory (1997), "Beyond Pleasure and Pain," *American Psychologist*, 52(December), 1280–1300.

Hirschman, Elizabeth C. (1983), "Aesthetics, Ideologies and the Limits of the Marketing Concept," *Journal of Marketing*, 47(Summer), 45–55.

Hirschman, Elizabeth C. and Morris B. Holbrook (1982), "Hedonic Consumption: Emerging Concepts, Methods and Propositions," *Journal of Marketing*, 46(Summer), 92–101.

Holt, Douglas B. (1995), "How Consumers Consume: A Typology of Consumption Practices," *Journal of Consumer Research*, 22(June), 1–16.

Kapferer, Jean-Noël (1997), "Managing Luxury Brands," *Journal of Brand Management*, 4(4), 251–260.

Kivetz, Ran and Itamar Simonson (2002), "Self-Control for the Righteous: Toward a Theory of Precommitment to Indulgence," *Journal of Consumer Research*, 29(September), 199–217.

Leibenstein, Harvey (1950), "Bandwagon, Snob, and Veblen Effects in the Theory of Consumers' Demand," *Quarterly Journal of Economics*, 64(May), 183–207.

Mandel, Naomi, Petia K. Petrova, and Robert B. Cialdini (2006), "Images of Success and the Preference for Luxury Brands," *Journal of Consumer Psychology*, 16(1), 57–69.

Merrill Lynch/Capgemini (2005), *World Wealth Report*. Available at https://www.no.capgemini.com/resource-file-access/resource/pdf/World_Wealth_Report_2005.pdf (accessed May 15, 2009).

Monga, Alokparna B. and Deborah Roedder John (2007), "Cultural Differences in Brand Extension Evaluation: The Influence of Analytic versus Holistic Thinking," *Journal of Consumer Research*, 33(March), 529–536.

Nueno, Jose Luis and John A. Quelch (1998), "The Mass Marketing of Luxury," *Business Horizons*, 41(November/December), 61–68.

O'Cass, Aron and Hmily Frost (2002), "Status Brands: Examining the Effects of Non-product-related Brand Associations on Status and Conspicuous Consumption," *Journal of Product & Brand Management*, 11(2), 67–88.

Park, C. Whan and Andreas B. Eisingerich (2008), "Managing a Brand's Extension Portfolio for Market Share Leadership and Shareholder Value," Working Paper, University of Southern California.

Park, C. Whan, Sandra Milberg, and Robert Lawson (1991), "Evaluation of Brand Extensions: The Role of Product Feature Similarity and Brand Concept Consistency," *Journal of Consumer Research*, 18(September), 185–93.

Patrick, Vanessa and Henrik Hagtvedt (2009), "Luxury Branding," In Joseph Priester, Deborah J. MacInnis, and C. Whan Park (eds.), *Handbook of Brand Relationships*, 607–618. New York: Society for Consumer Psychology and M.E. Sharpe.

Patrick, Vanessa M., Deborah J. MacInnis, and C. Whan Park (2007), "Not as Happy as I Thought I'd Be: Affective Misforecasting and Product Evaluations," *Journal of Consumer Research*, 33(4), 479–490.

Pham, Michel Tuan (1998), "Representativeness, Relevance, and the Use of Feelings in Decision Making," *Journal of Consumer Research*, 25(September), 144–159.

Phau, Ian and Gerard Prendergast (2000), "Consuming Luxury Brands: The Relevance of the 'Rarity Principle'," *Journal of Brand Management*, 7(5), 366–375.

Quelch, John A. (1987), "Marketing the premium product," *Business Horizons* 30(3), 38–45.

Research and Markets (2006), "The U.S. Luxury Market Continues to Boom," Retrieved from http://www.researchandmarkets.com/reports/c38174 (accessed May 25, 2009).

Rust, Roland T., Christine Moorman, and Peter R. Dickson (2002), "Getting Return on Quality: Revenue Expansion, Cost Reduction, or Both?" *Journal of Marketing*, 66(October), 7–24.

Schwartz, John (2002), "Supersize American dream: Expensive? I'll take it," *The New York Times*, December 16, p. 8.

Schwarz, Norbert and Gerald L. Clore, (1983), "How do I feel about it? Informative functions of affective states," In K. Fiedler and J. P. Forgas (eds.), *Affect, Cognition and Social Behavior* (pp. 44–62). Toronto: Hogrefe International.

Steinhauer, Jennifer (2005), "When the Joneses Wear Jeans," *The New York Times*, May 29. Available at http://www.nytimes.com/2005/05/29/us/class/when-the-joneses-wear-jeans.html?_r=0 (accessed May 15, 2009).

Silverstein, Michael J. and Neil Fiske (2003), *Trading Up: The New American Luxury*. New York: Portfolio.

Thomas, Dana (2007), *Deluxe: How Luxury Lost its Luster*. London: Penguin.

Thomson, Matthew, Deborah J. MacInnis and C. Whan Park (2005), "The Ties That Bind: Measuring the Strength of Consumers' Emotional Attachment to Brands," *Journal of Consumer Psychology*, 15(1), 77–91.

Tsai, Shu-pei (2005), "Impact of Personal Orientation on Luxury-brand Purchase Value," *International Journal of Market Research*, 47(4), 429–454.

Underhill, Paco (2000), *Why We Buy: The Science of Shopping*. New York: Simon and Schuster.

Unity Marketing (2006), "Luxury Report 2006: Who Buys Luxury, What they Buy and Why they Buy." Available at http://www.businesswire.com/news/home/20060612005131/en/Research-Markets-important-study-U.S.-Luxury-Market#.VamELEW_JKo (accessed May 15, 2009).

Veblen, Thorstein (1899), *The Theory of the Leisure Class*. Boston, MA: Houghton Mifflin.

Vigneron, Franck and Lester W. Johnson (2004), "Measuring Perceptions of Brand Luxury," *Brand Management*, 11 (July), 484–506.

Vigneron, Franck and Lester W. Johnson (1999), "A Review and a Conceptual Framework of Prestige-Seeking Consumer Behavior," *Academy of Marketing Science Review*, 3(1), 1–15.

Wong, Nancy Y. and Aaron C. Ahuvia (1998), "Personal Taste and Family Face: Luxury Consumption in Confucian and Western Societies," *Psychology & Marketing*, 15(5), 423–41.

Yeung, Catherine and Robert S. Wyer (2004), "Affect, Appraisal, and Consumer Judgment," *Journal of Consumer Research*, 31 (September), 412–424.

Yeung, Catherine W. M. and Robert S. Wyer, Jr. (2005), "Does Loving a Brand Mean Loving Its Products? The Role of Brand-Elicited Affect in Brand Extension Evaluations," *Journal of Marketing Research*, 42 (November), 495–506.

Chapter 10
The Dynamics of Brand Trust

Gregory Metz Thomas

PROLOGUE

Brand trust is an important concept and is applicable across all industries and regions. After conducting a literature review, it was found that there was a lack of literature providing a holistic view of brand trust at the macro level. Although many studies cover trust, they often use the concept without robustly defining its elements. And often, trust is viewed in literature as a static concept where the researcher is interested in understanding it at a specific point in time. This chapter helps to fill the gap by providing a robust model of trust and a view of trust as a dynamic element.

The chapter consists of five sections. The first section "Brand Trust and the Information Age" is an introduction on why trust is important in today's context. The second section "Brand Trust Literature Review" provides a background of literature on trust. The third section "Benefits of Brand Trust" covers the reason why the issue of trust is important for businesses. The fourth section "The Brand Trust Conceptual Model" provides a detailed conceptual model of trust. The fifth section "Brand Trust Dynamics" covers the dynamics of trust in brand relationships. And the last section provides a summary and suggests future directions on research.

BRAND TRUST AND THE INFORMATION AGE

The future is here.

We live in an age of distributed intelligence. Our world consists of smart cars, smart phones, smart food, smart bombs, smart drugs, and smart bots. Some Luddites amongst us may say they do not like computers without taking into consequence the digital clock radio that wakes them up, the microwave that makes their coffee, the car they drive to work, the lights that manage the flow of traffic, and the networks that manage their cell phones and rely on computer technology. Increasingly, these smart devices we rely on are connecting with the mother-of-all-networks known as the internet. Ours is an interconnected world where we can talk with a person anywhere instantly over the internet, send money over the internet, buy airplane tickets over the internet, post pictures of our latest vacation over the internet, and check our credit ratings over the internet.

The computer is an information machine. On entering the computer age, our world has moved to an era where an unprecedented amount of information is accessible, which makes all sorts of new possibilities come to life. Never before has so much information been available, yet this extraordinary information machine has potential to be both a blessing and a curse.

George Orwell (Orwell, 1950) was concerned about the future. His book *Nineteen Eighty-Four* is one of the most influential books of the 20th century. It is a cautionary tale about totalitarianism. In the book, the government is one that no longer honors the social contract—the idea that its power is justified by its abiding by its fiduciary duty to serve the will of the people. Orwell was concerned that when the government has absolute power, trust placed on it is overridden by the potential for abuse of its power. *Quis custodiet custodes ipsos?* ("Who watches the watchers?")

Power and trust can be viewed as opposites to a degree, for example, when power is absolute and exists without checks and balances, the government and society tends to degenerate into a lordship-bondsman relationship. The master is the consciousness that exists only for itself. The issue of corporate trust has become a huge concern with many companies generating revenues that are greater than the GDP of many countries today. Walmart earned

US$315 billion in revenue (from its company reports) for the year ending Jan 2006, which would have placed it among the top 30 if it were a country, ahead of Switzerland, Sweden, and Saudi Arabia (Economist Intelligence Unit).

Trust is not instantaneously affixed in a new relationship. It is something that is built over time in a relationship. A company that gains our trust has an advantage over an upstart, since trust accumulates over the span of the relationship. Therefore, trust in a brand is a switching cost an upstart needs to overcome. In essence, building brand trust is a possible competitive advantage, and therefore, enhances business performance.

To examine such issues in depth, the next section provides a background on prior work on the subject of brands, trust, and relationships.

BRAND TRUST LITERATURE REVIEW

Role of Brands

There are many perspectives on brands in literature including constructs from Kotler, Keller, Bennett, Brown, Ambler, de Cheratony, Morrall, Faust, Gardner, the American Marketing Association, and others (Gardner, 1955; AMA, 1960; Bennett, 1988; Kotler, 1991; Brown, 1992; Ambler, 1992; Faust & Eilertson, 1994; de Cheratony, 1999). Many of the weaker definitions equate a brand with a trademark. A trademark is a legal instrument that protects a brand identity, but it is only an element through which a brand is managed and not the brand itself. Many other definitions focus on the brand owner perspective of a brand, which is often limiting, since the manager compartmentalizes the notion of the brand, whereas the customer has a holistic view. Not reconciling these views can lead to managerial blind spots. This author proposes a dual definition of a brand from both the managerial as well as the customers' perspective.

Consumers' Perspective: A brand refers to a dynamic set of beliefs held by a consumer that establishes expectations pertaining to the relative utility of an offer, offer class, or set of offers. When brands fulfill a need effectively, customers tend to seek them out and develop relationships with them. Such brands evolve over time.

Relative utility typically consists of a blend of physically functional attributes and symbolic-emotional attributes, but in some cases, may only represent one of these categories. It represents the benefits derived less the cost of attainment of these benefits. Utility is relative, since it is gauged in the context of competitive offers. In establishing expectations, a brand becomes distinguished from other offers. Brand-based beliefs become dynamic over time when new information is acquired about it and its contexts, and beliefs about it are influenced. New information is acquired through multiple sources including direct experience of the brand and experience with other brands through media and interpersonal communication. Experience is influenced by all senses perceived by the sensory system. Brand beliefs are perceptions about a brand that may be misconstrued from the actual brand identity due to limitations in mental processing, judgmental biases, misattribution, inexperience, or lack of knowledge. Subjectivity provides a filter by which the meaning of a brand varies across individuals. In addition, a brand is in part co-created by consumers through its ownership and usage. Nonetheless, the brand is experienced holistically by consumers, and it does not matter if these perceptions are created by different points of contact with it, since these are unified in the mind of the consumers.

It is important to note that a brand is not its name. Its name is only its name. The brand is both the product distinguished and its distinguishing identifiers. It represents the entire system.

Bob Thacker, a former Vice President of Marketing for Target, put this very well. In simple terms, "Every step in the sand leaves a footprint." The significance is that every action (or even lack of it) of an organization creates its brand in the mind of the consumer.

Brand Management Perspective: A brand is a relationship-building asset representing a value delivery mechanism, which ideally provides a targeted level of value for customers, and enhances relationships with business partners. Ideally, brands are conceptualized, created, and maintained through defined business processes. In actuality, a brand is established through both intentional and unintentional actions. In practice, the sphere of influence of brand managers is often not extensive enough to control the entire process of brand delivery to customers. Managers aim to produce brands that provide superior relative utility to the customer as well as enhanced economic value to the organization. Economic value is derived through benefits such as acceleration of cash flows, market share premiums, pricing premiums, more persistent market dominance, reduced vulnerability to risks, decreased vulnerability to competitive moves, and enhanced opportunities to leverage a brand. A brand may be managed alone, in a portfolio of owned brands, and in conjunction with partner brands. In its weak form, it is a mere identified commodity. In its strong form, the brand consists of a relatively attractive and distinguished bundle of attributes.

Brands and Dynamic Relationships

Given the perspective above, customers develop relationships with brands. This view is supported by Fournier (1990), who explained that consumers anthropomorphize brands in a way that inanimate things can become richly associated with human qualities, and associations develop over time that result in consumers feeling they have a relationship with these just as though they were persons. Personification of a brand is sustained by marketing actions that help to engender human qualities in a brand, for example, characters such as the Michelin Man or Charlie the Tuna. It is also noted that people have relationships with movie stars as fans, with God as a mortal, with pets and even as a child with imaginary friends.

Relationships are by nature dynamic, and as such, are considered to progress across multiple stages of interaction (Dwyer, Schurr, and Oh, 1987; Fournier, 1990; Ford, 2001; Halinen and Tahtinen, 2002). In general, these stages include incubation, activation, development, decline, reactivation, and discontinuation. Incubation is a sort of pre-relationship stage. It occurs when knowledge of a brand starts and can take place long before any real interaction with it. Activation can be demarcated as beginning when a brand enters the consideration set or during the first usage experience. Development occurs when brand purchase becomes somewhat regular through brand reliance. Decline occurs when the brand is no longer consumed, often either due to changes in needs or in the brand offer. Reactivation of a brand occurs when either needs shift back toward the brand value or the company extends the value into a new domain that interests the consumer. And discontinuation occurs when the brand is no longer consumed, either due to a breakdown in the relationship or a shift in needs, or consumers' lack of access to it. These stages are generalized and therefore do not always occur in sequence. For some, the brand never transitions from incubation to activation. For example, many people want their own Lamborghini, but will never own one due to lack of affordability. These people become virtual consumers, which can be partially activated through purchase of posters, T-shirts, and so on, which feature famous cars.

Role of Trust and Relationships

The concept of trust has been assessed across multiple disciplines. This multiplicity of approaches means there is some divergence of thought. Economists tend to consider trust as being calculative (Williamson, 1993) or institutional (North, 1990). Typically, psychologists address it in terms of the attributes of those who trust and trustees, and dwell upon the internal cognitive processing that personal propensities yield (Rotter, 1967; Tyler, 1990). Sociologists view trust as being embedded within relationships among groups of people (Granovetter, 1985) or institutions (Zucker, 1986).

Trust also plays a central role in various areas of marketing literature, including services marketing (Berry and Parasuman, 1991), commitment formation (Morgan and Hunt, 1994, and Achrol, 1991), buyer-seller bargaining relationships (Schurr and Ozanne, 1985; Dwyer, Schurr and Oh, 1987), and inter-organizational relationships (Moorman, Zaltman, and Deshpande, 1992).

Morgan and Hunts' (1994) seminal article, "The Commitment-Trust Theory of Relationship Marketing," is one of the highest cited works in marketing literature. It builds on the social exchange theory (Blau, 1964; Cook and Emerson, 1978) and puts forth the concept that commitment and trust, not power or dependence, are the key focal constructs for understanding performance of inter-organizational relationships. The article emphasizes that commitment is the critical precursor to enhanced financial performance, and that commitment and trust are both fundamental for building strong relationships Commitment is an "enduring desire to maintain a valued relationship" (Moorman, Zaltman, Deshpande) and trust is confidence in an exchange partner's reliability and integrity that through commitment affects the exchange outcome (Morgan and Hunt, 1994, p. 23).

There are multiple ideas of trust put forth in marketing literature (Ambler, 1994). The following are quotations from pertinent authors:

Moorman, Deshpande, and Zaltman's (1993) "the willingness to rely on an exchange partner in whom one has confidence" may seem circular, since the word "trust" is replaced by "confidence," as does Morgan and Hunt's (1994) definition, "when one party has confidence in an exchange partner's reliability and integrity."

O'Shaughnessy (1992, pp. 154-5) states that "trust implies a willingness to accept vulnerability" and a sense of reciprocity that any short-term unfairness is evened out over time. Kumar (1996) similarly stresses on fair play and distinguishes an expectation of procedural justice (that disputes will be equitably dispatched) from an expectation of distributive justice (that rewards will be divided equitably). He sees trust as implying dependability and honoring of one's word; that it can be built through bilateral communications and interdependence, but is a separate relationship construct to power, and that trust is rarely all encompassing, but, one trusts some aspects but not others.

Ganesan (1994) makes the important point that understanding the customer's time orientation is of the essence in determining whether relational or transactional marketing is more relevant. Where long-term orientation applies, Ganesan proposes that mutual dependence and trust are the two key factors.

Geyskens and Steenkamp (1995) summarize 20 previous trust definitions as "the extent to which a firm believes that its exchange partner is benevolent and honest." In the context of a brand, this equates the extent to which a consumer expects it to provide satisfaction.

As these statements illustrate, the idea of trust is related to risk, which is a concept that spans literature on economic, sociological, and psychological conceptualizations of trust (Rotter, 1967; Coleman, 1990; Williamson, 1993). Risk is perceived probability of loss, as interpreted by the decision-maker (Chiles and McMackin, 1996). Sources of risk include financial risk, time risk, social risk, physical risk, functional risk, and psychological risk (Bauyer, 1967; Cox, 1974). In a perfect world with perfect information, a consumer would have all the information needed to evaluate risk. The need for trust would no longer exist. However, in the real world, with limited information and bounded rationality, trust acts as a method of reducing risk, based on a perception of a brand, and upholding its fiduciary agreement. Higher levels of perceived risk make trust more important. In the case of higher perceived risk, the person who trusts is more likely to examine the trustee's behavior to determine the limits of trust. See Table 10.1.

Trust is multidimensional. It can manifest itself at the individual (McAllister, 1995; Rich, 1997; Soule, 1998), group (Smith and Barclay, 1997), organization (Ganesan, 1994; Aulakh, Kotabe, and Sahay, 1996), network (Havila and Salmi, 2000), institutional (Fukuyama, 1995), and place-of-origin level. An individual customer-facing representative, for example, a salesperson, can make an impact on trust in a brand. The processes of an impact made by a

Table 10.1 Sources of Risk

Financial Risk	– Product is not worth price paid – Financial information is abused – Loss of productivity – Career risk – Loss of complimentary investments
Time Risk	– Time invested in building the relationship – Search cost for alternative – Time to pursue judicial enforcement
Social Risk	– Risk of embarrassment – Privacy loss of
Physical Risk	– Harm to self – Harm to others – Harm to things
Functional Risk	– Personal loss of utility – Loss of utility for others
Psychological Risk	– Personal well-being effected – Well-being of others effected

Source: Raymond Bauyer (1967), Donald Cox (1974), Author.

departmental group can affect brand trust, for example, employees' empowerment in Nordstrom's customer service. Through its actions and communications, the organization makes an impact on the brand, (and the corporation is often synonymous with the brand). The partners in a business network can affect trust in a brand, for example, when companies form alliances, their identities merge. The institutional system can affect trust in a brand, for example, the strength of the judicial system. Its place of origin (often recognized as the country of origin of a brand) can affect trust in it.

Based on this review, what is lacking in literature on trust is a detailed look at the factors that contribute to trust, and how it influences relationships over time. This chapter will explore a brand trust conceptual model in section "The Brand Trust Conceptual Model," but will first illustrate the reasons why trust is important in section "Benefits of Brand Trust."

BENEFITS OF BRAND TRUST

What is the goal in marketing? It is to create market imperfections that lead to a persistent superior financial performance. This is measured across the brand value chain from brand building, brand equity, and market performance to shareholder value (Srivastava, et al, 1998; Keller and Lehmann, 2003). In this section, we explore the brand performance benefits of brand trust.

In this information age, we find that customer-related knowledge provides the foundation for development and delivery of superior value. Gone are the days of interruption marketing or marketing activities that interpose on the prospective customer at an inconvenient time with an offer that is irrelevant. This a shotgun approach where most of the pellets are off-target.

Interruption marketing only serves to annoy the customer. For example, after moving recently, I signed up with BellSouth for telephone service. The company took this as an indication that I wanted to be called at all hours of the day with offers I was not interested in. It called about its DSL service with some innocuous message such as, "Did you know BellSouth is now offering a DSL service." Since I already have broadband service, I said I was not interested. Yet it kept calling back until I specifically asked to be taken off its prospect list. The company could have known that since I was already a phone customer, I subscribed to caller id in all probability, and I did this to avoid sales calls. Most people are uninterested in being interrupted by sales calls and are especially where an offer has no relative value. Calling a prospect and saying "We offer DSL" is tells you nothing. Evidently, the marketing program creator had not thought through customer-switching costs and the annoyance cost of invading the customer's privacy. And the golden rule of privacy is that the customer's preferences take precedent. When a customer signs up with a company for a telephone service, the purchase definitely does not authorize it to call any time of the day to interrupt his/her peace of mind with bland and unattractive offers.

The time of interruption marketing is gone. The information age has ushered in the practice of right-time marketing, which is the science of putting the right offer before right person at the right time. Brand trust is an integral component of effective right-time marketing. Without trust, all business becomes transactional; without trust, the consumer is unwilling to share information, and without trust, transactions remain anonymous, and this hampers development of relationships. According to Gartner, an industry analyst firm, highly targeted marketing communications, triggered by analysis and identification of prospects, and customers' life events or interactions between individuals and an enterprise, typically have response rates that are 4 to 10 times higher than those of conventional direct marketing efforts (Gartner, 2002). This is a compelling for carefully constructing a strong foundation for brand trust. See Figure 10.1.

With a strong foundation of brand trust, consumers are more willing to share information. Instead of remaining anonymous, they

Figure 10.1 The Personalization–Privacy Tradeoff

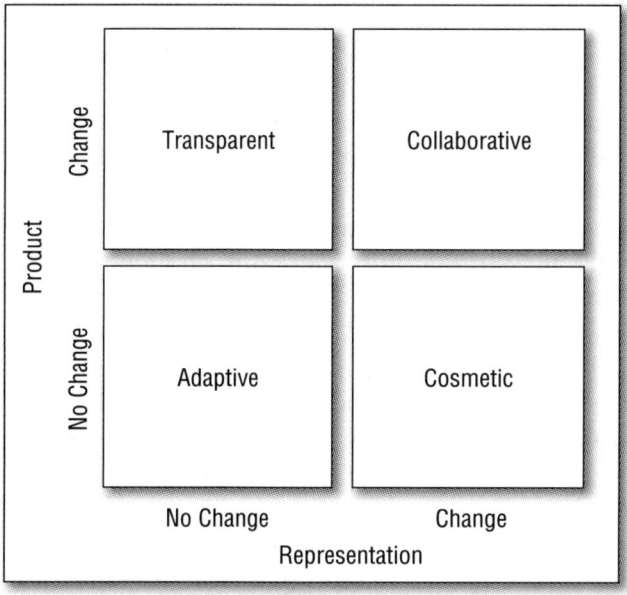

Source: Pine and Gilmore (1999).

Figure 10.2 Four Types of Mass Customization

customer consent to being identified. This process of identification permits discovery of factors that affect their needs, and this understanding becomes the basis for right-time marketing.

Based on the work of Gilmore and Pine (1999), we see there are four types of customization (Figure 10.2):

1. *Adaptive customizers* offer a standard, but customizable product that is designed so that customers can alter it.
2. *Transparent customizers* use standard packaging, but provide customers with unique products and services without letting them know explicitly that these have been customized for them.
3. *Collaborative customizers* work directly with customers to help them articulate their needs and then make customized products for them.
4. *Cosmetic customizers* present a standard product to different customers, but individually customize packaging, advertising, etc.

There are many benefits of building brand trust and pursuing right-time marketing and mass customization. Brand trust lowers risk for a customer. When perceptions of risk are reduced, there can be greater trust and lead to a potential for increased disclosure. An adept organization will solidify its relationship with consumers with right-time marketing and customization. This leads to higher levels of value for customers. With greater trust, there is added loyalty, more willingness to try new offers, and a greater chance of their recommending the brand to others. The Henley Centre (Ikalafeng, 2004) found that 89% of people in the USA agreed with the statement "When I trust a brand, I recommend it to others." Brand trust leads to increased customer empathy and willingness to tolerate a business error. A trusted brand is one for which customers are willing to listen and delve more in depth to understand the company, its mission and its offers.

Trusted brands drive higher performing businesses. They are able to set premium prices for their products and services. For example, research by Edelman (Edelman, 2007) shows that 8 out of 10 people they are willing to pay more for goods and services from companies with a good reputation. Additionally, trusted brands are more likely to end up with a market share premium. They see their new products reach a faster rate of time-to-market-penetration. And trusted brands are sought by a higher quality employment pool. For public companies, these benefits of brand trust are manifested in factors such as higher share price-to-earnings ratios.

Conversely, lack of brand trust leads to criticism of the brand to others. This negative word-of-mouth publicity is a multiplier of brand distrust. People refuse to purchase products and services of brands they distrust. Why would you consider doing business with a company you lacked trust in? Mistrusted brands may have high awareness, but they are not in the consideration set. Moreover, people refuse to invest in organizations they distrust. This reduces the market value of the stocks of such companies as well as their liquidity. Opinion leaders often criticize a mistrusted brand on the web. Feedback sites such as Amazon, Epinions and others expand the sphere of word-of-mouth publicity. Distrusted brands are caught in a vicious circle. People do not want to work for such brands. If you do not have trust in doing business with a company, why would you want to work there? And when you cannot hire the best, your organization is faced with a downward sloping performance. And in extreme cases, when people distrust a brand, they are prone to demonstrate against the organization through boycotts and public events.

It is plain and simple. Trusted brands have tremendous advantages over distrusted ones.

The next section provides some conceptual models to help you understand the elements of trust further. These models form the basis of how trust is developed and maintained.

THE BRAND TRUST CONCEPTUAL MODEL

A plethora of companies have found it attractive to position themselves on brand trust. The following is a sampling of advertising lines companies have used as slogans, taglines, endlines, straplines, or trademarks. Some such as US News and World Reports' "Trust matters" address the issue of trust directly. Others, especially in the tech industry, use words such as "secure," for example, in the case of Check Point, "We secure the internet." And another group of companies use the trust-related term "privacy," for example, Radica's "Privacy you control." See Table 10.2.

But what is behind this notion of trust? How can we explain what trust is all about? Brand trust has two main components. The first consists of values and the second competencies. These categories are adapted from Mayer and Davis (1995), who put forth a three-component model of trust with ability, benevolence, and integrity. However this author believes that simplifying this to a two-dimensional construct at the top level better organizes the concept of trust. Regarding the "value" component, we trust brands that stand for what is ethical, benevolent, and virtuous. Benevolence is typically established through visionary leadership, for example, the original Ben & Jerry's with its social mission. Organizations with a philanthropic mission are admired and respected for their altruistic goals.

Ethical organizations are lawful. However, although the law sets forth rules for governing a particular type of activity, it has its limitations. For instance, the legal system is often slow to adapt to new

Table 10.2 Examples of Advertising Lines Relating to "Trust"

Trust
• Securing the internet. Enabling trust—Indicii Salus
• Reach out on the wireless service America trusts—AT&T
• Websites you can trust—Librarians Internet Index
• Your trusted partner for the web—Easyspace
• The taste you trust—McCormick
• To earn trust every day—Schering-Plough
• Trust your car to the star—Texaco
• Trusted by generations—All the rage since 1913—Clorox Bleach
• Trusted to deliver excellence—Rolls Royce
• Your trusted, reliable partner for 20 year—Teleroute
• Dry protection you can trust—Stayfree Ultra Thin
• Trust matters—US News & World Report
• Trust the Midas touch—Midas
• Trusted by moisture obsessives everywhere—Vaseline Intensive Care Lotion
• Finely crafted. Trusted for generations—Carlisle Wide Plank Floors
• Strong—Trusted—Advil
• The more you know, the more you trust Bayer—Bayer Aspirin
• Trusted everywhere—Duracell
• The most trusted name in news—CNN
• Where 15 million investors put their trust—Fidelity Investments

Source: Company documents.

technologies. Ethics ascend law to include that which is fair, just and honest. For example, United States' largest distributor of soft drinks recently agreed to halt nearly all sale of sodas to public schools in an effort to reduce childhood obesity. Since 32 states have no legislative policy regulating the sale of such soft drinks to schools, this move by the company was beyond the call of the law. See Figure 10.3.

People also trust brands that are virtuous. Virtue is habitual excellence, something that must be pursued consistently and continuously over time. Virtues have many manifestations such as compassion, cooperation, respect, sincerity, generosity, kindness, diligence, and so on. See Figure 10.4.

The Dynamics of Brand Trust 251

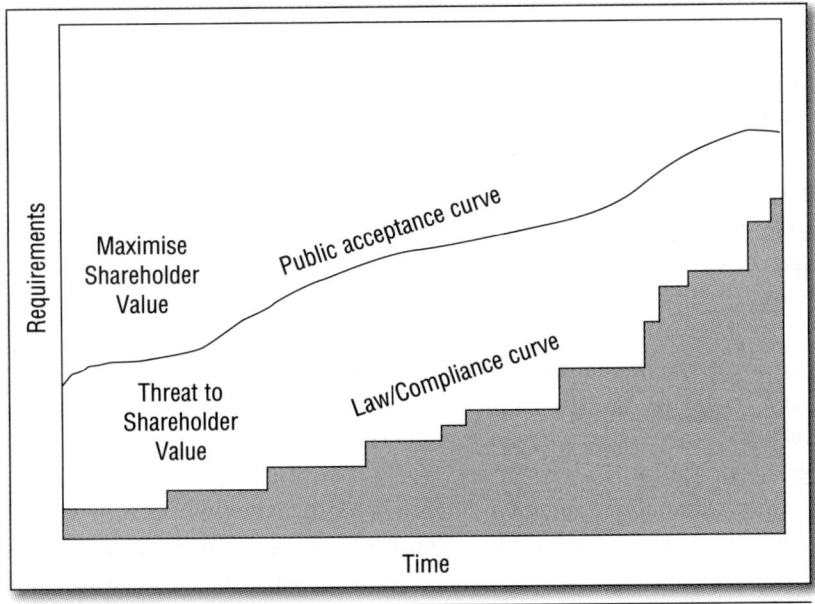

Source: WWF.

Figure 10.3 Law and the Court of Public Opinion

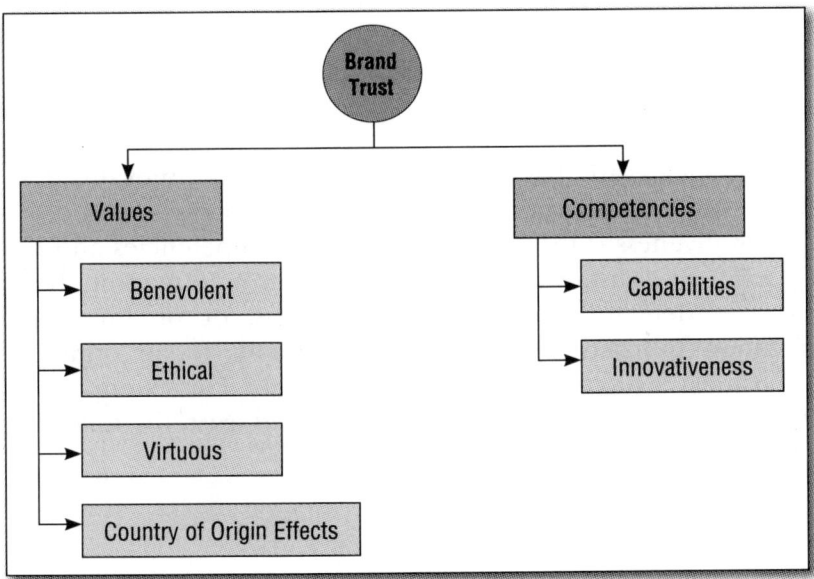

Figure 10.4 Brand Trust: The Conceptual Model

An additional component of values affecting brand trust is what is known as the country-of-origin effect—more widely as place-of-origin effect (Thomas, 2007). Brands have an affiliation with a country, which is usually the country of their corporate headquarters. Different countries vary on consumers' perceptions around the world. And these perceptions affect brand trust. For example, corruption is viewed as abuse of power for private gain. Transparency International (Transparency International, 2005), a coalition leading the fight against corruption, conducts an annual survey to measure corruption. In 2005, Iceland, Finland, New Zealand, and Denmark were countries that were perceived as being the least corrupt in the world. Haiti, Myanmar, Turkmenistan, Bangladesh, and Chad were perceived as being the most corrupt. Brands from Finland were perceived as embodying their country's values and were therefore considered as more ethical than those from Myanmar. Brand trust also varies by company in each region in which it participates. For example, UPS is trusted by 84% of people in the USA, but by only 53% of people in Europe (UK, France, and Germany) according to research conducted by Edelman in 2005 (Edelman, 2005). See Figure 10.5.

Brands that engender trust stand for doing the right thing. However, they also stand for doing things right. It is possible to know people who are always benevolent, ethical, and virtuous, but you may still not trust them in certain conditions. For example, you would not trust a person to fly a plane if he/she does not know how to.

Competencies are based on capabilities and innovativeness. Capabilities take the form of policies, system processes, and offerings. Innovativeness is the ability to improve competencies and has a temporal aspect. Innovation can take place around market offers, processes, a demand chain, business models, or organizations. Organization innovation involves improvements in an organization's business structure, practice and models. For examples, of policies, systems, and offerings that effect brand trust, the following list is provided. It is not however exhaustive.

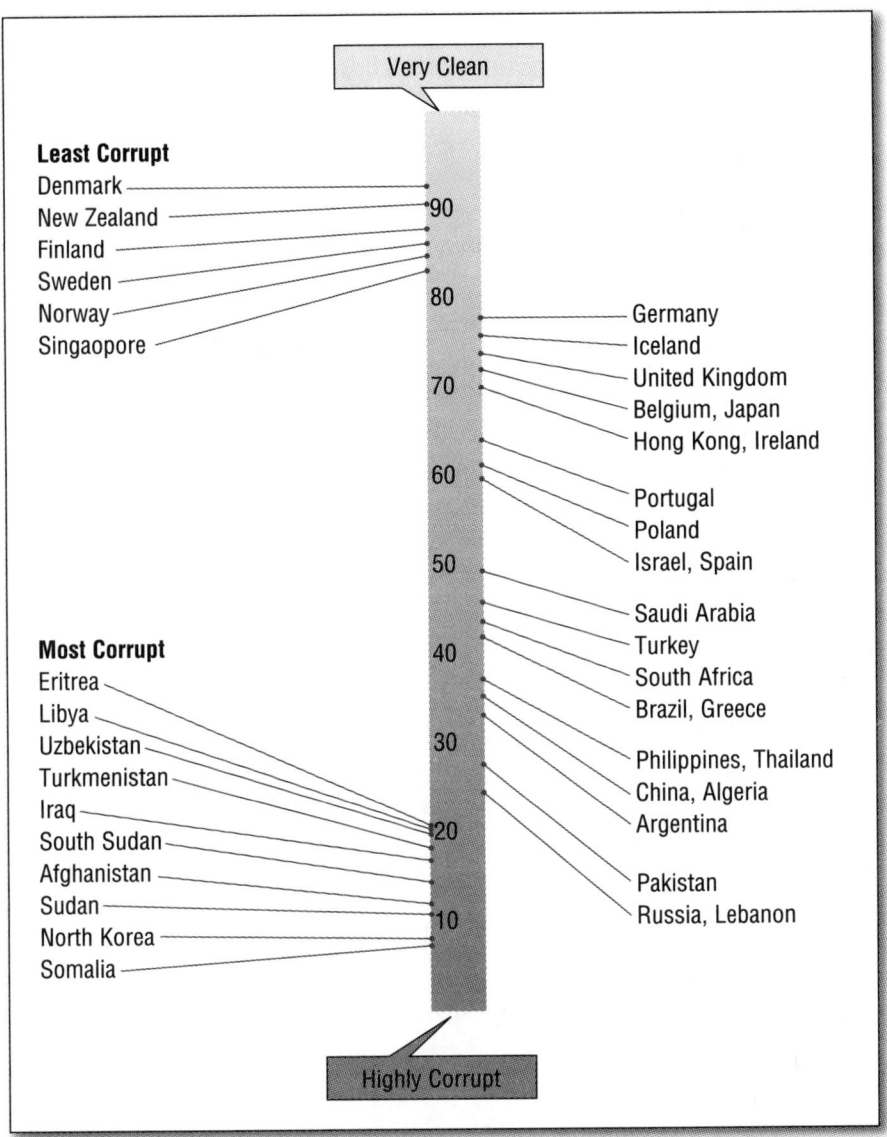

Source: Transparency International, transparency.org.

Figure 10.5 Corruption Perceptions Index 2014

Policies

Corporate Responsibility

1. Environmental policies
2. Fair trade policies

Employee policies
Customer policies

1. Return policies
2. Warranties
3. Guarantees
4. Privacy policy
5. Financial information security

Financial reporting policies

Systems

- Financial
- CRM
- Supply Chain

Processes

- Security processes

Offerings

- Product integrity
- Service integrity
    1. Pre-sales
    2. Sales
    3. Post-Sales
- Communications integrity

Trust is built through relational exchanges between buyer partners, supplier partners, lateral partners, the government, and internal partners. A brand's manifestations of trust lead to its treatment of its relations across all relational exchanges. It is not only a brand's direct interactions with its relational partners that establish its reputation of trust, but also interactions between indirect relations that promote the trustworthiness of a brand. Therefore, a company's relationship with its employees or its suppliers can affect its reputation of trust with its customers. See Figure 10.6.

In the next section, we will explore the dynamics of brand trust. Trust is built on the relationships brands can encounter and events that adversely impact trust in them. When this occurs, there are elements managers can keep in mind that will help them determine the effort and resources they need to allocate to rebuild trust.

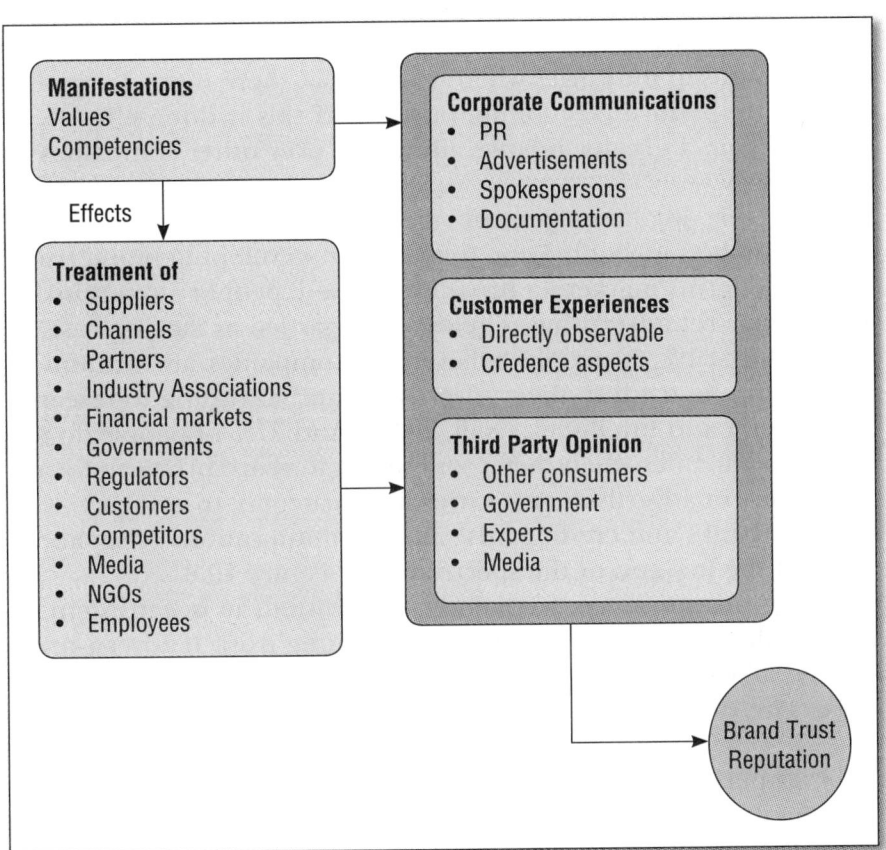

Figure 10.6 Brand Trust Reputation Building

BRAND TRUST DYNAMICS

Building Trust

Building trust is context-dependent on the industry. Inherent levels of trust vary across industries as well as by geography. Trust is generally highest in the retail and technology sectors across most geographic regions. However, trust in specific industries varies greatly from geography to geography. For example, brewing and spirits have high trust in the USA, whereas in APAC, they are ranked at the bottom. Whereas, technology companies are highly trusted across regions, in general, media, financial services, and banks are ranked the lowest. This means that companies need to make a more concerted effort to win trust in geographic regions where trust is lower for a specific sector. This could also indicate that in the case of organizations in industries where trust is low, there is greater potential for competitive positioning on trust. If this is done effectively, they will gain a greater relative advantage over other companies in the industry.

Now that we have conceptualized the model of brand trust, what is the best way of moving forward and developing brand trust? When the term "marketing program" is used, people often think of advertising. Yet advertising is generally regarded as lacking basis in truth. Only 24% of people believe that companies are truthful in presenting the truth in their advertisements, according to research by Forrester and Intelliseek (Nail, 2004). And 77% of people do not believe companies when they promise not to share private information. Trust in advertisements varies from category to category, with finance (banks and credit cards) and communications (telephony) being at the low end of the spectrum. See Figure 10.8.

Since advertising is frequently not trusted, it is consistent to believe that it is not the best mode of building trust. If advertising is not the method that should be utilized, how will customers develop trust? There are several ways of doing this.

- Experience-based Trust: Trust developed through customers' experience with the brand (Holmes, 1991; Lewicki and Bunker, 1995).

	USA	European Union	APAC	LATIN AMERICA	GLOBAL
High	Technology	Technology	Technology	Technology	Technology
	Brewing & Spirits	Consumer Electronics Manufacturing	Consumer Electronics Manufacturing	Consumer Electronics Manufacturing	Consumer Electronics Manufacturing
	Consumer Electronics Manufacturing	Automotive	Automotive	Entertainment	Automotive
	Food & Beverage	Entertainment	Banks	Automotive	Entertainment
	Consumer Goods	Brewing and Spirits	Consumer Goods	Food and Beverage	Food and Beverages
	Entertainment	Food and Beverage	Food and Beverage	Brewing and Spirits	Consumer Goods
	Automotive	Consumer Goods	Entertainment	Consumer Health	Brewing and Spirits
	Consumer Health	Telecom	Financial Services	Pharmaceuticals	Telecom
	Banks	Media	Consumer Health	Financial Services	Financial Services
	Chemicals	Financial Services	Brewing and Spirits	Media	Banks
Low	Media	Banks	Media	Banks	Media

Source: Edelman Annual Trust Barometer, January 2015.
*Global includes 27 countries.

Figure 10.7 Trust by Industry

- Calculative-based Trust: Trust choices based on rationally derived cost and benefits (Coleman, 1990; Williamson, 1993).
- Peripheral Cue-based Trust: Informational elements that convey trust when observed by a consumer (adapted from Petty, 1981)
- Expert-based Trust: Trust from word-of-mouth publicity or third parties

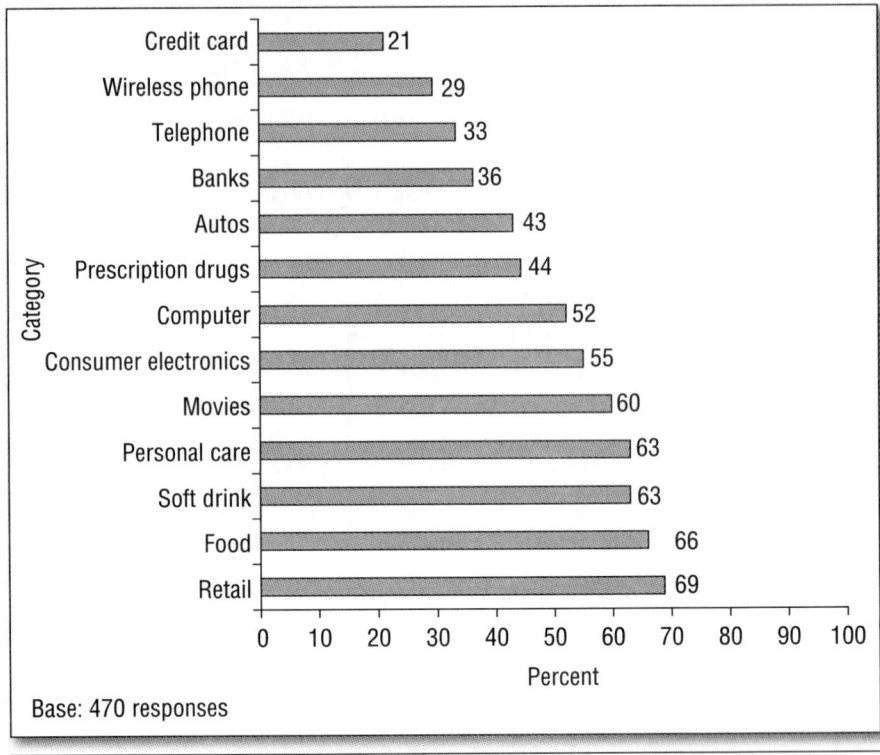

Source: Forester Research, Inc and Intelliseek.

Figure 10.8 Levels of Trust in Ads for the Given Products

- Capability-assessed Trust: Consumer developing trust based on evaluation of the trustee to perform as promised
- Transference-based Trust: Consumer developing trust based on transfer of trust from a third party

The most potent of these is experience-based trust, also referred to as relationship- based trust. It is the holistic customer experience from bumper-to-bumper that best forms bonds of trust. Cue-based trust often occurs when the customer is unable to directly observe elements of trust due to lack of access or expertise to evaluate the elements. Expert-based trust is in many forms, from testimonials and reviews to more casual word-of-mouth publicity.

When it comes to developing programs to support brand trust, there are three areas of consideration while dealing with breach of trust. These include prevention, mitigation, and restitution. Companies should recall the words of wisdom, "An ounce of prevention is worth a pound of cure." They need to focus on best practices to prevent breach of trust. A CMO is the keeper of the brand and when it is subjugated to breach, it is imperative to have a comprehensive program to mitigate risks and restore the peace of mind of the victims. See Table 10.3.

Revitalizing trust after a breach in trust can be difficult. In extreme cases such as Enron's, an incident causing the breach will dissolve the company. In more moderate cases, it is possible to rebuild trust, but this means overcoming perceptual anchors. People's beliefs tend to color the new information they come across regarding a brand. For example, research indicates that people "generally select, interpret, and recall information consistent with their prior beliefs or theories" (Greenwalt, 1980; Friske and Taylor, 1984). People's preconceptions also guide them to select information they think is relevant (Howard and Rothbart, 1980; Nisbett and Ross, 1980). When people come across information that does not confirm their views, they often discount it as being uninformative (Markus, 1977; Swann and Read, 1981; Taylor and Brown, 1988;

Table 10.3 Trust-building Programs

Exceptional guarantees	Customer service readiness
Warranties	Pioneering of new methods
Privacy policy	Disclosure policy in event of security breach
Security policy	PR on topic
Competency building	Sustainability practices
Consumer advocacy	Crisis response readiness
Third party consortiums	Information protection
Legislation support	Information parsimony
Legal and regulatory compliance	Reputation systems
Third party guarantees	Endorsements
Third party endorsements	CVV2 Codes
Allowing multiple paths of engagement	Internal policies
Buzz marketing (WOM)	Limit access
Monitoring WOM for issues	Employee empowerment
Data combining policies	In context cues
Institutes sponsorship (like "Internet Security Alliance")	Contracts
	CSR

Note: Not exhaustive.

Ross and Anderson, 1992). To counter such cognitive bias, the brand seeking to revitalize trust needs to overachieve in recovering from its weakness. For example, Odwalla, a manufacturer of natural bottled juice, would tout the benefits of its "live" juices that were unpasteurized (Layne, 2001). Things went well for the growing company until a breakout of e. Coli bacteria caused customers to fall ill by partaking of a batch of apple juice. After this incident, the Odwalla team went from being relatively naïve about health-control measures before the incident to becoming industry leaders. This turnaround did not go unnoticed, and eventually, the company was acquired at a premium by The Coca-Cola Company. Another example—Choicepoint, a consumer information company, lost a huge number of customer records from its database due to its lack of secure computing processes. The company also took a 180 degree turn when faced with adversity and is now seen as an advocate and industry leader in the area of data security (see PrivacyChoicePoint.com).

Even the most competent of companies are vulnerable to breach of trust incidents. Those who believe they are above this possibility need only think of the "unsinkable" ship known as the Titanic (Kirkpatrick, 1996). The Titanic was the largest passenger ship at the time it was launched and although it had the most advanced technology, 1,523 people tragically perished when it sank. The ship carried 20 lifeboats with a capacity for 1,178 people, but it held 2,223 passengers and crew. The extra boats needed to rescue everyone on board were part of the original ship design, but its management decided to reduce the number for aesthetic reasons. In the investigation that followed, it was found that many safety measures had not been implemented. As a result of the incident, improvements were developed, including safety in boat design, safety policies, and government support of safety at sea. The Titanic was a tragedy, but there would not have been such a loss of life if safety and the value of passengers' lives had been given greater importance by its management.

To develop and sustain brand trust, companies need to generate comprehensive response plans. Breaches happen. The impact of a breach depends on the factors involved. Some breaches are competency-based while others are values-based. The Enron scandal was a beach of values at the highest level. In 2004, Jetblue violated its privacy policy when it gave away information on 1.5 million customers to a defense contractor (Miller, 2004). The immensity of the breach of trust in the Enron case prevented recovery. Whereas, in the Jetblue case, we see that the event adversely affected the organization's market capitalization, but it has weathered the storm.

The degree of pervasiveness of a breach is a factor in its impact. If the beach is based on an isolated event, this is much better than if it were based on a systematic problem. For example, if a hacker gains access to an individual's account, this is not as devastating as in a case where all customer accounts are breached over an extended period of time. The cause of the breach is also an important factor. If the breach is intentional, such as employees reselling customer information to a third party in violation of a privacy law, this is more of a violation than if information were accidentally lost due to a hacker's intrusion via a previously unknown security flaw. The scope of the impact is another factor. Did the breach affect just a few people or millions of them? Naturally the latter is a greater problem. The cost associated with a breach is also important. If it means a loss of some harmless information such as color preferences, it is minimally disruptive as compared to if people's their life savings are withdrawn from their accounts or their credit damaged due to identity fraud. When a breach was obviously preventable, it is worse than an unforeseen security flaw. If it is internally initiated by an employee, it may be seen as being worse than it being perpetrated by an unidentified external cracker. If the breach is internal, it is deemed worse if executive management is involved rather than if it is merely a mistake made by line staff. And of course, a breach that is concealed or unknown is viewed as being less significant than a visible breach. If a company is unaware of a breach, this can later become quite serious. Furthermore, if a breach is committed by a person who is merely playing around with computer technology to access information for recreation without a malicious intent, this is less harmful than if the intrusion is motivated by a fraudulent intention. See Figure 10.9.

The response of a company to a breach event contributes to its impact. If the company is unresponsive or delays its response, this is detrimental for it. If it is at fault and merely offers basic reparation,

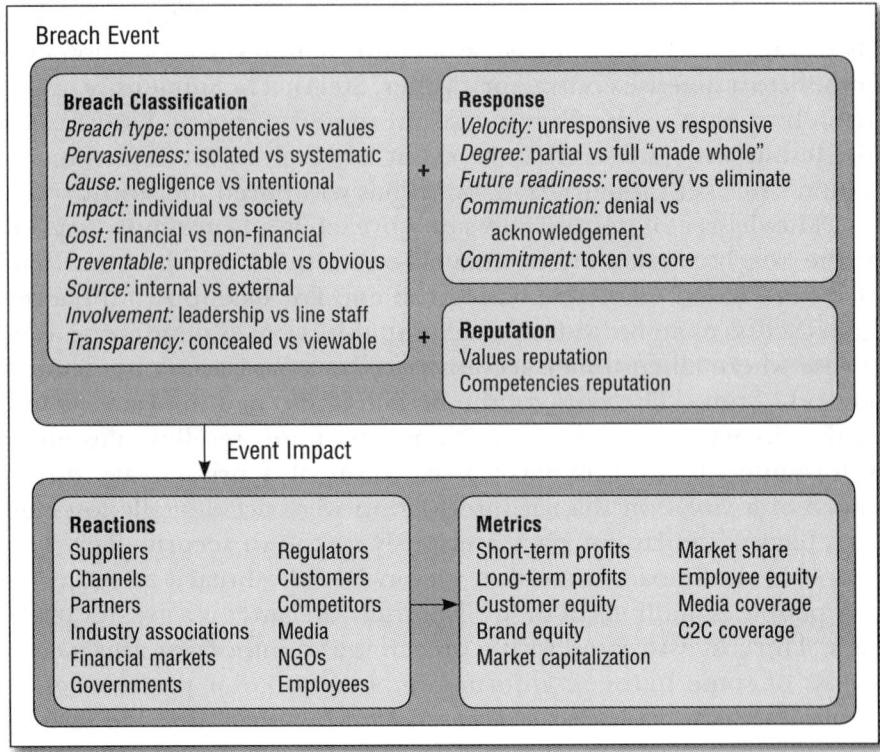

Figure 10.9 Brand Trust Breach Event and Impact

this is viewed as less attractive than when it is seen to sincerely endeavor to undo the damage in full. When it is recovering (if it makes a minimal recovery), this is viewed less positively than when it puts in full force its resources to prevent a recurrence of such an incident. When a company knowingly denies that the event has occurred, this is always viewed as being worse than if it acknowledges its fault. Its level of commitment to the issue is another factor. If a company only makes a token gesture, this is less effective than when it takes on making amends for the incident i as core to its mission. If the breach was purposely concealed by its management, this is seen as being worse than its admitting that such an incident has occurred or underestimating its impact.

In 1994, Intel (Sharangpani, 1994; Janeba, 1995) made the mistake of admitting that its Pentium processor had been found to be prone to making mathematical errors. Intel announced that "an error is only likely to occur [about] once in nine billion random floating point divides," and that "an average spreadsheet user could encounter this subtle flaw once in every 27,000 years of use." Yet this announcement seemed to underestimate the impact made on consumers. Within a month, IBM had to stop shipment of its Pentium-based computers and announced that "Common spreadsheet programs, recalculating for 15 minutes a day, could produce Pentium-related errors as often as once every 24 days." In November 1994, when the company first recognized the issue, it communicated it would only replace the Pentium chip for users who needed high accuracy. Only after a great outcry did it change its stance and announce that it would replace the chip for anyone who wanted it. Intel lost reputation points because of this incident and the way it handled it.

SUMMARY AND FUTURE DIRECTIONS

Trust plays a central role in the financial performance of a brand. It enables cooperative behavior (Deutsch, 1958), promotes adaptive organizational forms, reduces harmful conflict, decreases transaction costs (Williamson, 1993), promotes effective responses to crises, increases investment in relationships, fosters open communication, reduces the need for controls, and forbears opportunism (Smith and Barclay, 1997). Based on a review of trust literature, a value-competency model of trust is suggested in this chapter. It helps to identify the factors contributing to development of trust. Since trust is a core concept in development and optimization of relationships, this section should provide relevant information for future research.

The following are some directions for consideration in the brand trust research stream:

1. Determining to what degree brand trust is the core construct of brand development, or if there is another concept that works better (brand affect, brand loyalty, etc.)
2. Determining to what degree brand trust lead to price premiums and share premiums in the market

3. Gauging whether positioning on trust can provide a competitive advantage
4. Estimating to what extent a "reserve" of trust helps to buffer breach competency-related incidents
5. Determining at what level a company should place brand recovery and in what form it should be in response to breaches in its brand trust values; gauging whether unrelated value investment provides a halo effect to a breach of another type of values (for example, if social philanthropy can offset this if the company's agent is convicted of bribery charges)
6. Determining what causes levels of trust to vary across geographic regions or cultures
7. Estimating the effect of Place-of-Origin on overall trust In a company
8. Gauging what makes trust levels vary by industry and in which industries trust is a key success factor
9. Determining to what extent does trust explains a company's performance
10. Estimating what companies are doing to manage trust
11. Finding out whether they measure brand trust or use a proxy
12. Discovering the best practices in recovery from breach of trust
13. Determining to what degree partnerships affect brand trust
14. Finding out what types of internal branding are needed to optimally sustain trust

REFERENCES

Achrol, R. S. (1991), "Evolution of the Marketing Organization: New Forms for Turbulent Environments," *Journal of Marketing*, 55(4), 77–93.

Alexander, Ralph S. (1960), *Marketing Definitions: A Glossary of Marketing Terms*. Chicago, IL: American Marketing Association.

Ambler, T. (1992), *Need-to-know Marketing*. London: Century Business.

——— (1997), "How Much of Brand Equity is Explained by Trust?" *Management Decision*, 35(4), 283–292.

Aulakh, P., M. Kotabe, and A. Sahay (1996), "Trust and Performance in Cross-border Marketing Partnerships: A Behavioral Approach," *Journal of International Business Studies*, 27(4), 1005–1032.

Barton, S. A. (1994), *Statistical Analysis of Floating Point Flaw in the Pentium Processor.* Santa Clara, CA: Intel Corporation.
Bauyer, R. A. (1967), "Consumer Behavior as Risk Taking," *Dynamic Marketing for a Changing World,* 398. Boston: Division of Research, Harvard Business School.
Bennett, P. D. (1988), *Dictionary of Marketing Terms.* Chicago, IL: The American Marketing Association.
Berry, L. (1991), *Marketing Services.* New York: The Free Press.
Blau, P. (1964), *Exchange and Power in Social Life.* New York: John Wiley and Sons.
Brown, G. (1992), *People, Brands and Advertising.* New York: Millward Brown International.
Butler, J. K. (1991). "Toward Understanding and Measuring Conditions of Trust: Evolution of Conditions of Trust Inventory," *Journal of Management,* 17(3), 643–663.
Chernatony, L. D. (1999), "Experts' Views About Defining Services Brands and the Principles of Services Branding," *Journal of Business Research,* 46, 181.
Chiles, T. H. and J. F. Mcmackin (1996), "Integrating Variable Risk Preferences: Trust and Transaction Cost Economics," *Academy of Management Review,* 21(1), 73–99.
Coleman, J. S. (1990), *Foundations of Social Theory.* Cambridge, MA: Harvard University Press.
Cook, K. S. and R. M. Emerson (1978), "Power, Equity and Commitment in Exchange Networks," *American Sociological Review,* 43(5), 721–739.
Deutsch, M. (1958), "Trust and Ssuspicion," *Journal of Conflict Resolution,* 2(4), 265–279.
Dwyer, F. R., P. H. Schurr, and S. Oh (1987), "Developing Buyer-seller Relationships," *Journal of Marketing,* 51, 11–27.
Edelman (2007), *Trust Barometer.* Emory Marketing Institute Forum. Atlanta, GA: Emory University.
Faust, W. H. and A. Eilertson (1994), "You've Got a Logo, You Need a Brand," *ABA Banking Journal* 86.
Friske, S. T. and Shelley E. T. (1984), *Social Cognition.* Reading, MA: Addison-Wesley.
Fukuyama, F. (1995), *Trust: The Social Virtues and Creation of Prosperity.* New York: The Free Press.
Ganesan, S. (1994), "Determinants of Long-term Orientation in Buyer–Seller Relationships," *Journal of Marketing,* 58(2), 1.
Gardner, Burleigh B. and Sidney J. Levy (1955), "The Product and the Brand," *Harvard Business Review,* 33(2), 33–39.
Gartner (2002), *Gartner Research Note: How will marketing evolve to realize its potential?* Stamford, CT: Gartner.
Geyskens, I., J.-B. E. M. Steenkamp, and N. Kumar (1998), "Generalizations About Trust in Marketing Channel Relationships Using Meta-analysis," *International Journal of Research in Marketing,* 15(3), 223–248.
Global Corrupt Perceptions Index (2005), Germany: Transparency International.
Granovetter, M. S. (1985), "Economic Action and Social Structure: a Theory of Embeddedness," *American Journal of Sociology,* 91(3), 481–510.
Greenwald, A. G. (1980), "The Totalitarian Ego: fabrication and Revision of Personal History," *American Psychologist,* 35(7), 603–618.

Handy, C. (1995), "Trust and the Virtual Organization," *Harvard Business Review*, 73(3), 40–50.
Holmes, J. G. (1991), *Trust and the Appraisal Process in Close Relationships*. London: Jessica Kingsley.
Howard, J. W., Mayron R. (1980), "Social Categorization and Memory for In-group and Out-group Behavior," *Journal of Personality and Social Psychology*, 38(2), 301–310.
Ikalafeng, T. (2004), "A Better Life For All," *Adfocus*, May, 24.
Janeba, M. (1995), *The Pentium Problem*. Available at http://www.willamette.edu/~mjaneba/pentprob.html (accessed 2014).
Keller, K. L. (2003), *Building, Measuring, and Managing Brand Equity*. Englewood Cliffs, Prentice-Hall: New Jersey.
Keller, K. L. and D. R. Lehmann (2003), "How Do Brands Create Value?" *Marketing Management*, 12(3), 26–31.
Kirkpatrick, J. (1996), "I Survived the Titanic," *National Geographic World*, July, 24–29.
Kotler, P. (1991), *Marketing Management*. Englewood Cliffs, NJ: Prentice-Hall.
Kumar, N. (1996), "The Power of Trust in Manufacturer–Retailer Relationships," *Harvard Business Review*, 74, 92–106.
Layne, A. (2001), *How to Make Your Company More Resilient*. Harlan, IA: Fast Company.
Lewicki, R. J. and Barbara Benedict Bunker (1995), Trust in relationships: a model of trust development and decline, Jossey-Bass: San Francisco.
Lewis, J. D. and A. Weigert (1985), "Trust as a Social Reality," *Social Forces*, 63, 967–985.
Luo, W. and M. Najdawi (2004), "Trust-building Measures: A Review of Consumer Health Portals," *Communications of the ACM*, 47(1), 109–113.
Maccrimmon, K. R. W. (1988), *Taking Risks: The Management of Uncertainty*. New York: The Free Press.
Markus, H. (1977), Self-schemata and processing information about the self, *Journal of Personality and Social Psychology*, 35(2), 63–78.
Mayer, R. C., J. H. Davis, and F. D. Schoorman (1995), "An Integrative Model of OrganizationalTrust," *Academy of Management Review*, 20(3), 709–734.
McAllister, D. J. (1995), "Affect- and Cognition-based Trust As Foundations for Interpersonal Cooperation in Organizations," *Academy of Management Journal*, 38(1), 24–59.
Miller, L. (2004), "Government Finds no Violation in JetBlue Privacy Case," USA Today, February 20, 2004, Washington. Available at http://usatoday30.usatoday.com/tech/news/techpolicy/2004-02-20-jetblue-privacy_x.htm
Moorman, C., G. Zaltman, and R. Deshpande (1992), "Relationships Between Providers and Users of Market Research: The Dynamics of Trust Within and Between Organizations," *Journal of Marketing Research*, 29, 314–328.
Morrall, K. (1995), "Creating a Cohesive Image Through Branding," *Bank Marketing*, 27(8), 23–28.
Nail, J. (2004), *Plugging the Advertising Trust Gap*. Cambridge, MA: Forrester Research.

Narayandas, D. and V. K. Rangan (2004), "Building and Sustaining Buyer–Seller Relationships in Mature Industrial Markets," *Journal of Marketing*, 68(3), 63–77.

Nisbett, R. E. and Lee Ross (1980), *Human Interference: Strategies and Shortcomings of Social Judgments*. Englewood Cliffs, NJ: Prentice-Hall.

North, D. C. (1990), *Institutions, Institutional Change, and Economic Performance*. Cambridge: Cambridge University Press.

Orwell, G. (1950), *1984*. New York: Signet Classics.

O'Shaughnessy, J. (1992), *Explaining Buyer Behavior: Central Concepts and Philosophy of Science Issues*. Oxford: Oxford University Press.

Palmatier, R. W., R. P. Dant, and D. Grewal (2007), "A Comparative Longitudinal Analysis of Theoretical Perspectives of Interorganizational Relationship Performance," *Journal of Marketing*, 71(4), 172–194.

Petty, R. E. and John T. Cacioppo (1981), *Attitudes and Persuasion: Classic and Contemporary Approaches*. Dubuque, IA: William C. Brown.

Pine, B. J. and J. H. Gilmore (1999), *The Experience Economy*, Boston, MA: Harvard Business Press.

Reast, J. D. (2005), "Brand Trust and Brand Extension Acceptance: the Relationship," *The Journal of Product and Brand Management*, 14(1), 4–13.

Rich, G. A. (1997), "The Sales Manager as a Role Model: Effect on Trust, Job Satisfaction, and Performance of Salespeople," *Academy of Marketing Science*, 25(4), 319–328.

Romaniuk, J. and S. Bogomolova (2005), "Variation in brand trust scores," *Journal of Targeting, Measurement and Analysis for Marketing*, 13(4), 363–373.

Roselius, R. (1971), "Consumer Rankings of Risk Reduction Methods," *Journal of Marketing*, 35(1), 56–61.

Ross, L. and Craig A. Anderson (1982), *Shortcomings in the Attribution Process: On the Origins and Maintenance of Eroneous Social Assessments*. Cambridge University Press: Cambridge.

Rotter, J. B. (1967), "A New Scale for Measurement of Interpersonal Trust," *Journal of Personality*, 35(4), 651–665.

Schurr, P. H. and J. L. Ozanne (1985), "Influences on Exchange Processes: Buyers' Preconceptions of a Seller's Trustworthiness and Bargaining Toughness," *Journal of Consumer Research*, 11(4), 939–953.

Smith, J. B. and D. W. Barclay (1997), "The Effects of Organizational Differences and Trust on the Effectiveness of Selling Partner Relationships," *Journal of Marketing*, 61(1), 3–21.

Srivastava, R. K., T. A. Shervani, and L. Fahey (1998), "Market-based Assets and Shareholder Value: A Framework for Analysis," *Journal of Marketing*, 62(1), 2–18.

Swann, W. B. (1981), "Self-verification Processes: how We Sustain our Self-conceptions," *Journal of Experimental Social Psychology* 17(4), 351–372.

Taylor, J. W. (1974), "The Role of Risk in Consumer Behavior," *Journal of Marketing*, 38(2), 54–60.

Taylor, S. E. and Jonathon D. Brown (1988), "Illusion and Well-being: A Social Psychological Perspective on Mental Health," *Psychological Bulletin*, 103(2), 193–210.

Tyler, T. R. (1990), *Why People Obey the Law*. New Haven, CT: Yale University Press.
Williamson, O. E. (1993), "Calculativeness, Trust, and Economic Organization," *Journal of Law and Economics*, 36(s1), 453–486.
Zucker, L. G. (1986), *Production of Trust: Institutional Sources of Economic Structure, 1840–1920*. Greenwich, CT: JAI Press.

Section III
Leveraging Brands

Chapter 11
Branding and Emerging Markets

Martin Roll

A quick look at the major media outlets, be they newspapers, magazines, websites, professional conferences or consulting engagements, highlights the global obsession with emerging markets. The rather large bloc of countries in South America, Eastern Europe, and Asia constitute what is known as the emerging markets. Despite the geographic separation of these clusters of countries, they share some dominant and distinguishing characteristics. Most of them were either socialist or controlled capitalist economies. They were closed from the global economy for a long time. They are also characterized by their high populations, without improvements in physical, intellectual and financial capital. Many of these countries have opened their economies to foreign direct investment and thereby taken a step toward fuller integration with the global economy. Consequently, these economies seem very similar on many important dimensions.

Although many economies, such as Brazil, Dubai, and Turkey to name a few, are aggressively developing their economies, it is usually Asia that manages to capture global attention. Although at first glance, this obsession can be dismissed as yet another media-induced hype by curious onlookers, a deeper analysis of hard facts reveals the evolution taking place in the most important of all these emerging markets—Asia.

THE ASIAN LANDSCAPE

With a congregation of 49 countries, a total population of 3.6 billion, a rising middle class of over 300 million, economies growing at the average rate of 5%–7%, incredibly diverse customer segments, thriving home markets in which new products can be tested, the increasing integration of the rural population with the mainstream and rapidly developing markets with immense potential, Asia is indeed a region that attracts the ever-increasing interest of the global business community.

An increasing number of global brands are entering the Asian market to grab a piece of the pie. With the booming economies of China and India leading in the region, Asia is leaping toward global business dominance in coming decades. However, despite its impressive characteristics, Asia's potential is sometimes missed by those who are not knowledgeable about the region. Frequent political turmoil, the seemingly incredible diversity (in literally every aspect of life), the strong hand of the state, and differing cultures frequently instill fear and suspicion instead of open up an exciting vista of business opportunities. However, despite all this, the Asia is evolving into a booming market that may well become the global economic engine in coming decades. A comparison of some vital statistics of Western and Asian markets will help to reiterate this point.

The US market, with its around 319 million people, is a mature one.[1] However, the bulk of this population, the baby boomers, is retiring and thus is reducing their consumption. Moreover, the majority of the people in the country are over the age of 35. Furthermore, given the maturity of its capital markets, free competition and the presence of well-developed institutional intermediaries, US companies have been able to consistently penetrate various market segments. In addition, the penetration of the internet has empowered customers and society in general. Consequently, taken together, despite the business prowess of the US, its market potential is stable, but saturated.

---

[1] https://www.cia.gov/library/publications/the-world-factbook/geos/us.html (accessed October 2014).

The European market tells a much similar story.[2] Geographic clustering of some of the most advanced economies in the world such as Germany, the UK, and France has enabled their markets to reap the scale and scope of local economies and populations for a long time. However, much like in the USA, European markets are gradually slowing down. Countries in the continent have a combined population of around 742 million. Furthermore, Europe's population is forecasted to decline to around 696 million by 2025. Moreover, in addition to declining populations, Europeans are getting older, costs are continuously rising, and markets are fast maturing. And although the per capita income of people is high, with even higher disposable incomes in the advanced countries, the markets have become saturated.

BOOMING MARKETS IN ASIA

China and India are leading the pack. With a combined population of more than 2.5 billion, these countries are fast becoming the gold mine that all corporate organizations are eager to get a piece of. Added to this is the fact that apart from a handful of developed countries in Asia such as Japan, South Korea, Taiwan and Singapore, most of the others are still grappling with the challenge of morphing into developed economies.

China's gross domestic product surged from less than US$150 billion in 1978 to US$8,227 billion in 2012.[3] The country produced a mere 2.2% of the world's output in 1980, but this rose to 7% in 2000, 14% in 2011, and is projected to top 18% by 2016.[4]

China's foreign trade is expanding significantly, and since 1980, the country became the first to overtake the USA in attracting foreign investment—China attracted US$59.1 billion as against

[2] https://www.cia.gov/library/publications/the-world-factbook/geos/ee.html (accessed October 2014).
[3] http://blogs.hbr.org/2013/11/chinas-economy-in-six-charts/ (accessed October 2014).
[4] http://www.theage.com.au/national/china-to-lead-world-economy-20110424-1dt1j.html (accessed October 2014).

US$57.4 billion in the case of the USA in 2012.[5] The country has seen an average annual growth in its GDP of over 8%. With relatively low wages and a strong investment in manufacturing infrastructure, it has managed to become one the most favored manufacturing hub in the world.[6]

With a population of over a billion people, India's economy has grown at an average rate of over 7%–8% over the last couple of years. The country's GDP growth surpassed expectations to record 9.43% in 2005, but has slowed in recent years. It attracted over US$50 billion in foreign direct investment in 2005, second only to China, but has had to work much harder to attract foreign investors in recent years.[7] Most importantly, its English-speaking, technology-savvy labor force has made India the outsourcing hub of the world. Furthermore, more than 50% of the country's population is below the age of 25 and more than 65% below the age of 35. It is expected that the average age of an Indian will be 29 years in 2020, compared to 37 for China and 48 for Japan.[8] All these factors make India a potentially lucrative market for global companies, although foreign enterprises find it difficult to penetrate its market.

Apart from China and India, Asian countries such as Thailand, Malaysia, Vietnam, Indonesia and the Philippines present immense opportunities for growth. Myanmar, which is opening its economy to the world, is another example. All these countries share some basic characteristics. They have relatively small domestic markets, are still developing and are not completely integrated into the global economy as is the case with some of the other Asian countries. Most of these countries still have a nascent market and the majority of their population is still at, or in many cases, is below the poverty line. Their markets are neither matured not saturated. Their domestic markets have become the primary target of global companies.

Therefore, it is clear that the distinctive features of Asia countries make them the most lucrative among emerging markets. However,

---

[5] http://en.wikipedia.org/wiki/Foreign_direct_investment#China (accessed October 2014).

[6] https://www.cia.gov/library/publications/the-world-factbook/geos/ch.html (accessed October 2014).

[7] http://www.ft.com/intl/cms/s/0/a0f23c4c-cf57-11e3-9165-00144feabdc0.html#axzz32yB9Nk5W (accessed October 2014).

[8] http://en.wikipedia.org/wiki/Demographics_of_India (accessed October 2014).

the differences between Asian and developed Western markets are deeper than mere economic statistics.

THE ASIAN BRANDSCAPE

However, despite impressive statistics about the potential of Asian markets, Asia's presence in the global brandscape is fairly minimal. The annual Interbrand survey of the top 100 global brands features the most valuable ones in the world.[9] Out of these 100 brands, only 10 originate in Asia. Brands such as Samsung, Hyundai, and KIA (South Korea), and Sony, Nintendo, Canon, Toyota, and Panasonic (Japan) are the main ones that have made their mark. No other brands from Asia have really hit the jackpot yet.

Even beyond these 100 international brands, there are only a handful of global Asian brands such as Singapore Airlines (Singapore), Huawei (China), Mandarin Oriental (Hong Kong) and a few others that have made their mark. There are also many relatively smaller brands such as Banyan Tree Hotels & Resorts (luxury resort), Charles & Keith (shoes and bags), Jim Thompson (lifestyle) and Amorepacific (skincare and cosmetics) that are rising but are yet to become truly global.

It is disappointing that in spite of huge market opportunities for Asian companies, not many have built resonating brands that can successfully withstand competition in the global market. The reasons for this lack of branding are many, and the important underlying one can be traced to the historical origins of the dominant Asian mindset. While most of the Western world traces the origin of its dominant individualistic behavior patterns to Aristotle, most Asian cultures trace the origin of their dominant collectivistic behavior patterns to Confucius. The important traits of this collectivistic behavior pattern include avoidance of risk, collaboration rather than competition, and the community before individual. In line with this ideology, most Asian businesses have for a very long time been fighting to avoid risk. They have accomplished this by

---

[9] http://www.interbrand.com/en/best-global-brands/2013/Best-Global-Brands-2013.aspx (accessed October 2014).

diversifying their businesses to spread the risk; built tangible assets such as buildings, factories, assembly lines and companies, and focused on their immediate business gains.

The direct consequence of their actions has been their lack of conviction and commitment to building strong brands. The business mindset in Asia dictated that companies focused more on immediate tangible gains rather than on long-term intangible ones.

Branding, if practiced right, is an ongoing process that requires considerable allocation of financial, managerial, and technological resources. This, combined with the fact that results are not immediate, were reasons enough for companies' top management to relegate branding as yet another tactical tool in the hands of marketing managers who used it as an optional ingredient in their advertising campaigns.

In this chapter, we have examined the current state of affairs of branding in emerging markets, especially in Asia. It has three main sections. The first delineates the main reasons for Asia's earlier refusal to invest in building global brands. The second provides a toolkit for Western managers to effectively weave their brands into Asian markets. The final section offers Asian boardrooms strategies they can use to create global Asian brands.

BRANDING AND EMERGING ECONOMIES

In discussing branding -related challenges and opportunities facing companies in emerging economies, we have presented some examples from Asia that showcase both sides of the coin.

One of the greatest challenges for Asian companies, apart from the trading mindset alluded to earlier, is the "Made In" tag. Differences between the different Asian countries and their associations have a significant impact on brands. Japan, South Korea, and China are three Asian countries that represent the developed-developing spectrum. Japan had managed to build a very positive image as a country fairly early, and demonstrate that it was a country of high productivity, high quality and high technological prowess. This positive image gave a significant boost to Japanese brands. "Made in Japan" became an asset and Japanese companies leveraged this to the hilt. True to the perception of Japan being a quality and technological powerhouse, many companies such as Honda, Toyota, and Sony introduced breakthrough products and made a mark in the USA and the world market. Japanese companies and their global brands became benchmarks for other global companies, with their management skills and best practices.

Korea had to struggle (due to the Korean War) to create an alternative positive country image. The financial crisis in Asia in the mid 1990s came as a blessing in disguise for Korean companies. Many Korean *chaebols* (conglomerates) were highly diversified businesses with no strategic focus, and were fragmented in nature. The financial crisis forced these to prune their businesses and focus on quality and design to extract a premium. Samsung led with its single-minded focus on world-class design, quality and technological superiority and rose rapidly. The key to this change was the mindset of its owner and chairman, Lee Kun-hee, who believed in creating a market-driven and brand-focused company. Samsung broke the glass ceiling and became the first global Korean brand. Strong governmental support and enforcement of stringent intellectual property laws have also contributed to a conducive brand/business atmosphere for Korean companies.

China, on the other hand, has had to overcome many obstacles in its attempt to emerge as a brand giant. The country was isolated from the rest of the global economy for a long time because of its state-controlled economy and communist regime. When it did decide to open up its economy gradually, it had to counter the negative perception of the "Made in China" tag.[10] To add to this, is the huge counterfeit market thriving in the country. Moreover, lack of protection of intellectual property rights, supporting infrastructure outside the big cities, and transparency in business deals as well as the interference of its government have all been detrimental for China's aspirations to become a brand giant. However, a handful of companies such as Lenovo, Haier and Huawei have managed to break the glass ceiling and emerge in the global market.

As is evident from these examples, challenges to branding can be fairly idiosyncratic in different countries. Haier is a classic

---

[10] http://www.martinroll.com/resources/articles/marketing/how-nations-and-brands-overcome-country-of-origin-challenges/ (accessed October 2014).

example of sheer focus, tenacity and clever strategy. The company was one of the Chinese companies that broke away from the traditional state-owned enterprise paradigm, professionalized its operations and went international. Ruimin Zhang, a shrewd businessman, was appointed its Managing Director in 1984. His leadership contributed majorly to Haier's expansion and success.

The Haier brand is built on quality and the company's commitment to offer innovative products at a competitive prices. Haier's success in global markets is no surprise. It is one of the few Chinese companies that chose to follow a careful strategy that helped it first establish a leadership position in the domestic market before venturing into global ones. Moreover, unlike most players that concentrate on the low end of the market by offering cheap products, Haier has focused on both ends of the spectrum by offering innovative products at competitive prices—and this has paid rich dividends. The company is one of the leading brands in the USA in mini-refrigerator category. Haier's commitment to quality and innovation is evident in the streamlined operations of its five R&D centers in Beijing, Milan, Seoul, Tokyo and Los Angeles.[11]

A recent management book about Haier examined three decades of choices it made, which were linked by a common vision that enabled it to incorporated five main characteristics in its operations. These were responsible for the company's success:[12]

1. *Innovation:* Haier demonstrates cutting-edge innovation in its products, business model, and corporate culture.
2. *Speed:* The company acts more quickly than its competing companies.
3. *Customer-centricity:* It effectively communicates with customers and takes action based on their input.
4. *Ability to attract the right talent:* Haier attracts and unlocks talent
5. *Leadership:* The company's high-quality leadership has been instrumental for its success.

[11] http://www.chinese-champions.com/haier-group/ (accessed October 2014).
[12] http://as.wiley.com/WileyCDA/PressRelease/pressReleaseId-108177.html (accessed October 2014).

However, despite these few success stories, there are huge challenges facing the many aspiring companies in many of the emerging economies in their quest to create resonating brands. Some such important challenges are discussed in the following section.

REASONS FOR LACK OF BRANDING IN ASIA

Despite the innumerable opportunities that Asia offers to local, regional and global companies, it is still an evolving region. Many countries in Asia lag far behind the developed world in terms of their infrastructure, business frameworks, protection of intellectual property rights and established business practices. This complex mix of markets poses a humungous challenge for businesses. Therefore, in spite of its significant potential, Asia has for long remained the workshop for global brands. Leveraging low costs in the region, Asian companies have thrived as original equipment manufacturers (OEMs) supplying their products to well-known, global brands.

Added to all this has been the traditional mindsets of Asian managers and businesses that have valued tangible benefits and assets as compared to intangibles such as brands. A combination of these and certain other factors has resulted in hardly any global brands originating from Asia.

However, booming economic conditions in Asia in the past decade have compelled Asian companies to leverage their comparative cost advantage and emerge as the world's manufacturing and outsourcing hub. Asian managers have leveraged the low cost of labor and production to thrive as OEMs to global corporations. Although this phase in Asia's economic activity has facilitated its rise to global economic prominence, it has also become one of the major obstacles in the path of Asian companies trying to realize the importance of creating strategic advantages.

Asia remains one of the world's largest providers of commodities. Asian manufacturers mainly produce for other companies and the majority of these products are non-branded goods without any identity or personality. The direct result of this has been that the largest part of financial values is captured by manufacturers' customers—the next player in the value chain—primarily driven by strong brand strategies, and successfully planned and executed marketing programs.

There are many reasons for the emphasis on production of commodities in Asia. Asians are known to believe in what they see, feel and touch—tangible object. Historically, Asian businesses have invested heavily in accumulating physical assets—factories, assembly lines, companies, and so on. The focus has always been on short-term profitability and immediate turnover. Moreover, most Asian companies still view branding as advertising or logo designs. If they are to benefit from branding, they must recognize that it affects the entire business—the structure, goals, attitude and outlook of those in the boardroom. Managers will need to see branding not as an appendage to the ongoing business, but as an infusion that seeps through the very spirit of an organization as a healthy return on investment (ROI). Some of the main reasons for Asia's lack of branding include the following:

Trading mind set: Despite the rapid economic growth in Asia and its integration with the global economy, the business mindset is still predominantly driven by short-term sales and turnovers. Managers are more comfortable investing in tangible assets than in intangibles such as brands and innovation. Although such an orientation has helped many Asian economies achieve scale and scope in manufacturing sectors in the early part of the resurgence of the region, this orientation is a major deterrent in Asia's current effort to build strong brands. A conservative mindset that is focused on the tangible, the short-term and the risk-minimizing aspects of business has manifested itself by branding being relegated to the optional and tactical tool of marketing departments. Consequently, Asian companies have not fully realized the strategic role of branding and corporate management, especially of the CEO, in instilling branding as an organization-wide discipline in organizations.

Diversification of businesses: The origin of many Asian businesses can be traced to their founding families. Unlike in many advanced Western economies, where founding families gradually dilute their stakes in their businesses and such corporations evolve as a pure form of public corporations, Asian economies are still dominated by family-owned/controlled companies. Given the huge stakes of family wealth in such companies, for a long time the conventional wisdom has been to minimize risk by diversifying. As a result of this, many of the biggest corporations in Asia have very diversified operations—often in industries that have no connection with one another. Although this provides these conglomerates the opportunity to leverage their scale and power to dominate the market, it also puts immense pressure on them to maintain a focus and compete in the respective industries. More important, establishing their organizational identity becomes a challenge for them. Building brands is fundamentally about creating a strong organizational identity, and as such, such companies have had difficulties, given their multiple businesses.

Evolving economy: Apart from the developed economies of Japan, Singapore, Hong Kong, Taiwan, and South Korea, most other Asian economies are still evolving. A direct consequence of this is the increased participation of national and local governments in different roles in these economies. More often than not, it has been observed that such intervention may result in domestic companies being accorded a favored status, which can at times upset the business dynamics of an industry. For example, it is widely documented that the Chinese government has special, favorable lending procedures for Chinese companies compared to foreign ones. Furthermore, in many Asian countries, including China, India, Thailand, Indonesia, and Malaysia, government influence is both formal (through board appointments) and informal (through networks of influential personnel). Such influence, combined with socialist/communist ideologies, can mean that investing in branding may not be a priority.

Intellectual property rights: Lack of stringent enforcement of protection of intellectual property has been a major challenge in building brands. The counterfeit market in many Asian countries poses a huge challenge for both local and global companies, since counterfeit products not only undercut companies' profits, but also hurts their brands. One of the main reasons for such a thriving counterfeit market is the lack of stringent intellectual property right laws. In their own backyards, many Asian companies have faced rampant counterfeiting and infringement of intellectual property rights. Therefore, until and unless legislation and law enforcement improves in the region, these may be hurdles that hamper a deeper appreciation and respect for intangible asset management in Asian boardrooms. The World Customs Organization has estimated that

5%–7% of trade in global merchandise, amounting to US$450 billion, was due to counterfeiting in 2005. China alone is estimated to contribute a significant share of fake and pirated goods worldwide. In 2004, for example, French luxury house LVMH spent more than US$16 million on investigations, busts and legal fees against counterfeiting.

The counterfeit market has become one of the most pressing challenges in China's quest to build a strong country brand at a holistic level and for individual companies that have to combat this problem on a daily basis. Given such an environment, Asian corporations' hesitation to invest in building brands is understandable.

Diverse demographics: Asia is one of the regions that has the widest diversities in the world in terms of its demographic composition. Not only is its population diverse, it is also the youngest in the world—more than 50% of India's population of 1.1 billion is under the age of 30. Moreover, the majority of Asia's population still lives below the poverty line. There is a growing gap between the rich and the poor. At the same time, a larger number of people are being employed due to outsourcing and are joining the huge middle class category. All this makes it challenging for companies to strategize and build brands that appeal to a cross section of a society and are not only profitable, but also economically viable. In recent years, companies have been realizing the importance of serving the people at the bottom of the pyramid. Not only are companies formulating innovative strategies to reach such customers, they are also building their brand identities from the ground up. However, although such initiatives can offer companies opportunities to create awareness of their brands in diverse segments, they also create tougher challenges in terms of defining coherent brand identities and brand communication strategies. This demonstrates how diverse demographics in Asia can act as a barrier to branding.

Lack of CEOs' support: The one reason, more than any other mentioned earlier, which influences the creation of strong brands, is the mindset of the boardroom and the CEO. Branding is a boardroom discipline and successful brands can only be built when the boardroom, led by the chairman and the CEO, understands, appreciates and commits itself to treating branding as a strategic discipline and devotes the resources at the company's disposal to support brands continuously.

However, with Asian CEOs' complete lack of comprehensive understanding of branding discipline, it is no surprise that Asia has not been able to build many strong brands. Some of the best known global brands are led by their CEOs acting as their chief brand ambassadors. These brands are adequately represented in the boardroom. The corporate strategies of such brands are well aligned with their branding strategies. Brands are treated as strategic assets. Any strategic initiative is evaluated in terms of its potential detrimental effect on brand equity. These are decisions that are taken at the top of an organization, and consequently, the direct involvement of the corporate boardroom and the CEO is of paramount importance. However, given the dominant orientation of Asian CEOs and the institutional environment in Asian economies, Asian brands are not yet led effectively by CEOs.

The seven-step strategy to build powerful brands in emerging economies: Emerging economies, with their diverse cultures, business practices and customer segments, are much more complex than other any others in the world. The clusters are made up of certain highly developed countries such as Japan, South Korea, Taiwan, Singapore, and Hong Kong, which have ultra-urban and modern consumers with deep pockets. Moreover, there are a rapidly growing number of countries such as Brazil, China, India, Indonesia, Russia, Thailand and others with consumers who are willing to experiment with new products. However, there are several other still developing countries such as Vietnam, Cambodia, Sri Lanka and others, with people living below the poverty line and consuming only the bare minimum. Unlike markets in USA and Europe, where customers have reached a certain level of understanding and sophistication, these markets are still in their infancy in branding.

Diverse mindsets, the complexity of business structures, the diversity of demographic composition and the huge geographic extant requires certain unique branding strategies. The following are some essential steps to achieve this:

Create a strong differentiation: In many still developing countries such as Indonesia, China, Sri Lanka and Vietnam, Western brands are still looked up to, since people in these countries aspire to own global brands. With many local companies striving to create similar products at lower prices, Western brands would do well to create a strong differentiation by leveraging their brand equity.

Similarly, local brands that aspire to make it big must tap into unique cultural associations and local myths to weave their brands in the societal fiber.

Establish a strong distribution network: Brazil, Russia, India, Indonesia, and China, which are five of the largest economies in the emerging block, are vast countries, and distribution holds the key to success in many of their industry sectors. The major percentage of their population lives in rural areas, which are not usually covered by the major brands. However, with the increased migration of consumers from the rural to the mainstream economy, success in rural areas will prove critical. Some major brands such as P&G and Unilever have benefited from such a focus and localized many of their products to suit the needs of these emerging segments. Coca-Cola has also recognized this emerging phenomenon and has expanded beyond Shanghai and Guangzhou and into the heartlands of China.

Glocalize: As emerging economies mature gradually, they begin developing strong individual consumption identities. This is evident from the increasing demand for products that are localized to suit the preferences of customers. Global brands that enter these markets must retain their brand identities at the strategic level, but localize their tactical implementation such as their communication, product offerings, and so on. This combination of global brands with local products will enable global companies to weave their brands into the fabric of local society and make these a part of the community. Similarly, local brands must leverage their knowledge of local consumers to create brand identities that not only appeal to customers, but also create pride in the origins of the brands.

Leverage cross-border synergies: In spite of the many differences between these countries, companies can leverage their scale of operations and supply chains across borders to optimize their profitability. The relatively lower cost of production offers them a good platform to serve entire regions. By standardizing the major part of their products and fine-tuning the final offerings to suit local tastes, they can minimize their costs and gain scale.

Recognize and respond to unique regional markets: Asia, Eastern Europe and South America are mosaics of cultures and rich heritages. Each country has a unique pattern of consumption. Companies should be careful not to generalize across them as a homogenous region by ignoring their regional and national uniqueness. Managers aspiring to participate in these booming markets need to appreciate the challenges mentioned earlier. Since these countries are fast evolving and integrating with the global economy, none of these challenges and market situations are static. Businesses should develop the flexibility to quickly react to changes in the market and adapt their strategies to successfully compete and survive in it.

Collaborate and co-create: Many global and regional companies entering these new markets have collaborated and leveraged the resources of local companies. The combination of a strong brand equity, financial prowess, the business acumen of global brands, local networks, established distribution channels and a strong knowledge of the local customers of domestic companies offer a winning scenario. Such collaboration would not only facilitate a quicker entry into the market, but also enable a company to learn the nuances of the local business market.

Leverage the unique Asian culture: Companies that plan to build brands in these emerging economies must leverage unique local cultures to relate to their customers. Each country in the cluster has a very strong history and heritage that has for long influenced the local cultures and practices of companies as well as consumers. Companies should tap into these specific details and incorporate them in their brand personalities and identities so that their customers can be offered an authentic experience. See Brand Cases 1 and 2.

Brand Case 1: Unilever and Nokia—Glocalization as a Branding Strategy

Unilever is a classic example of a global brand that has pioneered offering products to locals that address their sensitivities. The company's Indian subsidiary, Hindustan Level Limited (HLL), has been the leader in recognizing the tremendous opportunity at the bottom of the pyramid. It serves a customer base that aspires to consume products, but in smaller quantities and at lower prices. HLL invented shampoo sachets—small plastic packets of shampoo for as little as INR1 (US$0.022). This became such a rage among rural consumers that many other brands started offering products such as detergents, coffee and tea powder, coconut oil and tooth paste in

(Contd)

(Contd)

> sachets. And even though the unit prices of these products were higher, rural consumers could afford to purchase smaller quantities at their convenience. This also illustrated that rural consumers are eager and ready to seek global brands and the benefits these provide in terms of their quality, value and emotional benefits.
>
> Another example is that of the mobile brand Nokia, which once dominated the mobile phone category before Apple and Samsung disrupted the industry. Nokia recognized the growing importance of rural customers in the Indian mobile telephone market, which grew from a mere 300,000 subscribers in 1996 to a whopping 55 million subscribers in 2004. Nokia introduced its dust-resistant keypad with an anti-slip grip and an inbuilt flashlight. These features, although minor, appealed to a specific target group of truck drivers initially and then to a broader segment of rural consumers including farmers and local shop-owners. They endeared Nokia to the Indian consumer, since the company demonstrated its genuine commitment to responding to local customers' needs and adapting its products accordingly.

> **Brand Case 2: Indo-Japanese Collaboration in the Indian Auto Market**
>
> Many Japanese brands have collaborated with Indian ones to enter the Indian market and have been highly successful. The Indian automobile market is a case in point—Kawasaki's collaboration with Bajaj (Indian motorbike brand) and Honda's strategic alliance with Hero (Indian automobile brand). Both Kawasaki and Honda entered the Indian market long before the current boom in it at a time when the market was still an enigma for many foreign brands. By strategically leveraging the capabilities of the local brands of Bajaj and Hero, respectively, the Japanese brands gained instant access into the complexities of the Indian market, its distribution channels, and the Indian consumers' mindset. These partnerships have also benefited Indian brands that rode high on the equity of Japanese brands, which have been traditionally recognized for their technological prowess and high quality. It will be such collaborations that will help brands in Asia's complex markets.

DOMINANT BRANDING STRATEGIES

Given these examples and brand cases, it is apparent that there is no one size fits all strategy for companies from emerging economies to build global brands. However, as comprehensively discussed earlier, there are three dominant strategies that can be adopted by such companies in their quest to build global brands.

Organic Growth Strategy

An organic growth strategy is one using which companies grow their brands based on their own potential without exploiting the possible synergies of other established brands. Companies strive to grow organically by expanding in the same market or other markets by having full management control over their brands. This strategy has its own advantages and disadvantages. Since a company is the sole owner of a brand, this gives it a lot of leeway in deciding on its positioning and personality. It also provides companies with the freedom to invest in and continuously manage their brands across all touch points. The disadvantage of this strategy is that companies may not be able to extend their brands beyond a certain set of product categories and market segments due to their high requirement of resources. This makes it challenging for them to launch new brands, since large investments are required. Moreover, since a brand would have built in certain entrenched personalities in consumers' minds, branching out into different product lines could prove challenging, depending on how large the resource requirements are, in order to establish and communicate this. See Brand Case 3.

Brand Case 3: Alibaba.com's Organic Path to Brand Dominance

In other parts of the world, Amazon and eBay may be the top e-Commerce players, but the online marketplace of Hangzhou, China's Alibaba, handles more sales than both the companies combined.[13] Not only are these global giants struggling to establish a competitive market position in China, they will have to begin looking over their shoulders in the global market place as well. Alibaba is not a Chinese brand for China, it is a China-based brand for the world.

(Contd)

[13] http://www.forbes.com/sites/walterloeb/2013/07/24/alibaba-a-threat-to-amazon-ebay-walmart-and-everyone-else/ (accessed October 2014).

(*Contd*)

The company's founder, Jack Ma, a former English teacher who founded the company in 1999 out of his apartment, calls it the "everything company." Already, a combination of Amazon, eBay, PayPal, and travel sites such as Zuji, Alibaba's affiliate site, also has an advertising business to challenge Google. The strategy, Ma admits, is to build a company that is so diversified that a consumer will not have to go anywhere else. In a difficult market, marred by global recessions, fears of a slowing Chinese economy, fleeting customers and competitors with deep-pockets, Alibaba has been able to continue grow and expand with help from strategic partnerships, mergers and acquisitions, and the steadfast leadership of its founder to build a company that truly serves its customers.

In 2005, Alibaba received US$1 billion from Yahoo! in exchange for 40% of the company—a figure that would not have been invested if it had not been for the aggressive and, at times, provocatively customer-centric philosophy of Jack Ma. While Ma's charisma has enabled him to sell a vision for his company, he has also earned the nickname "Crazy Jack" because of his animated personality.

In shareholder meetings, Ma has been known to announce his priority for customers, employees and investors, in this specific order. Although such announcements are quite rare in the Western world, where shareholders form the primary interest group of any company, Jack Ma has made a strategy of making his customers his primary priority. When the company filed for its US IPO in 2014, Ma wrote a letter to employees, which said, "We haven't survived because our strategies are farsighted and brilliant, or because our execution is perfect, but because for 15 years we have persevered in our mission of 'making it easier to do business across the world,' because we have insisted on a 'customer first' value system, because we have persisted in believing in the future, and because we have insisted that normal people can do extraordinary things."[14]

B2C service brands from developing Asia that achieve success on a global scale are extremely rare outside of the hospitality and airline sectors. Most giants in emerging markets, such as Lenovo, Infosys and Huawei, have a huge component of their brands based on B2B products and services. This makes Alibaba's ascent even more notable.

The most recent phase of Alibaba's growth has been defined by mergers and acquisitions. In 2012, Yahoo! reduced its ownership stake in Alibaba to 23%,[15] giving the latter more freedom to pursue its broader strategies. Since then, a flood of acquisitions have propelled Alibaba into new sectors including health care information systems, shopping mall operations, GPS navigation, ride-sharing, and banking and financial services. Next came Alibaba's push in the USA by launching a US

(*Contd*)

[14] http://www.businessinsider.sg/jack-ma-founder-alibaba-2014-5/#.U4M5m_mSyap (accessed October 2014).

[15] http://www.digitalstrategyconsulting.com/netimperative/news/2012/09/yahoo_sheds_half_of_alibaba_st.php (accessed October 2014).

(Contd)

e-Commerce website called 11 Main, and buying stakes in US retail site ShopRunner and 1stDibs, a marketplace for antiques, art, and furniture.[16]

However, despite its momentum, there is great risk in Alibaba's future. Many Chinese companies have not found North American markets worthwhile and face massive resistance in these. There is also a risk that Alibaba may be over-diversifying itself—a reality to which many Japanese giants have succumbed after their peak in the 1990s. Trying to do too many things, some of them have ended up doing nothing particularly well.

On the heels of filing for one of the largest IPOs in tech history[17] in 2014, it will be interesting to see whether Jack Ma can sustain his vision, based on his personal charisma and provocative ethos on a more global scale.

Alliance Growth Strategy

An alliance growth strategy is one in which companies enter beneficial strategic alliances that give both the companies the combined strengths of two brands. Furthermore, such a strategy optimally utilizes the synergies between the two companies with the result that the products and services offers made due to such an alliance has the backing of two brand names. However, as in the case of any strategy, this too has its advantages and disadvantages. When two companies decide to combine two distinct brands (or a portfolio of brands), both reap the advantages of access to new markets, distribution channels, customer segments and products. However, on the downside, it faces the risk of confused positioning and ineffective management of a brand's identity. This especially happens when two brands stand for two distinct things in the marketplace and cater to two distinct customer groups. Therefore, companies must ensure that they have regular brand-tracking procedures to help in maintaining a balance in their alliance.

---

[16] http://www.forbes.com/sites/ryanmac/2014/05/07/invading-china-alibaba-teams-up-with-amazon-rival-shoprunner-to-bring-american-goods-east/ (accessed October 2014).

[17] http://www.forbes.com/sites/russellflannery/2014/05/07/huge-u-s-ipo-is-a-pit-stop-for-alibaba-billionaire-chairman-jack-ma-tells-staff/ (accessed October 2014).

Costa Coffee: Brand alliance as a market entry mode

Being a quintessentially collectivistic society, China is significantly different from the Western world, and this creates some obvious challenges for Western brands entering the Chinese market. In order to overcome this seemingly obvious challenge, many companies either opt for the joint venture or strategic alliance route to establish their business in China. The British brand Costa Coffee is one of such example.

China's coffee market has grown by an estimated 10%–15% annually as compared to the worldwide average of a mere 2% over the past decade. In 2006, coffee consumption in China was roughly 45,000 tons. S some analysts predict this number could reach 300,000 tons annually by 2020.[18] Therefore, China is expected to become an attractive market for coffee and coffee retail brands in the future as Chinese consumption patterns evolve beyond the traditional preference for tea in the country.

Costa Coffee employs approximately 10.000 people and is part of the British leisure group Whitbread—the UK's largest hotel, restaurant and coffee shop operator. It has 1,755 coffee stores in the UK and over 1,000 coffee stores overseas and aims to increase this number to 2.200 stores by 2018.[19]

The global market leader Starbucks entered China in 1998 and has more than 800 stores in 58 cities on the Chinese mainland. It aims to have more than 1,500 stores in 70 cities by 2015.[20]

Costa entered the Chinese market in December 2006. The brand currently has over 300 stores in China and aims to take this number to a total of 500 stores by 2016—accounting for 8.9% of the country's coffee retail market.[21]

However, unlike Starbucks, Costa entered a joint venture with the Yueda Group, which is based in Jiangsu Province. The logic of such a partnership was simple—Costa being a new entrant to the Chinese market would take a long time to establish itself if it went alone, but a partnership with a local company would allow it to leverage the partner's knowledge of the local market and customers. However, as attractive as this may sound, such partnerships sometimes come with a price.

Costa Coffee's future in China will depend heavily on its strategic partners and how it builds and sustains its brand as competition heats up from global brands as well as aspiring local Chinese coffee brands.

---

[18] http://www.china-briefing.com/news/2013/10/09/chinas-coffee-industry-is-brewing.html (accessed October 2014).

[19] http://www.dailymail.co.uk/news/article-2616060/Costa-opens-three-outlets-week-taps-growing-coffee-shop-culture-backlash-against-US-rival-Starbucks.html (accessed October 2014).

[20] http://www.china.org.cn/business/2013-03/22/content_28327378.htm (accessed October 2014).

[21] http://www.china-briefing.com/news/2013/10/09/chinas-coffee-industry-is-brewing.html (accessed October 2014).

Acquisition Growth Strategy

An acquisition strategy is one where a company acquires another or its brands to leapfrog and grow. This strategy demands a huge financial outlay on the part of the acquirer, which can be an obstacle in its path. Furthermore, more than the acquisition, post-acquisition integration poses a huge challenge to such companies. Integration involves multiple functions within a company, including its people, processes, operations, and brand practices. In fact, the integration process often proves more challenging that the actual acquisition process. However, although fairly arduous, this strategy is very helpful for companies that venture new markets with well-known brands. See Brand Cases 4 and 5.

Brand Case 4: Lenovo's global leap

In 2005, Lenovo acquired IBM's Personal Computer (PC) division for US$1.75 billion. Its logic was simple and straightforward—it would ride IBM's brand equity in establishing itself as a credible brand in the PC industry. This acquisition was splashed across global media as the beginning of a Chinese global brand takeover. Instantly becoming the world's No.3 computer- maker in the world after Dell and HP (at the time), Lenovo jumped to second position in 2012, and finally became the world's largest computer-maker in 2013, accounting for 16% of PCs shipped worldwide.

Lenovo is replicating this strategy in two new business areas. It spent US$5.2 billion on mergers and acquisitions (M&A) in 2014 to purchase IBM's low-end data storage and server unit and the Motorola brand from Google. It must be remembered that although an after-thought in the case of smartphones, Motorola has remained a solid brand name in emerging markets, where the bulk of global growth in mobiles is expected, and this puts Lenovo in the third position behind Apple and Samsung in mobile hardware sales.

Lenovo now stands alone as the only major tech company with global product lines in consumer mobiles, PCs and tablets as well as business servers. As a brand leader in emerging markets, where 50% of its PC sales come from China alone, Lenovo has a strong chance of repeating its climb to global leadership through its dominance in emerging markets in its new business units.

> **Brand Case 5: Tata Motors: Brand legitimacy through high-profile acquisitions**
>
> Their country of origin can be a major liability for local brands in their effort to establish their legitimacy around the world. Brands have been found to either associate with global brands to establish their credibility, or in extreme cases, have acquired well-established the latter, hoping to achieve instant global recognition. Tata Motors of India is a good example of a high- profile acquisition. In 2008, Ratan Tata, the Chairman of the Tata Group, of which Tata Motors is a part, paid US$2.3 billion to acquire two of the most respected auto brands in the world—Jaguar and Land Rover.[22]
>
> Although Tata Motors is not traditionally considered as being among the major auto-makers in the world, this high profile acquisition immediately put the company on the global map. However, given the global recession that followed the acquisition, all has not gone as planned. It must be remembered that brands always operate on a long-term basis, and therefore, short-term losses in response to global recessions should mask the bigger strategic move that enabled Tata Motors to gain legitimacy in the global auto market.
>
> What remains to be seen is the extent to which Tata Motors will be able to leverage the addition of two of the world's most well-known brands to its portfolio in the long run.

Details of these three dominant strategies will give companies a wide choice in pursuing their branding blueprints, depending on their internal resource capabilities, core competencies, and the nature, tenor and character of the external competitive landscape in which they operate.

THE FOUR-STEP BRAND LEADERSHIP MODEL

Building brands is a strategic activity. As emphasized throughout this chapter, branding is based on some fundamental tenets. First, it is an organization-wide discipline. Second, it is a strategic activity that is directly led by the CEO and the corporate board. Third, branding encompasses multiple functional units in any company and thereby

---

[22] http://www.reuters.com/article/2008/06/02/us-tata-jaguar-idUSBMA00084220080602 (accessed October 2014).

spans different silos. Fourth, it requires long-term investment in building a distinct identity and value proposition. Finally, it is about creating an exciting experience for customers, which ultimately enhances companies' shareholder value.

Given these fundamental tenets, any company that aspires to establish itself as a brand leader in any segment, industry or country will have to simultaneously manage and excel at these multiple strategic activities. In the following section, a four-step strategic brand leadership model is proposed. This model encompasses the four main criteria that form the backbone of any global iconic brand—innovation, collaboration, sustainability, and strategic leadership.

Innovation

Innovation has become a word that is often misused in the business lexicon. Anything from the introduction of a new product, the creation of a new technology to a new advertising campaign is called innovative. However, in the context of brand leadership, the word is used in the sense of companies simultaneously investing in creating incremental as well as substantial improvements to their status quo, in addition to creating completely new offerings, be they products, services, technologies, or platforms.

There are many examples of some of the most iconic brands in the world actively making innovation a core part of their branding strategies. Apple is a classic example in the consumer electronics industry. What started as an alternative choice to then (and still) dominant PCs through Macintosh computers soon evolved into much beyond mere "Macs." Apple eventually revolutionized the digital music industry and moved into the mobile communications domain with the iPod, the iPhone and iPad, respectively. Not only did the company continuously invest in improving its existing technologies by upgrading the operating systems and features of its products, but also in creating new touchphone technologies and design capabilities. Simultaneous innovation of incremental and substantial aspects has helped Apple protect its global iconic status. Most importantly, its customers, stakeholders, investment analysts, and competitors around the world not only are aware of the Apple brand, but also value its equity very highly.

Companies that aspire to build iconic brands should make innovation a core part of their brand strategies. Not only does innovation help these brands remain in tune with the cutting edge of technologies, products, services, and customers' needs, but it also allows them to carve a strong brand identity as pioneers.

Collaboration

Competition is the hallmark of business. This is truer now than ever before. Flattening of the world, opening up of many hitherto closed economies, integration of more than a billion customers into the mainstream consumption market, the proliferation of the internet, and invention of new technologies have all combined to make competition extremely intense in markets. These factors have also ensured that any competitive advantage companies may gain is short-lived, as these tend to be effectively imitated.

Given such a scenario, companies are faced with difficult choices. An obvious way to face such a challenge is to intensify the competition through product and price wars, adverse advertising against competitors, and/or outbidding each other for the most prestigious endorsements. However, such competitive moves may only benefit them in the short term and may actually be harmful in the long term. Moreover, given that these competitive moves are very easy to replicate, there is no guarantee that the competitors will not imitate these. Consequently, the collaborative way of tackling such competition seems more promising. Collaboration here refers to partnering with another company with the intention of benefitting from this and also helping the partner benefit. Collaboration can be on multiple fronts—with customers, external stakeholders and even competitors. The concept may seem counter-intuitive to the dominant notion of competitive rivalry. However, collaboration has been time and again shown to result in the long-term health of companies.

Customers, external stakeholders and competitors are the three broad categories of actors a company interacts with. Collaboration with customers can entail a company taking a series of actions ranging from the highly involved to mere participation. For example, Harley Davidson is a classic example of effective collaboration with its customers to build an iconic brand. Through the many Harley Davidson communities, the company has not only brought the customer closer to the brand, but also enhanced the brand experience.

he Danish toy-maker LEGO is closely connected with the many global communities formed due to the popularity of the LEGO brand and products. The insights and feedback from these communities provide solid input to the innovation process in LEGO. Similarly, collaborating with external stakeholders is a common tactic. Companies form strategic networks with their suppliers, distributors, financiers and others to ensure that access to resources is easy and available. Such collaboration may take the form of exclusive agreements, co-option of actors by making them directors on the board, or the formation of joint ventures or strategic alliances with collaborators. The underlying purpose is to ensure that brands are entrenched in strategic networks that will eventually help to maintain companies' position in the industry.

Finally, although collaboration with one's competitors sounds absurd, many brands have been a success at this. Collaboration with competitors can result in multiple benefits for a company and at the same time expose it to multiple challenges. The main challenge is to decide what aspects of the brand strategy it wants to share. However, once this is decided, brands can collectively use resources, achieve scale and ensure efficiency in their cost structures. Although collusion between competitors is prohibited in most countries, selective collaboration is encouraged.

By collaborating with these three main constituencies, brands can effectively address increased competition. Furthermore, they can realistically move closer to leadership positions in their industries.

Sustainability

Sustainability is quickly becoming a strategic necessity for most businesses. Not only are they called upon to practice sustainable practices, but they are also being challenged in terms of ensuring that their strategies are sustainable. Such practices usually span the entire range—from initiation of local practices such as procuring raw materials from countries that are environment-friendly to such global practices as putting in place different strategies before entering industries in different countries as well as the kind of products to be launched.

This leads us to the question on whether companies can sustain their operations. In terms of competitive strategy, sustainability is fast becoming a thing of the past. Given the hyper competition discussed earlier, competitors are able to imitate practices very early, and thereby reduce the time lag between the pioneer and the late comer. Similarly, given the dominant focus on short-term and quarterly results, companies are forced to adopt certain practices only to later abandon these when external pressures cease. Consequently, sustainability sometimes ends up as merely a mirage.

However, some of the most iconic brands in the world such as Starbucks, Nike, Singapore Airlines, LEGO, and IKEA have succeeded in ensuring the sustainability of their practices. These as well their social practices have been sustainable over long periods. These companies actively adopt social responsibility as part of their corporate and branding strategies. In fact, all of them are known for adopting practices that are environment friendly, facilitate social participation and are ethical. Consequently, these brands have had a global cult following for a long time. They have also had a tremendous financial success.

Sustainability is one of the four fundamental pillars of achieving a global brand leadership position. When followed with innovation and collaboration, it can very effectively help a brand break through the clutter of brands and position itself powerfully to achieve a global leadership position.

Strategic Leadership

The final pillar in achieving brand leadership is probably the most crucial of the four. Much has been written, discussed and accepted about how organizations become the reflection their managers. It is clear that it is the senior management that shapes, guides, and implements a company's strategic brand vision, which serves as the strategic charter for a brand. However, the role of strategic leadership in the context of branding has been sidelined. Given that branding has mainly been relegated to a tactical activity that is managed by middle level and functional managers, the role of the corporate board and the CEO is often overlooked.

However, it is the CEO and the corporate board that shape the branding strategy and the overall brand identity of a company. A quick look at some of the most iconic brands in history attests this. Apple's Steve Jobs, Virgin's Sir Richard Branson, Nike's Phil Knight, Starbucks's Howard Schultz and many others made invaluable contributions to their brands as these grew. The important point to be noted here is that given the fact that branding is an organization-wide discipline, it is the CEO and the corporate board that should actively shape, support and sustain a company's strategic brand activities.

Many brands aspire to be leaders in their industries and achieve an iconic global status. However, very few are successful in doing so. Traditionally, companies have isolated one or two of the four fundamental principles discussed here and wondered why they failed. It is the coming together of the four principles that creates opportunities for companies to emerge as leaders in their industries. Consequently, when brands are guided by competent and enthusiastic top leadership that simultaneously invests in innovation and collaboration, which are sustainable over time, they are poised to emerge as brand leaders.

CONCLUSION

Changing market conditions have morphed branding from being a luxury for an elite few to becoming a strategic necessity for all businesses that wish to survive and thrive in the long run. Companies across Asia, South America and Eastern Europe are gradually beginning to understand that if they want to be serious contenders on the global platform and integrate with developed economies, they will have to invest in branding. This may also soon be true for Africa due to the continent's huge potential.

The dominant economic model in the previous era of closed economies does not seem to be effective today. Countries across the world are increasingly becoming connected. The world is indeed becoming flat. It is therefore important for companies to realize that given changing business norms in the global economic landscape, emerging economies cannot merely rely on established models of business and be complacent about their future strategies.

Among emerging economies, Asian companies have taken the lead to demonstrate that changing from the old to the new is possible. For a very long time, they managed to do business without building resonating brands due to a number of factors such as governmental protection from global competition, localized markets, low costs and the management mindset, which primarily focused on manufacturing.

However, Japan, Korea and Singapore showed the way and developed into modern, sophisticated economies where brands have become important assets in the management toolbox. Today, with China's rising economic power and to a certain extent India's in the global business scene, the confidence levels of many other Asian companies are growing and more business leaders are aspiring to venture into the global market by using branding and brands as effective strategies.

This is also the case with many South American companies. They not only realize the increased importance of interacting with developed economies, but are also gradually cruising along the stream of brand-building. Europe is also seeing some fundamental transformations. Moreover, the gradual integration of many Eastern European economies into the mainstream European economy is paving the way for learning as well as the development of new business models. However, the path may be strewn with obstacles, and will not be easy.

Companies would do well to remember that the addition of billions of people from emerging economies is bound to change the underlying character of global business. The integration of new producers and consumers into the mainstream economy, combined with capitalistic economic policies, globalization of trade and breaking down of trade barriers, is likely to bring about an enormous change in the global business order. However, if companies in these emerging economies realize the tremendous opportunities that lie ahead for them and embrace branding as a strategic tool in order to exploit these attractive opportunities, the next generation of economic superpowers may very well emerge from these economies.

REFERENCES

Business Week (2005), "Fakes!," *Business Week*, February 7. Available at http://www.bloomberg.com/bw/stories/2005-02-06/fakes (accessed October 2014). (By Frederik Balfour in Guangzhou, with Carol Matlack in Paris, Amy Barrett in Philadelphia, Kerry Capell in London, Dexter Roberts in Beijing, Jonathan Wheatley in Sao Paulo, William C. Symonds in Boston, Paul Magnusson in Washington and Diane Brady in New York.)

Business Week (2005), "Lenovo and IBM: East Meets West, Big-Time," *Business Week*, May 9.

Einhorn, Bruce (2009), "How China's Alibaba Is Surviving and Thriving," *Business Week*, April 9.

Gurhan-Canli, Zeynep and Durairaj Maheswaran (2000), "Cultural variations in country of origin effects," *Journal of Marketing Research*, 37(3), 309–17.

India Knowledge@Wharton (2007) "How Did Nokia Succeed in the Indian Mobile Market, While Its Rivals Got Hung Up?" *India Knowledge@Wharton*, August 23. Available at http://knowledge.wharton.upenn.edu/article/how-did-nokia-succeed-in-the-indian-mobile-market-while-its-rivals-got-hung-up/ (accessed October 2014).

Khanna, Tarun and Krishna G. Palepu (2010), *Winning in Emerging Markets: A Road Map for Strategy and Execution*. US: Harvard Business Press

Khurana, Rakesh (2004), *Searching for a Corporate Savior: The Irrational Quest for Charismatic CEOs*. US: Princeton University Press.

Knight, Gary, John R. Riesenberger, and Tamer S. Cavusgil (2009), *International Business: Strategy, Management and New Realities*. UK: Pearson Prentice Hall.

Lakshman, Nandini (2007), "Unilever Looks to Recover Lost Indian Glory," *Business Week*, September 26.

Nisbett, Richard (2004), *The Geography of Thoughts: How Asians and Westerners Think Differently ... And Why*. US: Free Press.

Prahalad, C. K. (2006), *Fortune at the Bottom of the Pyramid: Eradicating Poverty Through Profits*. US: Wharton School Publishing.

Roll, Martin (2005), *Asian Brand Strategy*. UK: Palgrave.

———— (2009), "Unleashing the Asian brand potential," http://www.martinroll.com/resources/articles/asia/unleashing-asian-brand-potential/ (accessed October 2014).

Williamson, Peter (2004), *Winning in Asia: Strategies for Competing in the New Millemium*. US: Harvard Business Press.

Yibing, Wu (2003), "China's refrigerator magnate," *McKinsey Quarterly*, August.

Zeng, Ming and Peter J. Williamson (2007), *Dragons at Your Door: How Chinese Cost Innovation Is Disrupting Global Competition*. US: Harvard Business School Press.

Chapter 12

Opportunities and Risks in Co-branding and Licensing

Jeffrey Parkhurst

INTRODUCTION

Co-branding and licensing are classic brand programs that date back to at least the early 1900s. They can be lucrative and even extend the brand's DNA. At the same time, success is elusive for most practitioners and the issue is often the duration. Appreciating the rigor of the business case of the world's best investors, there are five steps that can be taken to optimize a co-branding or licensing opportunity—quantifying your brand's opportunity space as well as the benefits and risks, testing the partner relationship for validity, introducing considerations that can reduce risk in the partnership, and quantifying hidden value with future options.

Co-branding and licensing are established brand extension techniques that are easy to understand and lucrative when successful. Yet, for most companies, economic gain is elusive and duration is often the issue.

If a co-branding or licensing idea cannot last three years, the probability of economic success is low. Technology products with high margins and 18-month lifecycles may be an exception. If an idea can last 10 years, it is probaly lucrative and may refine the DNA of the brand positively. These outcomes are obvious. Yet, duration is often not quantified well in the planning stages and that leads to the wrong go/no go decisions.

Historically, in a company's pool of intangible assets (brand, management, patents, customer lists, competitive advantage, and other intellectual capital) brand is the one asset that can stand the test of time. At the company level, the Coca-Cola brand dates back to 1886. The company has had 12 chairmen of its board from 1886 to 2009,[1] and many management teams. At the macro GDP level, brands have also grown in relevance; intangible assets as a percentage of the USA's total non-financial assets have increased from 24% in 1955 to 48% recently.

If a brand can last decades, our hypothesis is that a good co-branding or licensing relationship should last 5–10 years.

RECENT CASE STUDIES

The following are some case studies in best practices in co-branding and licensing:

Intel launched a brand ("Intel Inside"), about which very few consumers had ever heard, into the stratosphere by piggybacking on the equity of computer-makers such as IBM and Compaq. Within a year of the launching of the program, Intel was co-branded with some 300 computer manufacturers. This afforded Intel a unique business strategy, known as "commoditize the complement." The company garnered a market share of near or more than 80, while complementary PC manufacturers were commoditized. This helped to expand the total market.

Caterpillar, with a license as a key driver, has ended up as one of the world's more unlikely high-profile brands. The CAT logo is best known to the construction industry as the symbol of the leading global manufacturer of off-road trucks, tractors and other multi-terrain vehicles. To consumers, it is probably more familiar as a label on a range of high-priced heavy-duty designer boots and associated apparel. The latter, although the smaller of the two businesses, trades off its sibling's well-established values of rugged, durable, and dependable performance[2]. Royalties from licensing can supplement marketing budgets and enable some consistency versus the larger cyclical manufacturing business.

---

[1] Coca-Cola website under product descriptions, 2009 (us.coca-cola.com [accessed in 2009]).

[2] www.adbrands.net (accessed in 2009).

Disney has been in the licensing business for decades. An early entrant in the world of brand licensing was its cartoon character Mickey Mouse in the 1930s and 1940s, and its mass introduction of toys, books, and consumer products. Disney's characters have lasted for decades. The 2008 *License! Global* list of Top 100 licensing companies accounted for over US$135 billion in retail sales of licensed products—almost 75% of the estimated total of US$187.4 billion worldwide. Disney Consumer Products tops the list with US$26 billion in retail sales.

Habitat for Humanity International is both a co-branding and cause story. In its quest to build 300,000 homes, it leveraged its brand to enter a series of co-branding-type relationships, netting over US$100 million in support. Cause-related co-branding has been on the rise since 2000, with Susan G. Komen for the Cure (breast cancer) and St Jude's (children and medical research) being prime examples.

However, there are also failures. When the American Medical Association (AMA) was threatened with insolvency in 1997, it turned to corporate sponsors to bail it out financially. The AMA entered an exclusive agreement with Sunbeam, which permitted the company to put AMA logos on its healthcare products. Within a year, there was backlash from doctors who disagreed with AMA's endorsement of Sunbeam's products over other products. This resulted in the AMA breaking the agreement and having to pay US$9.9 million to settle a breach-of-contract lawsuit. The endorsement plan, which had no requirement that the AMA tested the products, was widely criticized by ethicists, physicians and newspaper editorialists who accused it of compromising its credibility.

One common trait of these stories is duration. Successes last for years, netting a significant cash flow over time, and failures have a short shelf life.

VALUE OF DURATION

Berkshire Hathaway's Class A stock appreciated by 31% annually since Warren Buffett and Charlie Munger took control of the company in 1964. Even under large market cap conditions, its stock appreciated by 28% annually from 1987–2007 and 25% annually from 1997–2007. This is well chronicled. If there is a rock star in the investment community, it is widely acknowledged that it is Warren Buffett.

A review of Berkshire's annual report letters and portfolio investments from 1978–2007 (30 years)[3] reveals repeated advertisements detailing its investment criteria. These shed light on how it makes investment-related decisions on long-term acquisitions and perhaps indirectly on short term arbitrage opportunities. Here is an advertisement from 1983:

"Last year in this section, I ran a small ad to encourage acquisition candidates. In our communications businesses we tell our advertisers that repetition is key to results (which it is), so we will again repeat our acquisition criteria. We prefer: larger purchases (at least $5 million of after-tax earnings), demonstrated consistent earning power (future projections are of little interest to us, nor are "turn-around" situations), businesses earnings good returns on equity while employing little or no debt, management in place (we can't supply it), simple businesses (if there's lots of technology, we won't understand it), an offering (we don't want to waste our time or that of the seller by talking, even preliminarily, about a transaction when price is unknown)."

As a side note on the brand, interestingly, the closest the advertisement gets to it is at best seen indirectly through another intangible: quality of management. Thus, we discover that the brand does not rank among Berkshire's top six investment criteria. We see ad-hoc discussions on the brand in the company's annual reports over the years, but these pale in scale versus other discussions including on its insurance business, investment-related decisions, management, and broad investment-related points of view. Buffett does not isolate brand as a key business driver, but it ultimately accounts for 20% or more of his long-term gains. The companies he holds for many years are one of the top two or three branded companies in the industry and net around 70% the real dollar gains he has made in equities. Some salient examples include those of the Coca-Cola Company, Disney, Gillette/P&G, American Express,

---

[3] Berkshire Hathaway Annual Report Letters, 1978–2007 (berkshirehathaway.com [accessed in 2009]).

Washington Post, GEICO, and Wells Fargo (see Figure 12.1). Net, our best investor does not formally endorse brand, but he relies on it for duration.

At the other end of the duration spectrum lies the Simmons brand. For most of the 133 years since its inception in a small city in Wisconsin, the Simmons Bedding Company and brand has enjoyed an illustrious history. The company has been sold seven times in the last two decades after being owned for short periods by private equity firms. In September 2009, Simmons announced its Chapter 11 restructuring plan. Its debt increased from US$164 million in 1991 to US$1.3 billion in 2009. Bondholders were set to lose US$575 million. In contrast, the private equity firms pocketed around $750 million in profits from Simmons over the years.

Net, if you had invested US$1,000 in Berkshire Hathaway in 1964, your investment would have grown to US$103,000 as of

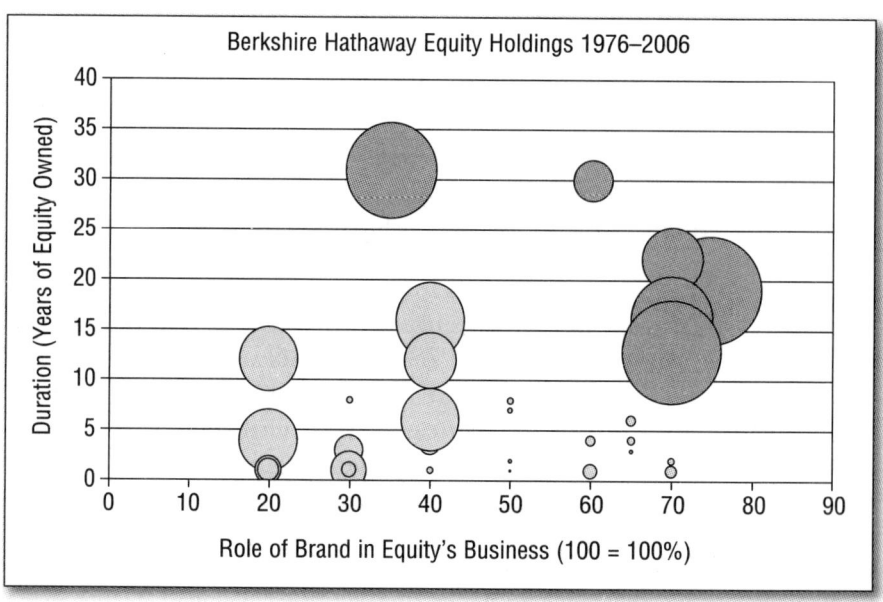

Note: Dark grey = Top 3 brand in category and has 10+ years duration; Grey = Less brand presence and/or less duration, or arbitrage; Size of bubble = Market cap gain of equity over duration.

Figure 12.1 Value of Duration with Brand

September 2009. If you had invested US$1,000 in Simmons, your investment would very likely have led to bankruptcy and become worth US$0.

CO-BRANDING AND LICENSING BASICS

Co-branding and licensing are common marketing activities in that they leverage a brand, and involve a contract between two organizations and a win-win financial gain for them. These are however unique in their terms. Co-branding combines two brands in support of a new product, service, or venture. Licensing is when a company allows a licensee to use certain of its business technology or intellectual capital (brand) under some form of measured control.

Sponsorships, ingredient branding, and cause marketing are similar to win-win partnerships, but different in their terms. Sponsorship is when finance is provided in exchange for brand visibility within the activity sponsored. Ingredient branding, as the name implies, involves a relationship where one company offers its brand as an ingredient in another company's brand for shared revenue (for example, Pillsbury brownies with Nestle chocolate). Cause marketing is where finance is provided to a non-profit organization in exchange for brand visibility with its cause.

A typical co-branding or licensing agreement includes provisions covering branding specifications, market plan strategy, licensing specifics, payments and royalties, representations and warranties, terms and termination, confidentiality, indemnification, and disclaimers. Among these, the most important provisions tend to relate to exclusivity, term and termination, licensing specifics, liability, co-branding partners, and branding and marketing specifications.

Forms of payment vary in co-branding and licensing. A sponsorship often involves an annual investment in certain rights. An ongoing license or co-brand may use a royalty rate, which can be computed by examining the operating earnings of the license, the capital employed, the role the brand plays in driving earnings, and its value described as a percent of sales. Calculation of royalty is fact-based and can therefore be reasonably accurate. A partner may promote a category royalty rate average in negotiations (It's always 3% in the X category), but by definition each brand is unique and calculation of its specific value is merited

HOW TO CAPTURE DURATION

As in a business case, there are five steps that can be taken to optimize a co-branding or licensing opportunity:

1. Quantify your brand's opportunity space.
2. Quantify the opportunities and risks.
3. Test the partner relationship for validity.
4. Introduce considerations that can reduce risk.
5. Quantify hidden value with future options.

If this is done well, the go/no go decision should be easy.

Quantify Your Brand's Opportunity Space

In 2005, *Forbes* magazine identified growth brands that outperformed their peers in their respective markets during the past four years. Apple, Google, and Amazon delivered annual brand value growth of more than 35% with an expanding opportunity space providing some support. What may be more noteworthy is that out of 5,000 companies studied, only 20 could deliver brand value growth of 12% or more annually over four years. In this regard, brand growth is difficult.

By one definition, a growth brand is one that has demonstrated exceptional recent growth and retains sustainable potential to grow in the future. Sustainable potential for future growth is a function of current momentum on a brand and three additional characteristics (see Figure 12.2).

Strong brand value that reflects the area in which a brand or business currently executes well. This translates into current growth, cash flow, and positive brand and customer relationship development. A significant portion of this brand value should be newly created (i.e., the net gain over the last four years).

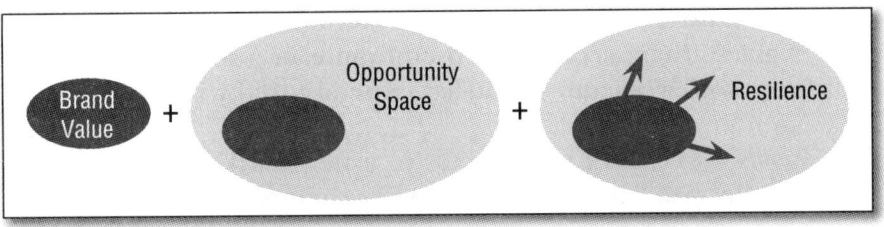

Source: Kurt Badenhausen (2005), "Brands Branching Out," *Forbes,* June 20.

Figure 12.2 Drivers of Future Growth: Brand Value, Opportunity Space, and Resilience

There should be an opportunity space in which a company can grow. In other words, there needs to be a number of new market opportunities that consumers and/or B-to-B buyers allow the brand to avail of.

A company should have the continuous capacity to develop, reinvent (its business model or business) and advance by constantly anticipating and adjusting to deep, secular trends and rapid changes in the customer and industry environment (strategic resilience).

When assessing potential co-branding and licensing partners, the effort often starts with ideation. Based on your brand's category, there are adjacent categories (for example, Disney movies and adjacent books, toys) that are obvious. There may be some that are less obvious (for example, Caterpillar bulldozers and shoes). One can start the process with lists, such as all industry SIC codes. A small investment in a session involving ideation processes may be pragmatic, and with success on the first license, it may make sense to revisit this annually.

Quantify Opportunities and Risks

There are many opportunities to be realized with co-branding and licensing, and the list is compelling:

> Opportunities
> *Royalties as Income*—direct income from partner for use of brand
> *Higher Sales*—high sales for licensor or co-brand partners for use of brand
> *Access to New Markets*—quick access of brand to new geographies, industries, and/or categories

Additional Consumer Benefits—few benefits for end consumers, given their access to licensed brands or a set of co-brands

Investment Minimized—reduced expenditure by brand owner to enter new market

Avoids Barriers to Entry—access to a new market that may have otherwise been unreachable For example, (A country's laws may mandate a maximum number of business operators.)

Risk Reduction—reduces brand and financial risk (Partner may have insight on the market. This is a value addition. Moreover, the co-brand partner may become an advocate instead of a competitor, and customers may buy-in more easily, knowing the co-brand partner who is already established.)

Quicker returns—rapid access to new markets and consumers for quick returns

Price Premium—ability to capture a high price via brand or co-brands

Communicates Quality—possibility of a new brand increasing perceived quality

Customer Reassurance—customers with technology products reassured with a familiar brand

Access to New Technology—ability to align with new technology

Market Priming—co-brand used to set stage for larger marketing strategy

Reinforcement of Advertising Messages—partnerships offering leverage of shared advertising

Brand Exposure—increased brand impressions in marketplace

Consumer Interest—new differentiation, leading to increased consumer interest

Adding Distinctiveness—a means to offset commodity conditions in market

Special Promotions—co-branding working as a seasonal promotion

Supplier Relations—suppliers affording co-branding economic wins

Enhancing of Brand Value—increases brand value

Assimilation of Positive Values from Partner Brand—partner with possible attributes that are high value, for example, chemicals changing image of company when partners demonstrate their many uses in downstream products

Communication Opportunities—new ways of talking to current and new consumers

Retailer Collaboration—new ways of aligning with retailers

There are also risks to be realized with co-branding & licensing, and these too are compelling.

Risks

Greed—focus of one or more parties on "quick buck," leaving gaps in the decision-making process and long-term problems with a brand

Incompatible Corporate Personalities—personality differences arising after signing of deal, which can hurt project and ultimately lead to litigation; personality differences in new management

Over-Extended Brand Franchise—over-extension leading to brand equity problems and falling income

Repositioning of Partner Brand—partner repositioning its main brand, which contradicts one's brand and/or co-branding and licensing goals

Change in Financial Status of Partner—partner suffering economically, including potential bankruptcy

Failure to Meet Targets—partner falling short on unit sales and revenue goals

Takeovers and Mergers—partner acquired or taken over, risking entire program

Changes in Market Attitudes—market shifting adversely on co-brand (which can happen to core brand as well)

Creation of Single Hybrid Name—co-brand going mainstream and beginning to overtake core brand

Loss of Exclusivity of Brand Features—differentiation transcending partner's core brand and weakening of differentiation

Increased Risk of 'Lookalikes"—co-branding with more than one partner (pharmaceuticals and retailers) who introduces lookalikes and creates confusion

Degeneration of Trademark into Generic Term—loss of exclusive right to core brand, based on how it is to be executed

Brand Separation—possibility of undoing co-brand taking unexpected effort and once undone, co-brand still existing in the grey market illegally

Disciplined Use of Trademark Vital—bad execution by partner hurting identity of core brand

Incompatibility with *Sibling Brand*—co-branding within company not always objective and wrong partnerships being forced on it

Anti-Trust and Other Legal Problems—legal issues

Test the Partner Relationship for Validity

If you look at co-branding and licensing as an investment decision, you can re-apply best in class investment rules. Insights from the operations of a company such as Berkshire Hathaway indicate that it may look at over 100 offers in a year, but only invest in one to three of them, which are worth the effort of doing so.

A partner should also be tested to meet certain standards. Leveraging the success of Berkshire's investment criteria, here are some possible partner outcomes that are desirable:

1. The partner market being accessed is reasonably large and a partner has a reasonable market share (with a multi-million annual co-branding or licensing revenue stream thus seeming plausible),
2. A partner has historical earning power (authenticated by history and not a mere forecast).
3. There are good returns with little or no debt (co-branding involving little or no debt by default).
4. Management is in place (with sustainable management quality and expertise).
5. Businesses are simple (a good sign if this is so) and offer the right terms.

If this sounds over the top or theoretical, consider all the litigation that occurs in licensing and broken intellectual property partnerships each year. Companies and management change over time and this can influence (lack of) duration.

Introduce Considerations That Can Reduce Risk

As you move forward with a business case that continues to hold merit, there are creative considerations to consider while helping the partnership reduce risk:

1. The licensor reduces short-term fees to enhance initial momentum and not jeopardize returns in the long term.
2. The licensor wants its brand in the market and will set a reduced rate to ensure that the right licensee is using it.
3. The licensee may offer marketing or trade mark protection or invest in brand development, and this should be netted off against any payment of royalty.
4. The license is awarded for a start-up operation, and during the early years, the licensor foregoes payment of royalty as a form of investment.
5. The licensee is obliged to purchase certain minimum quantities of raw material or finished products from the brand-owner at non-market rates, and this is netted off against royalties.
6. The economic conditions in which the licensee is operating are likely to worsen and the licensor wishes to minimize its exposure by reducing its expectations.
7. The licensor returns some of the royalty to the licensee, since the brand is being developed for the former's long-term benefit.
8. The licensee is spending more in marketing or brand development than could reasonably be expected of it and the licensor accepts part of this in lieu of payment of royalties.
9. The licensor recognizes that part of the underlying value of the brand is due to the actions of the licensee in the past (for example, investing in marketing in a new country), and this value, which is now being added by the brand, should remain with the licensee.

These considerations can help the partnership and increase trust.

Quantify Hidden Value with Future Options

When you invest in a project, a classic business case eventually offers a measure of value (outgoing investment, incoming cash flows over a duration, and present value adjustment for risk).

Investments made today can open doors tomorrow. These are options. Option value does exist and is the incremental value of the net present value of a business case. It is similar to the options market in the stock market, but harder to model in just one way in business or with brands, since options vary at the project level.

A significant example of future options is Apple (see Figure 12.3). Eventually, the market will catch up, but the run with options created since the launch of the first iPod in 2001 has been explosive, with 220 million cumulative ipods being sold since then till 2009. The iPhone followed in 2007 and saw sales of 35 million phones as of 2009, by when developers had created over 100,000 applications for the iPhone and iPod Touch App Store, and users had downloaded well over two billion apps. The store averages out to more than 200 new apps and a staggering 4,149,377 downloads a day. It almost seems as though Apple had a plan in place with future options all along.

Entering a new category via co-branding or licensing may introduce new options for a brand, perhaps not at the Apple level, but gaining access to just one new category or industry is not insignificant.

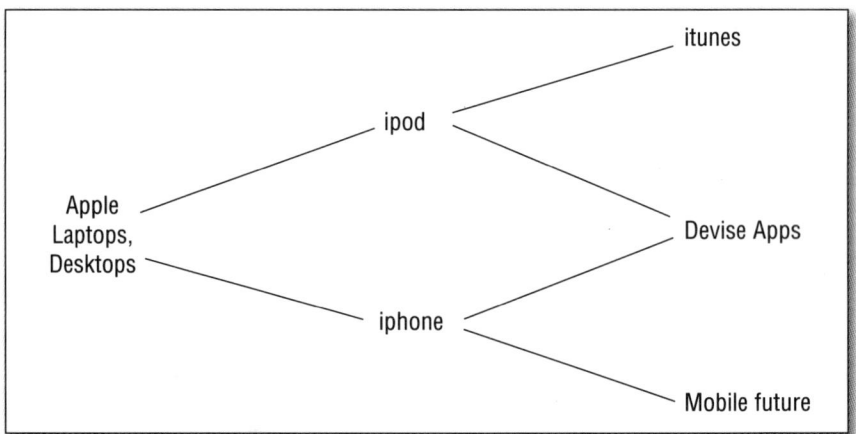

Figure 12.3 Creating Future Options

CONCLUSION

The effort and due diligence required for success is significant, but large corporations have succeeded with just one full time equivalent (FTE) individual in a co-branding and licensing role.

An indirect benefit from ideation, partner dialogues and due diligence is new insight for a company's core business. It is exciting when a business breaks through in co-branding or licensing. In some cases, it can almost mint money with minimal investment and arm's length management. The additional income can then be reinvested to strengthen its core business—a real luxury!

REFERENCES

Badenhausen, Kurt (2005), "Brand New World," *Forbes*, June 20, pp. 113–119.
Beezy, Miriam Claire (2005), *Co-branding: A Popular Form of Strategic Alliance*. Los Angeles, CA: Foley & Lardner LLP.
Blackett, Tom and Bob Boad (1999), *Co-branding: The Science of Alliance*. Macmillan Press Ltd.
Creswell, Julie (2009), "Profits for Buyout Firms as Company Debt Soared," *The New York Times,* October 5, page A1.
Ewalt, David M. (2009), "Apple's Shocking App Store Numbers," *Forbes*, November 4, p. 1.
Ip, Greg (2002), "The Rise and Fall of Intangible Assets Leads to Shorter Company Life Spans," *Wall Street Journal,* April 4. Available at wsj.com (accessed in 2009).
License! Global (2008), "Top 100 Licensors," Retrieved from www.licensemag.com (accessed in 2009).
Mckee, Steve (2009), "The Pros and Cons of Co-branding," *BusinessWeek*, July 10, pp. 1–3.
New York Times (1998), "Broken Deal Costs A.M.A. $9.9 Million," *New York Times*, August 3.
Quelch, John A., James E. Austin, and Nathalie Laidler-Kylander (2004), "Mining Gold in Not-for-Profit Brands," *Harvard Business Review*, April. Retrieved from www.hfhi.org (accessed in 2009).
World of Apple (2009), "Live Coverage from Apple's 'It's Only Rock and Roll' Event," Press Release, retrieved on September, 9, 2009. Available at worldofapple.com (accessed in 2009).

Chapter 13
Brand Revitalization*

Kevin Lane Keller

OVERVIEW

Because of changes or shifts in the marketplace or marketing environment, all brands experience ups and downs in their fortunes. Revitalizing a brand requires that lost sources of brand equity are recaptured (i.e., a "back to basics" strategy) and/or that new sources of brand equity are identified and established (i.e., a "reinvention" strategy). Two general approaches can help a brand achieve these goals—(1) expanding the depth and/or breadth of brand awareness by improving brand recall and recognition of consumers during purchase or consumption settings, and/or (2) improving the strength, favorability and uniqueness of brand associations making up the brand image (either in terms of existing or new brand associations). Guidelines for proper brand revitalization strategies are outlined in the context of industry examples on the following pages.

INTRODUCTION

Shifts in consumers' tastes and preferences, the emergence of new competitors or technology, or any change in the marketing

---

* This chapter is based in part on material from Chapter 13 of Kevin Lane Keller (2008), *Strategic Brand Management* (3rd ed.), Prentice-Hall.

environment can potentially affect the fortunes of a brand. In virtually every product category, there are examples of once prominent and admired brands that have fallen on hard times, or in some cases, even completely disappeared. Nevertheless, a number of these brands have managed to make impressive comebacks as marketers have breathed new life into their customer franchises. In recent years, brands such as Abercrombie & Fitch, Coach, Johnnie Walker, Olay, and Pabst Blue Ribbon have all seen their brands' fortunes successfully turning around in varying degrees.

Let us look at the fortunes of Lacoste. The brand, founded in France in 1933, became a style icon due to its tennis-themed sportswear and is credited with selling the first polo shirt. During the 1980s, Lacoste failed to keep up with prevailing fashion trends and saw its sales drop. In response, the company cut its prices and sold to discounters such as Wal-Mart and Kmart, which further damaged its brand image. It continued to suffer due to slow sales until 2002, when its new management stopped selling its products to non-luxury retailers. The company also regenerated its fading fashion line by introducing tight-fitting shirts for women. It went a step further and opened its own-brand boutiques in fashionable shopping locations to showcase its new look. As a consequence of these and other measures, Lacoste's revenues in the USA rose appreciably (Lindsay, 2006).

As the example of Lacoste illustrates, brands sometimes need to return to their roots to recapture their lost sources of equity. In other cases, the meaning of a brand has to fundamentally change to regain lost ground and recapture its market leadership position.

Procter & Gamble's brand, Old Spice, was fading in the early 1990s, with a reputation for being a great Father's Day gift—albeit for 1965! Revival of the brand's sales was due to its complete overhaul and the manner in which it was marketed, with the launch of new products in the form of body washes and sprays, antiperspirants, and deodorant; creation of a new Red Zone sub-brand, and irreverent, somewhat campy advertisements targeting a youthful 12–34-year-old male (Lauro, 2002).

Reversing a fading brand's fortunes either requires that lost sources of brand equity are recaptured and/or new sources of brand equity are identified and established. Regardless of which approach is taken, brands on the comeback trail have to make more "revolutionary" changes than the "evolutionary" ones to reinforce their meaning, and this requires effective long-term brand management. We begin our analysis by characterizing the nature of brand revitalization and alternative approaches available to marketers. We thereafter look at specific tactics that can be employed as part of brand revitalization strategies. Throught the chapter, we emphsize on examples of brands that have been successful (or unsuccessful) in their brand revitalization efforts.

CHARACTERIZING BRAND REVITALIZATION

Customer-based Brand Equity

We approach the topic of brand revitalization from the perspective of the customerbased brand equity model (Keller, 2008). This model defines brand equity as "the differential effect that customer knowledge about a brand has on customers' response to marketing of a brand." Customers may be actual or potential ones. Positive customer-based brand equity is possible when they respond favorably to a product, price, communication, etc., when a brand is identified rather than when it is not.

According to this model, the sources of customer-based brand equity arise from brand knowledge—all the thoughts, feelings, beliefs, attitudes, experiences, and other associations that become linked to a brand. In particular, two key dimensions of consumer brand knowledge include brand awareness and brand image. Brand equity occurs when consumers are aware of the brand and have strong, favorable and unique brand associations. There are a number of ways of creating these knowledge structures in the minds of consumers. They broadly they involve (1) choosing brand elements (for example, brand names, URLs, logos, packaging, signage, logos, and slogans); (2) developing marketing programs and activities for the brand, and (3) leveraging secondary associations by linking it to people, places, or things. There are a number of possible benefits for a company that has positive customer-based brand equity, for example, increased price premiums, enhanced loyalty relationships and more favorable customer responses to its marketing communications, in-store merchandizing and new product brand extensions.

THE BRAND REVITALIZATION CONTINUUM

-Often, the first place to look while turning around the fortunes of a brand is at the original sources of its brand equity and how current, former or possible future customers feel about it. In profiling brand knowledge structures to guide revitalization, it is important to accurately and completely characterize (1) the breadth and depth of brand awareness; (2) the strength, favorability and uniqueness of brand associations and brand responses held in consumers' memory; and (3) the nature of consumer-brand relationships.

A comprehensive brand equity measurement system should be able to reveal the current status of these sources of brand equity. If this is not possible, or to provide additional insight, a special brand audit that explores the health of the brand in terms of how consumers think, feel and act toward it may be necessary. Of particular importance is the extent to which key brand associations are still adequately functioning as points-of-difference or points-of-parity to properly position the brand. Are point-of-difference associations losing their strength, favorability, or uniqueness with customers? Have negative associations become linked to the brand, for example, because of a change in the marketing environment that requires a point-of-parity to be achieved? How do employees fit into the picture?

Decisions must then be taken about whether the same positioning should be maintained for the brand or a new one should be created, and if so, the positioning that should be adopted. These positioning decisions involve an analysis of the desirability, deliverability, and differentiability of different possible positions, based on acompany, consumers and competitive considerations, respectively. Thus, both internal and external factors must be considered while assessing positioning opportunities. Internal considerations may be especially crucial for the success of brand revitalization, since the entire organization must believe in and rally around the revitalization attempt (Light and Kiddon, 2009). In some cases, internal barriers in the path of success within a company may be as serious as external consumer barriers.

Sometimes a decision may be made that the brand positioning is still appropriate, but the marketing program is the source of the problem because it is failing to deliver on the positioning. In such instances, a "back to basics" strategy may help. For example, Harley-Davidson rode a back-to-basics strategy to icon status (Rifkin, 1997). The brand found its fortunes sagging in the 1980s when quality- and reliability-related problems resulted in the wide-spread belief that owners of Harley-Davidson bikes actually needed to have two bikes because "one Harley was always in the shop." Modern production processes improved the performance of the bike, and combined with its iconic image and rebellious personality, led to market leadership and a sustained period of profitability. Harley's grassroots marketing success is reflected in the over one million riders who belong to the Harley Owner's Group (HOGs) and the years of excess demand the company has seen. By going back to basics and delivering on its core brand promise, the company literally could not make enough Harleys!

In other cases, however, the old brand positioning is just no longer viable and a more radical "reinvention" strategy is required. For example, Mountain Dew completely overhauled its brand image to become a soft drink powerhouse. In the 1960s, PepsiCo marketed Mountain Dew with the countrified tag line "Yahoo Mountain Dew! It'll Tickle Your Innards." By the early 1980s, however, it had become neglected by retailers and overlooked by consumers. Its revitalization was driven by largely abandoning the rural, folksy image on which it had been built. Starting in the late 1980s, new packaging, an edgy new "Do the Dew" ad campaign, and a new emphasis on extreme sports all resulted in the brand becoming seen as being youthful, energetic and "hip." With its new image clicking with young adults, Mountain Dew became the No.4 soft drink in sales in the USA.

Revitalization strategies obviously involve a continuum, with a pure back-to- basics strategy at one end and pure reinvention strategy at the other. Many revitalization strategies combine the elements of both strategies. As the Mountain Dew example illustrates, it is often easiest to reinvent and revive a brand that has simply been forgotten rather than one that has decided negatives. Interestingly, marketing failures, which do not attract an adequate number of consumers to a brand, are typically much less damaging than product failures, in which a brand fails to live up to its promise to consumers. Product failures can create strong, negative associations that may be difficult to overcome. Such situations call for drastic actions, which we address on the following pages in the context of crisis marketing guidelines.

APPROACHES TO BRAND REVITALIZATION

With an understanding of current and desired brand knowledge structures, the customer-based brand equity framework can provide guidance as to how old sources of brand equity can be refreshed and/or how new sources of brand equity can be created to achieve the intended positioning. According to the model, two such approaches are possible:

1. Expand the depth or breadth of brand awareness, or both, by improving consumer recall and recognition of the brand during purchase or consumption settings.
2. Improve the strength, favorability, and uniqueness of brand associations making up the brand image. This approach may involve programs directed at existing or new brand associations.

More favorable responses and greater brand equity can be the result of enhancing brand awareness and brand image in such ways. Strategically, lost sources of brand equity can be refurbished and new sources established in the same three ways that sources of brand equity are created to start with—by changing brand elements or the supporting marketing program, and/or leveraging new secondary associations. We next consider some alternative strategies that affect awareness and the image of a struggling brand.

Expanding Brand Awareness

With a fading brand, it is often not the *depth* of brand awareness that is a problem—consumers can still recognize or recall the brand under certain circumstances. Instead, the *breadth* of brand awareness is the stumbling block and consumers only tend to think of it in narrow ways. Therefore, one potentially productive means of rebuilding brand equity is to increase the breadth of brand awareness, making sure that consumers do not overlook it and think of purchasing or consuming it in situations in which it can satisfy their needs.

There are a number of strategies that can increase usage of and find new uses for a brand. Assuming that a brand has a reasonable level of consumer awareness and a positive image, perhaps the most appropriate starting point for creating new sources of brand equity is with ways that increase its usage. In many cases, such approaches represent the path of least resistance because they do not involve potentially difficult and costly changes in brand image or positioning as much as easier-to-implement ones in top-of-the-mind brand salience and awareness.

Usage can be increased by either increasing the level or quantity of consumption (i.e., how much the brand is used) or by increasing the frequency of consumption (i.e., how often the brand is used). In general, it is probably easier to increase the number of times a consumer uses the product than it is to actually change the amount used at any one time. The consumption amount is more likely to be a function of the particular beliefs a consumer holds about how the product is best consumed.

A possible exception to the rule is in the case of "impulse" consumption products whose usage increases when these are made more available (e.g., soft drinks or snacks). For these types of products, marketing strategies to increase consumer stockpiling (for example, via promotions or changes in packaging) may increase the salience of the brand and thus usage of the product. For example, larger package sizes and price discounts, or a reduction in the perceived unit cost of the product have been shown to accelerate its usage (Wansink, 1996).

Increasing frequency of use, on the other hand, involves either identifying additional or new opportunities to use the brand in the same basic way or identifying completely new and different ways in which it can be used. Increasing frequency of use is a particularly attractive option for brands with a large market share that are leaders in their product category. Both of these approaches to increasing the frequency of product usage are examined next.

Identifying additional or new usage opportunities: In some cases, the brand may be seen as only being useful in certain places and at certain times, especially if it has strong brand associations to particular usage situations or user types. In general, to identify additional or new opportunities for consumers to use a brand more—albeit in the same basic way—a marketing program should be designed to include both of the following:

1. Communications to consumers about the appropriateness and advantages of using the brand more frequently in existing situations or in new ones
2. Reminders to consumers to actually use the brand as close as possible to such situations

For many brands, increasing their usage may be as simple as improving top-of-mind awareness about them through reminder advertising (for example, as with V-8 vegetable juice and its classic "Wow! I Could Have Had a V-8" ad campaign). In other cases, more creative types of retrieval cues may be necessary. These reminders may be critical because consumers often adopt "functional fixedness" with a brand such that it can be easily ignored in non-traditional consumption settings.

Another potential way of increasing the quantity used is to reduce the undesirable consequences of an increased usage level (Aaker, 1991). For example, a shampoo designed to be gentle enough for daily use may alleviate the concerns of those consumers who believe that frequent hair washing is undesirable, and thereby eliminate their tendency to conserve the amount of the product they use. Another potential opportunity for increasing frequency of use is when consumers' perceptions of their usage differ from the reality. For many products with relatively short life spans, consumers may fail to replace them in a timely manner because of their tendency to underestimate the length of productive usage (Cripps, 1994).

One strategy by which product replacement can be speeded up is to tie the act of replacing it to a certain holiday, event, or time of year. For example, several brands run promotions that tie in with the spring-time switch to daylight savings time (for example, Oral-B toothbrushes). Another strategy may be to provide consumers with improved information on either (1) when the product was first used or will need to be replaced or (2) the current level of its performance. For example, some batteries have built-in gauges that show how much power they have left. Some toothbrushes and razor blades also have color indicators on them to indicate when they are too worn out or blunt, respectively.

Finally, perhaps the simplest way of increase usage is when actual usage of a product is less than the optimal or recommended amount. In this case, consumers need to be convince of the merits of more regular usage, and any potential hurdles to increased usage must be overcome. In terms of the latter, product designs and packaging can make a product more convenient and easier to use.

Identifying new and completely different ways of using a brand: The second approach to increasing the frequency of use of a brand is to identify completely new and different usage applications. For example, food product companies have been advertising new recipes that use their branded products in entirely different ways for a long time. Perhaps the classic example of finding creative new usage applications of a product is Arm & Hammer's baking soda, whose deodorizing and cleaning properties have led to a number of new uses for the brand.

Other brands have taken a page out of Arm & Hammer's playbook. Clorox has run ads that stress on the many benefits of its bleach (for exmple, how it eliminates kitchen odors); Wrigley's chewing gum has run ads touting its product as a substitute for smoking, and Tums has advertised that its antacid is also a calcium substitute.

Coach managed to expand usage and increase frequency both of its brand and its category by filling "usage voids"—situations where existing bag options were not appropriate—through the introduction of a plethora of different bag options for almost every occasion, for example, evening bags, backpacks, satchels, totes, briefcases, coin purses, and duffels. Rather than owning a small number of bags suitable for limited uses, women were encouraged by Coach to treat handbags as "the shoes of the 21st century: a way to frequently update wardrobes with different styles without shelling out for new clothes" (Byron, 2004).

However, new usage applications may require more than just new ad campaigns or merchandizing approaches. Often, new uses can arise from new packaging (Wansink, 1996b). For example, Arm & Hammer introduced a "Fridge-Freezer Pack" (with "freshflo vents") for its natural baking soda. This was specially designed to better freshen and deodorize refrigerators and freezers. Trix Vereal used a side panel to feature complementary products (for exmple, ice-cream, yogurt, trail mix, etc.) on which Trix could be sprinkled. Murphy's Oil Soap printed a series of different usage ideas under peel-off stickers that were affixed to its spray bottles.

To uncover potential product consumption opportunities, Wansink advocates a number of different ways of identifying and communicating new usage situations (Wansink, 1996; Wansink and Gilmore, 1999). He maintains that an obvious starting point for generating potential expansion opportunities is through brainstorming meetings or focus groups with loyal or heavy users and less-loyal or light users. Contrasting the preferences and behaviors of the two groups can yield insights into potential barriers in their perceptions and usage that need to be overcome as well as to garner opportunities for further growth. He also notes how perceptions of potentially related products and situations can be uncovered through cluster analysis or other multivariate statistical approaches.

Improving Brand Image

Although changes in brand awareness are probably the easiest means of creating new sources of brand equity, more fundamental changes are often necessary. A new marketing program may be necessary to improve the strength, favorability and uniqueness of brand associations making up the brand image. As part of this repositioning—or recommitment to the existing positioning—any positive associations that have faded may need to be bolstered, negative associations created neutralized and additional positive associations created.

Repositioning the brand: In some cases, repositioning a brand requires more compelling points-of-difference, i.e., stronger, more favorable and more unique brand associations to be established. This may simply require reminding consumers of the virtues of a brand they have begun to take for granted. Ironically, the New Coke debacle from 1985, where a new formulation of the iconic cola brand was roundly rejected by consumers, accomplished just this in a round-about manner. In other cases, brand associations related to aspects of product performance or brand imagery (for example, user or usage imagery and brand personality) need to be improved in some way.

Sometimes a key point-of-difference may turn out to be the history and heritage of a brand rather than any product-related difference. Research indicates that nostalgic advertising can influence consumers positively. One empirical study confirmed that intentionally nostalgic advertisements prompted reflection among respondents and led to favorable attitudes toward the advertisement and the brand (Muehling and Sprott, 2004). Another study identified a potential source of nostalgic purchase behavior, called "intergenerational influence," or the influence of a parent's purchase behavior and brand attitudes on a child's behavior and attitudes (Moore et al., 2002).

However, not all young consumers want to emulate their parents. In some cases, they may want to do the exact opposite. Consider the Pabst Blue Ribbon (PBR) story (Cortissoz, 2004; Mullman, 2006). Years ago, the company became one of the major beer brands in America and remained so through 1977, when its sales peaked at 18 million barrels. As competition from Budweiser and Miller increased, the PBR brand suffered as a consequence of price cuts, quality problems and ownership changes. After years of decline, sales of PBR suddenly spiked in the Portland, Oregon, area in 2001. Management investigated and discovered that young trendsetters were adopting the beer as a "blue-collar, Americana" alternative to the big brands and craft beers favored by their parents. Rather than using above-the-line advertising, which it had not done since the 1970s, Pabst sought to capitalize on this market through word-of-mouth, on-premise promotions and event sponsorships, primarily via sponsorhips of local bands and concerts, and licensed merchandize aimed at "hipsters." As a result, PBR has seen renewed sales growth.

At other times, a brand needs to be repositioned to establish a point-of-parity on some key image dimension in which it is seen as lacking. A common problem for established and mature brands is that they need to be made more contemporary by creating relevant usage situations, a more contemporary user profile, or a more modern brand personality. Heritage brands that have been around for years may be seen as trustworthy, but also boring, uninteresting, and not that likable.

Updating a heritage brand may involve a combination of new products, new advertising, new promotions, new packaging, and so forth. For example, the 170-year-old regional beer Yuengling saw its sales virtually double by introducing lighter and fuller flavored versions, new labels that gave the beer an arty and nostalgic look, and new promotions that tapped into regional pride by focusing on the brewery's place in history. Its new image permitted higher prices and allowed the brand to gain more high-end and on-premise accounts.

Entering New Markets

Positioning-related decisions require the specifications of the target market and the nature of the competition in order to set the competitive frame of reference. The target market or markets for a brand do not typically constitute all the possible segments that make up the entire market. In some cases, a company may have other brands that target the remaining market segments. In other cases, however, these market segments represent potential growth targets for the brand. Effectively targeting these other segments typically requires some changes or variations in the company's marketing program, especially in its advertising and other communications, and the decision as to whether it should target these segments ultimately depends on a cost-benefit analysis.

To grow their brand franchise, many companies reach out to new customer groups to build their brand equity. For example, Johnson & Johnson's baby shampoo achieved greater success by promoting the gentleness and everyday applicability of its shampoo to an adult audience. Another example of a company seeking to boost sales of its high-margin pool tables is Brunswick Billiards, which targeted design-conscious women who may have previously rejected the idea of buying a pool table on aesthetic grounds.

Segmentation on the basis of consumer behavior variables or other means, and identifying neglected segments is therefore one viable brand revitalization option. In some cases, just retaining existing customers who may eventually move away from the brand, or recapturing lost customers who no longer use the brand can be a means to increase sales. The importance of retaining current or recapturing lapsed customers can be recognized by calculating the lifetime value of customers. This often turns out to be considerable.

Attracting a new market segment can be difficult. Brands with more masculine images, for example, Gillette, Harley-Davidson, Wrangler and ESPN, have sometimes struggled through the years to find the right blend of products and advertising to make their brands appear relevant and appealing to women. Creating marketing programs to appeal to women has become a priority of makers of products from cars to computers. Marketers have also introduced new marketing programs that are targeted at different racial groups (for example, African Americans, Asian Americans, and Hispanic Americans), age groups, and income groups. Attracting emerging new market segments, based on cultural dimensions, may require different messages, creative strategies, and media.

Of course, one strategic option for revitalizing a fading brand is to simply more or less abandon the consumer group that supported it in the past and target a completely new market segment. One of the hottest fashion brands in the 1990s, Tommy Hilfiger, was struggling to stay relevant by the early 2000s. Other labels such as Phat Farm, FUBU, Sean John, and Ecko had drawn customers away by adopting the young urban, hip-hop style on which Hilfigerhad built its success in the 1990s in more "authentic" ways. To recover its position in the market, Hilfiger chose to cut all its ties with the style that had made it popular earlier—oversized apparel, even more oversized logos, and an edgy urban aura. It even went so far as to remove the stylized American flag logo from many of its garments. Instead, the company struck out in a new direction with preppy styles inspired by the sun and surf (Rozhon, 2003).

However, in making these kinds of shifts, there is always the danger that the new target market will not take to the repositioned brand. If this is so, a "worse case scenario" can be the result, with the old target market being abandoned and the new one not being sufficiently attracted to the replacement. For example, faced with a steady decline in sales in the late 1990s, the Gap decided to embrace a more youthful, fashion-forward look in its apparel. Unfortunately, trendsetters did not take to its new look and the company's existing customer base, which valued the brand's simplicity and straightforward sensibility, felt alienated. This resulted in an even more dramatic drop in its brand revenue.

CRISIS MARKETING GUIDELINES

Not only will all brands experience ups and downs, marketing managers must assume that at some point in time, some kind of crisis will arise with their brands. Diverse brands such as Wendy's restaurants, Firestone tires, Tyco's diversified holdings and the Vioxx painkiller have all experienced a serious and potentially crippling brand crisis. In general, the higher the brand equity and the stronger the corporate image a company has established—especially with respect to its corporate credibility and trustworthiness—the more likely it is that it will be able to weather the storm. Careful preparation and a well-managed crisis-management program, however, are critical. Two classic examples of crisis marketing programs include that of Johnson & Johnson (in terms of the right way of handling a crisis) and of Exxon (in terms of the wrong way of doing this), as follows.

Johnson & Johnson (Tylenol)

Tylenol consists of acetaminophen, a drug that is as effective as aspirin in relief of pain and fever, but does not cause the stomach irritation that often accompanies aspirin (Deighton, 1996). By 1982, the brand's market share had risen to 37% of the pain reliever market. However, all its success came crashing to the ground with the news in the first week of October 1982 that seven people had died after taking Extra-Strength Tylenol capsules (which turned out to contain cyanide) in the Chicago area. Although it quickly became evident that the problem was restricted to this area in the country and had almost certainly been the work of a deranged person outside the company, most marketing experts believed that the damage done to the reputation of the Tylenol brand was irreparable and that it would never fully recover. Johnson & Johnson's response and the equity of the Tylenol brand and its strong and valuable "trust" association (built up over the years prior to the incident) made sure that that this was not the case.

- Within the first week of the crisis, Johnson & Johnson issued a worldwide alert to the medical community, set up a 24-hour toll-free telephone number, recalled and analyzed sample batches of the product, briefed the US Food and Drug Administration, and offered a US$100,000 reward to apprehend the culprit who had tampered with the brand.
- During the week of October 5, Johnson & Johnson began a voluntary withdrawal of the brand by repurchasing 31 million bottles with a retail value of US$100 million. The company stopped advertising, and all communications with the public were in the form of press releases. To monitor consumers' response to the crisis, it conducted weekly tracking surveys with 1,000 consumer respondents.
- The following week of October 12, it introduced a capsule exchange offer.
- During the week of October 24, Johnson & Johnson made its return to TV advertising with the goal of convincing users of Tylenol that they could continue to trust its safety and encouraged use of the tablet form until tamper-resistant packaging was available for the capsule form.
- Convinced that market conditions were now stable enough to commence regular advertising, Johnson & Johnson's ad agency developed three ad campaigns using the testimony of loyal Tylenol users with the goal of convincing consumers that they could continue to use new triple tamper-resistant packaged Tylenol capsules with confidence. The company's return to advertising was accompanied by additional promotional offers to consumers through coupons.

Incredibly, by February 1983, sales of Tylenol had almost fully returned to the lofty pretampering sales levels the brand had enjoyed six months earlier.

EXXON

Although Exxon spent millions of dollars advertising its gasoline and crafting its brand image over the years, it ignored marketing its corporate identity and image (Langford and Greyser, 1995). This decision haunted the company in the weeks following March 24, 1989. That morning, the tanker *Exxon Valdez* hit a reef in Prince William Sound, Alaska, resulting in around 11,000,000 gallons of oil spilling into the waters off the Alaska shoreline. The oil spill wreaked devastation on the fish and wildlife extending over around 1,300 square miles of the previously unspoiled waters.

Top Exxon officials declined to comment publicly for almost a week after the incident, and the public statements that were eventually made sometimes appeared to contradict information from other sources involved in the situation (for example, regarding the severity of the spill) or assigned blame for the slow clean-up efforts to other parties (for example, the U.S. Coast Guard). Exxon received withering negative press and was the butt of countless jokes on late-night talk shows. In frustration and anger, some of the company's consumers began to tear up their Exxon credit cards. On April 3, 10 days after the accident, Exxon's Chairman ran an open letter to the public in the form of a full-page message expressing the company's concern and justifying its actions in addressing the accident.

Most experts agree that the Exxon incident is a good example of how *not* to handle a brand crisis. On the other hand, Johnson & Johnson's nearly flawless handling of the Tylenol-tampering incident was a major factor in that brand's comeback. As Johnson & Johnson's crisis marketing program indicates, the two keys for effective management of a crisis is that the response of a company in a crisis should be seen by consumers as swift and sincere, as follows.

SWIFTNESS

The longer it takes a company to respond to a marketing crisis, the more likely it is that consumers can form negative impressions as a result of unfavorable media coverage or word of mouth publicity. Even worse, they may find out that they do not really like the brand that much after all and permanently switch to alternative brands or products. For example, Perrier was forced to stop its production worldwide and recall all of its existing bottles in February 1994 when traces of benzene, a known carcinogen, was found in excessive quantities of the bottled water. Over the course of the next few weeks, the companies offered several explanations on how the contamination had occurred, resulting in confusion and skepticism. Perhaps even more damaging, the product itself was off the shelves until May 1994.

Despite an expensive relaunch, featuring ads and promotions, the brand struggled to regain its lost market share, and a full year later found its sale less than half of what it had once been. A part of the problem was that during the time the product was unavailable, consumers and retailers found satisfactory substitutes (for example, waters such as Saratoga and San Pellegrino). With its key "purity" association tarnished (the brand had been advertised as the "Earth's First Soft Drink" and "It's Perfect. It's Perrier."), it had no other compelling points-of-difference over its competitors.[1] Finally, compounding the problems arising from its marketing crisis, the brand had been gaining an increasingly stodgy image and was seen as being much more appealing to the over-45 consumer market and much less so to those under 25 years. Eventually, the company was taken over by Nestlé SA.

SINCERITY

Swift actions must also come across as being sincere to consumers. The more sincere a company's response in terms of public acknowledgment of the severity of the impact on consumers and its willingness to take whatever steps are necessary and feasible to solve the crisis, it is less likely that consumers will take a negative view of its conduct and attitude. For example, although Gerber had established a strong image of trust with consumers, baby food is a product category characterized by an extremely high level of involvement and need for reassurance. When consumers reported finding shards of glass in some jars of its baby food, Gerber tried to reassure the public that there were no problems in its manufacturing plants, but adamantly refused to withdraw its baby food from grocery stores. Some consumers found Gerber's response unsatisfactory because the brand's market share slumped from 66% to 52% within a couple of months. As one company official admits, "Not pulling our baby food off the shelf gave the appearance that we aren't a caring company" (Alsop, 1989).

Another example is the public relations problems encountered by Intel Corp. with the "floating decimal" problem in its Pentium microprocessors in December 1994. Although the flaw in the chip resulted in miscalculation-related issues in only extremely unusual and rare instances, Intel was probably at fault—as company executives now admit—for not identifying the problem and proposing remedies to consumers more quickly. Once the problem became public, Intel endured an agonizing six-week period when it was the focus of media scrutiny and criticism for its reluctance to publicize the problem and its failure to offer replacement chips. Two key sources of brand equity for Intel microprocessors such as the Pentium—emphasized throughout their marketing program—are "power" and "safety." Although consumers primarily think of safety in terms of upgradability, perceptions of financial risk or other problems that may be due to a potentially flawed chip should have created a sense of urgency within the company to protect one of its prize sources of brand equity. Eventually, Intel recapitulated and offered a replacement chip. Perhaps not surprisingly, only a very small percentage of consumers—an estimated 1% to 3%—actually requested one. This indicates that it was Intel's stubbornness in taking prompt action and not the defect that rankled so many consumers.

Brand crises are difficult to manage because, despite a company's best efforts, it is difficult to be in control of the situation. To some extent, it is at the mercy of public sentiment and media coverage, which it can attempt to direct and influence, but which can sometimes take on a life of its own. Swift and sincere words and actions, however, can often go a long way in defusing a situation.

SUMMARY

Revitalizing a brand either requires that lost sources of brand equity are recaptured or new sources are identified and established. According to the customer-based brand equity framework, two general approaches are feasible—(1) expanding the depth and/or breadth of brand awareness by improving brand recall and recognition of consumers during purchase or consumption settings and (2) improving the strength, favorability and uniqueness of brand associations constituting the brand image. The latter approach may however involve programs that are directed at existing or new brand associations. (See Figure 13.1 for a summary of this.)

In the case of a fading brand, the depth of brand awareness is often not as much of a problem as the breadth due to consumers tending to think of it in very narrow ways. Strategies to increase usage of and find new uses of the brand need to be reviewed. Although changes in brand awareness are probably the easiest means of creating new sources of brand equity, a new marketing program may often need to be implemented to improve the strength, favorability and uniqueness of brand associations. As part of this re-positioning, new markets may need to be tapped. The challenge implicit in all such efforts to modify a brand image is that the equity that already exists should not be destroyed. A number of different possible strategies designed to acquire new customers and retain existing ones also need to be reviewed. Finally, guidelines in terms of swiftness and sincerity should be offered in terms of a how to handle a marketing crisis.

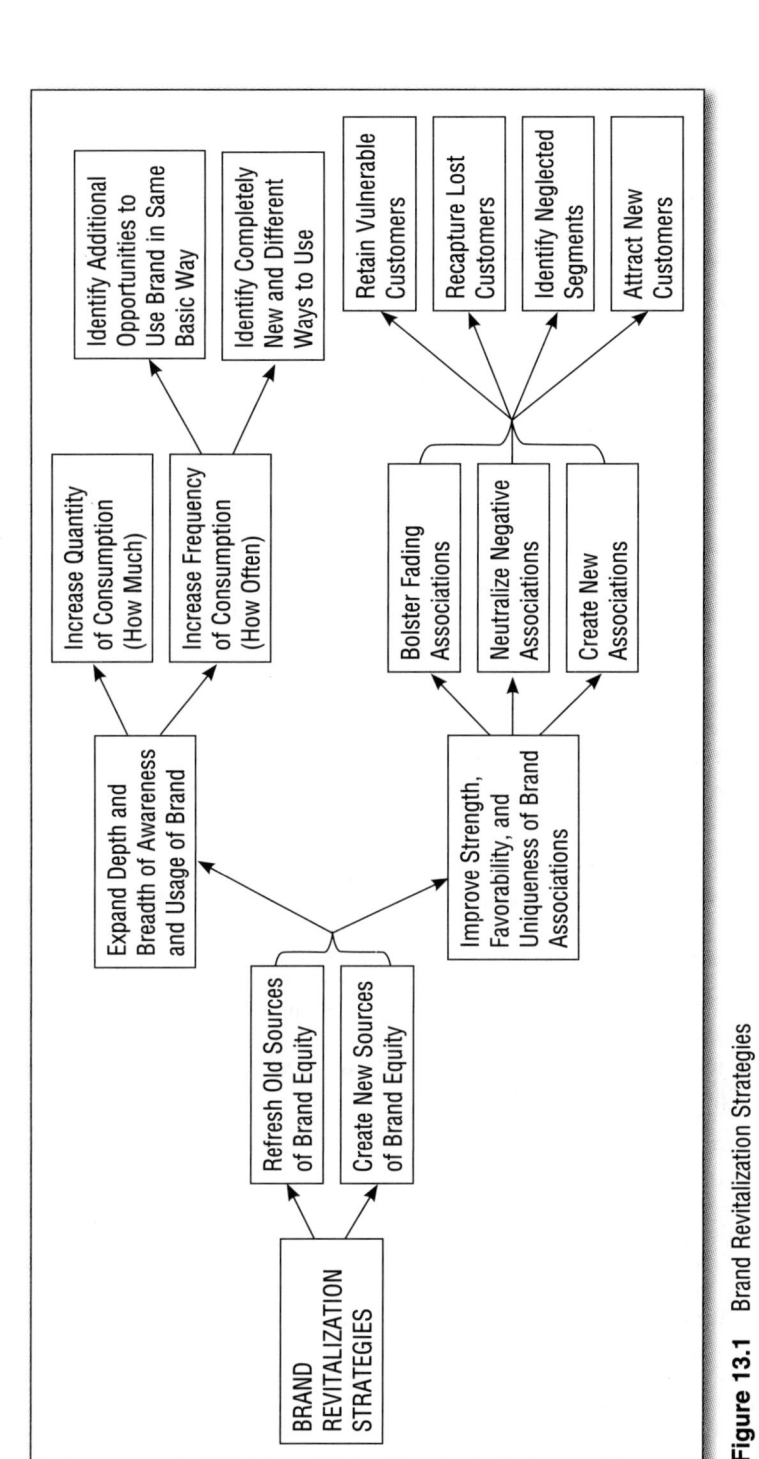

Figure 13.1 Brand Revitalization Strategies

REFERENCES

Aaker, David A. (1991), *Managing Brand Equity*. Free Press: New York.

Alsop, Ronald (1989), "Enduring Brands Hold Their Allure by Sticking Close to Their Roots," *Wall Street Journal Centennial Edition*.

Byron, Ellen (2004), "How Coach Won a Rich Purse by Inventing New Uses for Bags," *Wall Street Journal*, November 17, A1.

Charlier, Marj (1993), "Yuengling's Success Defies Convention," *Wall Street Journal*, 26 August, B1.

Cortissoz, Ann (2004), "Not Your Father's Beer: Your Grandfather's," *Boston Globe*, October 20, F1.

Cripps, John D. (1994), "Heuristics and Biases in Timing the Replacement of Durable Products," *Journal of Consumer Research*, 21 (September), 304–318.

Deighton, John A. (1996), "Features of Good Integration: Two Cases and Some Generalizations," In J. Moore and E. Thorsen (Eds), *Integrated Communications: The Search for Surgery in Communication Voices*. Lawrence Erlbaum Associates, Hillsdale: NJ.

Greyser, Stephen A. and Norman Klein (1990a), "The Perrier Recall: A Source of Trouble," Case 9: 590–104, Harvard Business School, Boston.

——— (1990b), "The Perrier Relaunch," Case Supplement 9:590–130, Harvard Business School, Boston.

Keller, Kevin Lane (2008), *Strategic Brand Management*, 3rd edition, Upper Saddle River, NJ: Prentice-Hall.

Langford, Nancy and Steven A. Greyser, (1995), "Exxon: Communications after Valdez," Case 9: 593–014, Harvard Business School, Boston.

Light, Larry and Joan Kiddon, (2009), *Six Rules for Brand Revitalization: Learn How Companies Like McDonald's Can Re-Energize Their Brands*. Upper Saddle River, NJ: Wharton School Publishing.

Lindsay, Greg (2006), "The Alligator's New Look," *Business 2.0*, April 2006, pp. 68–69.

Lauro, Patricia Winters (2002), "Old Spice Begins a Revival as a Body-Care Line for College-Age Men," *New York Times*, April 29, 2002.

Moore, Elizabeth S., William L. Wilkie, and Richard J. Lutz (2002), "Passing the Torch: Intergenerational Influences as a Source of Brand Equity" *Journal of Marketing*, 66, April 2002, 17–37.

Mullman, Jeremy (2006), "Schlitz Tries to Revive '50s Heyday," *Advertising Age*, April 17, 2006, 8.

Muehling, Darrel D. and David E. Sprott (2004), "The Power of Reflection: An Empirical Examination of Nostalgia Advertising Effects," *Journal of Advertising*, 33(Fall), 25–35.

Rifkin, Glenn (1997), "How Harley-Davidson Revs Its Brand," *Strategy & Business*, Fourth Quarter 1997.

Rozhon, Tracie (2003), "Reinventing Tommy: More Surf, Less Logo," *The New York Times*, March 16, 2003, 1.

Wansink, Brian (1996a), "Can Package Size Accelerate Usage Volume?" *Journal of Marketing* 60 (July), 1–14.

——— (1996b), "Advertising Strategies to Increase Usage Frequency," *Journal of Marketing* 60 (January), 31–46;

Wansink, Brian and Jennifer Marie Gilmore, "New Uses That Revitalize Old Brands," *Journal of Advertising Research* (March–April 1999), 90–98.

Chapter 14

Brand Identity Strategy for Mergers and Acquisitions

Srinivas Reddy and Anupam Jaju

OVERVIEW

In the past several years, there has been the increasing trend of companies changing their identities by redeploying their corporate or product brand names. Redeployment of corporate names due to a merger or acquisition take place in a variety of ways, ranging from elimination of one brand to concatenation of brand names. This chapter presents a framework of corporate brand redeployment approaches and highlights resource redeployment motives to hypothesize the choice of a brand name. We also showcase studies that examine the reactions of consumers to alternative redeployment strategies. Using both secondary and experimental data, we find evidence that consumers' beliefs, attitudes, and intentions relating to corporate brand names are often reduced due to M&A activities. Additionally, individuals react differently to mergers employing different redeployment strategies. These results call attention to the need for companies to evaluate the corporate branding component of M&A activities as part of the process of managing corporate brands as long-term and strategic assets.

INTRODUCTION

Corporate stakeholders routinely rely on the identity and equity of organizations while making investment- and career related decisions, and product choices (Dowling, 1986; Shimp and Bearden, 1982). These identities help stakeholders develop an overall perception about a company's capabilities and performance. Recently, there has been an increasing trend of organizations changing their identities by changing their corporate or product brand names. These name changes or brand redeployment are either the result of corporate action (for example, a merger or acquisition deal), or an attempt by a company to reposition itself or its offerings. Subsequent to M&A transactions, name changes occur in a variety of ways. In certain instances, the merged company decides to either keep the acquirer's or the target's name; in other circumstances, the merged organization decides to append/concatenate the acquirer and the target's name. For example, in the merger of the Bank of America and Nations Bank, the former's name was chosen for the merged company, whereas in the case of the automobile giants, Daimler Benz and Chrysler, the two names were concatenated to form "Daimler Chrysler." Such variations in companies' strategic choices motivate this investigation. The objective of this study is to develop an understanding of the antecedents that lead to such corporate brand name strategies.

The strategic and financial consequences of such redeployment of resources by a company could be substantial. While on one hand, organizations aim to achieve leveraged synergy, on the other hand, they risk losing the brand equity of the eliminated brand and even diluting equity in the case of a concatenated brand. In the Daimler Chrysler case, the merged company optimized between the equity loss of eliminating the Chrysler brand and the cannibalizing effect on the Daimler brand. The cost and frequency of such redeployment is significantly high. For example, Miles Inc. spent US$20 million on an ad campaign to promote its name change to Bayer (Rosendahl, 1995).

In 1999, a total of 2733 US companies changed their corporate brand names. Over 53% of these name changes were due to M&A transactions, which took place virtually across all the segments of corporate business. Such redeployment can cost US$20 million to more than US$200 million. Furthermore, problems such as deteriorating working relationships and low employee morale may occur in addition to financial expenses. Anecdotal evidence indicates that a sudden change in a name can cause confusion and frustration among a company's stakeholders (Wagner, 1981).[1]

During the past two decades, empirical research (although limited) indicates that the stock market seems to react to announcements of corporate brand name change (Howe, 1982; Horsky and Swyngedouw, 1987; Ferris, 1988, and Bosch and Hirschey, 1989). The reactions of the stock market have however been mixed or inconclusive. Signaling theorists argue that a corporate brand change may be a signal of an improvement in the growth prospects of a company. While such brand redeployment (corporate or product) promises to yield significant value to the merged company, the stumbling block is their enormous failure rates. Knudsen et. al (1997) studied a mix of complex and straightforward mergers and found that the market share was maintained in less than half of the cases. In the case of pure brand mergers, where two or more brands in the market are combined into one, the success rate fell to 25%. Similarly, Friedman (2000) showed that the subsequent (to the name change) stock market performance of such companies has been dismal relative to the S&P500 Index.

Despite the importance of corporate or product identity and its implications on the overall performance of companies, very little research is available on this area. While such brand redeployment strategies have been adopted for years, there has not been much academic discussion on it. Varadarajan et. al. (2001) suggests

> Resource redeployment is reflected in the brand rationalization activities that firms often undertake post-deconglomeration and subsequent acquisitions of competitors of the businesses retained in order to pursue focused growth ... Representative of brand related issues that such firms may be required to address include: (1) which brand names to retain and phase out, (2) opportunities for brand consolidation through brand fusion/dual branding (e.g., melding of currently owned brand names and

---

[1] It should be noted that brand redeployment subsequent to M&A activity is a unique phenomenon wherein a merging company cannot seek stakeholders' input on the naming process before the redeployment decision. Most M&A activity involves disclosing the new name on the day of the announcement of the merger.

inherited brand names), and (3) organizing of retained brand names into categories.

This article examines the overall motive of resource (brand) redeployment and relating these motives to a company, and market- and transaction-specific factors that lead to the strategic choice of corporate brand redeployment subsequent to an M&A transaction. Subsequently, we investigate the impact of corporate brand name redeployment after acquisition M&A activities from the perspective of consumers. At the outset, we would like to caution you that our focus is on examining redeployment of *corporate* brands (and not product or family brands). It should be viewed in light of the importance of corporate branding strategy and its link to a company's performance. As Rao, Agarwal and Duhlhoff (2004) empirically illustrate, corporate brands are more positively related to the intangible value of companies than any other branding approach. Undoubtedly, corporate branding strategy adds more value to customers' assets due to its cross-selling effect.

MOTIVES FOR BRAND REDEPLOYMENT

The motives behind the corporate strategy of brand or resource redeployment are fairly diverse, intriguing, and at times, vague. Some theorists argue that brand name changes are a result of a company's strategic decision to create synergies, (Jensen, 1986 and Dutz, 1989) leverage equity and/or "broaden the scope of business" (Berry, 1975; Steiner, 1975; Rock and Rock, 1990; Seth, 1990). Others ascribe the motive to the rather selfish nature of the executives and/or the companies (Stigler, 1964; Scherer, 1970; Yunker, 1983). A multitude of business perspectives provide the theoretical underpinnings of the motives of brand redeployment.

1. *Resource-based view (RBV) and Transaction-Cost (TC) perspective:* There has been ample evidence to indicate that companies use M&A transactions as a means to exchange organization-specific resources that otherwise are not easily redeployed (Wernerfelt, 1984; Hennart and Park, 1993; Mitchell, 1994;

Capron and Hulland, 1999). Resource redeployment enables companies to potentially reduce their costs by enhancing their productivity and enhancing the merging organizations' revenues. The desire to obtain resources (tangible or intangible) may be the motivation behind their decision to opt for an M&A transaction. However, an acquisition is likely to create synergistic value for the acquirer, only if this has the ability to generate significant economic benefits due to the combination. To exploit the value of these resources fully, companies need to redeploy the acquirer's resources into the target's markets as well as the target's resources for use in the acquirer's market. The redeployment process becomes particularly critical when resources (for example, the brand name) are immobile.

The immobility and inimitability of a brand as an asset (Hunt and Morgan, 1995; Srivastava et. al., 1998) inhibits competing companies from transferring, acquiring or copying them easily. These resources protect their ability to achieve a superior performance by sustaining resource heterogeneity across their competitors. Moreover, the effects cannot be readily or easily duplicated through the use of other strategic resources, i.e., substitutability is low. Therefore, the asset-seeking objective of M&A suggests that companies often turn to markets to "acquire or sell" their intangible resources (brand names) and consequently their goodwill and/or reputation.

From a transaction cost perspective, M&A transactions have been recognized as a means to internalize benefits. Given such opportunistic behavior, bounded rationality and low transaction costs may create a preference for external resource redeployment. Therefore, acquisitions can be a fundamental way of obtaining and internalizing such unique company-specific resources. M&A deals provide an opportunity for the acquirer company to rethink its own and its products' images and identities. Less advantaged organizations can attempt to neutralize or leverage the advantaged firm through a merger (in terms of their reputation). In certain instances, acquiring a brand name (and hence its reputation) may even be the primary motive of an

M&A transaction. Many companies acquire others with well-known and reputed brand names to avoid the high cost and risk of developing new identities. This also provides acquirers access to new markets and/or strengthens their position in existing ones. The advantage of such assets is that they can be deployed without consumption and used in several ways concurrently (Williams, Tsai, and Diana, 1991). To summarize, the RBV and TC perspective focuses on synergistic value creation, i.e., how companies enhance their performance or value by integrating/redeploying their resource via M&A transactions.

2. *Competitive strategy—market power perspective:* IO economists suggest that market power is one of the most important motives behind mergers and acquisitions. The asset-exploiting motive of M&A suggests that an acquirer has two forms of market control—(a) economic market power and (b) managerial power. Economic market power is the ability of a market participant or group of participants to control the price, quantity or nature of goods sold, thereby generating extra-normal profits (Eckbo, 1983; Stillman, 1983; Sheth, 1990). The argument is that mergers (especially, horizontal ones) increase market concentration, and thereby increase market power and consequently profitability. Organizations with a monopoly in a market can perform well in the short run, regardless of whether they modify their offerings to suit their customers' preferences.

The managerial power perspective, (unlike the RBV and TC perspective) advocates opportunistic behavior for companies and their executives during the resource redeployment process. A basic assumption in the microeconomic theory is that managers are strictly motivated by profits. The agency theory argues that executives work more for their self-interest than the collective interest of their organizations. Rhoades (1983) posits that business executives (and even government officials) are motivated by their desire for control over resources, people and events[2]. Some examples

---

[2] Berle and Means (1991) regard the modern executive as analogous to kings and Popes of former times, whose desire for power in the economic arena seems

of hostile takeovers strikingly illustrate this drive for power. Like social and political heritage, the source of power is attributed to a company's economic well-being, i.e., in terms of its size, assets, and resources. Yunker (1983) believes that corporate brand name changes are made after acquisitions because acquirers want their companies to gain prestige and visibility through recognition that previously independent organizations have become a part of them. Kahn (1981) states to this effect that:

> they (managers) may well be interested in the prestige, the public exposure and influence, and the higher remuneration that seems to go with their working for larger than smaller companies.

According to Russell (1983), companies and their executives use the opportunity created through M&A to satisfy their greed for power and prestige. This suggests that even if empire building may not be the primary motive for the transaction, the vulnerability of M&A engagements motivates opportunistic behavior. This phenomenon, consistent with "black widow" or "cherry picking" behavior, suggests that in an M&A, the acquirer considers the target company a resource cow. Therefore, an acquirer company is opportunist when it disposes of (resells) the target organization once it "picks" its useful assets/resources (for example, brand name) and achieves its desired objective.

3. *Signaling perspective:* Information-related asymmetry exists across the several stakeholder groups of companies. The signaling theory assumes that the majority of stakeholders do not have direct access to information or knowledge of many strategic management decisions taken within organizations. Some of these decisions and information pertain to issues such as the companies' long-term objectives and goals, their strategic posture, new products they plan to introduce, their financial health, etc. Disparities in access to information among stakeholders either make such strategies acutely sensitive to their beliefs and expectations, or they use some

---

likely to have been manifested in achievement of size, a wide range of unrelated operations, and access to large-scale financing.

market and/or financial signals as a proxy for companies' status/standing in the marketplace. Acquirers leverage information regarding resource redeployment to send out a "signal" to their stakeholders about strategic changes. Corporate brand name change is a tool that is frequently used for signaling the market and/or financial transitions of a company (Howe, 1982, and Bosch and Hirschley, 1987). Since companies do not release new information on asset redeployment or new potential sources of value while announcing mergers, changes in corporate names provide surrogate information on such developments.

Living in an era of high corporate visibility, stakeholders interpret any modification to the corporate name as a signal from its management (Karpoff and Rankine, 1994). The signals may not only be derived from the type of name change, but also from the implicit motivation behind the reasons or processes of the name change. Corporate name redeployment serves as a communication tool to convey not only the motive for a merger, but also to provide reassurance on future expectations. For example, if an acquiring company drops its own name and takes up the name of the target company, this may signal that the operations of the new company are dominated by the target company, and in all likelihood, the mission of the new entity will be similar to that of the latter.

4. *Bounded rationality (ease-of-transition) perspective:* The motives for resource redeployment mentioned above are pro-active and seek changes in current and future positioning of companies. However, it is prudent to acknowledge the contrary argument of bounded rationality (Simon, 1955), which posits that companies rely on "ease of transition" or "cost of operationalization" while making resource redeployment-related decisions. For example, Oliver (1997) suggests that managers commonly make normatively rational choices induced by cultural-cognitive (common beliefs, customs, etc.) regulations. Such actions are legitimized externally rather than in terms of efficiency (Meyer and Rowan, 1977). In an attempt to streamline the operations of a new/acquired entity, companies either maintain the status quo

of the acquired organizations' positions/brand names or choose strategies that require the least effort for and avoid the complications of redeployment. Such strategies not only offer operational ease (amid the complexity of M&A integration), but also eliminates anxiety among stakeholder groups. Due to the asymmetry of information between two companies, an acquirer may decide not to change/modify/eliminate the "unknown" until it acquires the target and confirms its market value. Brand redeployment in this instance may not be operationalized or implemented until a few months or years after the M&A transaction.

BRAND NAME REDEPLOYMENT APPROACHES

A cursory investigation of archived M&A anatomies indicates a wide variation in redeployment strategies or approaches. The following are six commonly used taxonomies:

Strategy 1: The acquirer and the target adopt the name of the acquirer as the final name.
For example: *Compaq + Digital Technologies → Compaq*

Strategy 2: The acquirer and the target adopt the name of the target as the final name.
For example: *Chemical Bank + Chase Manhattan → Chase Manhattan*

Strategy 3: The acquirer and the target concatenate their names with acquirer's name dominating the final name.
For example: Exxon Chemical + Mobil Chemical → ExxonMobil

Strategy 4: The acquirer and the target concatenate their names with target's name dominating the final name.
For example: *Farnell, PLC + Premier Industrial → Premier Farnell, PLC*

Strategy 5: The acquirer and the target adopt a completely new name.
For example: *Autocyte + Neopath, Inc.* → *Tripath Imaging, Inc.*

Strategy 6: The acquirer and the target continue with their respective corporate names, wherein the target becomes a subsidiary of the acquirer.
For example: *Gillette Company + Duracell International* → *Duracell (a subsidiary of Gillette).*

These brand redeployment approaches can be categorized, based on the dominant motive of resource redeployment (refer to Figure 14.1):

1. *Synergistic redeployment/non-synergistic redeployment:* The synergistic motive of redeployment assumes that the acquirer aims to capitalize on the synergies created through the concatenation of the acquirer's and the target's names or their simultaneous existence[3]. Rao and Ruekert (1994) state, "because brand names are valuable assets, they may be combined with other brand names to form a synergistic alliance in which the sum is greater than the parts." This particular strategy derives benefits by combining the equity of both the acquirer's and the target's resources. Synergies achieved through such redeployments are the consequence of (a) increased awareness (across markets), and augmented brand attitude and associations (across segments) of the combined brand, (b) the potentially reduced cost of creating brand equity by enhanced brand development and promotional efficiencies, and (c) efficient means of communication to various stakeholders (Rao, Agarwal, and Dahlhoff, 2004). However, on the other hand, non-synergistic redeployment indicates divestiture of brand equity of the acquirer or

---

[3] It is assumed that simultaneous existence of names (Strategy 6 or non-concatenated redeployment) may be synergistic. Such strategic actions enable cooperative interactions and leveraging of brand equity across the parent and subsidiary units both in the consumer and the financial marketplace. The non-concatenated redeployment strategy is similar to the mixed branding strategy proposed by Rao, Agarwal, and Dahlhoff (2004).

Brand Identity Strategy for Mergers and Acquisitions   345

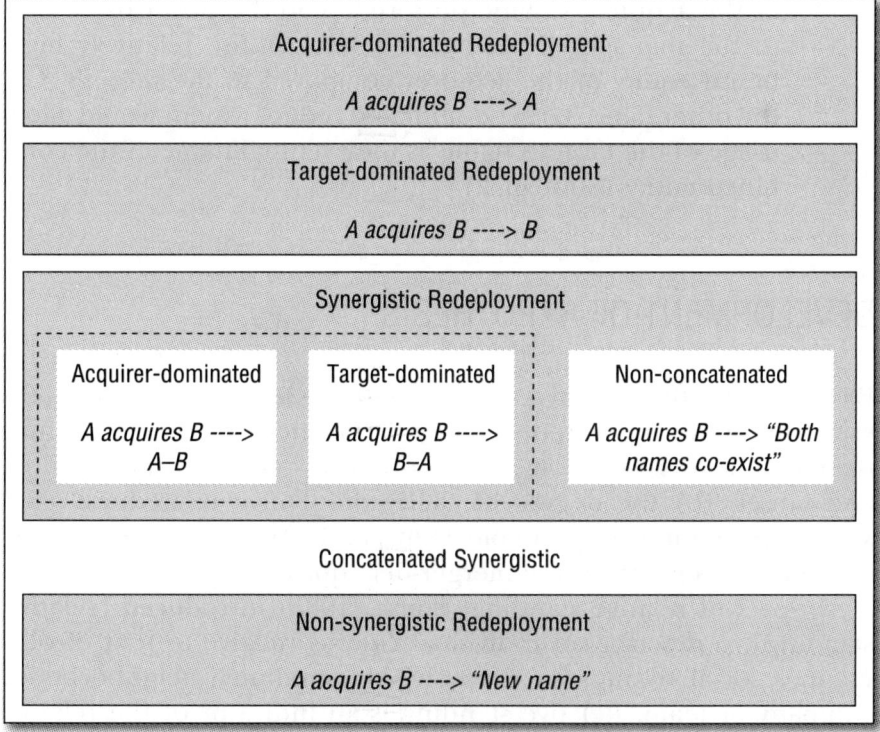

Figure 14.1 Framework of Brand Redeployment Strategy

target. It occurs in cases when either of the names (acquirer's or target's) cease to exist and/or the merged entity assumes a new name (Strategy 5).

2. *Acquirer-dominated redeployment/target-dominated redeployment*: The power motive denotes the dominance of the acquirer during the transaction process. This motive can be either through monopolistic dominance in the marketplace or managerial greed for empire building. Such motives incorporate actions wherein the acquirer's name dominates the ultimate name after the merger or acquisition[4]. The dominance

---

[4] It should be noted that the taxonomy of brand redeployment is not mutually-exclusive. Redeployment cases indicate a hierarchy of synergistic and dominating motives. For example, the synergistic motive can be sub-categorized as acquirer-dominated synergistic (Strategy 3) or non-dominated synergistic (Strategy 4). However, during the course of this research, discussions with corporate brand consultants revealed that the choice of acquirer-dominated synergistic versus

of the acquirer's name on a redeployed brand can be due to the managerial motive of power or the relatively high brand equity of the acquirer compared to the target's. On the other hand, target-dominated redeployment would allow usage of the target's name as the eventual name of the combined entity (Strategy 2).

DEVELOPMENT OF HYPOTHESIS

Based on the theoretical foundations discussed above, we hypothesize the brand name redeployment strategies based on four fundamental factors—(a) comparison of the resources of the acquirer and target, (b) the degree of their competitive relatedness[5], (c) signaling the motive of redeployment, and (d) the transactional or procedural elements of the merger or acquisition.

Impact of relative standing: Frank (1985) introduced "relative standing" to describe an individual's status relative to that of others in a social setting, for example, a community, neighborhood, company or team. Relative standing is an indicator of the relative status of the two companies over their resources, market-based credibility or reputation. While comparing two organizations, it is prudent to examine the sources by contrasting their performance. Our extant literature is replete with studies that examine the sources of the "bigness (or smallness)" or the reasons why one company is

---

non-dominated synergistic redeployment is primarily dependent on an issue relating to the "semiotics" or "schema (in)congruency" effects of the name and not on the synergistic or dominating motives. Therefore, these two strategies are combined into one choice option that is labeled as "Concatenated Synergistic Redeployment."

[5] Prior research in M&A and brand management has extensively evaluated the role of "fit" or similarity between companies, markets and product classes/brands. Scholars have identified that transfer of the perceived quality of a brand is enhanced when two companies or product-classes fit together in some way. Several theoretical perspectives are compatible with this view. The theory of cognitive consistency (Osgood and Tannenbaum, 1955; Heider, 1958), stimulus generalization (Bierley, McSweeney, and Vannieuwkerk, 1985) and the categorization theory (Fiske, 1982; Sujan, 1985; Cohen and Basu, 1987) support this phenomenon. The degree of perceived fit is a function of feature similarity perception and brand consistency perception (Aaker and Keller, 1990).

superior to the other. These studies indicate that larger firms have well-defined processes, organizational cultures, better capabilities, access to better resources, etc. These processes, cultures, capabilities and resources enable them to grow and prosper, and thus establish higher equity and brand recognition/reputation in the marketplace (Wernerfelt, 1984; Hennart and Park, 1993; Keller, 1993; Mitchell 1994; Capron and Hulland, 1999).

The phenomenon of the dominance of the "big fish" can be explained through a rational, resource-based and "capabilities" perspective (Very, Lubatkin, et. al., 1997). It can be fairly intuitively argued that a company with good resources and capabilities has a superior relative standing in terms of its equity and reputation. Therefore, it is prudent for the combined company to leverage the resources, equity and stronger reputation of the dominant one. Organizations have the incentive to redeploy resources from the company with a relatively stronger position to the weaker one (Capron, Dussuage, and Mitchell, 1998). In other words, a merger involving a strong acquirer leads to divestiture of the target's identities and vice versa.

Impact of market relatedness: Market relatedness within the M&A framework can be categorized as horizontal, vertical, congeneric, and conglomerate. A horizontal merger is one that takes place between two companies in the same industry. A vertical merger is one in which the buyer expands backward toward the source of raw materials or forward in the direction of the ultimate customer. A congeneric merger takes place between two diversified companies that aim for synergy in segments outside their core areas of operations (Brigham and Ehrhardt, 2002). A conglomerate merger, on the other hand, is enacted between companies engaged in unrelated lines of business.

1. *Horizontal M&A:* Such transactions take place between companies that are in direct competition in the same product lines and markets. Mergers between organizations that exhibit similar strategic characteristics result in better opportunities for scale efficiencies (Ramaswamy, 1997) or monopolistic collusion (Blair and Harrison, 1993; Stigler, 1968). This phenomenon motivates exploitation of shared resources, leading to divesture of redundant assets. Capron,

Mitchell, and Swaminathan (2001) illustrate that subsequent to horizontal mergers, resource redeployment occurs from the acquirer to the target and constitutes divestiture of the target's assets.

Economists have shown that horizontal mergers (between competing companies) often create monopolistic situations that result in enhanced profits for the acquirer (Stigler, 1964). Industrial organization (IO) economics emphasizes that market power is a primary incentive underlying horizontal acquisitions (Heflebower, 1963; Stigler, 1968, and Scherer, 1970). Therefore, it can be argued that subsequent to horizontal transactions, redeployment of the target's assets (in order to seek monopoly and market power) would have a competence-destroying effect. The underlying primary thesis is that the acquirer intends to increase its brand equity by capturing its competitor's (target's) market share.

2. *Vertical M&A:* Evolutionary theory suggests that as markets saturate and/or performance declines, companies tend to search and acquire new resources outside their core area of business. Vertical integration occurs when an acquirer expects to obtain synergies arising from backward integration to assimilate the sources of supply or forward integration toward the customer (Srivastava, Shervani, and Fahey, 1998). Such a strategic transaction is expected to create economies of scale by enabling more efficient coordination of the members of the vertical chain (increased internal efficiency) and even provide the acquiring company access to new (the target's) markets. Improved market access enables the combined entity to achieve revenue gains via increased market coverage. As mentioned earlier, the synergy perspective of mergers suggests that companies often leverage each other's resources to reconfigure themselves as part of the process of a broader strategic change. From the standpoint of brand reconfiguration, this synergy can be achieved when companies combine their identities and leverage their equities in their respective core markets. Consolidation of brand names following a vertical merger generates important efficiencies of marketing and promotional costs (Posner, 1976;

Bork, 1978, and Chatterjee, 1991). Leveraging the brand equity of the two brands increases their market coverage. Therefore, it is clear that vertically related M&A transactions motivate companies to adopt a synergistic brand redeployment strategy.

3. *Congeneric M&A:* Congeneric mergers or acquisitions are characterized by the acquirer sharing its peripheral (or secondary) markets of operations with the primary domain of the target. A frequently encountered situation involves a large and diversified acquirer (with multiple subsidiaries[6]) and a relatively small unified/undiversified target. The procedural objective of this transaction is to "accommodate and leverage" the target within an existing subsidiary or SBU of the acquirer. The merger is expected to generate synergies by leveraging the target's resources within the acquirer's processes. The motive for such mergers is to acquire a target that has a relatively higher standing than the existing subsidiary of the acquirer. Due to the target's specialization in its core area of business (and consequently its increased brand equity within that area), the acquirer intends to achieve synergy by acquiring and leveraging the resource and its equity (Mitchell, 1994). The post-acquisition integration of the target occurs in such a way that the target, while retaining its brand name, becomes a wholly owned subsidiary of the acquirer's company (a subsidiary merger). Therefore, the brand equity of both the acquirer and the target are synergistically combined while maintaining their respective (distinct) identities.

4. *Unrelated/Conglomerate M&A:* Typically, conglomerate mergers are affected between companies that are engaged in different or unrelated business activities. The primary motive is to diversify risk or seek above-normal gains by buying profitable companies and disposing of non-profitable ones." Blair (1958) contends that "of all types of merger activity, conglomerate acquisitions have the least claim to promoting

---

[6] Where a diversified company may already have several distinct brand names for each of its subsidiaries and product lines

efficiency in the economic sense." The effectiveness and efficiency of such mergers is questioned[7] due to economic and organizational risks in the post-merger consolidation process. Short-term profit- maximizing motives drive conglomerates' M&As. Gains in conglomerate mergers are achieved by acquiring the resources of profitable and high performance targets, which yield immediate cash flows. The acquiring company maintains the status quo of one enterprise by siphoning off its profits without interfering in its processes/operations or by making any effort/investments to integrate the resources of the two companies. As part of the same underlying phenomenon, the brand names of the two companies remain unattached such that their respective identities and equity is maintained and can be "resold" later. This argument is consistent with the "managerial synergy" perspective suggested by Matsusaka (1993), which suggests that conglomerate acquisitions tend to retain valuable target assets and not replace them. The main factor motivating redeployment of assets subsequent to a conglomerate merger is to maintain equity. Preservation of original brand names (of the acquirer and the target) ensures that individual brand associations and reputations are maintained intact, thereby avoiding the dilution affect or complexities arising during the eventual "disposal" of the acquired company.

5. *Impact of ownership status:* The ownership of a company and the phenomenon of resource redeployment can be explained through the fundamental principle of ease of transition/operationalization during the redeployment process. It can be argued that in instances when one of the merging entities is a public organization while the other is a private one, it is more prudient for the merged organization to adopt the brand name of the public unit. Since the public

---

[7] Klein (2001), Singh and Montgomery (1987), and Mueller (1977) suggest that conglomerate mergers yield below-normal or par- returns when compared with other transactions. This argument against their economic efficiency is supported by agency theorists, who debate that there appears to be a little incentive for managers who have little or no ownership interest in such conglomerate companies to pursue growth through gains in efficiency/synergies.

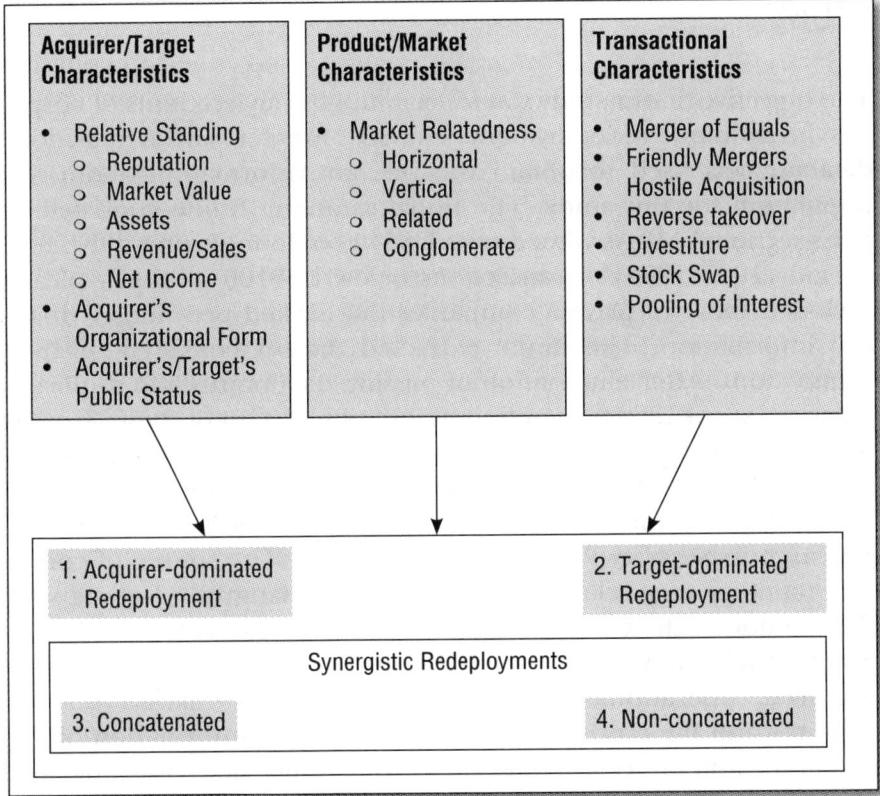

Figure 14.2 Antecedents of Brand Redeployment Strategy

entity has an additional stakeholder (shareholders) group (unlike the private entity), it is much easier to operationalize and implement the communication process of brand name redeployment. Therefore, in cases where one company is a publicly-owned one (and the other is privately owned), the brand name of the public entity is adopted as the redeployed name of the new company. The acquirer-dominated brand name redeployment strategy is more likely to be adopted when the acquirer is a public entity and the target a privately held one. Conversely, it can be argued that target-dominated brand name redeployment strategy is more likely to be adopted when the acquirer is a privately held company and the target a public one.

STUDY

The objective of our study was to examine the antecedents of corporate brand name redeployment. The SDC Mergers and Acquisitions database was used to obtain the relevant information about the population for this study. The initial sampling frame consisted of cross-sectional M&As valued over US$100 million during a five-year period (1995–1999)[8]. Transactions below US$100 million typically included those of private companies that lacked pre-merger financial information. The initial extracted dataset consisted of 1868 transactions. After elimination of missing data points and duplicate entries, a set of 1389 transactions was obtained. Out of these, around 361 transactions were cross-border deals and were eliminated, since they could be subject to special regulatory requirements. Name change-related information was obtained from the Center for Research in Security Prices (CRSP) database. The source of corporate name change-related information was triangulated along with the attitude of the transaction by validating it against archived news articles from the Lexis-Nexus database. The SDC database includes financial, operational, and market-related information on the acquirer and the target. Financial data includes information of the acquirer's and target's market value, total assets, sales/revenue, and net income. Companies' industries are identified by their operations in several industries/sectors, based on four-digit Standard Industrial Classification (SIC) codes (a total of 18 SIC codes per company). The primary/core businesses of the acquirer and the target are identified in the dataset and so is the categorical information on the ownership status of the two companies, i.e., "Public," "Private," or "Subsidiary," Additional procedural data (information about the transaction process) is obtained from multiple sources such as the *Mergers and Acquisitions Sourcebook* and the *Mergers and Acquisition Yearbook*. Each transaction is classified by using several procedures/M&A techniques—friendly or hostile, a merger of equals, pooling of interests, divestiture, stock swap, reverse takeover, etc.

---

[8] Mergerstat (2000) shows that the out of the total of 2439 disclosed M&A deals, more than 68% were valued at over US$100million. Therefore, it is safe to assume that deals valued over US$100million are a good representative sample of the overall population.

The final dataset contains 656 transactions after eliminating cases with missing values.

Measures

Relative standing: The relative standing construct is based on four[9] performance indicators—the market value, total assets, sales/revenue, and net income of the acquirer and the target. Relative standing scores are computed by using a ratio measure of the target's performance versus the acquirer's, based on each of the five indicators. Subsequently, an overall relative standing index is calculated as a mean of these four performance measures.

Market relatedness: Market overlap or relatedness is measured over four dimensions, based on the "type of relatedness" between the acquirer's and the target's areas of businesses. Over the years, the SIC system has served to measure relatedness objectively because its construction is based on similarities of technologies and principal input. A transaction is classified as a horizontal M&A if the primary SIC code of the acquirer is the same as the primary SIC code of the target. The vertical relatedness measure is obtained by using Lemelin's (1982) and Fan and Yang's (2000) vertical relatedness index. This index of relatedness is a continuous measure representing the degree of vertical relatedness and is based on the "Use Tables" provided by the Bureau of Economic Analysis[10]. Subsequently, congeneric M&A cases are identified as ones where the acquirer and the target are related in areas other that their pri-

---

[9] Reputation rankings from Business Week, Forbes, and Fortune (company rankings) were also extracted from the database. However, the reputation rank was not included in the overall relative standing index due to missing data on around more than 40% of the cases.

[10] The "Use Table" is a matrix (Input-Output or IO matrix) with the value of the commodity flows between each pair of over 500 industries. The table reports for each pair of industry, i and j, the dollar value of i's output required to produce industry j's total output, is denoted as aij. For calculating the vertical relatedness index, aij is divided by industry j's total output to get vij representing the dollar value of industry i's output required to produce one dollar's worth of industry j's output. Conversely, aji is divided by the dollar value of industry i's total output to get vji, representing the dollar value of industry j's output required to produce one dollar's worth of industry i's output. The vertical relatedness index is calculated as an average of vij and vji.

mary businesses. The degree of congeneric relatedness is a count measure of the number of common SIC codes between the acquirer and the target.[11] Finally, there are unrelated or conglomerate M&As, where no degree of relationship can be ascertained between the acquirer and the target.

Acquirer's degree of diversification: The acquirer's degree of diversification is based on the spread of an acquirer's business operations across industries.

The acquirer's degree of diversification (ADDI) is calculated as:

$$ADDI = \sum_{j=1}^{n} \sum_{i=1}^{n} ASIC_i - ASIC_j$$

Here, $ASIC$ = Acquirer 4-digit SIC code, n = number of businesses.

This measure, consistent with Rumelt (1974) and Christensen and Montgomery's (1981) conceptualization of a company's diversity, categorizes the extent of diversification of organizations, based on the relatedness between their business units (SBUs). Another dichotomous indicator of an acquirer's diversification also incorporated represents the presence or absence of its diversified portfolio.

DATA AND ANALYSIS

The dataset contains 261 horizontal mergers, and 31 vertical, 82 congeneric and 282 conglomerate transactions. Out of these, 40% of conglomerate M&As chose the Non-Concatenated strategy, compared to only 6.38% that chose the target-dominated redeployment

---

[11] Prior Studies have used SIC-based variable to classify relatedness between firms (Hoskisson, Hitt, Johnson and Moesel, 1993; Hambrick and Cannella, 1993). Fan and Yang (2000) compare the mean relatedness coefficients (obtained through Use Tables – IO matrix) between industry pairs classified into different SIC industries and between industry pairs classified into common SIC industries. Their comparison indicate that the results are better when the relatedness/complementarity between firms is calculated using SIC codes whereas the results are more valid when vertical relatedness is calculated using the IO matrix. Conclusively suggesting that SIC-based variables captures more complementarity and IO matrix variable captures more vertical relatedness.

strategy. Transactions that followed the Non-Concatenated redeployment strategy have the highest mean vertical relatedness. None of the vertically related M&As adopted the target-dominated redeployment strategy.

Table 14.1 provides descriptive statistics of the ownership status of the two companies. Out of the total of 656 transactions, 611 of them involve publicly owned acquirers and 492 publicly owned targets. About 18 (2.5% of the data) acquirers are also classified as subsidiaries to large publicly owned conglomerates. A total of 136 cases involved a publicly owned acquirer and a privately held target firm. Out of these 136 cases, 50% followed the acquirer-dominated redeployment strategy. None of the transactions in the entire dataset involved a privately held acquirer and a publicly owned target.

As discussed previously, the acquirer's organizational system or acquirer's diversification status is captured by using two measures— a continuous measure representing the degree of diversification and a dichotomous measure representing whether the acquirer has a diversified portfolio. The preliminary analysis of these two measures is presented in Table 14.2. A total of 531 (80.9%) of the acquirers have diversified portfolios and 49.93% adopt the non-concatenated strategy of brand redeployment. The means and standard deviations of the degree of diversification indicate insignificant differences across the various redeployment categories. The results indicate that acquirers with the highest degree of diversification tend to follow the concatenated redeployment strategy, closely followed by the acquirer-dominated strategy and the non-concatenated redeployment strategy.

The descriptive statistics of transactional characteristics are presented in Table 14.3. It should noted that out of 656 cases, 22 are mergers of equals, 94 hostile acquisitions, and 562 friendly mergers; 247 of M&A deals follow the pooling of interest accounting method and 402 the stock swap transaction. Additionally, 60 of the transactions involve divestiture of assets by the target and 27 are reverse takeovers. Please note that over 60% of hostile acquisitions and over 52% of stock swap transactions follow the acquirer-dominated brand redeployment method.

A multinomial logit model was estimated by using the four-brand redeployment strategies (acquirer-dominated, target-dominated, concatenated synergistic, and non-synergistic), since the dependent

Table 14.1 Descriptive Results: Categorical Measures (Market Relatedness, Ownership Status, and Diversification)
(Number of Cases and Percentages of Total)

	Dominating Redeployment			Synergistic Redeployment			TOTAL (656)
	Acquirer-dominated (265) (=41%)	Target-dominated (55) (=8%)	Concatenated (80) (=12%)	Non-concatenated (208) (=32%)	Non-synergistic Redeployment (48) (=7%)		
Market Relatedness							
Horizontal	118 (45.21%)	26 (9.96%)	37 (14.18%)	60 (22.99%)	20 (7.66%)		261
Vertical	12 (38.71%)	0 (0.00%)	4 (12.90%)	12 (38.71%)	3 (9.68%)		31
Congeneric	36 (43.90%)	10 (12.20%)	11 (13.41%)	19 (23.17%)	6 (7.32%)		82
Unrelated/ Conglomerate	100 (35.46%)	18 (6.38%)	31 (10.99%)	113 (40.07%)	20 (7.09%)		282
Acquirer Ownership Status							
Public	252 (41.24%)	50 (8.18%)	75 (12.27%)	42 (6.87%)	192 (31.42%)		611
Private	7 (25.93%)	4 (14.82%)	3 (11.11%)	10 (37.04%)	3 (11.11%)		27
Subsidiary	6 (33.33%)	2 (11.11%)	0 (0.00%)	5 (27.78%)	3 (16.67%)		18
Target Ownership Status							
Public	197 (40.04%)	41 (8.33%)	67 (13.62%)	144 (29.27%)	43 (8.74%)		492
Private	68 (41.46%)	14 (8.54%)	13 (7.93%)	64 (39.02%)	5 (3.05%)		164
Acquirer=Public & Target = Private	68 (50.00%)	12 (8.82%)	13 (9.56%)	40 (29.41%)	3 (2.21%)		136

Number of cases where acquirer is privately owned and target is publicly owned = 0.

Table 14.2 Descriptive Results: Continuous Variables (Relative Standing and Relatedness)

(Means and Standard Deviations)

Variable	N	Dominating Redeployment		Synergistic Redeployment		Non-Synergistic Redeployment
		Acquirer-Dominated	Target-Dominated	Concatenated	Non-Concatenated	
*Relative Standing**						
Reputation/Rank**	97	2.656 (3.614)	6.202 (15.738)	1.38 (0.815)	1.619 (1.791)	1.515 (1.276)
Market Value	597	0.343 (0.427)	0.796 (1.1023)	0.520 (0.426)	0.245 (0.254)	0.617 (0.369)
Total Assets	570	0.535 (0.661)	3.194 (11.744)	0.741 (0.948)	2.592 (19.715)	1.397 (1.498)
Sales	581	0.653 (0.876)	5.895 (18.857)	0.528 (0.084)	2.758 (19.362)	0.977 (0.819)
Net Income	553	0.265 (4.061)	1.170 (4.467)	0.339 (3.310)	1.509 (12.940)	0.899 (5.426)
Overall Relative Standing	633	0.316 (0.906)	2.008 (6.099)	0.811 (0.108)	1.349 (8.327)	0.550 (1.053)
(Degree of) Market Relatedness						
Vertical Relatedness	31	0.291 (0.426)	0.000 (0.000)	2.553 (4.744)	19.208 (59.322)	3.452 (5.724)
Congeneric Relatedness	82	1.51 (0.899)	2.29 (1.765)	1.59 (0.908)	1.53 (0.979)	1.36 (0.674)

* Relative standing is ratio of target characteristics by acquirer characteristics.
** Reputation/Rank indicator of the relative standing is eliminated owing to the high number of missing values.

Table 14.3 Descriptive Results: Categorical Measures (Control Variables)

(Number of Cases and Percentages of Total)

	Dominating Redeployment		Synergistic Redeployment		Non-synergistic Redeployment (48) (≈7%)	TOTAL (656)
	Acquirer-dominated (265) (≈41%)	Target-dominated (55) (≈8%)	Concatenated (80) (≈12%)	Non-concatenated (208) (≈32%)		
Transactional Characteristics						
Merger of Equals	5 (22.73%)	4 (18.18%)	7 (31.82%)	1 (4.55%)	5 (22.73%)	22
Hostile Acquisitions	57 (60.64%)	2 (2.13%)	5 (5.32%)	25 (26.60%)	5 (5.32%)	94
Friendly Merger	223 (39.68%)	53 (9.43%)	75 (13.35%)	168 (29.89%)	43 (7.65%)	562
Divestitures	34 (56.67%)	3 (5.00%)	7 (11.67%)	10 (16.67%)	6 (10.00%)	60
Pooling of Interest	118 (47.77%)	20 (8.10%)	37 (14.98%)	58 (23.48%)	14 (5.67%)	247
Reverse Takeover	6 (22.22%)	8 (29.63%)	6 (22.22%)	2 (7.41%)	5 (18.52%)	27
Stock Swap	210 (52.24%)	31 (7.71%)	63 (15.67%)	78 (19.40%)	30 (7.46%)	402

variable. The estimated parameters are presented in Tables 14.4 and 14.5. The results indicate that the overall relative standing, horizontal market overlap, "complementarity" between the acquirer and the target, the acquirer being a public entity, and transactional characteristics such as friendly mergers, hostile acquisitions, stock swaps, reverse takeovers and pooling of interest make a significant impact on the probability of choice of the (acquirer) dominated brand redeployment strategy. The results are consistent with the intuition that congeneric market overlap and pooling of interest transactions deter the strategic choice of acquirer-dominated brand redeployment. All of these factors tend to support a more synergistic type of redeployment strategy.

Similarly, estimates of the non-dominated redeployment model suggest that overall relative standing, and congeneric and conglomerate market overlap, have a significant effect on the probability of choice of non-dominated brand redeployment strategy. Consistent with our hypotheses, it was also found that the congeneric and conglomerate types of market overlap increase the likelihood of this strategy being adopted. The positive relationship between the conglomerate type of market overlap and non-dominated strategy may be explained through various underlying motives such as the acquirer's intentions of changing the focus of its own operations, organizational restructuring, etc. The results indicate that high vertical relatedness between the acquirer and the target significantly decrease the likelihood of choice of the non-dominated brand redeployment strategy.

Furthermore, the results show that the choice of the concatenated synergistic brand redeployment strategy is significantly influenced by vertically related, congeneric and conglomerate overlapping transactions. Apart from these factors, the interaction between the acquirer's diversification and relatedness was also found to have a significant positive effect on choice of this strategy. This relationship may suggest that there is a market overlap across multiple areas of business between the acquirer and the target.

Finally, the choice of non-synergistic redeployment is positively influenced by horizontal, vertical, and congeneric transactions. These results do not support our hypothesized arguments. The inconsistent ones can be attributed to a number of reasons relating

Table 14.4 Multinomial Logistic Model Results: Parameter Estimates—Acquirer-dominated versus Target-dominated

Variable	Acquirer-dominated [BRSTR=1]				Target-dominated [BRSTR=2]			
	Parameter Est. (β)	Std. Error	Wald's Stat	Odds Ratio [Exp(β)]	Parameter Est. (β)	Std. Error	Wald's Stat	Odds Ratio [Exp(β)]
Intercept (α)	1.593	2.011	0.628	–	4.372	2.336	0.061	–
Overall Relative Standing (ORS)	−1.011***	0.700	2.034	0.905	3.256***	0.958	2.297	1.246
Market Relatedness								
Horizontal (horizon)	4.348**	1.052	0.977	1.706	−0.192	0.545	0.124	0.826
Vertical (vertical)	−0.548	0.501	1.195	0.578	−14.536**	0.089	9.589	1.785
Congeneric (related)	−0.785**	0.172	20.778	0.456	0.038**	0.208	0.034	1.039
Conglomerate (conglom)	0.735	0.376	3.823	2.085	0.321**	0.620	0.268	1.379
Ownership Status								
Acquirer=Public, Target=Private (APTV)	0.470**	0.697	0.454	0.625	−1.083	0.961	10271	0.339
Acquirer=Private, Target=Public (AVTP)	–	–	–	–	–	–	–	–
Control Variables								
Acquirer's Diversification (ADIV)	−0.047	0.373	0.016	1.048	0.057***	0.621	0.008	1.058
Merger of Equals (MOE)	−0.989	1.116	0.708	0.391	2.241	1.186	3.569	0.106
Friendly Merger (Frndmerg)	−1.130***	0.825	1.875	3.094	19.757	0.005	1.874	0.056
Hostile Acquisition (HOSTACQ)	2.262**	1.115	2.754	1.294	−2.589**	0.256	1.347	0.851
Stock Swap (Stockswap)	0.687**	0.349	3.869	0.503	−0.773	0.564	1.876	0.462
Reverse Takeover (Revtake)	−0.978**	1.009	0.718	0.378	2.802**	1.021	5.915	0.006
Divestiture (Divest)	1.309	0.759	2.974	3.704	−0.087***	1.046	0.006	1.090
Pooling of Interest (POI)	−0.317***	0.316	1.002	0.729	−0.221***	0.473	0.218	1.247

** p<0.05, *** p<0.001

Table 14.5 Multinomial Logistic Model Results: Parameter Estimates—Concatenated Synergistic versus Non-synergistic

	Concatenated Synergistic [BRSTR=3]				Non-synergistic [BRSTR=4]			
Variable	Parameter Est. (β)	Std. Error	Wald's Stat	Odds Ratio [Exp(β)]	Parameter Est. (β)	Std. Error	Wald's Stat	Odds Ratio [Exp(β)]
Intercept (α)	4.430	2.221	3.979	–	−12.753	2.450	27.102	–
Overall Relative Standing (ORS)	0.054	0.087	0.383	0.947	0.117	0.165	0.506	0.889
Market Relatedness								
Horizontal (horizon)	−0.456	0.473	0.930	0.634	0.082***	0.617	0.018	1.086
Vertical (vertical)	0.180**	0.046	0.154	0.368	−0.016**	0.049	0.113	0.984
Congeneric (related)	1.000**	0.212	22.348	0.947	−18.364**	0.357	26.439	94.473
Conglomerate (conglom)	0.439***	0.515	0.727	1.551	0.638	0.640	0.994	0.319
Ownership Status								
Acquirer=Public, Target=Private (APTV)	−0.329	0.933	0.125	0.719	16.048	2.264	26.436	93.208
Acquirer=Private, Target=Public (AVTP)	–	–	–	–	–	–	–	–
Control Variables								
Acquirer's Diversification (ADIV)	0.603	0.449	1.802	0.547	−0.468**	0.545	0.737	0.626
Merger of Equals (MOE)	2.299**	1.112	4.274	0.100	−3.107	1.147	7.343	0.044
Friendly Merger (FRNDMERG)	0.542***	0.696	0.235	1.720	2.152***	1.109	1.612	8.606
Hostile Acquisition (HOSTACQ)	−0.291	0.002	0.714	0.028	−0.419	0.400	0.386	0.081
Stock Swap (STOCKSWAP)	−1.333	0.515	6.698	0.264	−1.295**	0.598	4.688	0.278
Reverse Takeover (REVTAKE)	−1.989	1.149	2.997	0.137	3.022	1.164	6.737	0.048
Divestiture (DIVEST)	−0.008**	0.945	0.000	1.009	1.292	1.661	0.605	0.437
Pooling of Interest (POI)	0.190***	0.396	0.229	1.209	−0.821***	0.482	2.898	2.271

** $p<0.05$, *** $p<0.001$

to methodological problems such as a smaller cell size (in a number of cases) to more conceptual issues such as non-synergistic redeployment being the irrational choice of executives. It is also plausible that the primary reasons for non-synergistic redeployment can be a complete restructuring of the merged entity or a change in its focus/direction in its future operations. Caution should be exercised in analyzing the results due to these inconsistencies.

Overall, the parameter estimates show fairly consistent results have been derived from an earlier analysis of individual hypotheses. The odds ratios provide an estimate of the change in the probability of choice that can be expected with each unit change in a particular independent variable. The results provide conclusive empirical evidence that the influence of relative standing, market overlap, and ownership status have a significant effect on the choice of brand redeployment subsequent to M&As.

CONSEQUENCES OF CORPORATE BRAND REDEPLOYMENT AFTER M&AS

Till date, in the bulk of empirical research on brand name redeployment in a variety of brand alliances or co-branding, contexts has focused on the product brand level of analysis1 (for example, Simonin and Ruth, 1998; Rao, Qu, and Ruekert, 1999; Levin and Levin, 2000; Rodrigue and Biswas, 2004; Washburn, Till, and Priluck, 2004). Regardless of what specific tactic is examined, these strategies are all based on the concept that since "brand names are valuable assets, they may be combined with other brand names to form a synergistic alliance in which the sum is greater than the parts" (Rao and Ruekert, 1994:87). Given the frequency of suich brand name redeployment, there has been increasing interest in the role of corporate brands in M&A transactions in the general business press (Gregory, 1999; Sampson, 2003) and on the part of academic researchers (Howe,1982; Horsky and Swyngedouw, 1987; Ferris, 1988; Bosch and Hirschey, 1989; Balmer and Dinnie, 1999; Capron and Hulland, 1999; Dacin and Brown, 2002; Karpoff and Rankine, 1994). Studies going back as far as 1969 have shown a positive relationship between a companys reputation and the performance of its stock. Additionally, several studies (Howe, 1982; Horsky and Swyngedouw, 1987; Ferris, 1988; Bosch and Hirschey, 1989) suggest that the stock market seems to react positively to announcements of corporate brand name changes. Others (Karpoff and Rankine, 1994) have failed to find any evidence that investors value name change-related information.

In contrast to earlier studies, we focus on the impact made by corporate brand name redeployment after M&A activities from the perspective of individual customers (cf. Brown et al., 2006). Unlike financial markets, which consider the consequences of a merger in terms of variables such as future cost savings and earnings, consumers are likely to react to brand name redeployment on the basis of associations they have formed with the two corporate brand names. For example, judgments on a newly merged company may reflect consumers' previous attitudes to each of the companies (Simonin and Ruth, 1998, and Washburn et al., 2000), the extent to which they see the corporate brands as fitting (Simonin and Ruth, 1998), or even idiosyncratic perceptions of the merger itself (negative images of "the big conglomerate engulfing the helpless independent").

BRAND REDEPLOYMENT, BRAND FAMILIARITY, PERCEIVED FIT, AND BRAND ATTITUDES

Brand familiarity: Research on product-level brand alliances (Levin and Levin, 2000, Simonin and Ruth, 1998) has found that if both brands are highly familiar, they contribute equally to consumers' evaluations of an alliance, whereas if one is more well known, it tends to dominate evaluations. Since the focus of this research was on alternative brand redeployment strategies, we selected corporate brands that were equally familiar to respondents in order to reduce the effect of familiarity.

Perceived fit: The concept of "fit" has been extensively researched in branding and M&A literature. On the basis of previous branding research (brand extensions: Aaker and Keller, 1990; Berens et al., 2005; Park, Milberg, and Lawson, 1991, and brand alliances: Simonin and Ruth, 1998), we expect that consumers' evaluations of a merged company will be higher when the two enterprises are perceived as being very similar to each other (high fit). However, the more interesting question is whether the effectiveness of alternative brand redeployment strategies is influenced by consumers' perceptions of fit. In other words, are certain branding strategies more effective when companies are seen as being more or less similar?

Attitude toward corporate brand: Individual corporate brands in an M&A transaction serve as the raw material for consumers' judgments about the combined entity. Prior research reveals that existing attitudes to individual brands are positively related to those to a brand alliance (Simonin and Ruth, 1998; Rodrigue and Biswas, 2004). This suggests that consumers' evaluations of a merged company are higher when two positively and similarly evaluated brands merge than when their corporate brand attitudes are dissimilar. However, as in the case of fit, the more interesting question is whether alternative brand redeployment strategies are more or less effective when two merging brands are similar or dissimilar to each other in terms of consumers' existing attitudes.

CONSUMER OUTCOME MEASURE: BRAND EQUITY

Research on branding alliances has often measured attitudes to brands as a way of evaluating general reactions to product branding strategies (Rodrigue and Biswas, 2004, and Simonin and Ruth, 1998). A number of researchers have made a strong case for looking at individual-level indicators of brand equity and brand identity (Aaker, 1996; Brown and Dacin, 1997; Kapferer, 1997; Keller, 1997; Washburn et al., 2004; Webster and Keller, 2004; Brown et al., 2006). We examined a general brand equity measure that consisted of measures of corporate brand attitudes, brand leadership beliefs, and purchase intentions (Aaker, 1996b). Our brand equity measure included an individual's overall evaluation of the corporate brands associated with the merger. In this particular context, corporate brand attitudes are an important component of the overall equity of a brand, with implications for future actions taken by a company. For example, overall corporate evaluations have been shown to influence evaluation of new products (Brown and Dacin, 1997; Gurhan-Canli and Batra, 2004). We have also included a measure of an individual's perceptions of a company's leadership in its industry. One of the links likely to exist in consumers' representations of corporate brands is a company's relative standing in the industries in which it competes. A corporate brand's equity is likely rise to the extent to which consumers' corporate associations include beliefs about the company as an industry leader (Aaker, 1996b). Finally, we have included a purchase intention measure, which captures the likelihood of purchasing focal brands. These measures were combined to form an individual level brand equity measure.

ANALYSIS AND RESULTS

The main study was conducted by using a $2 \times 2 \times 2 \times 2$ experimental design, with all the variables manipulated between the subjects. The design manipulated (a) the attitude to the two corporate brands (similar vs dissimilar brand-related attitude to the merging companies), (b) perceived fit (high vs low fit between the merging enterprises), (c) whether both the brand names have been maintained and concatenated subsequent to the merger (dominant vs synergistic redeployment strategy), and (d) which brand dominated the new name (acquirer-dominant vs target-dominant strategy).

Changes in the brand equity outcome measure before and after the merger were analyzed for all the strategies. The most surprising result was that across all redeployment strategies, a merger led to an overall decrease in our consumer-level measure of brand equity. Investigating this decrease further, we found that compared to the initial equity of the acquiring brand, the maximum change in brand equity (35%) occurred subsequent to a merger of brands with dissimilar brand attitudes and a low fit. When compared with the initial equity of the target brand, brand equity decreased by about 15% subsequent to the merger of brands with similar attitudes and a low fit. Our results indicate that the target brand suffered less in terms of equity loss than the acquiring brand subsequent to redeployment. In fact, in certain cases (for example, mergers between brands with dissimilar attitudes and a high fit), the merged company's brand equity ratings were actually higher than the target enterprise's ratings before the merger. However, when looking at consumers'

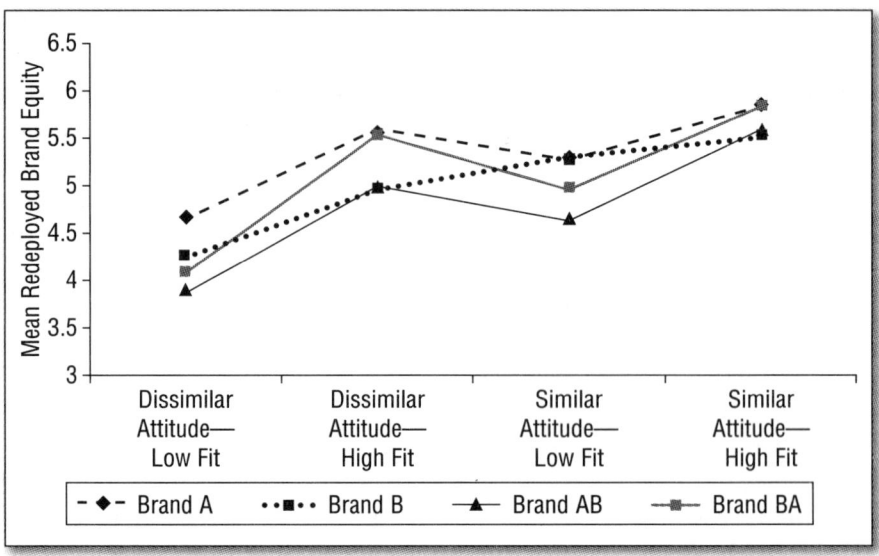

Figure 14.3 Post-merger Brand Equity: Comparison across Redeployment Strategies

perceptions of the target brand, there are numerous situations in which reactions were more negative subsequent to the merger.

It appears that joining of corporate brand names subsequent to an M&A does not yield synergistic gains with respect to changes in their equity measure. Previous research at the product level revealed that brand alliances positively affect not only consumers' perceptions of individual brands in the alliance, but also their perception of the brand alliance (Washburn et al., 2004). Our dependent variable fell subsequent to corporate name redeployment, regardless of the strategy used. This is a significant finding if replicated with other corporate brand stimulus. It suggests that there may be a "consumer-based" element that accounts for the frequent underperformance of companies subsequent to M&A transactions. We found that the acquirer-dominant and target-dominant strategies consistently outperformed those that maintained both the corporate brand names after a merger. No consistent pattern of difference was observed between the two kinds of synergistic redeployment (Brand-AB- vs Brand-BA-). This suggests that either of these strategies can be used interchangeably subsequent to mergers between companies with similar (and high) reputations.

For more details on customer-based studies and results exploring the consequences of corporate brand redeployment for customers (Jaju, Joiner, and Reddy, 2006).

CONCLUSION

The corporate brand is the cornerstone of a company's relationship with its stakeholder groups. It sets the attitude and tone, and is also the first step a company takes in its quest to establish its personality as well as that of its products and employees. A corporate brand and its equity represent the relationship between a company and its stakeholders and directly affects its value. While changing corporate brands is an extremely complex and costly process, companies undergoing mergers have no choice, but to redeploy.

This study presents the viewpoint that M&A transactions are valuable opportunities for companies to re-deploy their identities. Tauber (1988) notes that "[c]apitalizing on the equity in established brand names has become the guiding strategy of businesses." The brand redeployment phenomenon can be viewed as an extrapolated brand extension ("brand manipulation") across companies (rather than across product categories).In addition, our study illustrates of bridging corporate and functional strategies. The interdependencies between strategies at different levels (corporate, business, and functional) have received little attention in marketing literature. Deshpande, 1999 and Varadarajan, et.al., 2001 stress the need for examining multi-level or cross-level problems in strategies. Our study aims to partly fulfill this unmet need by providing salient examples of cross-level strategic interdependencies. It also supports power-based perspective of M&A transactions, and not only highlights this interesting outlook on the acquisition process and how acquirers engage in "assassination" of target companies, but also indicates the effect of managers' influence on redeployment of assets (Duhaime and Grant, 1984; Hitt, Hoskisson, and Ireland, 1990). Anecdotal evidence indicates that companies' executives treat corporate identity as an issue of vanity, and tie it to their personal esteem by associating themselves with "big" names. A large number of acquirer-dominated redeployment cases and their significant relationship with horizontal mergers indicate the pre-eminence of market power in brand redeployment-related decisions. This asymmetrical redeployment of resources suggests that changes linked to the integration process are one-sided, and primarily take place within the target company (Datta, 1993; Hambrick and Canella, 1993; Shanley and Correa, 1992; Paulo, 1994). Empirical evidence reveals that a target company frequently conforms to the acquirer's identity, culture, and managerial systems (Buono and Bowditch, 1989, and Chatterjee, et.al., 1992). This conformity is primarily due to the acquirer's power, ego, and arrogance (Jemison and Sitkin, 1986). It is based not only on the acquirer's confidence in its resources, but also on the strong pressure on a target company to break its previous routines/cultures (Hambrick and Canella, 1993).

The managerial implications of our study rest primarily on its prescriptive nature. Kumar (2003) suggests that subsequent to a hostile or controversial acquisition, most companies prefer quick redeployment of corporate brand names. Our collection of Lexis-Nexus news articles revealed that in over 94% of cases, companies announce their corporate name changes alongside their merger plans. However, given the legal nature of M&A activity, external validation of a redeployed name cannot be conducted at the time name change announcements are made. Our study, the first of its kind, aims to help corporate executives in their selection of new redeployed brands and stakeholders to predict the choice of brand names of merging companies. The analytical outcome of our study provides a set of four prescriptive models that help to determine the probability of choice of one brand strategy over another.

The results indicate that the target-acquirer's relative standing (financial characteristics), market overlap, transactional elements, and procedural characteristics have a significant effect on its redeployment-related decision. The results indicate that horizontal mergers or acquisitions lead to an acquirer-dominated redeployment-related decision. As discussed earlier, this supports the power motive of resource redeployment during M&A transactions. The results also indicate that congeneric mergers lead to non-dominated brand redeployment, which indicates acquirers' intentions of leveraging their targets' brand equity. Such a phenomenon suggests two procedural options for the acquiring company's redeployment-related decision—(a) the acquirer buys the target enterprise, combines it with its own overlapping subsidiary, and spins off the newly combined entity as a new company under the target's brand name, or (b) the acquirer buys the target to change its primary area of business and focus more on the overlapping subsidiary's business in the future. The latter strategy would entail it acquiring the target company, combining it with its own overlapping subsidiary, divesting its own primary area of operations, and leveraging the target's higher equity to change its focus in its operations. Our results also support the hypothesis that conglomerate mergers and acquisitions lead to non-concatenated brand redeployment and support the argument that conglomerate M&As rely more on financial gains from target companies and less on the strategic gains that may result from integration of assets. Our analysis also support our proposition that if an acquirer is a publicly owned entity and the target a private one, this will lead to an acquirer-dominated brand name choice. This indicates that redeployment-related decisions taken on brand names in such cases is influenced by (a) the dominance of the shareholders of the acquirer company, (b) ease of transaction during the merger process, and (c) the acquirer (as a public entity) having access to more resources and a higher brand awareness than the target. The positive relationship between vertical and congeneric market overlap and synergistic redeployment also highlights and offers evidence of the synergistic motive behind redeployment-relating decisions. As evident, most[12] of the derived propositions have yielded significant empirical support.

---

[12] The following are the relevant operational boundaries of this study:
 1. Unequal number of cases across the five redeployment categories that inhibit the ability to attain detailed insights into each strategy individually. This inconsistency in cell sizes, while on one hand provides us with evidence of the dominance of one type of redeployment activity (from target to acquirer), on the other hand makes the result difficult to analyze and interpret.
 2. One of the common anecdotal propositions for brand redeployments state that "... the new name was contemplated simply because the name of the target or the acquirer sounded better...." Such instances of "semiotics" or "schema (in)congruency", though important, are not included in the analysis
 3. The measure of relatedness/complementarity, based on SIC codes, is a simple additive measure used across all overlapping areas of operation between the acquirer and the target. A more comprehensive measure

One of the explicit contributions made by this study is the comprehensive taxonomy of brand redeployment strategies. Such taxonomy serves two primary purposes. (a) It provides a snapshot view of the motivation for brand redeployment and (b) it categorizes brand redeployment strategies into distinct groups to provide a basis for analytical comparisons for future studies in this field.

REFERENCES

Aaker, David A. and Kevin L. Keller (1990), "Consumer Evaluations of Brand Extensions," *Journal of Marketing*, 54(1), 27–41.

Aboody, D., R. Kasnik and W. Williams, (2000), "Purchase Versus Pooling in Stock-for-Stock Acquisitions: Why do Firms Care?" *Journal of Accounting and Economics*, 29(3), 261–286.

Agresti, Alan (1996), *An Introduction to Categorical Data Analysis*. New York: John Wiley & Sons.

—— (1990), *Categorical Data Analysis*. New York: John Wiley & Sons.

---

as suggested by Montgomery (1982) can incorporate a weighted mean measure of relatedness/complementarity based on the percentage of revenue associated with each SIC code.

4. The reliability of the friendly merger and hostile acquisition measure is questionable owing to the archival nature of the data.
5. The study could not incorporate measures of corporate reputation variable and measures of firm size (viz. number of employees). The data available for corporate reputation index was for very few companies (a pair of 97 firms in total).
6. Further one hypothesis incorporating ownership status (Target = public, Acquirer = private) could not be tested since no cases with this qualification could be found in the dataset. However, support for the converse hypothesis (wherein acquirer is a public entity and target is a private firm) provides theoretical justification for this proposition.

It is important to highlight some other seemingly less-related issues that effect corporate identity redeployments. For example, a company's redeployment decision may be influenced by the fact if a company's local or regional image detracts from its new strength in national or international market. Further, arguments for the motive of redeployment of resources would also include those offered by institutional theory, i.e., acquirers redeploy resources just because others do it and it is considered legitimate. However, as indicated earlier in this chapter, it is assumed that the acquirer and the target consider the corporate name redeployment decision proactively and consciously.

Berle, A. A. and G. C. Means (1991), *The Modern Corporation and Private Property*. New Brunswick: Transaction Publishers.

Berry, C. H. (1975), *Corporate Growth and Diversification*. Princeton, NJ: Princeton University Press.

Blair, John (1958), "The Conglomerate Merger in Economics and Law," *Georgetown Law Journal*, XLVI(Summer), 679–692.

Blair, Roger D. and Jeffrey L. Harrison (1993), *Monopsony: Antitrust Law and Economics*, Princeton, NJ: Princeton University Press.

Bosch, J.C. and Mark Hirschey (1989), "The Valuation Effects of Corporate Name Changes," *Financial Management*, 18(Winter), 64–73.

Brigham, Eugene F. and Michael C. Ehrhardt (2002), *Financial Management: Theory and Practice* (10th ed.). Harcourt College Publishers.

Buono, A.F. and J. L. Bowditch, (1989), *The Human Side of Mergers and Acquisitions*. San Francisco: Jossey Bass.

Campbell, Karen M. and Allan Donner (1989), "Classification Efficiency of Multinomial Logistic Regression Relative to Ordinal Logistic Regression," *Journal of American Statistical Association*, 84(406), 587–591.

Capron, Laurence and John Hulland (1999), "Redeployment of Brands, Sales Forces, and General Marketing Management Expertise Following Horizontal acquisitions: A Resource-Based View," *Journal of Marketing*, 63(1), 41–54.

Dussauge, Pierre and Will Mitchell (1998), "Resource Redeployment following Horizontal Acquisitions in Europe and North America," 1988–1992," *Strategic Management Journal*, 19, 631.

Mitchell, Will and Anand Swaminathan (2001), "Asset Divestiture following Horizontal Acquisitions: A Dynamic View," *Strategic Management Journal*, 22, 817–844.

Chatterjee, S., M. H. Lubatkin, D. M. Schweiger, and Y. Weber, (1992), "Cultural Differences and Shareholder Value in Related Mergers," *Strategic Management Journal*, 13(5), 319–344.

Chatterjee, S. (1991), "Gains in Vertical Acquisitions and Market Power: Theory and Evidence," *Academy of Management Journal*, 34(2), 436–448.

Christensen, H.K. and C. A. Montgomery, (1981), "Corporate Economic Performance: Diversification Strategy versus Market Structure," *Strategic Management Journal*, 2(4), 327–343.

Cohen, Joel B. and Kunal Basu (1987), "Alternative Models of Categorization: Toward a Contingent Processing Framework," *Journal of Consumer Research*, 13(4), 455–472.

Datta, D.K. (1993), "Organizational Fit and Acquisitional Performance: Effects of Post-Acquisition Integration," *Strategic Management Journal*, 12(4), 281–297.

Deshpande (1999), "'Foreseeing' Marketing," *Journal of Marketing*, 63(Special Issue), 164–168.

Dowling, Grahame R. (1986), "Managing your Corporate Images," *Industrial Marketing Management*, 15(2), 109–115.

Duhaime I. M. and J. H. Grant (1984), "Factors influencing divestment decision-making: evidence from a field study," *Strategic Management Journal*, 5(4), 301–318.

Eckbo, B., (1983) "Horizontal Mergers, Collusion and Stockholder Wealth," *Journal of Financial Economics*, 11(Apil), 241–273.

Fan, Joseph O. H. and Larry H. P. Yang (2000), "The Measurement of Relatedness: An Application to Corporate Diversification", *Journal of Business*, 73(4), 629–660.

Ferris, S. P. (1988), "The Effect of Corporate Name Changes in Shareholder Wealth," *Journal of Applied Business Research*, 4(Summer), 78–89.

Friedman, Josh (2000), "Any Value for Investors in Corporate Name Change?" *LA Times*, September 26, C6.

Hambrick, D. C. and A. A. Cannella, Jr. (1993), "Relative Standing: A Framework for Understanding Departures of Acquired Executives", *Academy of Management Journal*, 36(4), 733–762.

Hart, Oliver, (1995), *Firms Contracts and Financial Structure*. Oxford, UK: Oxford University Press.

J. Moore, (1990), "Property Rights and the Nature of the Firm," *The Journal of Political Economy*, 98(6), 1119–1158.

Heflebower, R.B. (1963), "Corporate Mergers: Policy and Economic Analysis," *Quarterly Journal of Economics*, 77(November), 554–557.

Heider, Fritz (1958), *The Psychology of Interpersonal Relations*. New York: John Wiley and Sons, Inc.

Hennart, Jean Francois and Young Ryeol Park (1993), "'Greenfield' vs. Acquisitions: The Strategy of Japanese Investors in United States," *Management Science*, 39(9), 1054–1070.

Hitt M.A., R.E., Hoskisson, and R. D. Ireland (1990) "Mergers and Acquisitions and Managerial Commitment to Innovation in M-form Firms," *Strategic Management Journal*, 11(Summer Special Issue), 29–47.

Horsky, Dan and P. Swyngedouw (1987), "Does it Pay to Change Your Company's Name? A Stock Market Perspective," *Marketing Science*, 6(4), 320–333.

Howe, John S. (1982), "A Rose by any Other Name? A Note on Corporate Name Changes," *The Financial Review*, 17(4), 271–278.

Hunt, S.D. and R.M. Morgan (1995), "The Comparative Advantage Theory of Competition," *Journal of Marketing*, 59(April), 1–15.

Jaju, Anupam., Christopher Joiner and Srinivas K. Reddy (2006), "Consumer Evaluations of Corporate Brand Redeployments," *Journal of Academy of Marketing Science*, 34(2), 206–215.

Jemison, D.B. and S. B. Sitkin(1986), "Corporate Acquisitions: A Process Perspective," *Academy of Management Review*, 11(1), 145–163.

Jensen, M.C. (1988), "Characteristics of Targets of Hostile and Friendly Takeovers: Comment," In Proceedings of Conference on Corporate Takeovers: Causes and Consequences, Alan Auerbach ed., Chicago: University of Chicago Press.

Karpoff, Jonathan M. and Graeme Rankine (1994), "In Search of Signaling Effect: The Wealth Effects of Corporate Name Changes," *Journal of Banking and Finance*, 18(6), 1027–1045.

Keller, Kevin L. (1993), "Conceptualizing, Measuring and Managing Customer-based Brand Equity," *Journal of Marketing*, 57(1), 1–22

Klein, Peter G. (2001), "Were the Acquisitive Conglomerates Inefficient?" *Rand Journal of Economics*, 32(4), 745–761.

Kumar, Nirmalaya (2003), "Kill a Brand, Keep a Customer," *Harvard Business Review*, 81(12), 86–95.

Lemelin, A. (1982), "Relatedness in the Patterns of inter-industry diversification," *Review of Economics and Statistics*, 64(1), 36–71.

Matsusaka, John G. (1993), "Takeover Motives during the Conglomerate Merger Wave," *Rand Journal of Economics*, 24(3), 357–379.

Mergerstat (2000), www.mergerstat.com

Meyer, J.W. and B. Rowan (1977), "Institutionalized Organizations: Formal Structures as Myth and Ceremony," *American Journal of Sociology*, 83(2), 340–363

Mitchell, Will (1994), "The Dynamics of Evolving Markets: The Effects of Business Sales and Age Dissolutions and Divestitures," *Administrative Science Quarterly*, 39(4), 575–602.

Montgomery, Cynthia A. (1982), "The Measure of Firm Diversification: Some New Empirical Evidence," *Academy of Management Journal*, 25(2), 299–307.

Mueller, Dennis .C. (1977), "The Effects of Conglomerate Mergers: A Survey on the Empirical Evidence," *Journal of Banking and Finance*, 1(4), 344.

Oliver C. (1997), "Sustainable Competitive Advantage: Combining Institutional and Resource-based Views," *Strategic Management Journal*, 18(9), 697–13

Paulo, A.L. (1994), "Determinants of Acquisition Integration Level: A Decision Making Perspective," *Academy of Management Journal*, 37(4), 803–836.

Penrose, Edith (1959), *The Theory of the Growth of the Firm*. Oxford, UK: Oxford University Press.

Ramaswamy K. (1997), "The performance impact of strategic similarity in horizontal mergers: evidence from the U.S. banking industry," *Academy of Management Journal*, 40(3), 697–716.

Rao, Vithala R. Manoj K. Agarwal, and Denise Dahlhoff (2004), "How is Manifest Branding Strategy Related to the Intangible Value of a Corporation," *Journal of Marketing*, 68(4), 126–141.

Rao, A.R. and R.W. Ruekert (1999), "Brand Alliances Signals of Product Quality," *Sloan Management Review*, 36(1), 87–97.

Rhoades, Stephen A. (1983), *Power Empire Building and Mergers*. Lexington MA: Lexington Books.

Rock, L. and R. H. Rock (1990), *Corporate Restructuring*. New York NY: McGraw Hill.

Rosendahl, I. (1995), "Out miles, in Bayer," *Drug Topics*, 139(3), 54.

Rumelt, R.P. (1974), *Strategy, Structure, and Economic Performance*. Boston: Division of Research, Graduate School of Business Administration, Harvard University.

Russell, Bertrand (1962), *Power: A New Social Analysis*. New York NY: Routledge.

Scherer, F.M. (1970), *Industrial Market Structure and Economic Performance*. Chicago IL: Rand McNally.

Seth, A. (1990), "Value Creation in Acquisitions: A reexamination of performance issues," *Strategic Management Journal*, 11(2), 99–105.

Shanley, M.T. and Correa, M.E. (1992), "Agreement Between Top Management Teams and Expectations for Post-Acquisition Performance," *Strategic Management Journal*, 13(4), 245–266.

Sheth, A. (1990), "Value Creation in Acquisitions: A Re-examination of Performance Iissues," *Strategic Management Journal*, 11(2), 99–115.

Shimp, T.A. and W.O. Bearden (1982), "Warranty and Other Extrinsic Cue Effects on Consumer's Risk Perceptions," *Journal of Consumer Research*, 9(1), 38–46.

Simon, Herbert A. (1955) "A Behavioral Model of Rational Choice," *Quarterly Journal of Economics*, 69(1), 99–118.

Singh, Jitendra V. and C.A. Montgomery (1987), "Corporate Acquisition Strategies and Economic Performance," *Strategic Management Journal*, 8(4), 377–386.

Srivastava, R.K.; T.A. Shervani, and L. Fahey, (1998) "Market-based assets and shareholder value: a framework for analysis," *Journal of Marketing*, 62(1), 2–18.

Stigler, G.J. (1964), "A Theory of Oligopoly," *Journal of Political Economy*, 12(1), 55–59.

(1968), "A Theory of Oligopoly," In G. J. Stigler, (Ed.), *The Organization of Industry* (pp. 39–63). Irwin, IL: Homewood

Stillman, R., (1983) "Examining Antitrust Policy Towards Horizontal Mergers," *Journal of Financial Economics*, 11(April), 225–240.

Steiner, P. O. (1975), *Mergers: Motives, Effects and Policies*. Ann Arbor MI: University of Michigan Press.

Tauber, E.M. (1988) "Brand Leverage: Strategy for Growth in a Cost-Control World," *Journal of Advertising Research*, 28(4), 26–30.

Varadarajan, Rajan P., Satish Jayachandran, and J Chris White (2001), "Strategic interdependence in organizations: Deconglomeration and Marketing Strategy," *Journal of Marketing*, 65(1), 15–28.

Varadarajan Rajan P. and V. Ramanujam (1987), "Diversification and Performance: A Reexamination Using a New Two-Dimensional Conceptualization of Diversity in Firms," *Academy of Management Journal*, 30(2), 380–393.

Very, Philippe, Michael Lubatkin, Roland Calori, and John Veiga (1997), "Relative Standing and the performance of recently acquired European firms," *Strategic Management Journal*, 18(8), 593–614.

Wagner, D. (1981), "Plan to rename Datsun drawing fire: auto maker's shift to Nissan vexes dealers," *The New York Times*, August 10, D4.

Wernerfelt, Birger (1984), "A Resource-Based View of the Firm," *Strategic Management Journal*, 5(2), 171–180.

Weston J. Fred, Chung, Kwang S. and Hoag, Susan E. (1990) *Mergers, Restructuring, And Corporate Control*. NJ: Prentice-Hall.

Williams, Mary L., Ming-Hone Tsai, and Day Diana (1991), "Intangible Assets, Entry Strategies and Venture Success in Industrial Markets," *Journal of Business Venturing*, 6(5), 315–333.

Yunker, James A. (1983), *Integrating Acquisitions: Making Corporate Marriages Work*. New York: Praeger Publishers.

Section IV
Brand Performance Management

Chapter 15

The Great Debate: Managing Brands versus Managing Customers

Werner Reinartz

In today's saturated product markets, where physical product differences are often marginal and customers expect their myriad desires and needs to be satisfied, companies need to make a clear choice with respect to their marketing strategies and tactics in order to make their offerings distinctive and achieve the required margins. They must decide what aspect they should stress on when they develop and roll out their marketing strategies, given that a go-to-market approach can focus on very different elements.

In the 1960s and 1970s, the focus was solely on the product itself, with little regard to targeting and positioning. Selling what was produced and what was in stock was the name of the game. During the late 1980s and 1990s, brand management was the obvious next step in responding to evolving markets and consumers' needs—particularly for differentiation and brand identification. Finally, in the late 1990s and during the first decade of the 2000s, customer management became the corporate *mantra*, with companies seeking to interact on a one-on-one basis with customers. However, although popular, this approach has not been adopted by all companies in all industries.

In view of this evolution, it is interesting to observe that while some companies take a predominantly brand management approach in today's environment, others have a customer management in dealing with the market, and a combination of both is used by yet a third group. From an organizational point of view, the two approaches, brand management and customer management, require very different capabilities and skill-sets. If an organization is to make the best use of limited resources, it needs to know under which conditions it should adopt brand management (as opposed to customer management) as its focal go-to-market approach and when it should not.

Take the case of a leading European manufacturer of branded detergents, which made significant investments in customer relationship management (CRM). Its intent was to strengthen its relationship with its end customers by communicating with them directly, customizing its promotions, and create meaningful interaction with consumers. Yet the outcome was disappointing. The company found that communicating individually with customers was difficult to implement, individually tailored promotions were expensive, and retailers were not always willing to share customer-related transactional data. While there was no lack of good ideas, the results were discouraging and internal acceptance lukewarm. Resources were lavished on the initiative with no obvious return. This would seem the case of an organization, despite its strong brand management capabilities, whose investment in customer management capabilities proved to be misplaced despite its good intentions.

The key issue underlying any successful go-to-market strategy is one that answers the question, "Should an organization predominantly use its brand as a platform to go to market, or should it center on (individual) customers as the unit of focus?" In this chapter, we seek to answer the question by probing the conditions under which an organization should use the brand management approach as opposed to a customer management focus. As we will demonstrate, the answer will depend on a company's internal cost structure (the specific nature of its variable and fixed costs) and the way it creates value around its products and customers.

TYPES OF GO-TO-MARKET STRATEGIES

Before answering the question, it is important to understand how a go-to-market strategy that focuses on a brand differs from one that targets the customer (Table 15.1), and to realize that these two approaches are not endpoints on a continuum, but orthogonal dimensions.

Table 15.1 Go-to-market Strategies

	Brand Management	Customer Management
Underlying Premise	Identify the need/desire of a (sizable) segment/market and serve that need with suitable branded offering (differentiation, communication, premium)	Customers are heterogeneous with respect to their value to the organization. Organizations recognize and accommodate this heterogeneity by differentially allocating resources across different customers/segments.
Unit of Analysis	Product/brand	Individual customer/segment
4P Execution	−By and large similar (identical) across customers −Key activities: advertising, R&D −Investments/costs: largely fixed	By and large varying across customers (or small segments) −Key activities: sales, pricing, servicing customers, direct response communication −Investments/costs: largely variable
Communication	Predominantly non-addressable media, mass communication ("above the line")	Predominantly addressable media, direct response communication ("below the line")
Main Objective	Maximize sales (top line)	Create profitable customer-level cash flows
Key Metrics	Consumer awareness, liking, market share, sales	Share-of-wallet, retention, customer profitability
Efficiency Achieved via	−Size of consumer target base −Size of shelf-space/distribution coverage obtained (leads to both communication and production efficiencies)	−Retaining/fortifying high value customers −Selectively growing customer share −Eliminating unprofitable customers −Allocating resources differentially between customers/segments
Distribution	Typically outsourced	Typically owned
Internal Focus	Predominantly marketing focus	Predominantly sales focus

Brand Management

In brand management, the underlying assumption is that the desires of a sizable segment or even entire market are served with a suitable branded offering.

Assuming that the offering is properly differentiated on meaningful dimensions and its positioning properly communicated, it will hopefully command a premium that more than compensates for the cost of branding. The unit of analysis is the individual brand (e.g., the product, product line, or company). In executing this strategy, managers communicate a selected message and positioning across the target market, within which the message is by and large identical.

The key activities that create significant costs are research and development (to create meaningful products) as well as communication of their respective benefits via advertising. Consequently, many of the significant cost elements behind a brand-focused strategy are fixed in nature, the implication being that managers will seek to recoup these investments from a large customer base. In line with this reasoning, the overriding goal is to maximize top line sale of the product because this will, given a sufficient margin, ensure the profit target is met. In order to achieve this, brand managers are preoccupied with monitoring key brand metrics such as consumer awareness and liking, market share, and sales.

> **Example of Brand Management Focus**
>
> Branding, at least at a certain level, is the prevalent approach in many if not most industries. Yet, there are still sizable differences in the degree to which branding strategies are used. Industries that rely principally on branding include many fast and slow-moving consumer goods (both manufacturers), for example, P&G and Nestle, as well as from a retailing point of view, for example, Ikea and Gap.

In this business model, efficiency, and consequently, return on investment, is achieved by ensuring a sufficiently large consumer target market and achieving the required distribution coverage (shelf space, number of outlets, etc Ataman, Mela, Heerde, 2008). Drawing on a sufficiently large target market ensures economies of scale in production. In most cases, distribution is outsourced due to long and elaborate supply chains as well as inefficient distribution. Internally, the majority of companies have a strong marketing focus, which is tied to their innovative and creative capabilities.

Customer Management

In customer management, the underlying assumption is that customers are heterogeneous with respect to their value to the organization (Werner, Krafft and Hoyer, 2004). This means that companies not only recognize that customers have significant value for them (typically lifetime value or a similar measure), but also that there are great differences between different customers. They accommodate this heterogeneity by differentially allocating resources across different customers/segments. The unit of analysis is the individual customer or segment.

When it comes to executing customer-related strategy, allocation of 4P varies across customers. A company's core activities are related to allocation of its sales force, pricing, customer service, and direct response communication. Many of the cost aspects of these activities are variable or semi-variable in nature. This means that rather than investing in fixed cost infrastructure, companies incur expenditure that can be adjusted easily across time and customers.

Direct response communication plays a central role in companies' communication with their customer base. This may include traditional communication as well as by email, telephone, and personal contacts. This is not to say that they will eschew mass advertising, but that the relative importance of the latter is diminished. Given the more individual nature of communications with their customers, companies can adjust the content and frequency of

> **Example of Customer Management Focus**
>
> During the last decade, many companies have embraced customer management strategies, at least to a certain degree. Industries that cater to adopters of customer management initiatives include financial services (for example, credit cards), travel and tourism (for example, hotels), and many organizations in the business-to-business (B2B) space.

their messages. This is a central element in a customer management approach because it is the key driver of an objective focus, which is to create profitable customer-level cash flows.

The core notion in this case is that because customers differ in their current and potential value to an organization, the organization should adjust its investments in such customers accordingly (Niraj, Gupta, and Chakravarthi, 2001). Since individual customers' behavior can be observed or tracked and resources allocated to each (or small customer segments), process metrics focus on drivers of profitable customer-level cash flows—share of wallet, retention, and customers' contribution. In this business model, efficiency, and consequently, return on investment, is achieved by ensuring retention and growth of high-value customers, selective growth of customers' share, differential allocation of resources between customers/segments, and possible elimination of unprofitable customers. In most cases, distribution (and therefore customer contacts) is the preserve of, for example, financial service providers, telcos, retailers, and B-to-B companies that typically have direct contact with their customers via their own distribution networks. Internally, many of these have a strong sales focus, which is tied to process, customer management, and service capabilities.

As earlier mentioned, these two approaches are not end points on a continuum, but distinct vectors along which organizations position themselves. Our conjecture is that while there is a certain degree of freedom in their positioning, the internal cost structure of the value creation process plays a significant role in companies determining their specific position.

BREAKING DOWN ORGANIZATION'S COST STRUCTURE

From the managerial accounting perspective, by looking at the value creation process within an unit of an organization one can identify several types of costs that are well known. The key distinction is between fixed and variable costs, and each can be further subdivided. If one allocates the costs that occur within a company on a per customer (segment) basis, the following three major types can be discerned:

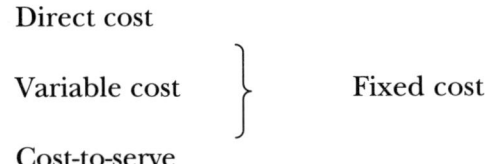

At the first step, these costs should be allocated to individual customers or defined segments—commensurate with their consumption of resources—with the goal of assessing individual customer's profitability, to use this in the second step to inform about and improve resource allocation.

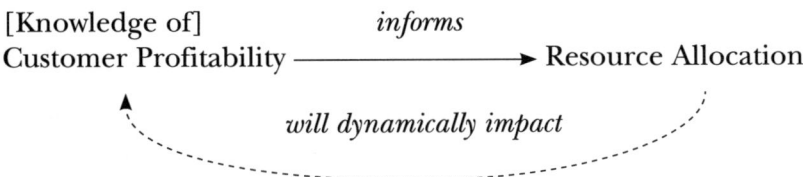

Hierarchically, the various cost components are linked to outcomes in the following manner:

Revenues per customer*	Example
-direct cost (or cost of goods sold (COGS))	Product procurement cost, direct production cost
= Gross profit per customer	
-cost to serve	e.g., marketing, sales, terms and conditions, returns, support and service, risk, warranties, etc.
= Contribution per customer	
-fixed cost	Plant overhead, head office overhead, R&D overhead, etc
= Operating profit per customer	

*All figures are in absolute terms with respect to a time period t.

However, achieving these outcomes can be challenging and complex. Typically, it is achieved by activity-based costing, (Kaplan and Bruns, 1987) where "consumption or use of resources" is allocated to objects, in this case the customer. Most large-scale enterprise CRM software systems typically include an activity-based cost component that performs these calculations.

As part of their customer management efforts, many organizations try to allocate resources to individual customers. For example, should not a customer who uses a customer support service regularly make an impact on the value he/she generates for an organization, compared to one who does not? Most organizations tend to allocate the operational cost of running call centers as an overhead proportionate to, for example, their customer-generated revenues. However, this is clearly not in line with the actual consumption of associated call center resources. Therefore, a thorough customer-level profitability view is required, especially in industries and companies where customers vary significantly in terms of their cost-to-serve consumption practices. In practice, however, arriving at the individual contribution a customer generates for a company is no small achievement.

Digging down to the customer-level contribution is sufficient for most practical purposes and applications, to make sound recommendations with respect to resource allocation. Consider the following example. A retail bank wants to know the degree to which its customers differ in their contribution levels. Its primary goal is to ensure that those who bring high value are recognized and treated accordingly. Its second goal is to investigate whether and how customers who bring low or negative value can be "grown." In a sample of 33,000 customers, the bank allocates the respective cost of goods sold (interest paid by the bank to generate funds for loans and credits) as well as the cost-to-serve (branch visits, call center usage, number of customer transactions, etc.). Starting from the revenues generated (income from interest, income from fees, etc.), it calculates the contribution (in absolute dollars) for all of such customers. The result is shown in Figure 15.1, where customers are ranked on the x-axis by their contribution, from the lowest to the highest. Their contribution (in dollars) is reflected on the y-axis.

In this example, 43% of the customers make a contribution that amounts to ≤0. And a meager 10% of the customer base represents the bulk of the total contribution, which is equivalent to more than

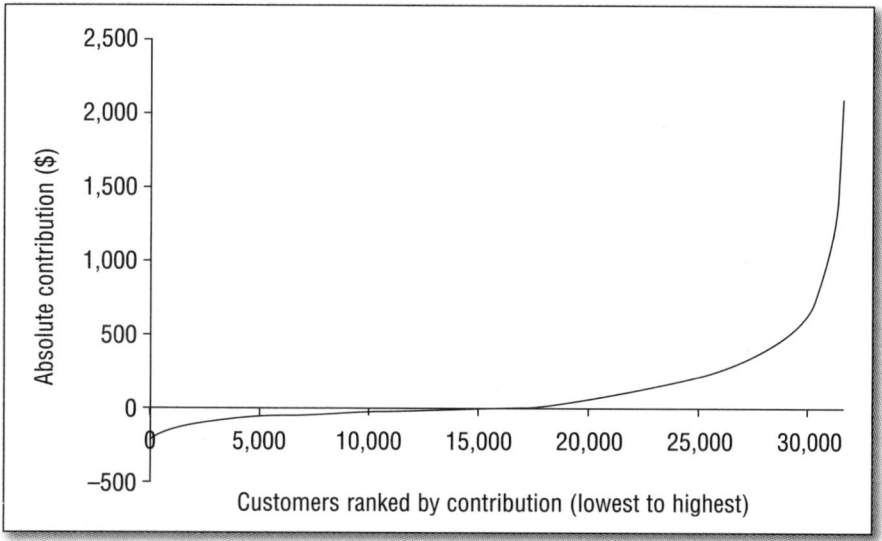

Figure 15.1 Distribution of Customers' Contribution

70%. Given that the bank now understands the value creators and value destroyers, it can now move to the stage of better managing these groups. This could entail, for example, a retention strategy for the high-value group and a growth strategy for the low-value one.

How can this analysis of the organization's cost structure help us determine its go-to- market strategy? In order to do this, we need to understand how contribution distribution patterns play out across different companies and industries. Therefore, we need to extend the earlier mentioned illustrative analysis across companies and look for underlying patterns.

ASSESSING DIFFERENCES ACROSS INDUSTRIES

After investigating customers' profitability empirically for many companies across a wide range of industries, a consistent picture starts to emerge (Werner, 2010). In particular, two basic models of customer profitability can be observed. Consider the two companies whose customers are depicted in Figure 15.2. In this example, each dot represents a customer. When the companies rank their respective customers by their absolute contribution (→ x-axis) and then depict each customer's absolute dollar contribution (→ y-axis), two

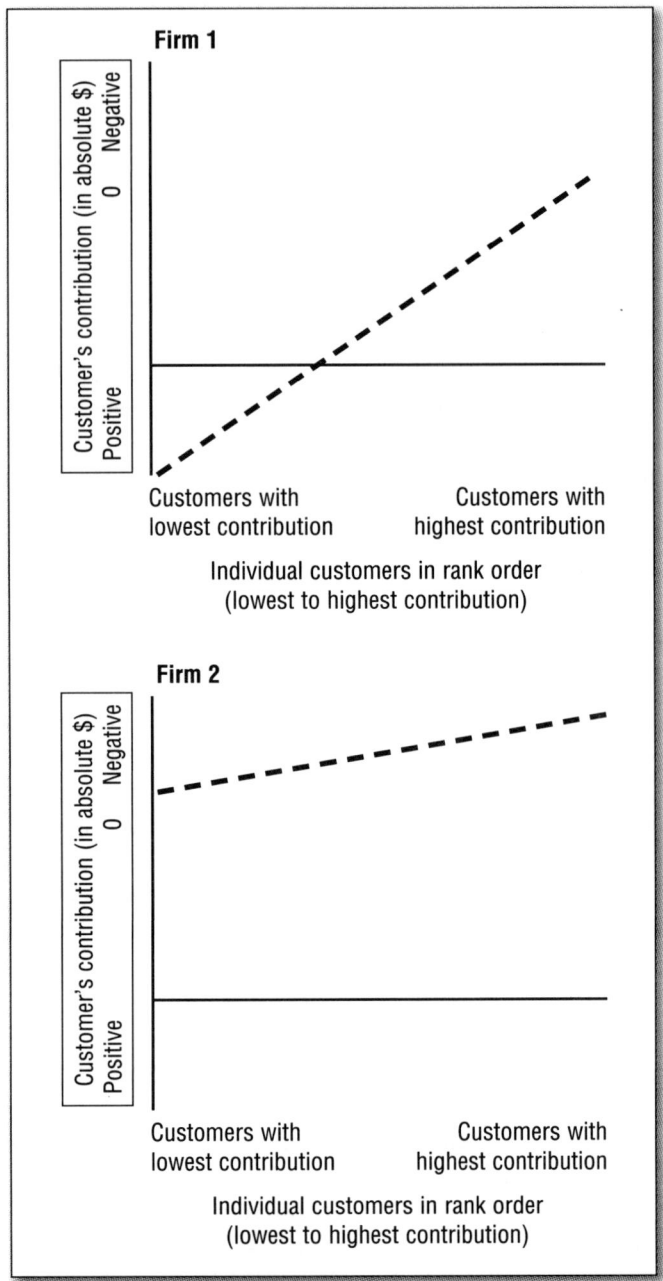

Figure 15.2 Distribution of Individual Customer's Contribution (in $) across Customer Base (Stylized Illustration)

prototypical patterns emerge. For the sake of clarity, the patterns have been stylized in the sense that we use straight lines. In reality, one regularly finds that the curve on the extreme right has a significant upward spike. In other words, there is a small group of customers that makes a very large contribution (in accordance with the 80/20 or 90/10 rule). However, for the sake of simplicity, we only use the straight line.

For Company 1, different customers generate very differential contribution margins. In other words, there is a large gap between the contribution of the best customer and that of the worst customer. On top, some customers generate a *negative* contribution. In contrast, for Company 2, customers generate relatively comparable contributions. In other words, the contributions of the best and worst customers are not that different. On top, every customer contributes to covering the fixed costs, as all contributions are positive.

The key to understanding the two patterns (or any intermediate pattern) is to grasp the link to the company's underlying internal cost structure. Remember that the revenues from a specific customer can essentially be broken down into (1) direct cost (i.e., cost of goods sold), (2) cost-to-serve (cost-of-sales, cost-of-marketing, product returns, after-sales service, terms and conditions, prospecting, client risk, etc.), (3) fixed cost and, finally, profits—all of which are associated with that same client.

Company 1, in this case, is an organization that has (in proportional terms) low fixed costs and high costs-to-serve. More importantly, when costs-to-serve are high, the potential for variation in cost-to-serve across customers also goes up. In other words, some customers need much hand-holding and attention whereas others are easy to satisfy. This means that a customer with a reasonable top line can end up being unprofitable. Company 1 operates in an environment where the contribution from the worst and best customers is very wide, i.e., underlying purchase volumes probably vary substantially. A typical example for Company 1 is a financial services company or a B-to-B manufacturer.

In contrast, Company 2 has (in proportional terms) high fixed costs and low costs-to-serve. Since its cost of goods sold and costs-to-serve are comparatively small, a given revenue will immediately contribute to its fixed costs. Similarly, there is negligible potential for variations in costs-to-serve to significantly perturb customers.

This means that whoever generates revenue will also make a positive contribution. Moreover, Company 2 is operating in an environment where the contribution range between the worst and best customer is very small—in other words, their underlying purchase volumes do not vary much. A typical example for Company 2 is a retailer or an FMCG manufacturer.

IMPLICATIONS OF THE GO-TO-MARKET STRATEGY

So what are the implications of these findings? Company 1 is operating in an industry where not every customer is a "good" one. It therefore "pays" for it to treat each customer differently, and in particular, to proactively manage unprofitable ones. For example, such a company should think about allocating resources in a differential manner across customers, for example, by rewarding high-value ones. In addition, it should be careful about whom it acquires as a customer because not every customer will end up contributing to fixed costs, and therefore selective acquisition is a must (Matthew, 2004). The company should begin by profiling its various groups of customers and look for common attitudinal or demographic patterns. It should then use this information at the acquisition stage. Finally (and critically), customers' loyalty is not sufficient as a business metric. In this scenario (Werner and Kumar, 2002), a loyal customer can in fact be unprofitable, therefore, measuring a customer's profitability is a necessity. In such a situation, a company would be well advised to use individual-level customer management strategies and technologies to manage its customer base effectively.

In contrast, Company 2 is operating in an environment where every customer contributes to covering fixed costs. Therefore, every customer is a "good" customer. Consequently, treating individual customers differently is not a priority. With respect to generation of new customers, our advice is to opt for all-out acquisitions. Moreover, customers' loyalty as a business metric is much more meaningful in this case, since their value only increases as long as they are retained. In this situation, organizations are not under pressure to invest in costly and complex customer management initiatives, and they should concentrate on brand-centric strategies that extend across segments of customers. Consequently, brand management should be at the center of their go-to-market strategies.

> A caveat is warranted at this point. A number of industries, such as telcos and airlines, should come under pattern 2 (and thereby avoid investing heavily in customer management) due to their high fixed costs and comparatively low costs-to-serve, but in fact are seen to practise customer management extensively. The reason for this is that while the majority of their customers come under pattern 2, these industries have small groups of customers who are very valuable to them (for example, business travelers who use roaming call plans extensively, platinum-level flyers, etc.). In order to ensure that such clients are satisfied and retained, companies have to pay special attention to these groups. Therefore, over and above their brand-based go-to-market strategies, they embed differential treatment at the client level—customer management.

As previously indicated, brand management and customer management are not polar opposites, but orthogonal dimensions. Companies have a certain degree of freedom to practice one and/or the other, as described in Figure 15.3. Those that operate in quadrant (A) use brand management as their predominant go-to-market strategy, and those that operate in quadrant (C) adopt customer management as their principal go-to-market strategy. Finally, organizations that operate in quadrant (B) practice both brand management and customer management.

This latter scenario in quadrant (B) is an ongoing dynamic development. It is interesting to observe that an increasing number

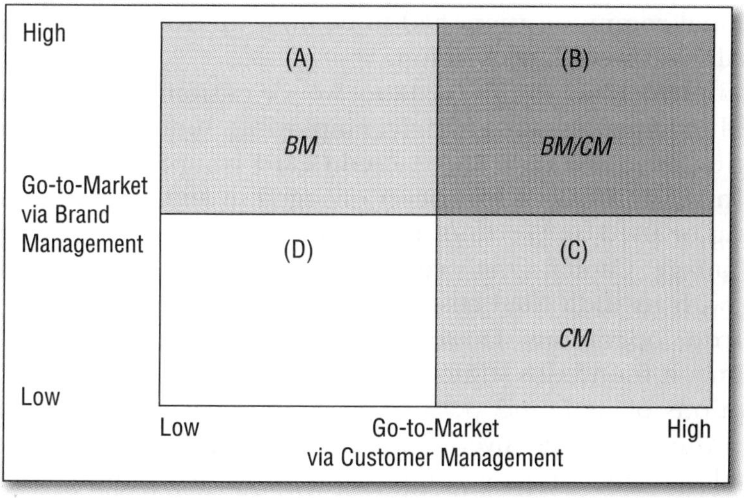

Figure 15.3 Link between Brand Management and Customer Management

of companies are moving toward a hybrid approach. In other words, brand management-dominated organizations are increasingly adopting customer management approaches in addition to their brand management strategies.

Let us take, for example, the case of the German luxury car manufacturer BMW. Traditionally, the company pursued a wholehearted brand-focused approach, and accordingly, its customers only communicated with its dealers. The overall BMW brand was its only one-directional communication with the end-consumer from the BMW Group's perspective. Today, customer management strategies play a critical role in the company's go-to-market approach. More and more of its end customers expect to communicate directly with the BMW Group. Therefore, the challenge for BMW (and any carmaker) is to establish a bi-directional individual relationship between itself and its end customers, coming from a brand management mindset.

Another case in point is Procter & Gamble, the well-known consumer goods brand with its Tremor.com offering. Realizing that traditional mass communication via print and TV advertising was becoming less and less efficient, the company tapped into the power of word-of-mouth communication by reaching out to opinion leaders in the youth market. To this end, it set up a massive database of opinion leaders who received messages from the company about its new product launches. Naturally, the capabilities required for this approach, such as individual customer data management and bi-directional communication, had to be built up from scratch, either internally or through acquisition.

Complementary to this scenario, we see customer management-focused companies increasingly employing brand management strategies, as in the case of the credit card company Capital One. Until the early 2000s, it had never engaged in any proactive brand-building or used any form of mass communication to build up its brand image. Capital One's communication focused on communicating with its individual customers via its massive call center and mail order operations. However, after having seen stellar growth over time, it found this strategy to be too limiting, with consumers' perceptions of its brand positioning being hazy at best. In order to pave the way for its diversification into retail banking and insurance selling, the company found it useful to first build up a solid and distinct brand image. Starting around 2005, it began investing heavily in creating a brand image via massive public advertising (McCarthy, 2005).

EPILOGUE

The challenge, when moving from pure go-to-market strategies (quadrants A and C) to a hybrid one (quadrant B), is in creating the right internal capabilities and mindset. Apart from recruiting the right talent to execute its strategy, a company needs to open itself to existing mental go-to-market models to create synergistic springboards. It is not parallel execution of brand management alongside customer management that yields the key benefits, but their close integration and cross-fertilization. This target seems to be the next to be achieved within the great debate on managing brands vs managing customers.

REFERENCES

M. Berk Ataman, Carl F. Mela, and Harald J. van Heerde (2008), "Building Brands," *Marketing Science*, 27(6), November–December, 1036–1054.

Reinartz, Werner, Manfred Krafft, and Wayne D. Hoyer (2004), "The Customer Relationship Management Process: Its Measurement and Impact on Performance," *Journal of Marketing Research*, 41(3), 293–305.

Niraj, Rakesh, Mahendra Gupta, and ChakravarthiNarasimhan (2001), "Customer Profitability in a Supply Chain," *Journal of Marketing*, 65 (3), 1–16.

Kaplan, Robert S. and Bruns, W. (1987), "Accounting and Management: A Field Study Perspective," *Harvard Business School Press*, p. 204.

Kaplan, Robert, "Dakota Office Products" by, *Harvard Business School* Case 102–021.

Reinartz, Werner (2010), "CRM Practices across Industries," Working Paper, University of Cologne, p. 6.

Swibel, Matthew, (2004), "Where Money Doesn't Talk: Think ING Wants Your Cash? Don't be so sure. This Bank Cherry picks Customers—and Fat Cats Aren't Among Them," *Forbes*, May 24.

Reinartz, Werner and V. Kumar (2002), "The Mismanagement of Customer Loyalty," *Harvard Business Review*, 80 (July), 86–94.

McCarthy, Michael (2005), "Capital One's 'What's in your Wallet?' Ads Filling Airwaves," *USA TODAY*, March 13.

Chapter 16

Brand Imperative: Protecting Your Most Valuable Assets

Jeffery Andrien, Paul Benoit, and Philip C. Zerrillo

INTRODUCTION

Increased globalization in today's business environment, and the resulting commoditization of products and services, have spotlighted brands and branding as essential components of successful corporate strategies. Moreover, technological advances, container shipping, outsourcing of labor, and opening up of world economies have upped the requirements of businesses and enabled products to be made with enhanced efficiency. Consequently, competition has increased and products have become more homogeneous than ever before.[1] To combat this trend, companies are often forced to find a way to differentiate their products and services from the large number available in the marketplace. Many are turning to branding as the solution.

Interestingly, some of the same factors that have spurred the current emphasis on branding have also made brands more vulnerable to attack. Counterfeiting, infringement of trademarks, "cybersquatting" and other assaults on brands have been increasing in frequency and severity during the past few years. This has put companies in a bit of a quandary, and the board room question is, "We need to invest heavily in brands and branding to be successful in the global economy, but how do we ensure that our investments are

---

[1] http://www.unescap.org/ttdw/Publications/TFS_pubs/pub_2194/pub_2194_ch2.pdf

providing the appropriate returns?" In other words, organizations need to be able to successfully protect their brands. The greater the certainty around brand protection, the greater the probability that managers will be willing to invest millions of dollars in developing brands.

It has been estimated that the average cost of protecting a trademark by bringing a suit against an infringer is US$600,000,[2] and although recent damage awards have been significant (exceeding US$300 million in the matter of Adidas v Payless), the bulk of damages awarded for trademark infringement have been less than US$10 million.[3] Accordingly, it is important for companies to actively manage their brand value and take action to protect it from a business and a legal perspective.

This chapter reviews the various methods, including legal and business remedies, available to companies to protect their brands and assesses their effectiveness in developing a best practice approach to address the quandary mentioned earlier.

BRANDS

Before we can adequately develop best practices for brand protection, we must first define what we are trying to protect and uncover the means by which this adds value (i.e., why we are trying to protect it).

Definition

The word "brand" is used in many different ways. This can create confusion when there is an attempt to define it or understand the ways in which it drives a company's value. For example, the word brand can simply connote a named product or service, for instance, "What brand of toothpaste do you use?" It can also refer to a trademark, for example, "What brand should we use for the new toothpaste we have developed?" While both of these examples highlight a specific characteristic of a brand, they are too narrow in scope and

---

[2] 2003 Report of Economic Survey published by the AIPLA.
[3] "Intellectual Property: Valuation, Exploitation, and Infringement Damages," Gordon V. Smith Russell L. Parr.

breadth to suffice as a working definition. They are merely parts of a larger whole. To eliminate confusion and serve as the basis for our discussion on brand protection, this chapter relies on the broader and more inclusive definition of a brand as an intangible asset that encompasses all of the ideas, perceptions and expectations that consumers have of a particular product or service. In the words of a well-know leader in the field of branding, Walter Landor, "Simply put, a brand is a promise. By identifying and authenticating a product or service, it delivers a pledge of satisfaction and quality."[4] Under this definition, brands extend beyond the corporation and can be effectively used by individuals, charitable organizations, scholastic institutions, and even countries (for example, Brand USA, Amazing Thailand, or The Colors of Malaysia). Moreover, brands can be either positive or negative. In other words, the satisfaction and quality Mr. Landor refers to can be either high or low. One only has to think of the Edsel to understand the concept of a negative brand.

Brands have many different components because of the myriad of means by which a company can identify and authenticate its products. More specifically, the pledge or promise a brand offers its customers can be communicated via names, products, trademarks, trade-dress, characters, colors, smells, tastes, textures, logos, slogans, and distribution channels, and so on.

How Brands Add Value

Because brands are intangible assets, their values are not generally found on financial statements (the portion attributable to the goodwill associated with acquisitions). Moreover, under current accounting rules, investments in brand-building need to be recorded as expense items, rather than capitalized on a balance sheet. The intangible nature of brands, coupled with the accounting rules that regulate brand investments, often obfuscate their value and result in managers to underestimating their importance. This can be a grave error, since brands often represent the single most valuable asset a company has. One need only review the market valuations of Altria and Philip Morris after their split. Figure 16.1 created by using the Interbrand valuation methodology shows brand values as a percentage of the market capitalization of 49 well-known US companies:

[4] http://answers.yahoo.com/question/index?qid=20070821043257AACEvSS

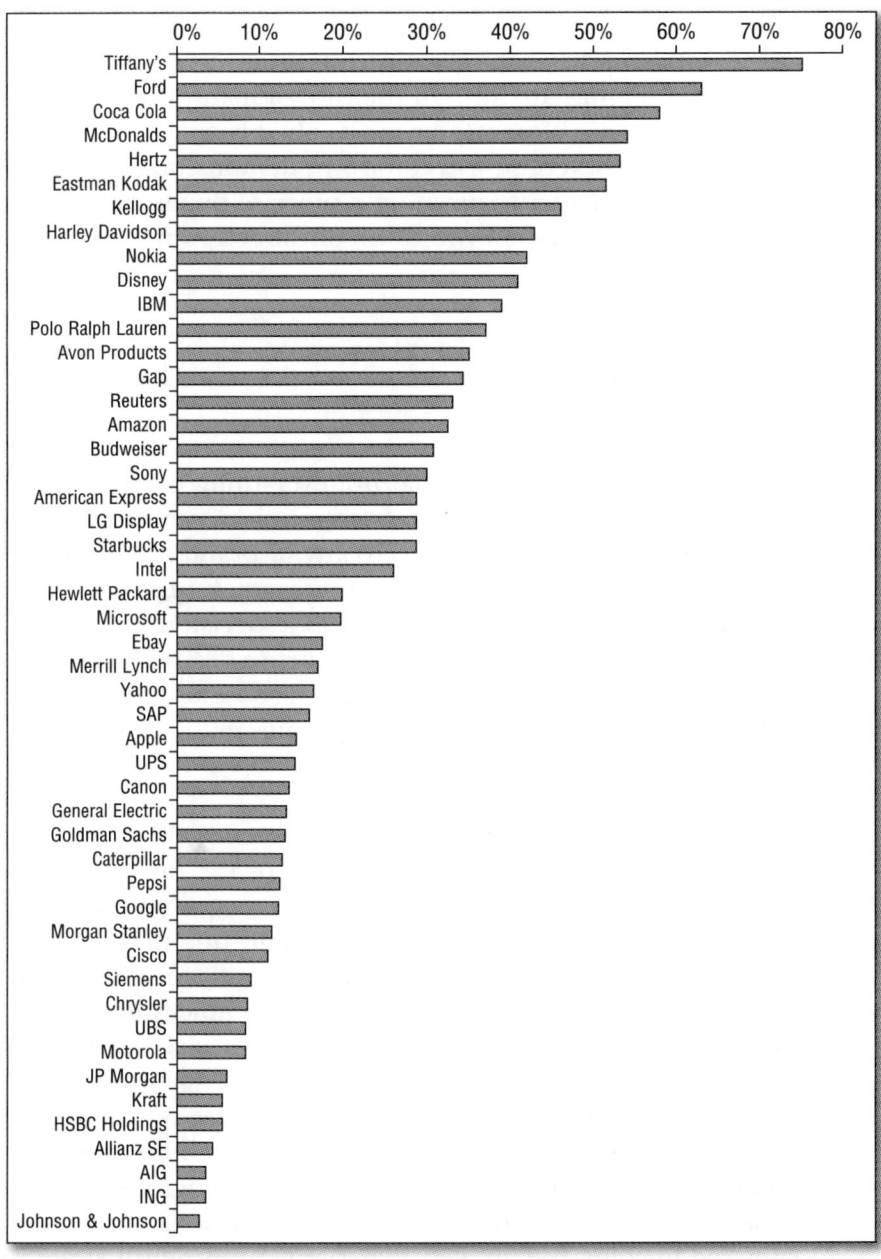

Source: http://www.customersandcapital.com/book/2007/09/the-interbrand-.html

Figure 16.1 Brand Value as a Percent of Market Capitalization[5]

[5] Figure uses interbrand valuation methodology, which is discussed in "Brand Protection" section of this chapter.

On an average, the brands in the figure represent more than 17% of the total market capitalization of these companies, with Tiffany's leading the way at 75%.[6] In the case of many of these companies, their brands are clearly their most valuable assets.

There is a simple exercise you can do to demonstrate the value brands can have. Simply write down on a piece of paper everything that comes to your mind when you think of the following:

- The Nike Swoosh
- Habitat for Humanity
- Ronald McDonald
- The King of Beers

While the authors are certain that not everything on your list is positive, how nice it must be to have communicated all the information to a consumer so easily. In actuality, a brand is a shortcut into a consumer's mind. As judicious processors, humans tend to use brands as a means of easing the purchase decision, since they reduce the search, evaluation, and choice portions of the process.

As might be seen in the lists you created, some of the tangible ways in which brands add value to the companies that own them are by the following means:

- *Differentiating their products from competing ones:* Based on the popular quotation, "An apple a day keeps the doctor away," one might surmise that every apple is endowed with the same power to keep away doctors. While this may or may not be true, not all apples look, taste, or even feel the same. Accordingly, consumers have multiple of choices in procuring their daily dose of medicine—green ones, red ones, tart ones, and sweet ones. In addition, there are small ones, big ones, crispy ones, and mealy ones. Fortunately, there are brands to help consumers differentiate between the available choices. For example, Braeburn apples are medium-sized and crisp, with a sweet and tart taste. Red Delicious apples are ruby red in color and are very sweet. A Granny Smith apple is

---

[6] http://www.customersandcapital.com/book/2007/09/the-interbrand-.html

green and tart. A primary function of a brand is to differentiate commoditized products, such as apples.
- *Reducing transaction costs:* A byproduct of product differentiation is reduction of transaction costs. Determining that products match their tastes and preferences is not a costless endeavor for consumers; it takes time, effort, and experience. Brands can reduce these costs by informing consumers about a product's quality, value, durability, consistency, and/or other product characteristics, making it "cheaper" for them consumer to make purchase decisions and reduce the probability of poor ones.
- *Providing negotiating power with suppliers/vendors:* In general, companies seek to be associated with other organizations that have strong and reputable brands. The increased demand to do business with branded companies can result in an improved negotiating position for the branded enterprise. In the absence of a means of distinguishing their products from those of another, producers' products become commoditized. At this point, the most efficient means of differentiation is via pricing or point of sale promotion/services, either of which can be accomplished more easily by a downstream vendor.
- *Shifting supply curve upwards:* Brands are bridges that connect products to markets. In doing so, they enable markets to attract the goods and services desired and enable these to reach their target audiences. In their infancy, marketing ideas were housed within economics departments. Until the "Marginalist" movement, economic theory could not explain why consumption was not solely driven by income. However, advertisers had realized long before that when provided with product-related information, consumers were willing to purchase more goods at all levels of incomes. In general, such value-added services enable branded products to have price premiums over their non-branded counterparts as well as a higher sales volume.
- *Fostering customer loyalty:* Good brands make it difficult for customers to switch to competitive products. According to Aaker (1993), "If customers are indifferent to brands, and in fact buy with respect to features, price and convenience with little concern for the brand name, there is likely little equity. If, on

the other hand, they continue to purchase the brand even in the face of competitors with superior features, price, and convenience, substantial value exists in the brand and perhaps in its symbols and slogans (Aaker, 1991)." Additionally, this results in reducing the cost of customer reacquisition and a greater likelihood of future sales to existing customers.
- *Providing stability:* The stability provided by brands helps to ensure the certainty of future demand for them. From an investor's standpoint, it establishes the perception of continuity of cash flows into the future, thereby increasing the multiple over the company book value that investors are willing to pay for stock. Moreover, the low perception of risk to future cash flows results in reduced borrowing/financing costs.

While it seems abundantly clear that brands create value for companies, they have been greeted with a much cooler reception socially. It is an interesting dichotomy that when brands effectively achieve their goal of providing companies with increased economic power, global reach and iconic status, they do so at the cost of their social perception. For example, many large mega-brands such as Wal-Mart, Nike, and McDonalds have been linked to issues relating to monopolization, exploitation of labor, and culture genocide, to name just a few. Without taking a position on these criticisms, it is important to note that there are numerous positive externalities associated with brands. The social benefits of brands include the following:

- *Consumer protection (quality control):* For brands to be effective, associated products have to consistently deliver on the promises they make to consumers. This requires extensive quality control, which can protect consumers from defective or harmful products. A good example of the extent to which a corporation's management will go to protect their relationship with the consumer is the famous Tylenol case. In 1982, a person in Chicago laced Extra Strength Tylenol capsules with cyanide. This resulted in seven deaths. In response, Johnson & Johnson ceased all production of the capsules, recalled more than 31 million bottles of the product and replaced them with tamper-resistant ones. The company's response was unprecedented and demonstrated to its customers its commitment to safety and quality. A non-branded manufacturer may not have gone to such lengths. The effort, expense and ability to track, identify and remove a product from the shelves is difficult, requires great effort and compliance from not just from a company, but trade as well.

- *Innovation:* Good brands effectively communicate their quality and value to consumers, and appeal to the tastes and preferences of their targeted customers. Once their bridges to consumers are established and fortified, companies are freer to innovate, because they not only have a method to associate their efforts with their innovations, but they also have in place an installed customer base that makes innovation less risky. For example, Apple Inc.'s brand is synonymous with innovation. Steve Jobs and Apple are known for thinking differently from the rest of the computer industry and for creating original and user-friendly products. The brand has enabled Apple to expand from computers to musical devices to cell phones. Think how difficult the transition to a cell phone-maker would have been for Apple had it not been for its brand.
- *Wealth creation:* If businesses are the key drivers of wealth creation and brands are fundamental components of successful businesses, then the latter are by definition the key drivers of wealth creation.
- *Corporate responsibility:* A tenet taught in almost every entry-level microeconomics course is that companies[7] are profit maximizers, and do not undertake actions unless they reasonably expect these to move them toward their goal of maximizing their corporate profits. As profit maximizers, companies produce output at the level where marginal revenue equals marginal cost (MR-MC).[8] In a perfectly competitive market, organizations are price-takers whose economic profits are computed away to nothing and prices are equal to marginal

---

[7] This assumes that the firms are "for-profit" firms in the private sector (not universities, government entities, charitable organizations and/or religious organizations, etc.).

[8] See http://www.econ.ilstu.edu/ntskaggs/ECO105/readings/profit-max.htm for discussion on companies as profit maximizers.

revenues (P=MR=MC). If prices are equal to companies' marginal costs, why do we continually see them incurring costs on altruistic endeavors such as charitable contributions, green manufacturing, and public service announcements? It is because such activities are linked to the profit motive. Investments such as these help a company build a positive brand image, which enables it to escape from the "perfect competition" constraint previously discussed. By differentiating their products from available substitutes along lines of quality, value, social responsibility, etc., companies are able to compete more effectively and garner price premiums over their non-branded counterparts, i.e., the brand reduces the primacy of price in the decision-making process (Aaker, 1993). In the mid-1990s, the President of Samsung stated, "Competing successfully in the 21st century will require more than just outstanding product and quality functions. Intangibles such as corporate and brand image will be crucial factors for achieving a competitive edge." Manufacturing high-quality products in a socially responsible manner helps a company develop a positive brand image. As such, brands provide social value by fostering corporate responsibility.

While these are only some of the social benefits attributable to brands, they provide significant food for thought for those who eschew the notion that brands can be a social good.

Risks to Brand Value

According to real estate agent, Marc Davison, "a brand is the most valuable real estate in the world, a corner of the consumers' mind."[9] However, managers need to be aware that this particular real estate market is very fickle; brands can be and are often evicted from their valuable perch. Eviction can come swiftly without notice and can continue over a long time with a large number of subtle (and sometimes not so subtle) warnings. Either way, the result can be devastating with squandered investments, loss of brand value, and

---

[9] http://answers.yahoo.com/question/index?qid=20070821043257AACEvSS

decreased profitability just being starters. It is therefore incumbent upon managers to understand the risks to which their brands are vulnerable, so they can appropriately manage the risk and protect themselves against the erosion or complete destruction of brand value.

As previously defined, a brand is a promise made between a product and consumers. It communicates information, such as product value, quality, and satisfaction. Therefore, any increase in price sensitivity is in essence synonymous with erosion of brand value. Risk to brand value, therefore, can be defined as the sensitivity a brand's value has to shortfalls on its promise. In general, there is an exponential relationship between the risk to brand value and the importance of the brand as a differentiator. The logic is that the more influential a brand is as a differentiator, the greater the percent of corporate value concentrated in it, and the more value concentrated in the brand, the more important is its promise, and the more important a brand's promise, the more catastrophic the effect of a breach of the promise can be to its value, since trust is not easily or cheaply rebuilt, if at all. Bear Stearns is a recent example of this. The Bear Stearns brand was built over decades of providing exceptional performance and service to its customers. It elicited trust by communicating its professionalism, intelligence, diligence and integrity, and so on. This trust was the foundation of the success company achieved over such a long period of time. However, once news of its risky investments on sub-prime mortgages came to light, this trust was broken and the company quickly crumbled. What took years and years to build was destroyed in a matter of days. This effect is compounded by the speed and ease with which information travels to prospective consumers.

Brand value has become more important than ever before in a marketplace where commoditization of products is inevitable. With flexible manufacturing, and computer assisted design and manufacturing, the ability to solely differentiate on products' features has lessened. Additionally, many product categories are operating in "dark markets," where they are not allowed to be advertised on public media or be available on shelves, etc. (for instance, the message placement options of liquor and cigarette companies have been minimized and in some markets become completely "dark.) Additionally, cigarette companies are often forced to increase the size of their warning messages on packs, which are being relegated to under the counter. Therefore, in this environment, it is virtual necessity to have in place brand awareness, recall and loyalty. In fact, even a small breach in a brand's promise can push consumers to readily available substitutes.

There are many ways in which a brand's promise can be broken and, accordingly, there are many different risks to a brand's value. Some of these risks are a function of companies' specific actions and decisions, while others are due to external events such as changing market conditions and the criminal activity of competitors. A more detailed list of these risks is presented in the following table:

Brand Protection

Because brands have unique functions and value drivers, and operate in a variety of industries across a plethora of products and services, it is virtually impossible to provide a comprehensive and exhaustive

Table 16.1 Brand Risks

Internal Risks	External Risks
Poor product quality	Commoditization (price competition/substitutes)
Poor customer service	Changes in social values
Lack of distribution channel control	Changes in political climate
Over-stretching brand (Genericizing)	Changes in consumer tastes and preferences
Mismanaged brand alliances	Changes in market conditions
Ineffective risk management policy/procedures	Illegal activity by competitors:
Lack of employee buy-in	Intellectual property infringement
Dilution from mergers/acquisitions	Counterfeiting
Lack of competitive responses	Breaches of contracts
Outsourcing brand-relevant activity	Cybersquatting
Lack of understanding of brand value	Phishing
Brand performance not systematically measured	Slander/Libel

list of all of the steps managers should take to protect brand value. Similarly, because there are infinite ways in which brands can be eroded through illegal activities. Listing all the laws and case precedents that aim to preserve brand value is difficult. There are, however, some general precautions managers can take, regardless of the industry, product or service involved, to protect brand value. Moreover, there are a few general laws and case precedents that comprise the bulk of the legal framework within which managers can seek legal protection for their brands. Understanding these laws and interpretations provided by historical cases can help them take steps to better position brands for successful courtroom protection. The balance of this chapter outlines our views on the best practices for brand protection from a business and legal perspective.

BUSINESS

One of the primary steps managers should take with respect to brand protection is to periodically and systematically value their brands. Use of a rigorous methodology can result in the brand valuation process uncovering the value drivers of a particular brand, and force managers to assess the risks associated with these drivers. They can then use this information to identify and prioritize appropriate methods for to protect their brands. Moreover, understanding a brand's overall value enables managers to perform cost/benefit analyses of the various protection methods they are considering.

As Table 16.2 indicates, there are many different approaches to brand valuation; each with its own inherent limitations and weaknesses. Managers should understand and consider these limitations and weaknesses when choosing the method they wish to use. The approach that seems to best overcome impediments to an accurate and relevant brand valuation, and the one most used by marketing professionals, and auditors and tax authorities, is the "economic use" method. This method is an income-based, discounted cash flow (DCF) approach that combines financial and competitive analyses with forecasts of branded sales to calculate the present net value of future profits attributable to a brand. Perhaps the most famous and widely used version of the economic use methodology till date is the

Table 16.2 Brand Valuation Methodologies

Approaches	Description	Weaknesses
Replacement Cost	NPV of all historical investments in marketing and promotions incurred in developing the brand.	Historical cost or replacement cost may not be well correlated with current value. The method ignores any return on brand investment than may have been realized by the firm.
Comparables	Utilize market comparables to derive brand value.	Hard to find good comparables given that brands are unique. Similar metrics, such as investment levels, etc., do not necessarily equate to similar values.
Price Premium	The NPV of the future price premiums that the branded products are expected to achieve over their non-branded counterparts.	Many brands do not have the function of generating price premiums, but provide other valuable benefits, such as customer loyalty, demand stabililty, and increased sales volume.
Royalty Relief	Assumes that brand is licensed and applies a royalty rate to the branded sales over time, then discounts it to get the NPV of the revenue stream generated by the royalty.	Difficult to determine appropraite royalty rate.
Goodwill	Calculates the difference between the firms market value and book value, then attributes that difference to brand value.	Goodwill includes intangible assets that are not brand-related, such as expected synergies. Moreover, the book value may underestimate the market value of many tangible assets.
Economic Use	A DCF methodology that calculates the return earned as a result of owning the brand. The Economic Use method integrates consumer research, financial analysis and competitive analyses with forecasted branded earnings.	Does not consider any "hope value" based on new uses of the brand.

Source: "Brand Valuation." *Brands and Branding: An Economist Book* and "Current Practices in Brand Valuation," prepared by Brand Finance.

Interbrand approach, which has been used to value more than 4,000 brands since its inception.[10]

In addition to conducting a brand risk assessment and establishing brand value, other business measures that can help to protect against the erosion of brand value include at least the following:

- *Making the brand concept a corporate philosophy:* For brands to be effective and maintain their value, corporations need to deliver on their promises. This implies that the brand concept must be part of a company's core values and permeate every aspect of its business. To this end, its management should ensure that there is buy-in at every level of the organization by every employee, vendor and business partner. This requires extensive training and communication, as well as continued development of the brand and its associative meanings. Stakeholders should be aware of the brand's promises prior to and during its launch and corporations must strive to maintain brand integrity and the integrity of its core differentiators at all times. Once this takes place, the brand moves from a mere slogan to a deep-seated philosophy that drives corporate decisions, organizes strategies, and provides clear guidance in the event of brand-related catastrophes. For instance, when one thinks of the Volvo brand, safety is the first thing that enters one's mind. Recognizing the company's reputation and position in the marketplace, Volvo's management has consistently resisted the temptation to use lower cost suppliers to preempt superior safety performance being offered to its customers. A public misstep on this dimension could have debilitating effects for a company such as Volvo.
- *Control of distribution channels:* Inadequate control of distribution channels can have a disastrous effect on brand value. It can result in proliferation of counterfeit goods, poor customer service, large disparities in retail price, and other discrepancies that negatively affect perception of a brand. By controlling their distribution channels, companies are better able to protect their product integrity and ensure that customers

---

[10] For more information regarding the Interbrand valuation methodology, see http://www.ourfishbowl.com/images/surveys/060830_CBV2006_En.pdf

receive the requisite support and service at the point of sale. Methods to control distribution channels include, among others, resale price maintenance agreements, selective or exclusive distributorships, independent distributor audits, co-opting of counterfeit manufacturers, and use of overt and covert technologies to identify, track and authenticate branded products throughout the downstream market. Some of the more common uses of overt and covert technologies to police markets for counterfeits are as follows:

○ Overt technologies:

- Optically Variable Devices (OVD) such as holograms and optically variable inks
- Security papers with special fibers and/or chemical reactive properties
- Microtext—small text, usually in a 3-point font or smaller, embedded into the background of a tag, label, or packaging
- Tamper-proof/Tamper-evident packaging to visibly alert consumers of a breaches in product integrity
- Bar coding

○ Covert technologies:

- Ultraviolet and infrared taggants involving embedding of transparent light elements that are only visible in the presence of ultraviolet or infrared light
- Microscopic nanotext and hidden images
- Radio-frequency identification (RFID) tags—a technology that encompasses transmission and reception of data via radio waves

- *Maintaining market vigilance:* Markets are dynamic entities that are capable of changing in at moment's notice. Carefully monitoring those in which a brand operates will help to keep it at the forefront of market movements, and thereby maintain or even increase its relevance and value. Companies that do not remain vigilant in their markets are called into court to defend their lax policies when counterfeiting cases are heard.

- *Engaging in strategic brand extension:* Brand building is costly and fraught with risks. Accordingly, rather than continuously developing new brands, companies often attempt to extend successful brands into new markets. For example, the Polo brand was originally developed for a line of clothing, but it has successfully been extended into eyewear, bedding, bath towels, and other home and lifestyle products. However, while brand extension can result in cost savings and promote new product development, it is not without its own risks. Managers must be careful not to cannibalize or "genericize" their brands by overextension. Failed extensions can negatively affect a brand's image in core product markets and diminish its overall value. Accordingly, brand managers should strive to only extend brands to strategic products that are consistent with the brands' associative meaning and that can deliver on their promises to consumers. Focus groups, surveys and other research methods can be used to analyze consumers' perceptions and brand associations prior to brand extensions.

LEGAL

Although it should be management's goal to protect brand value through the use of business strategy; certain acts of competitors and suppliers, such as those listed in Table 16.1, cross legal boundaries and leave the court system as its ultimate protector. The court's role is to enforce property rights and compensate a brand owner for loss of value.

However, relying on the court system for protection of brand value is not without risk. Although protection of branding rights outside of the USA is governed by the WTO under the Trade-Related Aspects of Intellectual Property Rights (TRIPS) agreement, this only requires members to comply with certain minimum standards for protection of intellectual property rights. The agreement also gives member countries the freedom to determine the appropriate method for implementing its provisions within their own legal systems. Accordingly, it is critical for companies doing business outside the USA to understand the rights afforded to them in each country as well as enforceability of these rights.

Within the USA, companies run the risk of investing significant resources to bring legal action against perceived infringers as well as suppliers of defective products in order to protect brand value or recover lost brand value. However, no outcome in litigation is certain. Results often depend on the uniqueness of a brand, how well it was developed and supported in the market and other discretionary factors decided by the "trier of fact." Adding further risk in recovery of brand value, damage awards frequently require quantification of future lost profits (or lost brand value), which by nature require additional estimation and projection of future events than calculations of lost profits incurred in the past. Consequently, some courts have found claims for future lost profits and damage to goodwill to be overly speculative, and do not award future damages to the brand owner.[11]

While there are a myriad torts and statutes under which a company may seek legal protection of its brand value, in the USA, many of these actions are filed under the Lanham Act of 1946 and the Federal Trademark Dilution Act of 1995. The Lanham Act provides for protection of trademarks in the event of infringement arising from customers' confusion, whereas the Federal Trademark Dilution Act protects famous marks from losing their value due to customers' disassociation with these, i.e., it guards against genericization of famous (distinctive) marks. By understanding the precedents and nuances of these laws, a manager can better position a brand for successful prosecution, if forced to seek legal remedy as a means of protecting brand value. Figure 16.2 outlines the basic legal protection afforded to trademarks under the law.

THE LAW

Legal protection of trademarks has progressively moved from protecting the tort of fraud, whereby the intent of the law was to protect

---

[11] Lifewise Master Funding v. Telebank, 374 F.3d 917; Lithuanian Commerce Corp. v. Sara Lee Hosiery, 23 F. Supp. 2d 509; Pharmanetics, Inc. v. Aventis Pharms., Inc., 2005 U.S. Dist. LEXIS 45768.

consumers from inferior and counterfeit goods made by those who would tread upon the good names of others in an effort to dupe the unsuspecting consumer. Prior to the 20th century, American brands and marks died with the owner of a mark. However, with the advent of corporate structures and publicly traded companies, there was a need to expand trademark protection to enable continuance of trading names. However, while the courts recognized the dual purpose of protecting the consumer from the counterfeiter as well as the property owner from those that would trade in their names, it was not until the passage of the Reasonable Fields Doctrine of 1916 that protection of owners' marks was extended to what the courts believed were related fields. In the case of Rigby Flour (a company launching a new pancake batter) vs Aunt Jemimah (a syrup company), the court held that there were fields so closely related to the primary business of the former that protection of its name should extend to these related fields. This was a clear sign that protecting the mark owner was a primary emphasis.

The Lanham Act (1946) is contained in Title 15 of the U.S. Code, and includes regulations for registering trademarks, as well as injunctive relief[12] and monetary recovery for violation of rights. Protection under the Lanham Act extends to three basic forms of branding—trademark, trade name, and trade dress. The Lanham Act defines "trade mark" as

> any word, name, symbol, or device, or any combination thereof... [used] to identify and distinguish ... goods, including a unique product, from those manufactured or sold by others and to indicate the source of the goods, even if that source is unknown.[13]

Unlike a trade mark, which is used to distinguish goods, the Act defines "trade name" as any name used by a person to identify his or her business or vocation.[14] "Trade dress," although not specifically defined by the Lanham Act, has been defined by the courts as

---

[12] Injunctive relief is a court order that forces the recipient to refrain from certain activities.

[13] U.S. Code Title 15, § 1127.

[14] The terms "trade name" and "commercial name" mean any name used by a person to identify his or her business or vocation (U.S. Code Title 15, § 1127).

the total image, overall design, or appearance of a product or its packaging.[15]

Continued demonstration of the movement toward protection of property, and possibly the most significant development affecting US brands (and arguably worldwide brands) in the past half century has gone virtually unnoticed in marketing research. The January 16, 1996, signing of Public Law 104-98 [h.r.1295], titled the Federal Trademark Dilution Act of 1995 is to be referred to from here onward as "the dilution act". This statute provides for protection of brands through adoption of anti-dilution principles. It reduces the burden of trademark infringement from potential confusion to "lessening of the capacity of a famous mark to identify goods or services, regardless of the presence or absence of (a) competition between the parties, or (b) likelihood of confusion, mistakes, or deception" (p. 1030). In this law, the Government set forth a statute that could have a tremendous impact on naming, valuation, development, and more directly, protection of brands.

This Act made it easier for owners of marks to preempt others from using their marks, because plaintiffs were no longer required to demonstrate the likelihood of customers being confused, but only to show that a defendant's use of a mark would result in "blurring" or "tarnishment" of a famous mark. Blurring is defined as reduction of the distinctiveness of a famous mark in the minds of the plaintiff's customers, tarnishment as an association between a famous mark and a defendant's mark, which harms the former.

Following the enactment of the 1995 Act, courts were split as to whether a plaintiff was required to show actual economic injury or only a likelihood of economic injury to a famous mark. The Supreme Court clarified the issue in the 2003 matter of Moseley v. Secret Catalogue, Inc., ruling that a plaintiff must show actual economic injury to the famous mark in order to obtain protection under the Federal Trademark Dilution Act. However, this standard was revised when President Bush signed into law the Trademark Dilution Revision Act of 2006, which states that the owner of a famous mark

---

[15] Two Pesos, Inc. v. Taco Cabana, Inc., 505 U.S. 763, 765 (1992); American Greetings, 807 F.2d at 1141; Rose Art Industries, Inc. v. Raymond Geddes & Co., 31 F. Supp.2d 367 (D.N.J. 1998).

shall be entitled to an injunction against another person who, at any time after the owner's mark has become famous, commences use of a mark or trade name in commerce that is *likely* to cause dilution by blurring or dilution by tarnishment of the famous mark, *regardless of the presence or absence of actual or likely confusion, of competition, or of actual economic injury.*[16] (emphasis added)

POSITIONING BRANDS FOR LEGAL PROTECTION

Whenproactively seeking to protect brand value or ex-post legal remedies to re-establish brand value under the Lanham Act or the Federal Trademark Dilution Act, managers should consider the positions taken by the courts in deciding what constitutes an established and protectable mark.

According to the courts, ownership of a trademark, trade name or trade dress (collectively "mark") is established through the use of the mark. The first company to use a mark in economic commerce, regardless of whether that company has federally registered the mark, has the right of ownership.[17] Registration of a mark, however, has several advantages. First, federal registration issues a constructive notice nationwide so that a second user cannot claim innocent use due to lack of notice. Second, registration of the mark provides the registrar with a presumption of ownership, dating to the filing date of the application for federal registration. Any challengers to ownership rights of the mark must overcome this presumption by a preponderance of the evidence, showing that the non-registrant can used the mark in commerce first.[18]

When establishing a mark, it is important for managers to understand the types of marks that are afforded protection by the courts, and to avoid the pitfalls that might render a mark unprotected. Figure 16.2 summarizes the conceptual categories of marks, and identifies which marks have the highest protection under the law.

As shown earlier, marks tend to fall within a spectrum ranging from the generic to the fanciful. Generic marks identify a product

---

[16] Trademark Dilution Revision Act of 2006, p. 1.

[17] Sengoku Works Ltd. v. RMC Int'l, Ltd., 96 F.3d 1217, 1219 (9th Cir. 1996).

[18] Vuitton et Fils S.A. v. [**6] J. Young Enterprises, 644 F.2d 769, 775-76 (9th Cir. 1981); Rolley, Inc. v. Younghusband, 204 F.2d 209 (9th Cir. 1953).

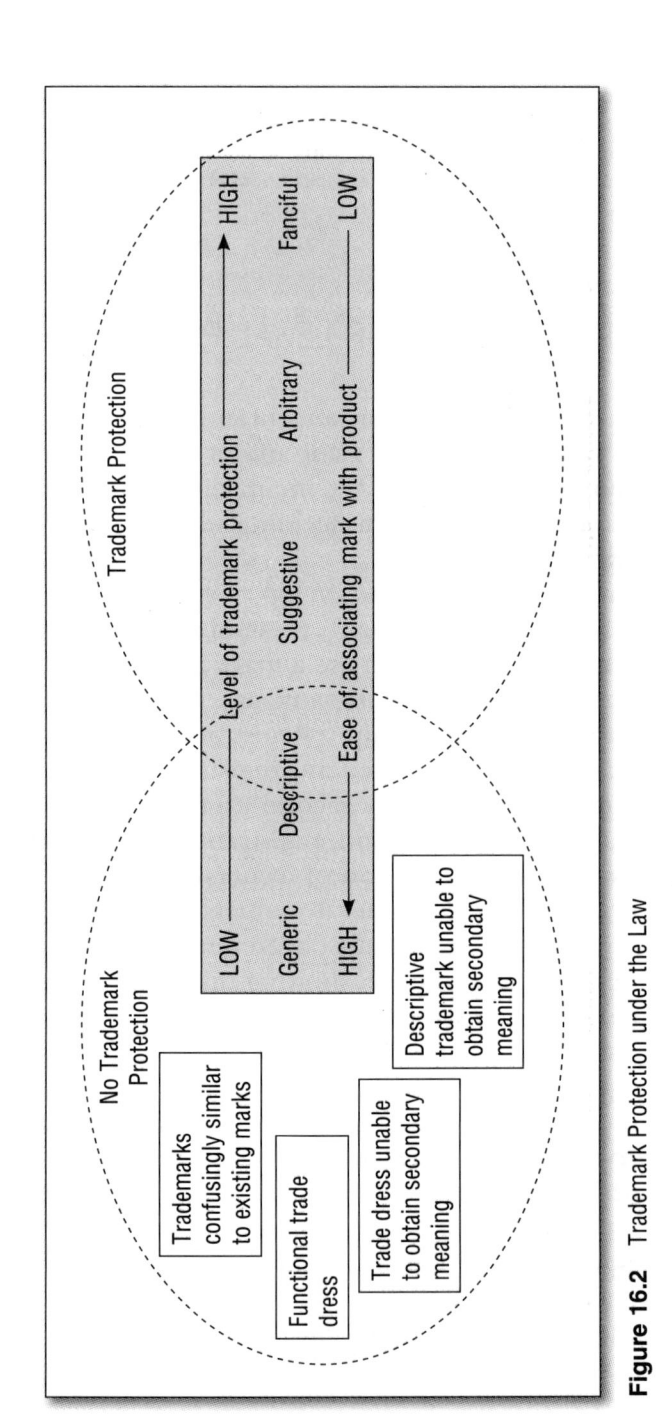

Figure 16.2 Trademark Protection under the Law

category such as trampolines, kerosene, and cellophane. Although these marks instantly associate a product category in the mind of the customer, and therefore assist in the marketing effort of the product, they do not help customers identify the mark with the manufacturer of a product. At the extreme end of the spectrum, fanciful marks consist of words that are created for the sole purpose of associating a manufacturer with a product. Common examples of fanciful marks include Clorox and Exxon. These marks do not describe the products, and therefore do not help in their initial marketing, but become associated with these over time. Accordingly, when selecting a mark, managers need to balance the marketing benefit of selecting a mark that is naturally associated with a product and helps in the marketing effort with the legal protection that may be sacrificed by using such a mark. The following paragraphs elaborate on the pitfalls that should be avoided when selecting a mark.

- *Avoid generic names:* As previously discussed, trademarks exist to provide an assurance of consistency and quality to consumers. It follows that generic trademarks or trademarks that describe categories of products rather than identify those manufactured by specific companies cease to convey the intended meaning.

    It is important to note that trademarks deemed to have been generic when initially introduced in the market are not capable of subsequently obtaining legal protection by developing a secondary meaning through the use of advertisements and other means. In Microsoft Corp. v. Lindows.com, the court held that determination of whether a mark is generic should be measured from the time it was first used in commerce, even if it was not generic at the time of trial. The court specifically instructed the jury to "consider whether the WINDOWS mark was generic before Microsoft Windows 1.0 entered the marketplace on November 1985." However, even if a trademark is not generic when originally introduced in the market, owners run the risk of losing protection if the mark becomes generic over time.

- *Avoid descriptive marks:* Descriptive trademarks describe a products or service. Examples of descriptive trademarks include "Sharp" for televisions, "World Book" for encyclopedias and

"Honey Roasted Peanuts" for roasted peanuts. Similar to generic marks, descriptive marks are not initially capable of securing trademark protection because they do not serve the purpose of a mark, which is to enable consumers to efficiently identify a producer's goods and services. However, unlike generic trademarks, descriptive trademarks can obtain protection if they are able to achieve a secondary meaning in the minds of customers such that the mark becomes associated with the supplier of the product or service.

In assessing whether a mark has obtained a secondary meaning, the courts have considered (1) advertising expenditures, (2) consumer studies linking the mark to a source, (3) unsolicited media coverage of a product, (4) success in sales, (5) attempts to plagiarize the mark, and (6) the length and exclusivity of the mark's use.[19]

An example of descriptive trademarks that have acquired a secondary meaning can be seen in the 2004 matter of Hearts on Fire Co., LLC (HOF) v. L C Int'l Corp. (LCI). HOF, a Massachusetts-based distributor of branded diamonds, began using the marks "The World's Most Perfectly Cut Diamond" and "The Most Perfectly Cut Diamond in the World" while advertising cut diamonds in January 1997. LCI, a New York-based distributor of diamonds, which were similar to the specialized cut of HOF's diamonds, began using the phrase "the most perfectly fashioned diamond in the world" in its promotion of yjr "Hearts and Arrow Ideal Cut" diamond.

HOF asserted dilution of its marks "The world's most perfectly cut diamond" and the "Most perfectly cut diamond in the world" was a takeoff on LCI's use of the phrase "The most perfectly fashioned diamond in the world." LCI filed a motion to dismiss this, arguing that "the phrases are generic and descriptive, and thus, even if they have acquired a secondary meaning, they are not entitled to protection under the Lanham Act." The court denied LCI's motion to dismiss, noting that HOF had "pleaded facts supporting all elements of the Lanham Act cause of action," effectively rejecting LCI's

---

[19] Centaur Communications v. A/S/M Communications; Jewish Sephardic Yellow Pages, Ltd. v. DAG Media, Inc.

argument that the marks were not afforded protection under the Lanham Act.
- *Avoid use of surnames:* Just as descriptive marks are not initially capable of obtaining trademark protection, surname marks also require secondary meaning to obtain protection. Reluctance to allow surname marks to be protected appears to stem from the concern that such protection would prohibit others from using their names in their own businesses, and potentially prohibit useful information from reaching customers.[20]

  In Brennan's, Inc. v. Brennan's Rest, the court found the mark "Brennan's," used in connection with a well-known New Orleans restaurant, was a common last name, and therefore, an inherently weak mark that was not entitled to the protection of the Lanham Act. The court noted that the mark Brennan's had acquired a secondary meaning in New Orleans, but not in New York, the state in which the defendant's restaurant operated.

  Interestingly, although surname marks require their secondary meaning to be protected, marks based on first names receive more favorable treatment. In the 2004 matter of Peaceable Planet, Inc. v. Ty, Inc., the court noted that 15 U.S.C. § 1052(e)(4) prohibits registration of a mark that is "primarily merely a surname" without demonstrating its secondary meaning, but makes no mention of first names. The court also completely disallowed the use of personal names as trademarks and absent secondary meaning on grounds that it would lead to absurd results.
- *Avoid selecting marks that are confusingly similar to existing ones:* In order to obtain a protected mark (and be held liable for trademark infringement), it is important to select a mark that is not confusingly similar to an existing mark. In determining whether two marks are too similar, courts apply what has become known as the "eight factor Polaroid test," based on analyses conducted by the United States Court of Appeals Second Circuit in the 1961 matter of the Polaroid Corp. v.

---

[20] Peaceable Planet, Inc. v. Ty, Inc., 362 F.3d 986, 70 U.S.P.Q.2d (BNA) 1386 (7th Cir. 2004).

Polarad Elecs. Corp. The eight factors considered by the Second Circuit in determining customer-related confusion of a trademark are discussed subsequently.

(1) Strength of the trademark: The strength of a mark measures its capacity to indicate the source of the goods or services with which it is used, and is related to the degree to which the marks are arbitrary or fanciful, and has resulted in a high degree of consumer recognition.[21]

(2) Similarity of the marks: Depending on the type of confusion claimed, courts can assess whether differences are easily discernible on simultaneous viewing, or memorable enough to dispel confusion on serial viewing.[22]

(3) Proximity of the products and their competitiveness with one another: In determining the proximity of products and their competitiveness with one another, the courts consider the nature of the products and the structure of the relevant market. Among the considerations germane to the structure of the market are the classes of customers to whom the goods are sold, the manner in which the products are advertised, and the channels through which the goods are sold.[23]

(4) Likelihood a plaintiff will bridge the gap: This factor considers the likelihood that the plaintiff will enter the defendant's market, and seeks to protect the plaintiff's interest in being able to enter a related field at a future time.[24] However, it is not sufficient that a plaintiff merely speculates about the possibility of a future customer overlap.

(5) Evidence of actual consumer confusion: Although not essential for a finding of infringement, this factor has significant weight in determining whether marks are confusingly similar.[25]

---

[21] Pan American World Airways, Inc. v. Flight 101, Inc., et al.
[22] Louis Vuitton Malletier v. Burlington Coat Factory Warehouse Corp.
[23] Pan American World Airways, Inc. v. Flight 101, Inc., et al.
[24] Vista Food Exchange, Inc. v. Vistar Corporation.
[25] Louis Vuitton Malletier v. Burlington Coat Factory Warehouse Corp.

(6) Evidence that imitative mark was adopted in bad faith: This factor relates to whether the defendant knew of the plaintiff's mark and intended to capitalize on the latter's brand value.
(7) Respective quality of the products: This factor is primarily concerned with whether the plaintiff's reputation could be injured due to the defendant selling a product of inferior quality.[26]
(8) Sophistication of consumers in the relevant market: In accessing the likelihood of confusion, the courts consider the customers' level of level of knowledge of the accused products. Customers that are highly trained professionals are less likely to be misled than untrained customers.[27] Additionally, the purchase of expensive items is likely be scrutinized closely by customers, suggesting a level of sophistication among customers of these products.[28]

- *Avoid design functionality:* In order for trade dress, or the overall design or appearance of a product or its packaging, to obtain protection under the Lanham Act it must be non-functional. This requirement of non-functionality under § 43(a) of the Lanham Act prevents blurring of the line between patent law and trademark law. If the functional elements of a product design were allowed protection under the Lanham Act, inventors would be able to protect their inventions indefinitely, rather than through the 20-year life of a patent.

  The Supreme Court has defined functionality of trade dress to consist of a product feature that is "essential to the use or purpose of the article or if it affects the cost or quality of the article"[29] in such a way that exclusive use of the feature would put competitors at a significant non-reputation-related disadvantage.[30] Additionally, the Supreme Court has looked at expired patents to determinate trade dress functionality.

---

[26] Arrow Fastener Co. v. Stanley Works.
[27] Virgin Enters. Ltd. v. Nawab.
[28] Dan-Foam A/S and Tempur-Pedic, Inc. v. Brand Named Beds, LLC D/B/A Brandnamebeds4less.
[29] *Inwood Laboratories, Inc., et al. v. Ives Laboratories, Inc.*
[30] Qualitex Co. v. Jacobson Prods. Co.

According to notes in the Supreme Court matter of Traffix Devices v. Mktg. Displays:

> An expired patent has vital significance in resolving a claim of trade dress infringement concerning the features that were patented; a utility patent is strong evidence that the features therein claimed are functional; if trade dress protection is sought for those features, then the strong evidence of functionality, based on the previous patent adds great weight to the statutory presumption that features are deemed functional until proven otherwise by the party seeking trade dress protection; where the expired patent claimed the features in question, one who seeks to establish trade dress protection must carry the heavy burden of showing that the feature is not functional, for instance, by showing that the feature is merely an ornamental, incidental, or arbitrary aspect of the device.

- *Seek suggestive, arbitrary and fanciful marks:* As indicated by the first Polaroid Factor, the strength of a mark increases if it is arbitrary or fanciful.

  A term is suggestive if it requires imagination, thought, and perception to reach a conclusion as to the nature of goods. For example, the mark "Coppertone" is suggestive of suntan lotion because it hints at the nature of the connected product.

  An arbitrary mark consists of a word or symbol that is in common usage in the language, but is arbitrarily applied to goods or services in question in such a way that it is not descriptive or suggestive. The mark "Apple" is arbitrary for computer-related items because its common definition is a fruit, which is unrelated to its use in connection with computers and other technological products.

  A fanciful mark is a term coined for the express purpose of functioning as a trademark. It could also be any obscure or archaic term not familiar to buyers. The mark "Exxon" is fanciful because it was invented and designed solely to designate petroleum and other related goods. It has no other meaning.

CONCLUSION

In the new world economy, where technological advances, corporate mergers, and the increasing legal convergence across nations have spurred competition and commoditization, brands have arguably become the most valuable of all corporate assets. They can confer great power on their owners and provide significant competitive advantages in the marketplace, but they are expensive to develop and maintain, and their value is often obscured by their intangible nature. Additionally, they are subject to a multitude of risks that threaten to erode or completely destroy their value. These risks are compounded by the increased reliance companies are placing on brands, and the speed at which news regarding even small breaches of brand-related promises permeate the marketplace. Consequently, brands are more vulnerable than ever and require vigilant managerial protection.

To effectively provide this protection, managers should (1) systematically value their brands and perform risk assessment, which will enable cost/benefit analyses and prioritization of brand investment decisions, as well as identify value drivers and specific risk categories; (2) ensure that the brand philosophy permeates the entire organization and that employees fully understand and support it; (3) make certain that they fulfill the brand promises that have been made; (4) in the world of physical products, consider the technological tools and products available to enhance brand protection, and (5) finally, develop their brands in light of the legal precedents that govern their protection. In addition, they should have strong communication and contingency plans to preempt a catastrophic brand-related occurrence. While these are just some of the steps managers can take to protect their most valuable assets, they are fundamental for implementation of a successful brand strategy.

Chapter 17

Hidden Value of Brands: Brands in Mergers and Acquisitions

S. Cem Bahadir

INTRODUCTION

Brands are companies' strategic assets. Practitioners and academics focus on brands as one of the key drivers of companies' long-term performance. Over the years, academic research has investigated diverse facets of the brand-performance relationship. Traditionally, researchers explored the relationship between marketing mix strategies (for example, pricing, advertising, and promotions) and market performance (for example, market share and sales). More recently, they have been studying the impact of brand strategies on financial performance (Rao, Agarwal, and Dahlhoff, 2004; Mizik and Jacobson, 2007). Although brands have been at the center of marketing executives' and academics' attention, their focus has primarily been on management of brands where there was no change in ownership of brands. Frequently, brands are key considerations in M&A deals. For example, during the negotiations before InBev's recent acquisition of Anheuser-Busch, Anheuser-Busch's top management rejected InBev's first offer on grounds that it did not appreciate the value of Anheuser's brand portfolio sufficiently.

It is intuitive to assume that brands make up a large portion of the overall value of a company. However, a detailed analysis of M&A transactions paints a different picture. There are significant variances in the proportion of value brands account for in M&A transactions. At one end of the spectrum, 49% of a company's value is attributed to brands, for example, the purchase of Gillette, while at other end, less than 1.51% is attributed to the brand value, for example, the acquisition of Latitude by Cisco Systems (Table 17.1). In this chapter, I will discuss the factors that explain this variability beyond the obvious value drivers such as market share or sales growth.

Which Factors Explain the Value of Brands in M&As?

The dollar values in Table 17.1 reflect the acquirer's cash flow-related expectations from the target's brands. In the context of an M&A, the performance of the target company's brand would be the first set of factors to come to mind as the driver of brand value. Brands that have persistent sales growth and market share affect the acquirer's cash flow-related expectations from the acquired brands. However, acquirers have cash flow-related expectations from acquired brands, based on what they can do with these. When Triarc Beverages acquired Snapple from Quaker Oats, Snapple was experiencing serious problems in the marketplace. Triarc was able to improve the performance of the brand and sell it at three

Table 17.1 Illustrative Transactions and Brand Portfolio Value

Acquirer	Target	Target Company's Value (in millions)	Target Company's Brand Portfolio Value (in millions)	Value of Brand Portfolio/ Company
Checkers Drive-in Restaurants	Rallys Hamburgers	40	19	49.72%
Procter and Gamble	Gillette	53,457	26,251	49.61%
Constellation Brands	Robert Mondavi	1,042	186	17.85 %
Cisco Systems	Latitude	86	1	1.16%

Source: Bahadir, Bharadwaj, and Srivastava (2008).

times the price it had paid for it. There are many other examples of acquirers reviving brands. Therefore, it is my contention that the acquirer's characteristics affect the value of brands in M&As.

In order to understand the factors that determine the value of brands in M&As, we collected data on a wide variety of industries. Out of the target companies, 31.58 % operate in the business services industry and 9% in the measurement instruments industry. Among the acquirer organizations, 24.81% operate in the business services industry and 12.78% in the industrial, commercial machinery, and computer equipment industries.

Findings

Acquirers' Characteristics

Diversity of Brand Portfolio: The diversity of an acquirer's brand portfolio affects its cash flow expectations from its target's brands. We find that, as we have hypothesized earlier, acquirers with high diversity in their brand portfolios attribute a high value to their targets' brand portfolios. I will now discuss the concept of diversity in brand portfolios and why the diversity in acquirers brand portfolios affect their cash flow-related expectations from their targets' brand portfolio.

Companies follow one of the following brand portfolio strategies —corporate brand strategy, house-of-brands strategy, or mixed brand portfolio strategy (Laforet and Saunders, 1994 and 1999). These strategies affect the structure of companies' brand portfolios. We have tried to capture the aspect of a brand portfolio that is affected by a company's branding strategy with the concept of diversity in a brand portfolio, i.e., the extent to which a company chooses to serve markets with different brands. For example, those that follow a corporate branding strategy tend to have one or a few brands. Since these companies enter new markets or product categories, they use the same brand name (for example, General Electric). In such cases, the diversity of their brand portfolios is very low, because only a few brands are used in a wide variety of businesses. At the other end, some companies follow the house-of-brands strategy. In this case, they use different brands across markets. If such a company enters a new product market, it creates a new brand that is positioned to serve the particular product market. The diversity of a company's brand portfolio that follows a house-of-brands strategy is high due to its using different brands across markets.

Our analysis indicates that an acquirer's brand portfolio strategy has an important effect on its cash flow-related expectations from its target's brands. The direction of the effect is such that acquirers with a high diversity in their brand portfolios tend to attribute higher value to their targets' brands. This confirms our expectations about the relationship between the diversity of acquirers' brand portfolios and their targets' brand value relationship. Acquirers with a high diversity in their brand portfolios are more likely to retain their targets' brands following M&As. On the contrary, acquirers that have a low diversity in their brand portfolios generally divest most of, if not all, their targets' brands following the transactions. This difference is the outcome of variations in companies' branding strategy approaches.

The choice between having a high vs low diversity in brand portfolios is affected by a company's preference for customized benefits over economies of scale, or vice-versa. Those with a high diversity in their brand portfolios enjoy the benefits of customizing each brand to their target markets' needs. Such companies tend to spend more on marketing than those that have fewer brands. Their key strategy is to generate higher revenues by enhanced positioning. Therefore, such companies are more likely to retain more of their acquired brands. Consequently, their cash flow-related expectations from their targets' brands are also higher. On the contrary, companies that have a low diversity in their brand portfolios spend less on marketing because they only own one or a few brands. They are not able to customize their brands to the specific needs of different markets. Such companies are more likely to divest most of their targets' brands following M&As. A recent review of 207 M&As completed since 1995 reveals that target brands are divested in 39.6% of transactions (Ettenson and Knowles, 2006). A case in point, following the merger between AT&T and SBC, AT&T (which has a very low diversity in its brand portfolio) decided to abandon its popular Cingular brand and logo in 2007 (Cuneo, 2006)

Marketing capability: We found that that acquirers with strong marketing capabilities attribute a higher value to their targets' brand portfolios. An acquirer's marketing capability refers to its ability to efficiently combine a number of marketing resources in order to engage in productive activity and attain its marketing objectives (Amit and Schoemaker, 1993). Companies, even ones that operate in the same industry, have varying degrees of marketing capabilities (Dutta, Narasimhan, and Rajiv, 1999). One of the reasons for the variability in acquirers' bids for the same target or strategic assets is the difference in the capabilities of potential acquirers of the assets. Some companies have superior marketing skills compared to their competitors. "Marketing competent" acquirers can leverage their targets' brands more effectively by (1) earning the same or higher revenue by spending fewer marketing dollars, thereby leading to expectations of an increased cash flow; (2) extending targets' brands to new markets more efficiently by enabling the expectation of a higher growth in their cash flow; (3) co-branding targets' brands with existing brands more efficiently, leading to higher expectations of cash flow, or (4) withstanding competitive pressures from other brands better, leading to reduced volatility/vulnerability of expected cash flows, and consequently lower discount rates. The analysis confirms all of this. On an average, acquirers with strong marketing capabilities attribute a high value to acquired brands.

Target Characteristics

Brand Portfolio Strategy: The diversity of a target's brand portfolio affects the acquirer's cash flow-related expectations from the former's brands. We find that (as we have hypothesized) acquirers attribute a higher value to more diverse brand portfolios. Their intuition tells them that brand portfolios with low diversity provide lower growth opportunities, and that brand portfolios with lower diversity do not provide many extension opportunities because the few brands in the target's brand portfolio are already extended to many markets. However, when the diversity of a target's brand portfolio is high, i.e., it serves markets with multiple brands, an acquirer has the flexibility to choose one it would like to extend to new markets. The importance of extension-related options has been also voiced by executives involved in M&As. For example, when Liz Claiborne acquired Prana (a maker of apparel for climbing, yoga, and outdoor activities), Paul Charron, CEO of Liz Claiborne, argued that Prana provided strategic brand extension-related opportunities in non-apparel categories (Ryan, 2005). Similarly, following AOL/Time Warner's acquisition of IPC Media, Michael Pepe, CEO of Time International Inc., contended that IPC Media had a brand portfolio in the publishing business that provided extension-related opportunities (Brech, 2001). Therefore, it is clear that the presence of extension-related options increases an acquirer's level and growth of cash flow-related expectations from an acquired brand portfolio.

Marketing capability: We find that, as we have already hypothesized, a target's marketing capability positively affects the acquirer's cash flow-related expectations from the former's brand portfolio. However, the relationship has two caveats. First, a target company that has a stronger marketing capability will be more profitable than its competitors. This is supported by prior empirical findings (Dutta, Narasimhan, and Rajiv, 1999). Second, the target company's marketing capability may be an insurance against existing and potential competitive pressures. Consequently, the acquirer's volatility- and vulnerability-related expectations associated with cash flows from the target's brands will be much lower. Less risky cash flows lead to higher brand value.

Do These Factors Affect Brand Value in the Same Way under All Conditions?

The short answer is no. If the acquirer is buying a competitor, the impact of the diversity of the former's brand portfolio and the target's marketing capability on brand value changes. We find that when the acquirer and the target operate in the same industry, the impact of the diversity of the acquirer's brand portfolio and the target's marketing capability on a brand value is lower. These findings are based on the concept of redundancy.

When the acquirer and the target operate in the same industry, the redundancy between the acquirer and the target's brands are greater (Varadarajan, DeFanti, and Busch, 2006). Acquirers with diverse brand portfolios suffer more from redundancy compared to acquirers with less diverse brand portfolios because the former have more brands targeted at different consumer segments within the same industry. The overlap among brand portfolios causes cannibalization of cash flows. Consequently, to minimize this, the acquirer's propensity to retain its target's brands is lower. Only a few brands retained lead to a lower level of cash flow-related expectations from target brands.

In order to understand the impact of redundancy on the relationship between the diversity of an acquirer's brand portfolio and brand value, we performed a simulation. As illustrated in Figure 17.1, when the acquirer and the target operated in the same industry, the value attributed to the latter's brands decreased (on an average by 43.22 %—from US$163.8 million to US$93 million). On the other hand, when the acquirer and the target operated in different industries, the value attributed to the latter's brands increased by 76.11% (from US$20.1 million to US$35.5 million) when the diversity in the acquirer brand portfolio changed from low to high. When the acquirer and the target operate in the same industry, this situation leads to redundancy between the acquirer's and the

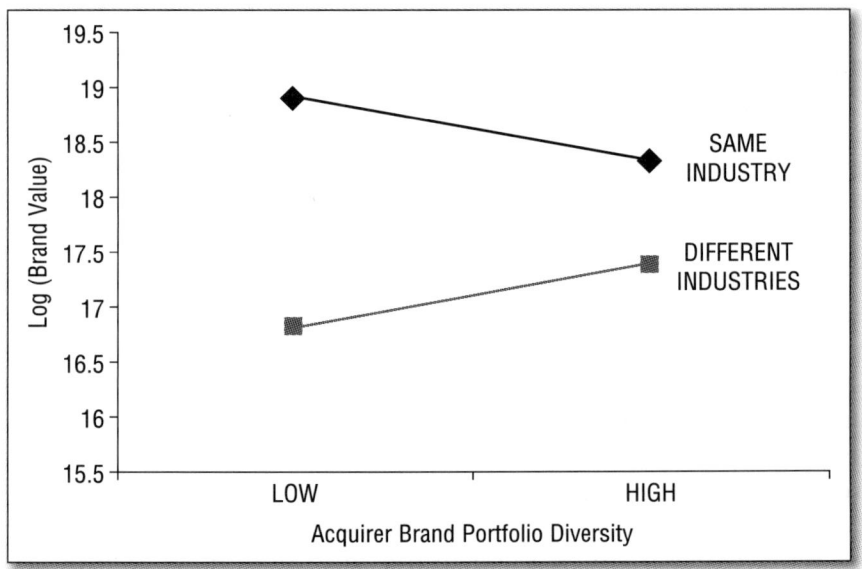

Source: Bahadir, Bharadwaj, and Srivastava, 2008.

Figure 17.1 Diversity in Acquirer's Brand Portfolio—Brand Value Relationship: Impact of Redundancy

target's marketing capabilities. There may also be overlaps between the skills of the acquirer's and the target's marketing personnel. In such cases, the acquirer may put less of a premium on the target's marketing ability to generate additional cash flows since the former as similar capabilities. In extreme cases of overlap the the marketing capabilities of the target and the acquirer, the latter may deploy the former's marketing personnel elsewhere (Capron and Hulland, 1999). In the case of redundancy between the target and the acquirer's marketing capabilities, the target's ability to affect the acquirer's cash flow-related expectations from the former's brand portfolio will be inhibited.

In order to understand the impact of redundancy on the relationship between target marketing capability and target brand value, we performed a simulation. The impact of target marketing capability on the brand value of a target is lower when the target and the acquirer operate in same industry, compared to when they conduct their business in different industries. As shown in Figure 17. 2, when the acquirer and the target operate in the same industry, the value of the target's brands decreases as its marketing

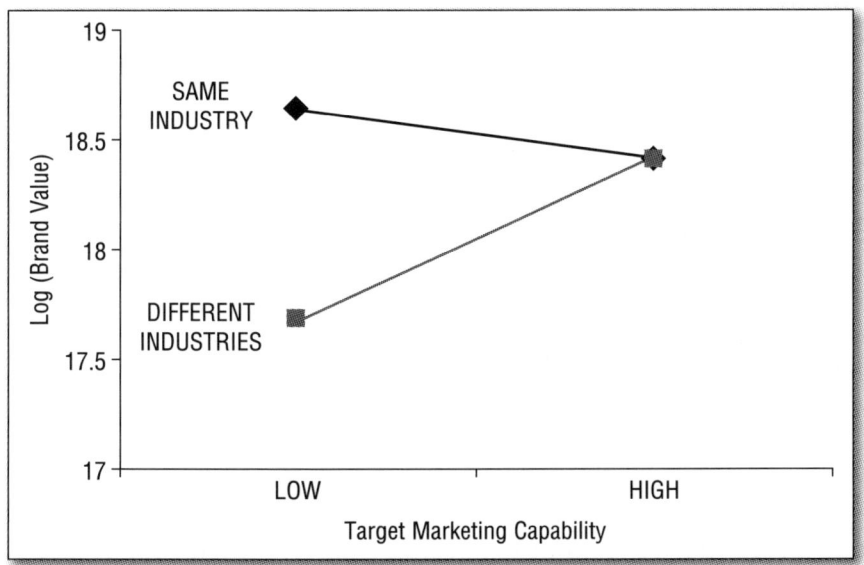

Source: Bahadir, Bharadwaj, and Srivastava, 2008.

Figure 17.2 Target Marketing Capability: Brand Value Relationship—Impact of Redundancy

capability increases. The average reduction in value placed on the target's brands is 20.48% (from US$125.1 million to US$99.5 million). This suggests that the acquirer operating in the same industry as the target places a lower premium on the target's marketing capabilities due to the redundancy between the acquirer's and the target's marketing capabilities. However, when the target and the acquirer operate in different industries, the average increase in value attributed to the target's brands was 108.16% (from US$47.7 million to US$99. million) when its marketing capability increased from low to high.

Managerial Implications

Our findings have managerial implications, especially for companies planning to be involved in M&As. First, executives who are grooming their companies for an M&A transaction need to be cognizant of their potential acquirers' marketing capabilities as well as their brand portfolio-related strategies. They may seek acquirers with strong marketing capabilities and a high diversity in their brand portfolios in order to get a higher price for their brands. However, if the potential buyer is a competitor of the target company, then a high diversity in its brand portfolio may reduce the price due to potential redundancies between the brand portfolios of the two companies.

Second, target companies need to recognize the significance of an organization's marketing capabilities as well as the diversity of its brand portfolio. Targets with strong marketing capabilities can negotiate higher prices for their brands because this assures acquirer companies about the future performance of its brand portfolios. Targets with diverse brand portfolios can charge higher prices for their brands (or acquirers may be more willing to pay) because diverse portfolios provide strategic options for an acquirer. If a company follows a single brand strategy, it could consider limiting the number of businesses to which its brand is extended, and after a certain threshold of extension, it may be better for it to use new brands.

REFERENCES

Amit, Raphael and Paul Schoemaker (1993), "Strategic Assets and Organizational Rent," *Strategic Management Journal*, 14(1), 33–46.

Bahadir, S. Cem, Sundar G. Bharadwaj, and Rajendra K. Srivastava (2008), "Financial Value of Brands in Mergers and Acquisitions: Is Value in the Eye of the Beholder?" Journal of Marketing, 72(6), 49–64.

Brech, Poppy (2001), "Brands Behind the Time-IPC Deal," *Marketing*, August 2, 19.

Capron, Laurence and John Hulland (1999), "Redeployment of Brands, Sales Forces, and General Marketing Management Expertise Following Horizontal Acquisitions: A Resource-Based View," *Journal of Marketing*, 63(2), 41–54.

Cuneo, Alice Z. (2006), "AT&T Plans to Kill Cingular Brand," *Advertising Age*, May 2. Available at http://adage.com/article/news/t-plans-kill-cingular-brand/108937/

Dutta, Shantanu, Om Narasimhan, and Surendra Rajiv (1999), "Success in High-Technology Markets: Is Marketing Capability Critical?" *Marketing Science*, 18(4), 547–568.

Ettenson, Richard and Jonathan Knowles (2006), "Merging the Brands and Branding the Merger," *Summer 2006 Research Feature*, July 1. Available at http://sloanreview.mit.edu/article/speaking-in-tongues/

Laforet, Sylie, and John Saunders (1994), "Managing Brand Portfolios: How Leaders Do It," *Journal of Advertising Research*, 34(5), 64–76.

——— (1999), "Managing Brand Portfolios: Why Leaders Do What They Do," *Journal of Advertising Research*, 39(1), 51–66.

Rao, Vithala R. and Manoj K. Agarwal, and Denise Dahlhoff (2004), "How Is Manifest Branding Strategy Related to the Intangible Value of a Corporation?" *Journal of Marketing*, 68(4), 126–141.

Ryan, Thomas J. (2005), "Liz Claiborne Acquires Prana," *SGB*, 38(12), 15.

Mizik, Natalie and Robert Jacobson (2007), "Myopic Marketing Management: Evidence of the Phenomenon and Its Long-Term Performance Consequences in the SEO Context," *Marketing Science*, 26(3), 361–379

Varadarajan, Rajan P., Mark P. DeFanti, and Paul S. Busch (2006), "Brand Portfolio, Corporate Image, and Reputation: Managing Brand Deletions," *Journal of the Academy of Marketing Science*, 34(2), 195–205.

Chapter 18
Role of Brands in Managing Innovations

Rajendra K. Srivastava

INTRODUCTION

Brands play a critical role in creating perceived value in innovations for customers. They also develop competitive advantages and extract financial value for their owners. Companies need to learn how to leverage their brands, or these will continue to be unutilized—or at least underutilized—tools that could benefit them but do not because their value and use are not understood by their owners.

INNOVATION AND INVENTION

Today, innovation is both overused and misinterpreted. It is confused with invention and development of technology. However, invention means scientific discovery. Henry Ford did not invent an automobile. He did find ways to manufacture them more efficiently in the assembly line mode. Sustainable business innovation has three requirements—they must create value for businesses and customers, overcome societal challenges while conserving resources, and be in tune with markets' needs and contexts. Innovation is simply finding ways of adding value by making and/or marketing effective products, processes, new uses of existing technologies or pathways to markets. Simply put, innovation is doing things better.

BRANDING INNOVATIONS

The dramatic rise and recent decline of Apple's stock is a case study of the inseparable link between innovation and branding on a company's pathway to success—in doing things better. However, it is not only about technology. Other organizations have access to or have developed similar technologies earlier than Apple. But Apple developed a more attractive design, encouraged an army of collaborators to formulate applications for Apple products by creating a win-win platform where the partner (and, of course, Apple!) can make money. And, Apple's strong brand has held this "eco-system" together. If we were to ask whether the company's brand has:

- Enhanced its profitability?
- Provided a platform for its future growth?
- Provided protection against competition?

The answer to each would be a resounding "yes." Apple's string of successes across its iPod, iPhone, iPad, computer, and laptop stores have embued the company with an aura of near invincibility so that customers and investors understandably think it is bound to succeed "disruptive innovation" in any market it enters. Although the company's recent decline is perhaps due to its failure to disrupt the television market via iTV, it can also be attributed to the combined success of two of its key competitors, Google and Samsung, collectively and individually.

BRANDING AND VALUE CREATION

Nevertheless, Apple is selling at the time book or balance sheet value. This is if the market value is in excess of property, plant and equivalent, and other traditional assets (including cash). What is this incremental value? Apple is not alone in accumulating and leveraging these intangible, off-balance sheet or market-based assets (MBAs) (Srivastava, Shervani, and Fahey, 1998). These include brands, customers (for example, subscription services such as Telco's), distribution (for example, Coca-Cola's) and partner networks (for example, Microsoft and Google's) as well as human capital (for example, Accenture's) and intellectual capital. Brands, as intangible assets, enable companies to grow, to ward off competition, and negotiate with distributors.

Srivastava, Shervani, and Fahey (1998 and 1999) underscore the importance of the ability of companies to enhance their market value on which depends their future profitability, growth and risk. This involves the role of the brand in "selling a vision of the future" to relevant stakeholders (shareholders, partners, employees, and partners). It also includes a belief in the ability of Apple and now the Samsung brand to grow by disrupting markets, as well in convincing stakeholders that a company is taking the right steps (in its investments and targeted growth) to make its future more sustainable and predictable, less vulnerable to competitive moves or technological surprises and by putting in place "de-risking" strategies (for example, increasing brand loyalty, customer switching costs, or engaging customers in long-term contracts).

The research, development and engineering community has long used the concept of technology or product platforms to justify investment in intangible assets—by assessing the role of these platforms in containing costs, and enhancing growth and profitability while reducing competitive risks, especially opportunities with long-term payoffs. Since brands provide the same business performance-related benefits, it is important for marketers to demonstrate how investments in customer platforms provide an even more compelling opportunity in emerging networked markets, and how connectivity with customers can be managed across related markets to develop sustainable competitive advantages. This is achieved by developing the concept of brand platforms that can enable marketers to better manage their organic growth and business risk, while simultaneously reducing their go-to-market costs.

ROLE OF BRANDS IN INNOVATION PROCESSES

Companies are slowly recognizing the fact that innovation is not only about technology and new products, but about transforming the management of their businesses. It is also clear to them that their erstwhile business models will not work unless they keep pace with and innovate with the changing marketplace. While research on such innovation is becoming popular, for the purpose of this chapter, innovation carries the more traditional connotations of not just technological breakthroughs for the production of a commercially viable product, but also use of technology to improve existing situations. It discusses and analyzes in depth the ways in which a strong brand helps in the innovation process.

So what is the connection between branding and innovation? In one sense, both, particularly product innovation, serve the same purpose, i.e., to enable the development of a profitable, strong and well-differentiated product from others in the market. A great brand is far better than a great product because it not only satisfies customers' practical needs and service aspects, but also goes beyond to gauge their desires and deliver on an unwritten, yet expected reputational promise.

BRANDS CREATE MARKET IMPERFECTIONS

Therefore, brand equity is important because it moves a customer along a continuum of expectations—starting from the functional benefit of a product (which is provided by technological innovations, but can perhaps be reproduced by another product) to the benefits that accrue due to positive experiences that translate into emotional attachment to a product or service. A final component of brand equity is attributable to aspirational benefits (owning a Porsche as opposed to a Toyota), which another brand of the same product category cannot reproduce. Therefore, it is clear that the experiential and aspirational components of brands create strong market imperfections (barriers to competition), providing opportunities for pricing flexibility, as well as offering leverage of both offensive and defensive strategies. The brand creates a powerful attachment for the product.

Brands that are off-balance sheet assets can thus affect key value drivers in several ways. An ultimate commodity product is one where the slightest change in price would result in a substantial change in demand. However, by creating differentiation, a strong brand ensures that such commoditization is overcome, which leads to a period of competitive advantage. It is the constant cycle of innovation that creates this differentiation. Strong brands improve share and margin premiums. For example, Samsung can charge more than HTC for products with similar features. Companies with market clout can be leveraged to negotiate lower distribution costs. Nike uses its brand to negotiate better terms with distributors such as Footlocker. Strong brands such as Apple and Samsung have a loyal following. Other robust "family brands" that stretch across multiple product categories (for example, Honda across cars, motor cycles, wet-bikes, power generators, snowmobiles, and other products) and have large customer bases witness higher productivity in their marketing efforts across products and channels. Leading brands are able to penetrate markets for new products faster than less popular ones—an invaluable advantage in short-cycle environments.

Collectively, these competitive and financial benefits create market imperfections or structural barriers to competition, i.e., brands "de-commoditize" markets and serve as legal monopolies. They enable incremental cash flows that are more predictable and stable, less susceptible to competition, and therefore, more sustainable. In addition, they increase profitability and growth while "de-risking" corporate performance. Research has clearly shown that brands and marketing make a clear impact on financial performance. For instance, when Proctor & Gamble purchased Gillette, around 85% of the payment was considered to be due to the latter's brand name.

Therefore, as summarized in Figure 18.1, compared to low equity brands, high equity ones enable companies to charge a price premium, garner an additional market share and have the potential to improve negotiation terms with suppliers, and thereby, contribute directly to improve their revenue growth rates, cash flows and earning margins.

COST OF NOT INNOVATING

While the key foundation stone for ongoing brand equity is undoubtedly the creation of innovative products, as is clear in the case of Apple, this chapter focuses on the reverse phenomenon—how does

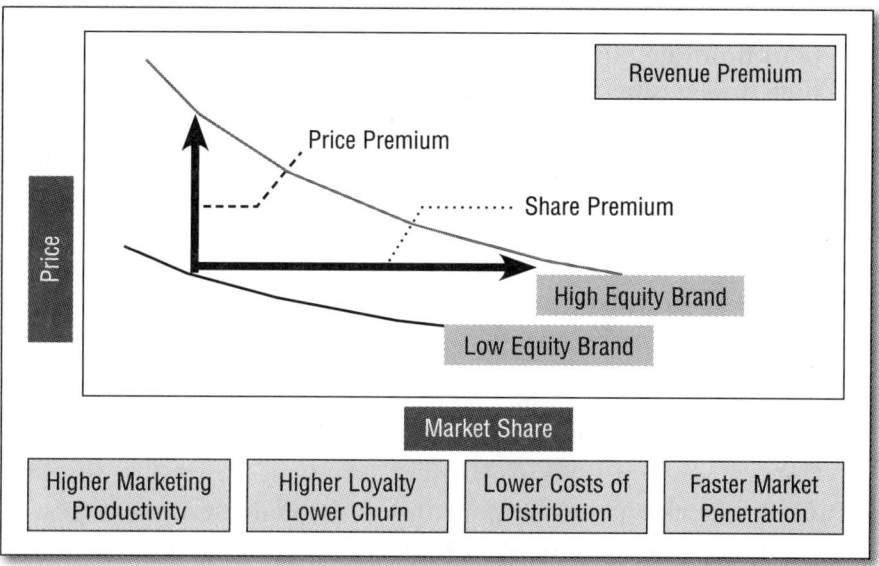

Figure 18.1 Impact of Brands and Marketing on Financial Performance

a strong brand help in the innovation process? This is an important question, because a company may often not taste success, despite having a highly innovative product, due to lapses in the ensuing steps to ensure that maximum possible value is captured out of the product. A frequently cited example is that of Xerox, which many believe lost out on its viability, since it could not successfully convert some of its excellent technological innovations into commercially viable product offerings. Therefore, over and above creation of innovation-based new ventures, successful innovation depends on market insights and knowledge of processes on how to bring these to market. And this is where a brand, particularly one recognized as being innovative, is far more successful in extracting value out of the innovation.

Brands and technological innovation are complementary strategic components that rely on each other. In the long run, brands cannot be a substitute for technological incompetence. This has been demonstrated by the disappearance of many a brand. This year, we have seen the last Kodak moment. Philips has conceded defeat in consumer electronics. Panasonic and Sony are at Samsung's mercy. Dell and HP are now under threat from Lenovo, a company rising from the earlier shrinking IBM Thinkpad. These companies largely failed to innovate. In part, they did not innovate and adapt their products and business processes to the requirements of growth segments or for emerging markets.

In the next few sections, we will discuss the role of brands as a platform to launch and manage innovation. We will elaborate on how the strength of a brand enables an innovative company to penetrate a market faster, and thereby ensures far greater extraction of value from its product innovation.

STAGES OF PRODUCT LIFE CYCLE

Generally speaking, a company goes through several stages of innovation. At inception, its focus is on product innovation or technological leadership, targeting and attracting customers by offering products that are "different" with an improved perceived value over those of competing products. It may also innovate by finding new applications for its existing products. At the height of technological prowess, it could opt for disruptive innovation to bring about such a dramatic change in a product or service that the existing market is completely unsettled. An example of this is when Nintendo launched its Wii game, which was a small, cheap and easy to use product, which completely disrupted the video-game industry that was then dominated by the technologically superior Sony's PlayStation and Microsoft's Xbox.

During the middle phases, a company focus on innovation shifts to business and market innovation through several means such as by expanding the range of the products it offers or improving its cost structure by integrating/bundling products, etc. At this stage, innovation is not relates to product design, but is also of a process innovation type, which looks at pursuing and optimizing efficiencies in productivity. This is seen in the case of Zara, which has created a business model of strong value to deliver its upscale and high-fashion apparel and accessories at reasonable prices. The brand is kept rejuvenated by Zara ensuring that its constant product innovation with fresh and differentiated designs, along with its process innovation strategy of maintaining low inventories, fast design cycles

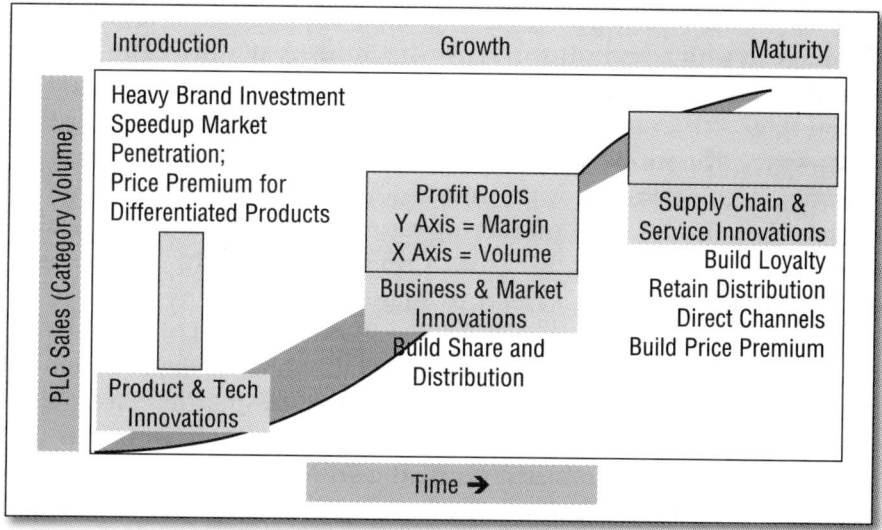

Figure 18.2 Role of Brands at Different Stages of the Product Life Cycle (Contingent Strategies and Relevant Metrics)

and flexible manufacturing enable it to achieve a high degree of operational excellence. With superior customer management skills as the third key prong of its strategy, it comes as no surprise that Zara continues to be the favorite of its shareholders.

At the tail end, a company can also look at category renewal either through organic innovation or acquisitions.[1] An apt example is that of Cisco, which has frequently outsourced innovation to enhance its product lines through acquisitions. Another approach may be for a company to focus on service innovation to augment the value of its offering by bundling maintenance services and complimentary product upgrades into the price, thereby increasing its margins. Figure 18.2 summarizes earlier discussed points relating to the role of brands at different stages of the innovation life cycle, and how profit pools move from high-margins and low volume to low margins and high volume over their lifecycles.

The stages of innovation we have already discussed can also be linked to the cycles in the industry or market in which a brand

---

[1] Moore, G. (2005) "Dealing with Darwin: How Great Companies Innovate at Every Phase of Their Evolution", scpd.stanford.edu/dtu/pdf_courses/Dealing%20With%20Darwin/CHAPTER4.pdf (accessed 10 May 2010).

operates, since the degree of acceptance of innovation depends on the stage at which an industry is. As the industry matures, the impact of innovation in terms of risk and value decreases. Therefore, at the initial stage, for example, when a disruptive innovation bursts into a white space, the innovation is at high risk, but also typically gets high rewards. With market growth, innovation generally shifts to focusing on business model- and marketing-based innovation that is geared to capture share during the growth phase. Finally, with a slowdown in the market, there is a need to manage profitability in the face of increasing competition and decreasing demand. This requires a focus on supply-chain innovation (operational excellence), where the risk-return rates tend to become more moderate. Moreover, when the market is becoming saturated, a product begins to get commoditized, and innovation introduced invariably comprises low risk and low return services and solutions.

ROLE OF BRANDS IN EXTRACTING VALUE FROM INNOVATION

A company (brand) chooses to follow a different strategy, depending on what stage its product is in its life cycle as well as the maturity of the market. The role of the brand shifts with the company's strategy at each of these stages because a strong brand plays a key role in supporting its initiatives at innovation management and also in extracting value from its innovation. This is illustrated in Figure 18.3 in the context of Samsung Electronics.

ROLE OF BRANDS AT THE LAUNCH (INTRODUCTION) STAGE

How does a powerful brand enable fast and successful extraction of value from a newly innovated product? To begin with, at the very inception or product development stage, powerful brands are known to reduce the capital cost of their entry into new categories, thereby lowering their capital expenditure outlay.

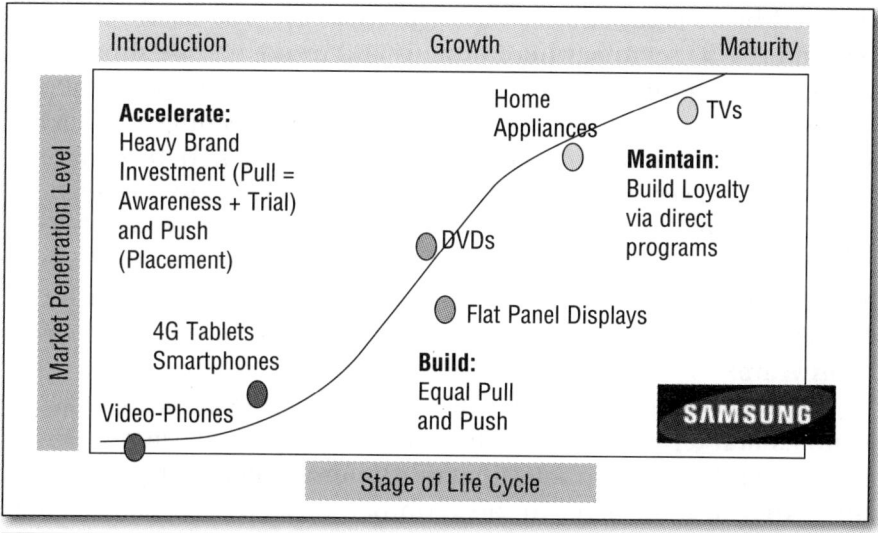

Source: Samsung Electronics—Worldwide Marketing Operations, 2004.

Figure 18.3 Strategies, Relevant Metrics Depend on Stage of Product Life Cycle and Competition

However, most importantly, strong brands also typically witness fast market penetration, which is particularly true in the case of new product innovation. Customers are more willing to try out new products, or as seen in the case of an Apple product, even queue up to do so. When Starbucks decided to enter China, and more recently, announced its plans to enter India, its entry became relatively easy, since most of its target consumers were already aware of its brand. This is extremely important, because on the whole, markets tend to resist new concepts and products, and only accept a select few—and that too reluctantly. However, for a company, the potential for reaping attractive rewards from innovation is a prospect that it finds difficult to resist, despite the risks involved,.

Another significant benefit of a strong brand while launching a product is that it offers the company an opportunity to enter a market late, which may be essential in some instances where the larger eco-system required to support the product has to first be developed before it can gain acceptance. This naturally has to be balanced by the advantages it would gain from riding on a first mover advantage and creating a strong market for its product before it is imitated by its competitors. This is particularly true in the technology and FMCG sectors, where designs and trends can be short-lived. However, sometimes, as seen in the case of Apple, a company may choose to delay its entry into the market and pushing for accelerated market penetration. As Steve Jobs commented on catching technology waves in 2008, "Things happen fairly slowly, you know. They do. These waves of technology, you can see them way before they happen, and you just have to choose wisely which ones you're going to surf. If you choose unwisely, then you can waste a lot of energy, but if you choose wisely, it actually unfolds fairly slowly. It takes years."[2]

While a strong brand offers a company the opportunity to accelerate its market penetration, and thereby helps it develop a strong position early in a product's life cycle, it also offers the brand-owner the luxury to enter late. In fact, companies such as Coca-Cola and General Electric, with their strong brands and channels, often rely on other, generally smaller, more entrepreneurial companies to take market risks associated with innovation. Only when they are assured of the market demand and prospects, do they enter the market. Therefore, as seen in Figure 18.4, the time factor is an important contribution made by a brand when a company launches a new innovation.

However, at this stage, it is also important to consider the differences between innovation in short-cycle markets and long-cycle ones. In short-cycle markets such as fashion and technology, speed may be of the essence. A brand would need to quickly penetrate the market through its existing customer base and awareness-related benefits. However, in long-cycle markets, such as insurance, it is building customer loyalty that is important. A strong brand pulls innovation out of a short-cycle market and pushes it into a long-cycle one by making customers hesitant to switch loyalties. This was seen in the case of Microsoft Word when it was launched in 1983 and was one of the many word-processing programs available at that time. However, by leveraging the brand across its many launches, and bundling its products and services to create unique

---

[2] Excerpted from *The Wide Lens* by Ron Adner, Portfolio Penguin, 2012.

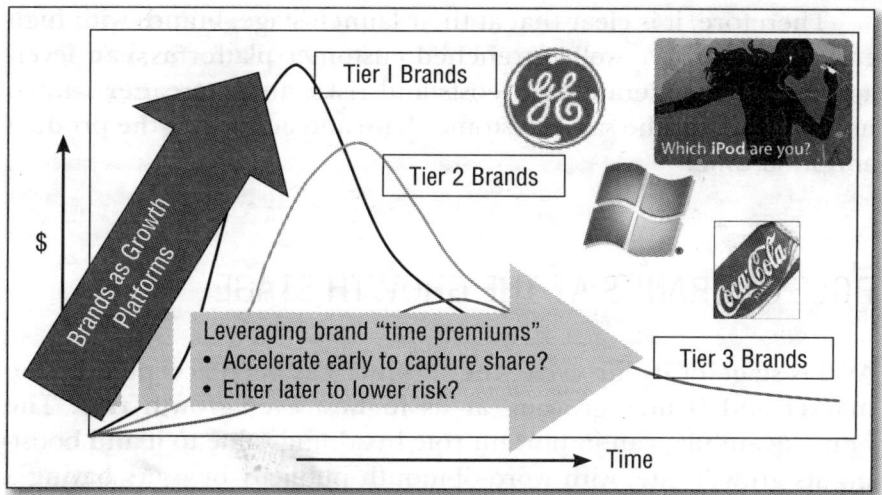

Figure 18.4 Brand Platforms as Strategic Growth Options

value, it has since proved to be one of the most durable products from the Microsoft suite by making it difficult for customers to switch to other brands.

Another key factor to consider while discussing the role of a brand in creating value from a company's innovative product launch is its influence on the larger environment or network of assets required to sell the innovation. After all, it is not the best products that win, but the best networked ones that lead the race. Chief among these would include the company's relationship with its distribution channels and the other players in the supply chain. Shelf space allocated to a new product is perhaps one of the most tangible measures of the value of a brand.

A successful brand also enables a company to enter multi-lateral relations, as seen in the case of Google. Because the brand can expand the market horizon, this also enables it to increase its global reach. Another example of such a brand is Dell Computers, which decided to base its business model on volume and innovation in terms of its just-in-time inventory and supply chain management processes. The company went online, and soon found that over 30% of its customers resided in locations where they had been no distribution network earlier.

Therefore, it is clear that at their launch stage, brands with high equity, which have well-entrenched customer platforms, can leverage these to moderate their costs and risks, and thereafter launch new products to the same customer base and accelerate the product adoption time.

ROLE OF BRANDS AT THE GROWTH STAGE

At this stage of its life cycle, the product has been accepted by the market and is now growing at its highest ever growth rate. The brand again plays an important role in adding value to it and boosting its growth rate, with word-of-mouth publicity by users having a far greater influence on non-users than in the case of an unknown brand. At the acceptance stage, the value of the brand was more visible in the speed at which it enabled penetration of the new product in the market. However, at this stage, the principal role of a strong brand is providing protection to a company against competition and thereby controlling its market share by acting as a clear differentiator from other products. The new product now begins enjoying the many benefits of the brand because it has become valuable to its distributors.

It is at this stage that a company begins to look at process innovation. One of the most well-known brands in the world and a business model that is often spoken about is Southwest Airlines. While many companies have tried to replicate the original low-cost, no-frills, fun and easy services Southwest Airlines offered, they have not achieved significant success in their endeavors. This is because Southwest Airlines has continued to innovate its processes, ensuring that these maintain consistent operational excellence through its various strategies of keeping overheads low. It should also be noted that by this stage, as suppliers have also probably started taking advantage of economies of scale, process innovation is further hastened. A company should now be typically offering increased margins to its strategic partners, since it has more to share. In some instances of original equipment manufacturers with strong brands, their partners are offered funding for research to enable technical support that supports further innovation at the growth phase of products.

A successful recognizes that to capture true value out of its innovation, it needs to demonstrate clear and tangible gains to its supply chain partners. It has to accept that it is not the most innovative product that wins, but the best networked ones that do so. Otherwise, the market would hesitate to accept products. A prime example of this is television, which gained extensive acceptance as a mass media product in the USA almost 30 years after it was first introduced in the late 1920s—only when people were convinced that there were an adequate number of media partners and channels to make the purchase of product television a worthwhile proposition. Consequently, in the current scenario, there is an even greater need to move toward innovation in business models with a focus on multi-process excellence and exploitation of networked markets.

ROLE OF BRANDS AT THE MATURITY/SATURATION STAGE

At this stage of the market's life cycle, a strong brand is of great value because it helps to stem the product's decline. The brand also protects the product's market share, which would have otherwise declined fairly rapidly. It ensures that existing customers continue purchasing the product due to their loyalty to the brand. Therefore, at this stage, one can really appreciate the difference between a product's life cycle and a brand's life cycle, with the brand offering protection to the product and thereby extending its life. This was observed in the case of Sony's cassette-based Walkman. From its launch in 1979, the company has sold almost 220 million such devices.[3] However, by the late 1990s, it was becoming increasingly evident that the product was becoming obsolete in the wake of emerging digital technologies with compact discs and MiniDiscs. However, it was only as late as October 2010 that Sony discontinued manufacturing Walkmans in Japan for its various overseas markets.

---

[3] CBC News (October 25, 2010), "Sony stops Walkman production in Japan," http://www.cbc.ca/news/story/2010/10/25/con-walkman-manufacture.html (accessed July 1, 2012).

It is therefore clear that strong brands enable products to maintain their position in challenging times. It also makes it easier for companies to explore new markets and enables alternative distribution channels to be sourced. In addition, this ensures that organizations can fully exploit their networks of strategic partners and come up with new ideas to innovate further and thereby further reinvention of their products.

WHAT WE CAN CONCLUDE

Brands have an definite and key role to play in extracting from and adding value to an innovation. If we analyze Apple's strong performance, it is evident that its strong growth is not only on account of its well thought out and tightly innovative products, but also because of its strong brand, which enables its products to penetrate the market quickly, and diversify and cross-sell with ease by providing a platform for their global growth. By opting to control its distribution channels and the entire customer experience, Apple ensures that its brand has remained one of the most trusted and wanted brands in the world. Furthermore, please note that Apple Stores contribute to customers' satisfaction and comfort in doing business with the company. Their experiences translate into a brand dimension that competitors such as Dell or HP cannot match. This makes it far easier for Apple to commercialize its next new product innovation.

The value a brand brings may differ in certain scenarios, such as in a short- cycle market versus a long-cycle one. However, it is clear that a strong brand reduces the perceived risk of trial for a customer, who may hesitate to try out an unknown product made by an unknown manufacturer. A robust brand therefore accelerates its acceptance rate by creating a circle of trust into which customers are willing to venture, and thereafter through accelerated trials and referrals. The brand improves the market productivity of the new product by allowing trust in the marketplace to be leveraged. It also affords a company the luxury of entering a market late when its required eco-system is in place.

A robust brand name enables reduction of the cost of innovation. It makes easier negotiations with distributors, who are comfortable providing additional shelf space to the new product. In addition, it benefits the company by improving the availability and reach of the product, and also hopefully kick-starts a virtuous cycle where word-of-mouth promotion increases its reach. Consequently, the new product is able to reach out rapidly, and because the brand can expand the market horizon, the former is able to increase its global reach significantly.

BRANDS AS PLATFORMS FOR MANAGING PROFITABILITY, GROWTH, AND RISK

The R&D and engineering community often uses "product platforms" as a means to justify long-term investments in new technology. A relevant example of this is Honda's small engine technology platform, because the same engine can be used in motorcycles, wet-bikes, lawnmowers, snowmobiles, power generators, and so on, investments in the core technology can enhance product differentiation. Moreover, Honda's profitability across its products reduces its risks. Its competitors cannot match the company's investments in its core technology, its lower costs and investments due to shared R&D and inventory, and accelerated time to market. It can also outspend its competitors with fewer products on the same base technology. Brands provide the same competitive and financial benefits to a company. This is achieved through shared sales and distribution costs across products; faster time to market, acceptance and penetration; reduced risks due to brand loyalty, and transference of brand equity due to shared attributes and experiences. Quantification of these benefits will go a long way in justifying investments in brands and other market-based assets (Srivastava et al., 2010).

To conclude, it is clear that strong brands with their inbuilt promise of quality, reliability, and replicability are perhaps the best platform in a company's armory to create, extract and deliver value from its innovative products, and thereby promote excellence and add substantial value to it overall business model.

REFERENCES

Srivastava, Rajendra K., Tasadduq Shervani and Liam Fahey (1998), "Market-based Assets and Shareholder Value: A Framework for Analysis," *Journal of Marketing*, 62 (January), 1–14.

―――― (1999), "Marketing, Business Processes and Shareholder Value: An Organizationally Embedded View of Marketing Activities and the Discipline of Marketing," *Journal of Marketing*, 63 (Special Issue), 168–179.

Srivastava, Rajendra K., et al. (2010), "Brand Platforms as Strategic Investments: Leveraging Customer Connections to Manage Profitability, Growth, and Risk." In *The Connected Customer: The Changing Nature of Consumer and Business Markets*, 203. New York: Routledge. Available at https://www.worldcat.org/title/connected-customer-the-changing-nature-of-consumer-and-business-markets/oclc/419792840&referer=brief_results

About the Editors and Contributors

EDITORS

Rajendra K. Srivastava is Provost and Deputy President, Singapore Management University. A leading authority on the impact of marketing on business performance, he is frequently invited as a keynote speaker on topics such as business model innovation, marketing metrics, value of market-based intangible assets (brands, channels), and management of growth and risk. His work on assessing the impact of marketing strategies on business and financial performance has influenced both theory and practice on topics ranging from marketing accountability to strategic metrics across the globe. His paper linking market-based assets and market-facing processes to shareholder value in the *Journal of Marketing* received the Maynard Award for the article judged to contribute the most to the development of theory in marketing, the MSI/Paul Root Award for the article judged to contribute the most to the practice of marketing, as well as the AMA/Sheth Foundation Award for its long-term impact on marketing.

He has worked closely with industry and has provided executive training and consultancy services, largely in the technology/B2B and services sectors, to companies' executives spanning North America, Europe, Asia, and Africa. He has also served on the faculty of the University of Texas, Austin, and the Emory University, Atlanta, and has been a visiting faculty member at the London Business School, the Indian School of Business, and the Helsinki School of Economics. He has done B.Tech. (Mechanical Engineering) from the Indian Institute of Technology, Kanpur, MS (Industrial Engineering) from the University of Rhode Island, and MBA and PhD in business from the University of Pittsburgh.

Gregory Metz Thomas drives organic growth with evidence-based marketing, a vast portfolio of proven marketing methods, and excellent go-to-market execution. These include:

- Marketing strategy: value proposition, business models, and business strategy
- Brand management: 360 degree brand audit, brand identity, brand positioning, and brand architecture
- Digital marketing: platforms, social media, Search Engine Optimization (SEO), Search Engine Marketing (SEM), Electric Direct Marketing (EDM), and analytics
- Consumer insights: consumers' attitudes, preferences, and decision making
- Innovation management: innovation process, open innovation, and high-tech innovation

Gregory has worked in the USA and Asia, bringing to life issues of importance to managers. This includes his engagement on 70+ projects with several Fortune 500 brands such as Coca-Cola, Kimberly Clark, DuPont, Milliken & Co., Marriott, Leading Hotels of the World, Banyan Tree Hotels, Avaya, Lucent Technologies, InterContinental Hotel Group, Computer Sciences Corporation, Palladium, Sprint, Home Depot, ING, UPS, Electronic Arts, CMO Council, and Equifax.

He completed MBA from the McCombs Business School, the University of Texas and BSc from the University of California, Santa Cruz.

CONTRIBUTORS

Jeffrey Andrien is Managing Director of The Claro Group, a privately held financial advisory and management consulting firm in the United States. In this capacity, he provides expert witness testimony and consulting analyses on a wide range of litigation and business consulting matters, including those related to antitrust, intellectual property infringement, securities fraud and valuation. His clients include Fortune 500 companies, government agencies, international conglomerates, and major law firms.

In addition to his responsibilities as a consultant, he works as a visiting professor in the Masters in Marketing Program at the Thammasat University in Bangkok, Thailand, a post which he has held since 2006. He has also taught graduate-level courses at the Olin School of Business, the Washington University, St Louis, and at the McCombs School of Business, the University of Texas. He holds a BA degree in economics and an MBA degree from the University of Texas.

S. Cem Bahadir is Assistant Professor of Marketing at Ozyegin University. He previously served on the faculty at the University of South Carolina. His current research interests include strategic brand management, financial value of market-based assets, global brand management, and marketing issues in the initial public offering context. His research is published in journals such as *Journal of Marketing, Journal of International Business Studies, International Journal of Research in Marketing,* and *Journal of the Academy of Marketing Science.* A graduate of Istanbul Technical University, he holds an MS degree from the Marmara University, and PhD in business from the Emory University.

Paul Benoit is Founder and President of Nouvelle Analytics, LLC. He specializes in the valuation and licensing of intellectual property. He has provided economic testimony and consulting services in matters involving allegations of patent infringement, theft of trade secrets, breach of contract, business interruption, and fraud. His education includes BSc in Accountancy from the University of Mississippi and MBA from the Louisiana State University. He is a Certified Public Accountant and Certified Fraud Examiner.

Leslie de Chernatony has made a significant contribution to advancing knowledge about brand management. He now bridges the advancement of brand knowledge in his academic role with the application of brand knowledge in his consultancy role. He has undertaken pioneering work on brand management which has an international reputation. His cutting-edge work on strategically building brands has helped many organizations develop more effective brand strategies.

His research on brand marketing is globally disseminated through books, frequent international conference presentations, and a significant stream of international journal articles, some of which have won best paper prizes.

Leslie's work has resulted in TV programs and radio broadcasts. He is a frequent speaker at management conferences. Several major research grants helped him and his team investigate factors associated with brand success.

He has run many highly acclaimed management development workshops throughout Europe, the USA, the Middle East, Asia, and Australia. His advice has been sought by numerous organizations throughout the world on developing more effective brand strategies. On several occasions he has acted as an expert witness in court cases over branding issues.

Henrik Hagtvedt's primary research interests are in experiential consumer behavior, including art, aesthetics, and luxury. His research has appeared in *Journal of Marketing Research, Journal of Marketing, Journal of Consumer Research, Journal of Consumer Psychology, Journal of the Academy of Marketing Science, International Journal of Research in Marketing, NeuroImage,* and *Personality and Social Psychology Bulletin,* among other outlets.

His teaching interests include consumer behavior, luxury marketing, brand management, and international marketing. Having lived in seven countries on four continents, and having traveled extensively in dozens of countries around the world, he brings an international perspective to the classroom.

Prior to his doctoral studies, he studied painting at the Academy of Fine Arts in Florence, Italy, and he worked full time as an artist and exhibited internationally for several years. During these years, he had more than 25 major exhibitions in Europe and Asia. Additionally, he obtained a Cand. Mag. degree in art history at the University of Oslo, Norway, before completing an MBA (Marketing) and PhD in Business Administration (Marketing) at the University of Georgia. The initial art-related experiences sparked his interest in marketing and consumer behavior, and today this background still informs his research and areas of expertise.

Anupam Jaju is Associate Professor of Marketing in the School of Management at the George Mason University. He received his PhD in Business Administration (Marketing) from the Terry College of Business at the University of Georgia.

His research papers have been published or are forthcoming in *Journal of Academy of Marketing Science, Journal of International Management, Marketing Theory*, and *Marketing Education Review.*

His corporate experience includes working for ITW Signode (I) Ltd as Regional Sales Manager and Business Development Manager. Over the past several years, he has consulted for corporate clients such as NIIT (USA), memoryBLUE, Inc., AutoSmartCard, etc.

Jean-Noël Kapferer is acknowledged as one of the international forerunners in the study of brands and strategic brand management. He is the author of the original leading textbook *Strategic Brand Management*, now in its fifth edition. Known for his inspirational advanced work on brand identity, brand portfolio management, brand architectures, and most recently on prestige and luxury management, he is co-author of *The Luxury Strategy*, author of *How Luxury Brands Can Grow Yet Remain Rare* and of more than 100 articles published in American, European, and Asian journals. He won the American Marketing Association Award for the most influential contribution to marketing thinking for his article on "Local versus Multinational Brand Strategy" (2004).

An HEC Paris graduate and PhD from the Kellogg Business School, the Northwestern University, USA, he teaches strategic brand management all around the world: HEC Paris; Tsing Hua University, Beijing; Luxury Business Institute, Seoul.

Advisor to the President of INSEEC business schools, he is an active consultant to leading international corporations on brand strategy and also a sought-after speaker for conferences and executive seminars all around the world.

Kevin Lane Keller is the E. B. Osborn Professor of Marketing at the Tuck School of Business at the Dartmouth College, USA. He has degrees from Cornell, Carnegie-Mellon, and Duke Universities, and is acknowledged as one of the international leaders in the study of brands, branding, and strategic brand management. With over 90 published papers, his research has been widely cited and has received numerous awards.

Actively involved with industry, he has served as a consultant and advisor to marketers for some of the world's most successful brands, including Accenture, American Express, Disney, Ford, Intel, Levi Strauss, Procter & Gamble, SAB Miller, and Samsung. He has also served as executive director and academic trustee for the Marketing Science Institute.

Professor Keller is currently conducting a variety of studies that address strategies to build, measure, and manage brand equity. His textbook on those subjects, *Strategic Brand Management*, in its 4th edition, has been adopted at top business schools and leading firms around the world and has been heralded as the "bible of branding." He is also the co-author with Philip Kotler of the all-time best selling introductory marketing textbook, *Marketing Management*, now in its 15th edition.

V. Kumar is Regents Professor, Richard and Susan Lenny Distinguished Chair Professor of Marketing, and Executive Director, Center for Excellence in Brand and Customer Management, at the J. Mack Robinson College of Business, the Georgia State University, and Chang Jiang Scholar, the Huazhong University of Science and Technology, China. He has been recognized with eight lifetime achievement awards in marketing strategy, inter-organizational issues, retailing, business-to-business marketing, and marketing research from the American Marketing Association (AMA) and other professional organizations. He has also had the privilege and the honor of being named as the Editor-In-Chief of the *Journal of Marketing*, the number one ranked academic journal in the field of marketing.

He has published in many scholarly journals in marketing including the *Harvard Business Review, Sloan Management Review, Journal of Marketing, Journal of Marketing Research*, and *Marketing Science*. His books include *Managing Customers for Profit, Customer Relationship Management,* and *Marketing Research.*

He has been chosen as a "Legend in Marketing" where his work is published in a 10-volume encyclopedia with commentaries from scholars worldwide. He spends his "free" time visiting business leaders to identify challenging problems to solve. He plays tennis and basketball to relieve his stress arising out of being in academics.

Lluis Martinez-Ribes is Associate Professor at Esade Business School for the subjects Marketing Innovation and Retail Innovation. He has been a visiting professor at SDA Bocconi (Italy), and has lectured at the University of Edinburgh (UK), the University of St Gallen (Switzerland), HEC (France), the University of Vienna (Austria), ANE (Russia), amongst others.

He is a member of the Scientific Committee of the Channel and Retail Academy sponsored by IBM. He has been a speaker at some world conferences, such as the Neuromarketing World Forum, Barcelona, March 2015. He is also an active writer of marketing posts on his blog martinez-ribes.com and on LinkedIn.

One of his publications is on retail customer experience: www.thecustomerexperience.es/en/

He has been a consultant for companies in 25 countries: AbbVie, Asics, Bayer, Coca-Cola, Desigual, Zara, Ikea, Nestlé, Roca, Sentosa, Pepsico, Heineken, Mercadona, Migros, Tata retail, Unilever, etc.

He was awarded with the Global Electronic Marketing Award in 1999, with SUPSA; in 2009, Aqui é was one of the six most innovative shops at World Retail Awards. In 2013, the European Union appointed him as Retail Innovation Expert.

Jeffrey Parkhurst has an established expertise in branding, marketing, analytics, and strategy. Over the last 15 years, he has led analytic teams on major brands and overseen practices including brand valuation with WPP, Omnicom, and independent agencies in New York. Prior to that he spent 17 years with The Procter & Gamble Company, Kraft Foods, and A.T. Kearney.

He has worked in a brand capacity across over 50 companies in 19 industries including American Express, BlueCross BlueShield, Chevron, Duke Energy, Easter Seals, Kellogg Company, Levi Strauss, MasterCard International, P&G, Sprint, Verizon Communications, and World Economic Forum.

His work has been cited in cover stories with *Forbes* and *BusinessWeek* as well as other regional and national periodicals. A Harvard Business Case Study and Harvard Business Review article has been written about his co-branding work with Habitat for Humanity International. He has an MBA with Honors from the University of Chicago and a Bachelor of Computer Science from the University of Minnesota.

Vanessa M. Patrick is Professor of Marketing and Director of Doctoral Programs at the Bauer College of Business at the University of Houston. She has a PhD in business from the University of

Southern California, an MBA in marketing, and a BS degree from the Bombay University.

Her research deals with the psychology that underlies the two sides of the pleasure coin. On one hand, the pursuit of pleasure dealing with art, aesthetics, hedonics, and luxury, and on the other, strategies to successfully manage and control the pull of pleasure.

Her research has appeared in the *Journal of Consumer Research, Journal of Marketing Research, Journal of Consumer Psychology, Journal of Retailing,* and other academic journals. She was named one of the top 50 most productive marketing scholars worldwide by DocSig (AMA), an MSI Young Scholar by the Marketing Science Institute, and has won numerous research awards.

She is on the editorial board of *Journal of Consumer Research* and *Journal of Consumer Psychology* and is an Associate Editor for the *Journal of Retailing.* She has been featured on ABC News and NPR as an expert in self-control and her work has been covered by news outlets such as the *Los Angeles Times, Forbes, Huffington Post,* and *Scientific American.*

Bharath Rajan is Associate Research Director for the Center for Excellence in Brand and Customer Management at the J. Mack Robinson College of Business. His primary responsibilities include overseeing the research productivity, supporting research and business proposal writing efforts, and disseminating research publications in academic and trade-related journals and magazines for the Center.

He has published in business and marketing journals such as the *Sloan Management Review, Journal of International Marketing, Journal of the Academy of Marketing Science, Industrial Marketing Management, Management Accounting Quarterly, Strategic Finance,* and *Marketing Intelligence Review.* His current research interests include customer relationship management, group-buying behavior, international marketing research, and international trade. He holds undergraduate and graduate degrees in business and economics.

Srinivas Reddy is Professor of Marketing and Director, the Center for Marketing Excellence, and Academic Director, LVMH-SMU Luxury Brand Initiative, the Lee Kong Chian School of Business, the Singapore Management University. He served as the Associate Dean of General Management overseeing the MBA and the Executive MBA programs. Previously, he was the Robert O. Arnold Professor of Business and the Director of the Coca-Cola Center for Marketing Studies, Terry College of Business at the University of Georgia. He holds M.Phil and PhD degrees in Business Administration from the Columbia University. He was on the faculties of the New York University's Stern School of Business, the Columbia University, the University of California (Los Angeles), and the Stanford Business School.

His research on innovation, brand, and marketing strategy has been published in *Journal of Marketing, Journal of Marketing Research, Management Science, NeuroImage, Social Networks, Statistical Science, Journal of International Business Studies, Marketing Letters, Journal of Retailing, Journal of the Academy of Marketing Science, Decision Support Systems,* and *Journal of Business Research.*

He has consulted and taught executive programs for IBM, Coca-Cola Company, United Parcel Service, Miller Brewing, Pfizer, Eli Lilly, Bristol-Myers-Squibb, Satyam Computer Services, Chase, Turner Broadcasting, Cox Interactive Media, Equitable, Ford Foundation, Pricewaterhouse Coopers, MasterCard, and Unilever.

Werner Reinartz is Professor of Marketing at the University of Cologne, Germany. He also directs the Center for Research in Retailing (IFH) at the University of Cologne.

His research interest and expertise focuses on the subjects of marketing strategy, retailing, customer management, and service strategies. His work in these domains has been recognized with major academic awards, such as the 1999 AMA Doctoral Dissertation Competition, the 2001 Don Lehmann Award for the Best Dissertation-Based Research Paper to be published in *Journal of Marketing Research* or *Journal of Marketing,* the 2003 and 2005 MSI/Paul Root Award of the *Journal of Marketing,* finalist for the 2009 O'Dell Award, and the 2011 Sheth Foundation/Journal of Marketing Award for long-term contribution to the marketing discipline. He has published extensively in journals such as *Journal of Marketing, Journal of Marketing Research, Journal of Consumer Research, Journal of Retailing, International Journal of Marketing,* and *Journal of Service Research.* Furthermore, he is an area editor at the *Journal of Marketing, International Journal of Research in Marketing,* and *Journal of Marketing Behavior* as well as a member of the editorial board of *Marketing Science*. In addition, he has conducted extensively executive training programs for many Fortune 500 and EuroStoxx50 companies.

Professor Reinartz is a PhD in marketing from the University of Houston (1999).

Martin Roll delivers the combined value of an experienced global business strategist, senior advisor, and facilitator to Fortune 500 companies, Asian firms, and family-owned businesses on how to build and manage strong, global brands as well as leadership of high-performing, marketing-oriented businesses.

He is very experienced in engaging and advising clients at all management levels from business owners and C-suite leaders to functional staff across multiple industries and cultures.

He is a keynote speaker at global conferences, an experienced conference moderator, and executive workshop facilitator. He also teaches MBA, Executive MBA, and Executive Education programs at Nanyang Business School (Singapore), and is a frequent guest lecturer at INSEAD and other global business schools.

He is the author of global bestseller *Asian Brand Strategy*, a business columnist with INSEAD Knowledge, a prolific management writer, and a regular commentator in global media. He holds an MBA from INSEAD.

His specialties include branding, marketing, strategy, leadership, change and transformations, business family transition, business coaching, and Asia and emerging markets.

Bernd Schmitt is Robert D. Calkins Professor of International Business at the Columbia Business School in New York. He is also the Faculty Director of the Center on Global Brand Leadership at Columbia and Executive Director of the Institute on Asian Consumer Insights at Nanyang Technological University in Singapore. He is author of several books including *Big Think Strategy* and *Customer Experience Management*. His research, which focuses on language, brands, and experience, has been published in more than 50 articles in leading marketing journals.

About the Editors and Contributors

Don E. Schultz is Professor (Emeritus-in-Service) Integrated Marketing Communications, the Medill School of Journalism, the Northwestern University, Illinois, and President of Agora, Inc., a global marketing, communication, and branding consulting firm.

He has done BBA from the University of Oklahoma and MA and PhD from the Michigan State University. He consults, lectures, and holds seminars on integrated marketing communication, marketing, branding, advertising, sales promotion, and communication management in Europe, South America, Asia/Pacific, the Middle East, Australia, and North America. He is the author/co-author of 28 books and over 150 trade, academic, and professional articles. He is a featured columnist in Marketing News and Marketing Insights.

Jean Yannis Suvatjis holds a BSc degree in economics and finance, a masters degree in marketing, a masters degree in management, and an MBA in operations management from American universities. He also holds a PhD degree from the University of Birmingham in Marketing/Corporate Brand Identity.

He worked in the United States for 25 years holding various managerial and executive positions in various industries such as manufacturing, retailing, service, and consulting. He taught marketing, management, and logistics in various academic institutions and universities in the United States.

He has advised several private and public companies around the world. In Greece, he has advised The Greek Post Office, The Greek Telecommunication Company, The Greek Water Supply Company, The Association of Northern Greek Exporters, and many other large companies in Greece and Northeastern Europe. He undertook and successfully implemented a number of European projects assigned by the European Union. Also, he worked as the director of academic studies at the Athens Graduate School of Management/NTU.

Shi Zhang is Associate Professor of Marketing at the University of California, Los Angeles. He holds PhD degrees in both linguistics and marketing. He has done innovative research in the area of market-entry strategy and marketing communications, and in the area of brand naming and positioning in the international market. His research has been published in all the major marketing journals.

Index*

acquirer's brand portfolio
  brand value relationship
    diversity in, 426f
  hidden, brand value, 420–421
acquirer's degree of diversification (ADDI), 354
Asia
  lacking of branding in
    collaborate and co-create, 285
    diverse demographics, 282
    diversification of businesses, 280–281
    dominant economic model, 297–298
    evolving economy, 281
    glocalize, 284
    healthy return on investment (ROI), 280
    intellectual property rights, 281–282
    leverage cross-border synergies, 284
    leverage, unique Asian culture, 285
    no CEOs' support, 282–283
    original equipment manufacturers (OEMs), 279
    seven-step strategy, 283
    strong differentiation creation of, 283–284
    strong distribution network, establishment of, 284
    trading mind set, 280
    unique regional markets, recognition and, 284–285

Asian
  branding and emerging economies challenges, companies, 276–278
  brandscape
    branding and emerging markets, 275–276
average growth rate (AGR), 201

BAV consulting, 203
BAV measures
  and brand strength
    cereal brands, positioning map, 204f
    cosmetics brands, positioning map, 205f
  brand stature
    cereal brands, positioning map, 204f
    cosmetics brands, positioning map, 205f
    OTC allergy brands, positioning map, 206
benefits of brand trust, 245–249
  information age, 245, 246
  interruption marketing, 245–246
  personalization–privacy tradeoff, 246f
brand
  and customer management, 389
    CRM, 378
    customer's contribution, 386f
    go-to-market strategy, types, 378, 379t
    industries differences assessment, 385–388

*"t" signifies table and "f" signifies figure.

Index 459

organization's cost structure, 382–383, 384–385
brand-building and management tools
  need of, 207
  primary purpose of, 205–206
brand architecture
  brands innovations, 25–27, 28f
    Gillette for women, 26, 27
    umbrella architecture, 26
    Venus by Gillette, 27
  brands portfolios, rationalizing of, 23–25
    corporate one, 24
    market-driven one, 24–25
    one brand policy, 24
  building blocks, 6–21
    brand, 7
    brand image, 7
    brands, integrative role of, 9f
    business growth, 7
    company's business model, tying, 18–19
    corporate culture and, 19–21
    issues, 8
    masterbrand, 8
    organizational structure, 8–10
    situation based, 15–17
    types of, 10–14
  business-to-business (B2B), 3–4
  company's business model, 18–19
  corporations visibility, 21–23
  innovations
    disruptive, stepwise integration of, 28–29
    new masterbrand, launch of, 29–31
    progressive integration of, 29f
  issues, 4, 5–6
  new masterbrand, launch, 29–31
    innovation in, 29–31
  selection of, 12, 14
  six type, 13f
    positioning of, 16f
  strategic decisions of, 4–6
    establishment of, 18
    parameter, 18
  types of, 10–14
    endorsement brand, 15–16
    house of brands, 11, 14, 17
    house of brands *vs* branded house, 17
    situation based, 15–17
    source brand, 15
brand development, 149
  brand association ratings, examples of, 154t
  brand audit, 150–151
  key steps for, 150
  qualitative
    brand audit research, 151–153
    research, 153–154
    techniques, summary of, 152t
brand elements, 163–164
  choice criteria, 164–165
  deciding, 174
  development of, 166–167
  future considerations, 167
brand equity
  consumer outcome measure, 364–366
    changes in, 365–366
    post-merger, 366f
brand equity charter, 168–169
  report, 169–171
  responsibilities, 172–174
  sample customer-performance scorecard measures, 171t
brand experiences, 177
  act experience, 183
  concept of, 179–180
  consumers conception, 184–186
  dimensions of, 180
  feel experience, 182–183
  management, 195
  marketing issues, address, 192
    innovation management, 194
    positioning, 193
    segmentation and targeting, 193
    service management, 194
  measuring of, 190–192
  pleasure dimensions, 181
  project based framework
    designing of, 188–189
    experience platform, 187

experiential world of customer,
analyzing, 186–187
relate experience, 183–184
sense experience, 182
staged experiences, 182
think experience, 183
traditional marketers, 178–179
brand familiarity, 363
brand identity strategy
mergers and acquisitions for, 335
brand keys, 203
brand management
and customer management, 377
business model in, 380–381
examples of, 380
reinventing, research agenda
connections and inclusion, 213–214
factors to work on, 207–208
financial focus, 212–213
longitudinal analysis, 209
multi-dimensional models, 211–212
networked systems, 210–211
shift to behavioral data, 208–209
brand name redeployment
approaches, 343–344
acquirer-dominated, 345–346
synergistic/non-synergistic, 344–345
data and analysis, 354
continuous variables, 357t
multinomial logit model, 355–359, 360t, 361t
hypothesis, 346–351
market relatedness, impact of
congeneric M&A, 349
horizontal M&A, 347–348
ownership status, impact of, 350–351
unrelated/conglomerate M&A, 349–350
vertical M&A, 348–349
non-dominated redeployment model
estimates of, 359
parameter estimates, 362
relative standing, impact of, 346–347

study, 352–353
study measures
ADDI, 354
control variables, 358t
market relatedness, 353–354, 356t
relative standing, 353
brand naming
complex process, 99
consumer's perspective, 101–102
efforts and process, 100
positive brand identities, 116–117
brand platforms
strategic growth options, 441
brand portfolio strategy
findings
target characteristics, 424–425
managerial implications, 428
brand positioning
Accenture's
competitive positioning map, 158f
straddle positioning, 159f
brand mantra, 159–160
bullseye model, 160
codifying, 174
hypothetical Starbucks positioning worksheet, 162f
key components of, 155–156
other considerations, 157
worksheet, 161f
brand redeployment
acquirer-dominated
horizontal mergers, relationship with, 367–368
brand attitude, 364
brand familiarity, 363
M&A transactions, 367
motive for
bounded rationality perspective, 342–343
competitive strategy, 340–341
resource-based view (RBV), 338–340
signalling perspective, 341–342
transaction-cost (TC) perspective, 338–340
perceived fit, 363–364
strategic and financial consequences, 336–338

strategy, 370
study
    managerial implications of, 368
    results, 368–369
brand redeployment strategy
    antecedents of, 351f
    framework of, 345f
brand revitalizing, 314–316
    approaches, 319, 332
        brand awareness, expanding, 320–323
        brand image, improvement, 323–325
        new markets, entering, 325–327
    characterization of
        customer-based brand equity, 316–317
    continuum, 317–319
    marketing guidelines, during crisis
        Exxon, 329
        Johnson & Johnson (Tylenol), 327–329
        sincerity, 330–332
        swiftness, 330
    strategies, 333f
brand trust
    benefits of, 245–249
        information age, 245, 246
        interruption marketing, 245–246
        personalization–privacy tradeoff, 246f
    brands, role of
        literature review, 239–241
    competencies, 252
    concept of, 237
    conceptual model, 249, 251f
        advertising lines, example of, 250t
        law and court of public opinion, 251f
        virtue of, 250
    corruption perceptions index 2014, 253f
    customers relationship with, 241–242
        reactivation of, 242
    customization, types of
        adaptive customizers, 247
        collaborative customizers, 247
        cosmetic customizers, 247
        transparent customizers, 247
    directions for consideration, 268–269
    dynamics of
        building trust, 256–263
    information age and
        nineteen eighty-four, 238
        power and, 238–239
    policies, 254
    process, 254
    reputation building, 255f
    role in financial performance, 268
    sources of risk, 244t
    systems, 254
    Transparency International, 252
    trust and relationship, role of
        reactivation of, 242–245
    values, component of, 252
brand trust dynamics
    building trust
        breach event and impact, 262f
        breaches, 260–261
        by industry, 257f
        calculative-based, 257
        capability-assessed, 258
        experience-based, 256
        expert-based, 257
        holistic customer experience, 258
        Intel, mistake, 262–263
        levels of, ads for, 258f
        marketing program, 256
        peripheral cue-based, 257
        programs, 259t
        transference-based, 258
branding and emerging economies
    challenges, 276–278, 279
        Asian companies, for, 276–278
    characteristics in
        customer-centricity, 278
        innovation, 278
        leadership, 278
        right talent, ability to attract, 278
        speed, 278
branding and emerging markets, 271
    Asian landscape, 272–273
        booming market in, 273–275
brands
    business, 403–407

measures, 405–407
definition, 393–394
evaluation of
    market place in, 113–115
growth and risk, 445
information society, 69
law, 408
    Lanham Act (1946), 409–410
legal
    Federal Trademark Dilution Act, 408
    TRIPS agreement, 407
limitation of
    language proficiency, 115–116
platforms for managing profitability as, 445
protection, 402–403
valuation methodologies, 404t
value addition by, 394
    corporate responsibility, 399–400
    creating difference between competing ones, 396–397
    fostering customer loyalty, 397–398
    innovation, 399
    percent of market capitalization, 395f
    providing negotiating power with suppliers, 397
    providing stability, 398
    quality control, 398–399
    reducing transaction costs, 397
    shifting supply curve upwards, 397
    wealth creation, 399
value, risks to, 400–402
brands innovations, 25–27, 28f
    brands portfolios, rationalizing of, 23–25
    Gillette for women, 26, 27
    umbrella architecture, 26
    Venus by Gillette, 27
brands portfolios
    rationalizing of, 23–25
        corporate one, 24
        market-driven one, 24–25
        one brand policy, 24

brands value
    brand portfolio value, 421t
    factors explaining
        M&As in, 421–422
    findings
        acquirers' characteristics, 422–424
        target characteristics, 424–425
    hidden, 420–421
brands, role
    extracting value from innovation in, 438
    growth stage at, 442–443
    innovating, cost of, 434–436
    innovation, 430–431
    innovation process, 432–433
    launch stage at, 438–442
    literature review, 239–241
    market imperfections creation, 433–434
    marketing on financial performance, impact, 435f
    maturity/ saturation stage at, 443–444
    technological innovation and, 435–436
    value creation, 431–432
building blocks
    brand, 7
    brand image, 7
    brands, integrative role of, 9f
    business growth, 7
    company's business model, tying, 18–19
    corporate culture and, 19–21
    issues, 8
    masterbrand, 8
    organizational structure, 8–10
    situation based, 15–17
    types of, 10–14
business-to-business (B2B), 3–4

co-branding and licensing, 300–301
    basics, 305–306
    brand's opportunity space
        quantification of, 306–307
    case studies of, 301–302
    future growth, drivers of, 307f

future options, 312f
hidden value quantification, 312
opportunities, quantification of,
    307–309
risks
    quantification of, 309–310
    reducing considerations, 311
validity
    partner relationship test for, 310
value of duration with brand,
    302–305
conceptual model, 249
    advertising lines, example of, 250t
    brand trust, 249, 251f
        advertising lines, example of,
            250t
        law and court of public opinion,
            251f
        virtue of, 250
consumer information processing
    phonographic and logographic
        systems
            differences between, 105–107
consumer outcome measure, 364–366
    changes in, 365–366
    post-merger, 366f
corporate brand, 367
corporate brand redeployment
    after M&AS, consequences of,
        362–363
corporate identity
    concept as, 119–120
    confirmatory factor analysis,
        145t–147t
    contribution to, 136–137
    investigation of
        C-SEG audit, 134
        corporate strategy audit, 134
        exoteric and esoteric visual
            audits—E2VA, 135
        MIA audit, 135
        MV2 audit, 134
        situ analysis, 134
        SWOT matrix, 136
        tailor-made audit, 135
    issues related to
        and performance, 139

appropriate implementation of,
    139–140
clear goals, 137–138
open and interactive approach,
    139
relationship with stakeholders,
    138–139
synergy-oriented environment,
    138
new model, 120–123
    criteria of, 121–123
positive brand identities, 116–117
quantitative phase, 141
quantitative research, synoptic
    presentation of, 141–147
rotated factor matrix, 142t–144t
six-station model, 123, 124–126
    structure of, 124
total variance, 144t
corporation alignment
    people and system, 189–190
customer brand value (CBV), 34
    calculation of, 41–44
    components of, 50f
    concepts of, 40, 49
    constituents, 34
    customer deciles,
        telecommunications company
        for, 60
    definition of, 40–41
    drivers of, 44–45
        customer characteristics, 44–45
        exchange characteristics, 44
    implementation between
        linking between, 53–54
    lifetime value of customers, linking
        to
            SURs, 52
    linking of
        lifetime value of customers, 52
    managerial implementation of
        link between, lifetime value and,
            55
    measures of
        brand attitude, 49
        brand behavior, 50
        brand behavior intention, 50
        brand knowledge, 49

optimized, 54
sample output of customer A's observed brand value, 51f
strategies and implications
   customer attrition, prevention of, 47–48
   customer equity and, 48–49
   customer selection, 45
   loyalty and profitability, 45
   multichannel shoppers management, 48
   pitching, 47
   profitable customers, acquisition of, 48
   resources, optimal allocation of, 46–47
   wheel-of-fortune, 45, 46f
customer management, 389
   core notion, 382
   CRM, 378
   customer's contribution, 386f
   direct response communication, 381–382
   examples of, 381
   go-to-market strategy
      types of, 378–379
   industries differences assessment, 385–388
   organization's cost structure
      customer contribution, 384, 385f
      types of, 382–383
customer referral value (CRV), 34
   calculation of, 56–60
   concept of, 56
   customer deciles of, 60t
   implementation
      link between, lifetime value and, 62–64
   linking to
      lifetime value, 60–62
   managerial implementation
      link between, lifetime value and, 64–65
   measures of, 56
   misers campaign for
      telecommunications company for, 65, 66t

referral program
   AT&T from, 61f
   DIRECTV from, 62f
   telecommunications company for
      advocates campaign, 65t, 66t
      affluents campaign, 65t, 66t
      customer deciles, 60t
customer relationship management (CRM), 35, 378
customer value, 34–35
   customer brand value (CBV)
      calculation of, 41–44
      concept of, 40
      constituents, 34
      definition of, 40–41
      drivers of, 44–45
   definition, 34
   forward-looking metrics
      CBV, 38
      CLV, 38
      CRV, 38, 39f
   inter-linkages between
      CLV, CBV, and CRV, 39f
   maximizing, strategies and implications of, 45–49
   measures
      primary customer-based metrics, 36–37
      strategic customer-based value metrics, 37–38
      traditional marketing metrics, 36
   measuring, need for
      CRM programs, 35
      CVM approach, benefits of, 35, 36
   primary customer-based metrics
      measures
      customer acquisition, 37
      customer activity, 37
      customer win-back, 37
   strategic customer-based value metrics
      past customer value (PCV), 38
      recency-frequency-monetary value (RFM), 38
      share of wallet (SOW), 37–38
customer value management (CVM), 35

customization
    types of brand trust
        adaptive customizers, 247
        collaborative customizers, 247
        cosmetic customizers, 247
        transparent customizers, 247

dominant branding strategies, 286–287
    acquisition growth, 291–292
    alliance growth, 289
    organic growth, 287

fast-moving consumer goods (FMCG), 70–71
    decline preferences, factors involved in, 202–203
Federal Trademark Dilution Act, 408
four-step brand leadership model, 292
    collaboration, 294–295
    innovation, 293–294
    strategic activity, 292
    strategic leadership, 296–297
    sustainability, 295–296
full time equivalent (FTE), 313

globalization
    business environment, impact on, 392
go-to-market strategy
    challenge, 391
    implications of, 388–391
        brand and customer management, link between, 389f
    types of, 378–379
golden age of branding, 199

industrial organization (IO)
    economics, 348
innovations, 28–31
    in brand architecture
        disruptive, stepwise integration of, 28–29
        new masterbrand, launch of, 29–31
        progressive integration of, 29f
internal branding, 167–168

international brand linguistics
    conceptual analysis, 102–105
investigation of corporate identity
    C-SEG audit, 134
    corporate strategy audit, 134
    exoteric and esoteric visual audits—E2VA, 135

lacking of branding in Asia
    reasons of
        collaborate and co-create, 285
        diverse demographics, 282
        diversification of businesses, 280–281
        dominant economic model, 297–298
        evolving economy, 281
        glocalize, 284
        healthy return on investment (ROI), 280
        intellectual property rights, 281–282
        leverage cross-border synergies, 284
        leverage, unique Asian culture, 285
        no CEOs' support, 282–283
        original equipment manufacturers (OEMs), 279
        seven-step strategy, 283
        strong differentiation creation of, 283–284
        strong distribution network, establishment of, 284
        trading mind set, 280
        unique regional markets, recognition and, 284–285
Lanham Act (1946), 409–410
luxury branding
    associations of, 223–225
    consumer choice, drivers of, 226–228
    consumer of, 225–226
    definition of, 222–223
    democratization of, 220–221
    future research areas on
        aesthetics benefits of, 229–230
        benefits and risks of, 231–232

hedonism benefits of, 229–230
investigates processing, concepts, 230–231
psychological benefits of, 229–230
new luxury, 218
and old luxury, comparison between, 219–220
promise of pleasure, as, 217–218
recession, management in, 221–222
market
brand name redeployment, impact
congeneric M&A, 349
horizontal M&A, 347–348
ownership status, impact of, 350–351
unrelated/conglomerate M&A, 349–350
vertical M&A, 348–349
market performance
stores and products of, 201t
market relatedness, brand name redeployment
congeneric M&A, 349
horizontal M&A, 347–348
ownership status, impact of, 350–351
unrelated/conglomerate M&A, 349–350
vertical M&A, 348–349
marketing capability
average reduction in, 428
brand value relationship
redundancy, impact of, 427f
findings
target characteristics, 425
marketing guidelines
brand revitalizing
Exxon, 329
Johnson & Johnson (Tylenol), 327–329
sincerity, 330–332
swiftness, 330
marketing issues in brand experiences, 192
innovation management, 194
positioning, 193
segmentation and targeting, 193
service management, 194

motive for brand redeployment
bounded rationality perspective, 342–343
competitive strategy, 340–341
resource-based view (RBV), 338–340
signalling perspective, 341–342
transaction-cost (TC) perspective, 338–340

net promoter score-type measurement system, 200
nineteen eighty-four
brand trust
information age and, 238
no brand preference (NBP), 200
research framework, 200
non-dominated redeployment model
estimates of, 359

positioning brands
legal protection, for, 411
managers' role, 419
pitfalls, selecting a mark, 413–418
trademark protection, 412f
positioning map
BAV measures, using
cereal brands for, 204f
cosmetics brands for, 205f
product life cycle
competition and strategies/relevant metrics, 439f
stages of, 436–438
project based framework for brand
designing of, 188–189
experience platform, 187
experiential world of customer, analyzing, 186–187

qualitative brand development
brand audit research, 151–153
research, 153–154
techniques, summary of, 152t

resource-based view (RBV), 338–340
retail branding
brand positioning, 92
brand score, 93

branded goods, 70
   type of, 77
branding process, 93
chain in portfolio, 78–79
facts, 70–73
   AC Nielsen report, 70–71
   FMCG, 70–71
formats, 78
future challenges, 79–80
   possible customer expectations trend, 80
missing elements, 81–82
misunderstandings, 89–91
natural set of benefits
   advantage of, 84–86
   complete control of, 83–84
   direct knowledge of customers, 84
   improved economic performance, 84
origins and evolution, 73–75
paradigm, breaking of, 91–92
Planet Retail's reports, 71
potential variation, 82–83
preconceptions, 93
private label, 80–81
stages in
   generics or "no-name" products, 75
   own branded products, 76
   private label products, 76
   retail branded products, 76–77
suppliers
   impact of, 86
   responses of, 87–89
   trade associations, 86

seemingly unrelated regressions (SURs), 52
six type brand architecture, 13f
   positioning of, 16f
six-station corporate identity model
   architecture of, 124–126
   assessment of
      qualitative findings of, 130–131
      quantitative research, 132–134
   left stage of
      communication station, 128–129
      critical triplet station, 130
      human corporate power station, 129
   mechanisms of, 124–126
   right stage of
      creativity station, 127–128
      head station, 126–127
      strategy station, 127
   structure of, 124
   topology of, 124–126
sound and meaning, critical test
   2 by 2 scheme, 107–113
      brand name evaluation, 112f
      stimuli brand names, 110t
stages in retail branding
   generics or "no-name" products, 75
   own branded products, 76
   private label products, 76
   retail branded products, 76–77
store brand
   consumers, preference by, 201
strategic decisions
   in brand architecture, 4–6
      establishment of, 18
      parameter, 18
strategies and implications of CBV
   customer attrition
      prevention of, 47–48
   customer equity and, 48–49
   customer selection, 45
   loyalty and profitability, 45
   multichannel shoppers
      management, 48
   pitching, 47
   profitable customers, acquisition, 48
   resources
      optimal allocation of, 46–47
   wheel-of-fortune, 45, 46f
study
   brand redeployment
      managerial implications of, 368
      results, 368–369
study measures
   in brand name redeployment
      ADDI, 354
      control variables, 358t
      market relatedness, 353–354, 356t
      relative standing, 353

top leading brand categories
 characteristics of, 202t
Trade-Related Aspects of Intellectual
 Property Rights (TRIPS) agreement,
 407
Transparency International, 252
types of brand architecture, 10–14
 endorsement brand, 15–16
 house of brands, 11, 14, 17
 house of brands vs branded house,
  17t
 situation based, 15–17
 source brand, 15

value addition by brands, 394

corporate responsibility, 399–400
creating difference between
 competing ones, 396–397
fostering customer loyalty, 397–398
percent of market capitalization,
 395f
providing negotiating power with
 suppliers, 397
providing stability, 398
quality control, 398–399
reducing transaction costs, 397
shifting supply curve upwards, 397
wealth creation, 399

wheel-of-fortune, 45, 46f